APPLIED MARKETING
AND SOCIAL RESEARCH

SECOND EDITION

APPLIED MARKETING AND SOCIAL RESEARCH

SECOND EDITION

Edited by
Ute Bradley

Department of Business Studies
City of London Polytechnic

Foreword by
John Downham
Honorary Member of Market
Research Society

JOHN WILEY & SONS

Chichester · New York · Brisbane · Toronto · Singapore

Library of Congress Cataloging in Publication Data:

Applied marketing and social research

   1. Marketing research — Case studies.   2. Marketing
research — Great Britain — Case studies.   I. Bradley,
Ute.
HF5415.2.A654   1987   658.8′3   86–32447
ISBN 0 471 91356 1
ISBN 0 471 91475 4 (pbk.)

British Library Cataloguing in Publication Data:
Applied marketing and social research. —
   2nd ed.
   1. Marketing research
   I. Bradley, Ute
658.8′3   HF5415.2

ISBN 0 471 91356 1
ISBN 0 471 91475 4 (pbk.)

Typeset by Dobbie Typesetting Service, Plymouth, Devon
Printed and bound in Great Britain by Anchor Brendon Limited, Tiptree, Essex

Contents

Foreword   **xiii**

Introduction   **xv**

1. **The Contribution of Research to General Motors' Corporate
    Communications Strategy in the UK**   **1**
    E. Fountain, I. Parker, J. Samuels
    Summary   1
    Background and genesis of the research programme   2
    The research programme   4
       Research objectives   4
       Details of the project   5
       Methodology for the General Public sample   7
       Some results   7
       Other 'Publics'   17
    The Contribution of the research programme   18
    Further reading   20
    Acknowledgment   20
    Appendix 1.1 Questionnaire content and order   20

2. **The Fresh Cream Cake Market: the use of qualitative research as
    part of a consumer research programme**   **23**
    J. Dickens
    Introduction   23
       What is qualitative research?   23
       Uses of qualitative research   25
    The Fresh Cream Cake Market: a consumer research programme   28
    Project 1: A qualitative study of consumer attitudes and behaviour
    in relation to fresh cream cakes   29
       Stage 1: Planning   30
       Stage 2: Recruitment   38
       Stage 3: Fieldwork   41
       Stage 4: Analysis   48
       Stage 5: Verbal Presentation   50
       Stage 6: Written Report   53
    Project 2: A quantitative study of consumer attitudes and behaviour
    in the fresh cream cakes market   57

Project 3: A qualitative creative development study   59
   Stage 1: Planning   59
   Stage 2: Recruiting   60
   Stage 3: Fieldwork   60
   Stage 4: The findings   61
Conclusions   63
References   63
Appendix 2.1 Research brief   64
Appendix 2.2 Fresh Cream Cakes—concepts explored during the group discussions   67
Acknowledgment   68

3.   Clover New Product Development   69
S. Day
Introduction   69
Stage 1—Desk research (1979)   70
Stage 2—Product research   72
   Exploratory product research (March 1979)   72
   Quantitative blind product test (July 1979)   73
Stage 3—Concept research   73
   Concept research I (August 1979)   74
   Concept research II (October 1979)   74
Stage 4—Packaging and name research   75
   Pack shape test (November 1979)   75
   Pack design test I (January 1980)   76
   Name and pack exploratory groups (March 1980)   76
   Pack design test II (April 1980)   77
Stage 5—Mix assessment (May 1980)   77
Stage 6—In-home concept/product placement (September 1982)   79
Stage 7—Clover 'Sharescale'   80
Stage 8—Launch of Clover   81
Reference   84
Appendix 3.1 Usage and Attitude study: 1979   84
Appendix 3.2 Concept research I—questionnaire   85
Appendix 3.3 Pack shape test—questionnaire   89
Appendix 3.4 Clover launch script   92
Appendix 3.5 Illustrations and questionnaire for in-home concept/product placement   94
Appendix 3.6 Sensor models   107

4.   The contribution of research in the development of the BBC's computer literacy project   113
V. Marles, P. Mills
Origins   114
Research and production   115
Production questions   115
Postscript on the approach   117
Pre-production research   119
   Defining the target audience   119
   Characteristics of the likely target group   119
   Refining the target audience and the production approach   123

Evaluating the project   129
  Audience size   129
  Audience reaction   131
  The rest of the package   133
References   135
Appendix 4.1 'Hands on Micro-Electronics' questionnaire   136
Appendix 4.2 Recruitment questionnaire: 'Hands-on Micro-
electronics'   138
Appendix 4.3 Pre-questionaire   140
Appendix 4.3a Post questionnaire   142
Appendix 4.4 'The computer programme'   154
Appendix 4.5 'The computer programme' survey questionnaire I   156
Appendix 4.5a 'The computer programme' survey
questionnaire II   165
Appendix 4.6 BBC Microcomputer System—questionnaire   177

5.   **Assessing what is being measured by a readership survey**   **185**
   H. A. Smith
   Introduction   185
   The needs of the advertiser   186
   Comparative data essential   187
   The National Readership Survey   189
   Pragmatic approach preferred   193
   Design of study   194
   Allowing for genuine differences in response   195
   Summary of results   197
   General implications   201
   References   201
   Acknowledgment   201
   Appendix 5.1 Readership questions from NRS Readership Survey   201
   Appendix 5.2 Specimen answer page from NRS questionnaire   204

6.   *Ad-hoc* **pricing research**   **207**
   R. P. Morgan
   Introduction   207
   Available techniques   208
     Monadic tests   208
     Case History 1   208
     Comparative tests   210
     Case History 2   211
   Selecting and adapting techniques for markets   211
     Problems concerning the market context   212
     Case History 3   214
     Problems concerning the product field   215
     Case History 4   216
     Case History 5   217
     Case History 6   218
   Some final considerations   218
   The outcome   220
   References   221

7. **Product Testing** 223
   K. T. Boyd
   Why test products? 223
   Who should assess them? 225
   The kinds of test available 226
   Extensions of comparative testing 230
   How many products should each person assess? 235
   Order of testing 237
   Attributes 238
   Test conditions 239
   Blind or branded? 240
   Sample size 241
   Conclusion 243
   References 243
   Further reading 243
   Appendix 7.1 Factorial tests 244
   Appendix 7.2 Sequential monadic testing 245
   Appendix 7.3 A Product development research programme 249

8. **A cost-effective use of research to evaluate**
   sales promotions 251
   M. Drake
   Summary 251
   An outline of the problem 252
   Promotions should be pre-tested before committing to the final package 253
   Promotions must be evaluated against specific objectives 255
   Summary and conclusions 262
   Appendix 8.1 Questionnaire 263

9. **The tracking study in market research** 265
   I. P. Sampson
   Introduction 265
   Continuous advertising tracking 268
   Tracking and sales forecasting for one brand 269
      Data collection 270
      The BASES calibration model 270
      The volume calculation model 273
      Data input 273
      Analysis and modelling 274
      Case Histories 275
      BASES experience 277
   Tracking and sales forecasting—several brands 277
   The future of tracking 278
   References 278

10. **On-line data bases: their role in information retrieval** 281
    D. Holmes
    Introduction 281
       The development of on-line data bases 282
    Benefits and problems with 'on-line' survey data bases 283
       Benefits 283
       Problems 284

Creating an on-line data base — a case study   285
  Background   285
  The basic concept   286
  Some important considerations   287
The interactive system   290
  The basic concept   290
  An example of an enquiry   290
  Examples of the system in use   291
Summarising the pros and cons of an interactive data base   291
The application of an interactive data base   292
Notes   292
Acknowledgement   292
Appendix 10.1 Confidential prescription record   293
Appendix 10.2 Example of an enquiry   295
Appendix 10.3 Example results from an enquiry   296

11. The Research Benefits of Scanning   301
    L. Morris
What is Scanning?   301
Customer viewpoint   305
Manufacturer viewpoint   306
Retailers viewpoint   307
Promoting the benefits of Scanning data   308
Scantrack   309
Scantrack applications   309
What data does Scantrack show?   310
Scantrack uses   310
  Case 1 — Allied Lyons — Port   310
  Case 2 — Confectionery market   310
  Case 3 — New product   313
  Case 4 — Promotions   314
Further Scantrack uses   315
Future plans for Scanning services   316
References   316
Appendix 11.1 Specimen of ANA 4-week report   317
Appendix 11.2 Specimen Scantrack 4-week report   318
Appendix 11.3 Specimen Scantrack Trend report   319

**12. Assessing the effectiveness of computer-
    based training   323**
    R. J. Mortimer & R. J. Stubbs
Summary   323
Introduction   324
Barclay's traditional training methods   325
  Centralised courses   325
  Local courses and seminars   325
  In-branch training   325
The Viewdata project   326
  Student interactivity   327
  Reference facility   327
  Test reports   327
  The effectiveness of viewdata as a training medium   328

The findings   329
  Physical acceptability   330
  Structure of Viewdata training   331
  Effectiveness of computer-based training   331
  Importance of supervisors' views   334
Action as a result of MORI survey   335
Problems   336
  The siting of terminals   336
  Time   337
  Education   337
Development of computer-based distance learning in Barclays Bank 338
Further reading   338
Acknowledgment   338
Appendix 12.1 Supervisor's questionnaire   339
Appendix 12.2 Retrospective questionnaire   346
Appendix 12.3 Immediate questionnaire   352

13. Multi-Country Research   359
       D. N. Aldridge
       Introduction   359
       Who does it?   360
       The benefits of co-ordination   361
       Some considerations   362
         Life-style, habits, market structure   362
         Religion and culture   362
         Language   364
         Sampling   364
         Data collection   365
       How is it done?   365
         Local agency selection and initial briefing   366
         Communication   367
         The proposal   367
         Costs   367
         The questionnaire   368
         Final briefing   368
         Data processing   369
         Presentation and reports   369
         Qualitative research   370
       Research in developing countries: additional considerations 370
         Diversity   370
         Religion and culture   372
         Language and literacy   373
         Sampling   374
         Scaling   375
         Costs   376
       Conclusion   376
       References   377

14. Evaluating the effectivness of anti-drinking and driving advertising:
       increasing the cost efficiency of research   379
       R. Jones & T. Twyman   379
       Summary   380

Introduction   380
Discussion of repeat interviewing   380
Drinking and Driving   382
    The role of research in these campaigns   383
    Description of the experiment   384
The survey results   386
    Introduction to the results   386
    Drop-out between the two stages of the repeat interview survey   387
    Comparison of the absolute levels of the results between the
    repeat interview and independent sample methods   388
    Comparison of changes between stages from different methods   389
    Attitudes, knowledge and advertising awareness   390
    Sensitivity of measurement of behavioural change in the two
    methods   391
    The connection between attitudes and behavioural change   392
Conclusion   393
An application of the results   395
References   396
Acknowledgment   396
Appendix 14.1 Precision of pre-post changes in reported behaviour   397
Appendix 14.2 Behaviour study—questionnaire   398

15. **Developing a new index of crime: the British crime survey**   **415**
     M. Hough
     The rationale for crime surveys   416
     Some features of the BCS design   418
         The questionnaire   418
         The sample   419
         Fieldwork   420
         Weighting   420
         Series victimisation   421
         Classifying and counting incidents   421
     Findings from the BCS   422
         Reporting to the police   425
         Recording by the police   425
         Changes in crime over time   427
         Other findings   428
     Taking stock   431
     References   432
     Acknowledgment   432
     Appendix 15.1 BCS questionnaires   433
     Main questionnaire   433
     Victim form   449
     Follow-up questionnaire   470
     Demographic questionnaire   484

Foreword

In my Foreword to the first edition of this book I commented that good case-history material is a vital element in market research training. Survey research must of course be based on a sound understanding of the theory and principles underlying the craft, but this by itself is insufficient. Any given project has to be designed to answer a specific set of real-world problems. It inevitably involves balancing various very practical considerations of timing, available resources, sometimes incompatible objectives, etc. The imaginative adaptation of ideas and approaches used in other research situations, and compromise based on experienced judgement, are therefore an essential part of the trained researcher's skills. One of the best ways of acquiring such skills is to study exactly how other experienced researchers have tackled different types of research problem.

The fact that this is now the second edition demonstrates that the book has successfully met a real market need. It has in the event proved to be of interest and value to people already working in marketing and social research as well as to those still studying to enter the field. This is not surprising in view of the continuous demand for good case-histories at conferences and other gatherings of practising researchers. There is always something new to be learnt in marketing research; and other people's successful (and sometimes their *less* successful!) experiences are one of the most valuable as well as interesting ways of learning. This applies to the users of research as much as it does to researchers themselves. Beyond this, the relevance and usefulness of the book to students and teachers — naturally a key objective from the outset — has since been proved by the fact that it is now on recommended reading lists such as that of the Market Research Society's Diploma Course.

One or two of the chapters in this second edition appeared also in the first, although they have been added to and updated. However, most of the case-histories are new — partly in order to provide fresh and more recent examples wherever this seemed appropriate, partly in order to cover additional areas of interest. This time it has also been possible to include extra details of the technical aspects of many of the cases — for example more of the actual questionnaires used. The value and interest of the book should thereby be further enhanced. It is to quite a large extent a new book, not simply a marginally amended new edition.

Dr Bradley must be congratulated on persuading a group of very busy practising researchers to prepare the case-histories included in this volume. Many of the contributions have of course been specially written for the book. Even where the chapters are based on papers presented elsewhere, the authors have had to rework and add to these for the purposes of this textbook. In every case they have specific skills and experience in the fields about which they write. We must be grateful to them for all their efforts, as well as to Dr Bradley for her initiative in organising and editing the work as a whole.

John Downham

Market Research Consultant, previously Head of Market Research, Marketing Division in Unilever London Headquarters.

Honorary Member & former Chairman of the Market Research Society; closely involved with various ESOMAR activities.

Co-editor *Consumer Market Research Handbook 3rd edition*, 1986

Introduction

The first edition of *Applied Marketing and Social Research* was published in 1982 as there was a real gap in the market for UK-based market research case material, providing full details of the methodology employed. The emphasis on the details of the methodology provided students of marketing research with experience of research as practised and practitioners with examples of the way other researchers approach problems of the type they had themselves tried to solve. By allowing researchers to speak for themselves in the cases, it was possible not only to show up personal differences in approach—what aspects of a problem were regarded as important—but also indicate some of the problems of confidentiality imposed on the writer of case histories. The emphasis on detail also meant that the market or product being researched became of secondary importance, merely a vehicle for demonstrating the ways and means, thus making the cases relevant for a longer period of time.

However, marketing research methodology is developing and in some areas quite fast, to such an extent that there is scarcely time to write up the theoretical approach, much less the practice. Also, international co-operation can be detected in many of these instances (e.g. building decision support systems and developing decision models like pre-test market models). It is that international link, as well as the quality of much of UK research, which hopefully will be of value to students in this second edition.

The cases in the second edition are just as detailed as those in the first edition and cover a wide range of marketing applications, mainly in the commercial area, but also in media and social research. In most cases too, markets and brands are disclosed. The first case illustrates the value of marketing research at the corporate decision-making level:

1. Fountain, Parker & Samuels: The Contribution of Research to General Motors' Corporate Communications Strategy in the UK.

The next case introduces the wide-ranging contributions research can make to the development of future marketing strategy:

2. Dickens: The Fresh Cream Cake Market: The Use of Qualitative Research as Part of a Consumer Research Programme.

This case has been revised and updated from the first edition and concentrates mainly on the role of unstructured research.

The third contribution:

3. Day: Clover New Product Development

covers a complete new product development, using different approaches and methodology to solve the problems involved.

4. Marles & Mills: The Contribution of Research in the Development of the BBC's Computer Literacy Project

is not really concerned with developing a new product, but a new programme and so introduces media research, where a specific contribution is made by:

5. Smith: Assessing what is Being Measured by a Readership Survey.

This case details the current nature and developments being undertaken on the National Readership Survey.

The marketing mix elements are, of course, covered in many ways in the new product development cases listed above. But particular important aspects are further developed in the following cases:

6. Morgan: *Ad-hoc* Pricing Research

surveys the current knowledge and expertise in this important area.

7. Boyd: Product Testing

is updated and republished from the first edition.

8. Drake: A Cost-Effective Use of Research to Evaluate Sales Promotions

is concerned not only with assessing the effectiveness of a single promotion, but develops the argument for strategies for promotions and their evaluation.

9. Sampson: The Tracking Study in Market Research

contributes to our understanding of tracking by underlining the connections between Usership and Attitude studies, tracking and pre-test market models.

Information Technology and marketing research have become inseparable. Many of the previous cases stress this aspect but three cases concentrate on it:

10. Holmes: On-Line Data Bases: Their Role in Information Retrieval.

11. Morris: The Research Benefits of Scanning.

12. Mortimer & Stubbs: Assessing the Effectiveness of Computer-Based Training within a service company.

Research in sophisticated and developing markets can provide many interesting problems, especially when research results need to be comparable. The problems and some solutions are discussed in:

13. B. Aldridge: Multi-Country research.

Social researchers will find two contributions of major interest:

14. Jones, Godfrey & Twyman: Evaluating the Effectiveness of Anti-Drinking and Driving Advertising

15. Hough: Developing a New Index of Crime: The British Crime Survey.

    Developments in methodology are evident in both cases and these are of value to all researchers.

To aid the student and teacher alike, each case is preceded by an introduction, giving some major points of interest and some suggestions for follow-up work or discussions. It should also be stressed that cases can be used in part or in total — for example, for teaching questionnaire design or exploring approaches in developing and testing new products. Further, it is suggested that the student can profit by following up the references provided. Other points which the individual student might wish to pursue may be covered in a general up-to-date UK text and its references, e.g. Worcester, R. M. and Downham, J. (Eds), *Consumer Market Research Handbook*, 3rd ed., Elsevier North-Holland (1986).

The diversity of the material in this collection shows the many potential applications of research and many new research developments. The difficulties of bringing together suitable case material has not diminished since the first edition of this book and I should like to thank the authors, their companies and institutions for their co-operation and effort which made this second edition possible. I hope that students and teachers alike will find this text helpful and that it will encourage others to publish case material giving the problems and techniques used in solving them in detail.

Ute Bradley

1. The Contribution of Research to General Motors' Corporate Communications Strategy in the UK

Eric Fountain *General Motors Ltd.*
Ian Parker *Charles Barker City Ltd.*
John Samuels *BMRB Ltd.*

Many companies recognise that they need successfully to communicate with their publics. General Motors set up a full-scale research programme with its advertising and research agencies, to find out how best to communicate. The programme covers all stages of the research process and can therefore be useful in understanding the parts (e.g. the dissemination of research results), as well as how to set up a comprehensive programme. The research can also demonstrate how to deal with interesting and complex concepts, e.g. the meaning and importance of 'British' in the making and buying of cars.

This was the first study in a series and the authors indicate subsequent developments.

SUMMARY

This paper, prepared jointly by a client company, an advertising agency and a research agency, is designed to demonstrate the contribution of a major programme of research to policy decisions in the area of the corporate communications of a worldwide marketing company, in relation to its operations in the UK. It is in three parts.

The first part of the paper details the background to the research and the genesis of the research programme. General Motors is the largest manufacturing company in the world and markets cars, trucks and other automotive products in the UK via Vauxhall, Bedford, and several other companies engaged in components manufacture. In its deliberations on corporate communications strategy, and specifically the value of the GM connection to the local operating companies, the Public Affairs Council and its advisors, Charles Barker, delineated five key question areas to be addressed by a programme of research.

The second part of the paper is devoted to the research programme itself. Details of the project are given which, in the scope and scale of investigation of the general public and a wide range of specialist audiences, make it one of the largest ever undertaken in the UK in this area. Selected results are given from just one of the surveys, the General Public survey. They are used as an illustration of the sort of findings that emerged. The results shown build together into an argument that GM has a very low profile in the UK but that, properly handled, a higher profile and a more strongly perceived relationship between the UK companies and their American parentage would be beneficial to their operations.

Finally, the third part of the paper assesses the contribution of the research programme. It indicates the ways in which the findings were disseminated among senior management and how they took them on board in devising the strategy of the individual operating companies. It concludes that research has made a significant contribution to the thinking about and development of current GM corporate strategy in the UK and looks forward to it being used as the baseline against which to assess that strategy.

BACKGROUND AND GENESIS OF THE RESEARCH PROGRAMME

General Motors is the largest manufacturing company in the world with a turnover of more than $84 billion in 1984 and some 750 000 employees worldwide. It has distinguished technological and manufacturing record going back to the earliest years of the century.

Although the Corporation has always been particularly strong in the USA, General Motors has in fact operated round the world for the major part of its history. This is a relatively little known state of affairs because in many markets GM's local companies have operated through their own brand names which have established national identities. Thus in the UK, the British companies Vauxhall and Bedford have for over half a century been manufacturing British cars and trucks for sale in the UK and for export, as members of the GM international family of companies. Similarly, there are other GM companies in the British Isles, most of which are involved in the manufacture of a variety of automotive components for incorporation into both Vauxhall and Bedford vehicles and into those made by non-GM companies. These companies are: AC Spark Plug, Delco Products, Fisher Body, and Saginaw Steering in the UK, as well as General Motors Distribution (Ireland) Ltd., and Packard Electric in the Republic of Ireland, and the Corporation's financing arm, General Motors Acceptance Corporation. Components are also sold directly to the public for the maintenance of vehicles under the AC Delco brand name. Altogether in the British Isles, the GM companies employ in excess of 27 000 people and with a combined turnover in excess of £2 billion they are amongst the largest manufacturing groups in Britain.

The various GM companies in the UK operate largely independently of each other under their own brand names with their own marketing plans, production facilities, distribution networks and so forth. However, they do co-operate with one another through the Public Affairs Council (PAC) of GM in the UK and Ireland, on which they are all represented and through which they can speak with one voice on all matters of overall relevance and common concern.

It was the PAC which took the lead to initiate the research programme described later in this paper. Individual GM companies' fortunes were on an ascending path. There had been the introduction of the Vauxhall Cavalier which had been supremely successful and mounted a major challenge to Ford in the massive fleet vehicle area. Bedford had developed a new range of commercial vehicles. The components companies were going from strength to strength. The PAC was concerned to investigate the potential for linking these successful developments with each other by identifying the companies and their products more closely with General Motors.

It was not of course clear that such identification would be beneficial. There was concern that too close a connection with an American parent might be detrimental to companies seen as solidly British. The PAC therefore set up a Working Party who in turn appointed the advertising and public relations group Charles Barker. Against the background described in outline above, the brief to Charles Barker was to identify the specific questions to which answers should be sought and to recommend how these answers should be obtained.

As a result of the dialogue between the Working Party and Charles Barker five key questions were identified:

  (i) Would it be a good thing to upweight the General Motors corporate connection to provide a greater sense of identity, cohesion and purpose to the UK operations?

 (ii) Would such an upweighting be detrimental to the identity of the UK operating companies? Would there be any adverse effects on opinions about or loyalty towards the GM companies in the British Isles?

(iii) If such a development were to be indicated as a feasible corporate strategy, what would be the relative strengths and weaknesses of the General Motors image that might be utilised or avoided?

(iv) In such a corporate strategy, what would be the key problems which corporate *communications* might be employed to help overcome?

(v) What effect would such corporate communications have overall on the corporate standing of both GM and its individual operating companies?

As a major contribution to the answering of these questions, Charles Barker developed detailed research objectives and a broad outline of the scope and scale of the research programme. The British Market Research Bureau was appointed to carry out the programme.

The wide-ranging nature of the questions being asked, and the likely impact of the answers on the future strategy of GM companies in the UK meant that the survey had to investigate a very wide range of audiences. These are set out in full in the next section but they included considerable emphasis on opinion-forming audiences both inside and outside the motor industry: not only motor dealers and fleet buyers, but MPs, trades unionists, pressure groups and the like. They also included, as a very special and vitally important group, the companies' own employees. The project took place in 1983. It produced a vast amount of detailed information and led to action on a number of fronts. In the restricted space allowed here, an excellent flavour of the nature of the important role of the research can nevertheless be obtained by presenting findings in relation to just one of the surveys, that among the general public. The main body of the paper now provides some of the key results from that survey that are central to one of the major questions the research addressed, namely the value or otherwise of upweighting awareness of the GM corporate connection with its operating companies. Following this exposition, the last part of the paper returns to a discussion of the value of the research and how it has been utilised in the formation of GM's corporate strategy and communications.

THE RESEARCH PROGRAMME

Research Objectives

The basic parameters of the research programme had been set by Charles Barker in its brief to BMRB. Its first essential was that it should be *comprehensive* in two ways. It was to be comprehensive in its coverage of all of GM's activity. It was not intended primarily to assist GM in its marketing operations, but act as a guide to GM management in taking future corporate decisions in relation to any or all of its UK operations. It was also to be comprehensive in its coverage of the full range of audiences — from the general public at large through to the most senior and specific specialist audiences (such as senior civil servants, top trade-union officials, influential journalists, etc.). The objectives of the research programme were therefore formally stated as:

> To provide information on awareness of General Motors and attitudes to the Corporation and its constituent operating companies in Great Britain and Ireland in order:
>
> — to serve as input into the thinking about and the determination of corporate strategy;
> — to serve as a baseline against which to monitor change in the position and standing of the organisation over time, and to assess the impact of corporate communications.

Thus from the outset the research was envisaged as having the dual role of *contributing to the decision-making* on corporate strategy, and being part of *the basis of evaluation* of the strategy subsequently adopted.

Details of the Project

The research project comprised the three 'classic' phases of exploratory qualitative work, a pilot operation, and main quantitative work. However not all of the audiences were covered in all phases. For some of the smallest groups of specialist 'opinion-forming' publics (e.g. trades union leaders) there was only one phase because their number was so small and their degree of intimate knowledge so considerable that only qualitative methods could properly obtain the wealth of information that was there to be unearthed.

The full details of the content of each phase are given below. In perusing the wide range of specialist and non-specialist audiences investigated, the reader will observe that the project met the specification of being comprehensive.

Phase I: Qualitative

Group Discussions	*Number*
General public with emphasis on motorists	14
Local audiences, i.e. people living within the catchment area for the workforce of a GM plant	6

Depth Interviews	
Vehicle dealers	10

Vehicle fleet operators	10
Repair garages—fitters and managers	5
Motor insurance specialists	2
Pressure groups with pro and anti-motoring biases	5
'Government' (relevant Senior Civil Servants and Members of Parliament)	6
Motoring press	5
General editorial press and TV	5
Trades union leaders	4
Suppliers to GM operating companies	5

Phase II: Pilot Surveys

Pilot surveys to test the quantitative questionnaires among:
General public, UK
General public, Eire
Local audiences
Fleet operators
Dealers
City
Employees

Phase III: Quantitative Surveys

Representative samples of several universes with the following sample sizes:

General public, UK	1232
General public, Northern Ireland	250
General public, Eire	258
(All the above with oversampling of motorists)	
Local audiences—people living within the catchment area for the workforce of each of six main GM plant locations in UK	619
Local opinion formers (businessmen and others in key positions in local government and local affairs) in same geographical areas (semi-structured)	60
Fleet operators (cars and commercial vehicles)	274
Dealers and repairers (cars and commercial vehicles)	274
Specially selected sample of very large fleet operators (semi-structured)	31
GM employees	889
City panel	100

The last two elements were conducted by subsidiaries of the Charles Barker group; that among GM employees using self-completion, and that among the City panel by telephone. All of the remainder of the project was conducted by BMRB by personal interview. In all, the project constituted one of the most comprehensive overviews by a major company of its corporate standing ever undertaken in the UK.

Although the whole project is set out systematically above, the three basic phases overlapped somewhat in time. Data collection spanned the period January–July 1983 with the quantitative survey of the General Public (results of which are given below) taking place in June.

Methodology for the General Public Sample

The sample for the main quantitative survey comprised 650 adults representative of the population of Great Britain aged 16–64, plus a booster sample of 582 motorists (defined as people who have a car available for them to drive nowadays). They were interviewed in a representative sample of 80 areas which were pairs of Enumeration Districts (containing on average 300 households). The areas were selected with probability proportional to the number of motorists after stratification by ACORN neighbourhood type within Standard Region. Interviewers were given a quota of eight adults to interview with controls for sex. Within the female quota there were controls for working vs. non-working housewives, and for housewives with and without children. Interviewers were issued with a list of addresses which made up the Enumeration Districts for their sample. They had to interview their general public quota at the odd-numbered addresses only. They then had to obtain a further eight interviews with motorists, as defined above, with controls for age and sex within the same streets but from the even-numbered houses only. This sample design of working within a small, strictly defined geographic area and further restricting interviewers as to where the general public and motorists sample should live, introduces a degree of control that is much greater than in the average quota sample used in market research.

The over-sampling of motorists and minor demographic imbalances were corrected by weighting at the analysis stage.

Some Results

The project was so comprehensive in its coverage that only a flavour of some of the findings can be given. Moreover, of course, the commercial implications of many results are such that they must be treated as confidential. However, we feel we can give a good idea of the type of information that was collected and the sort of findings which emerged and subsequently contributed to the detail of the corporate communication programme GM has adopted in the UK since the research. For this purpose we will use a fascinating series of results from the quantitative survey among the general public, which together build into a particular argument in relation to a really key issue: namely, the extent to which it would be advantageous to the UK operating companies to establish a more strongly perceived corporate link with their American parent.

Step 1: The 'Profile' of GM in the UK

The first step was to establish the 'profile' (i.e. current awareness and standing) of GM in the UK.

Information on awareness and knowledge of GM was collected in a number of ways. The very first question, before respondents knew that the survey was about motor companies, presented respondents with a series of cards, on each of which was printed a company commonly known by its initials. These included two other motor companies: BL and VW, two other American companies: IBM and TWA, and three other British companies, chosen in the expectation of their having very differing levels of recognition: BP, GEC and TI. The question read: 'Each of these cards shows a set of initials which stand for the name of a large company. Could you sort the cards into two sets for me—those which you have heard of before, and those which you have never heard of'. This question gives a first measure 'Initial Recognition'. The next question produced a measure called 'Correct Identification' by asking the respondents, for each set of initials they claimed to recognise: 'Can you tell me what the initials . . . stand for?' Finally, 'Prompted Recognition' was derived from a third question which gave respondents a card with all the full information on it (e.g. GM = General Motors, etc.) and asked them: 'This card shows what each of these sets of initials actually stands for. Now that you can see their full names, which of these companies have you *not* heard of?'.

Thus we have three measures of 'awareness' and to these we added two measures of 'familiarity'. Those who recognised the company at all were given a card listing four options ('Know very well', 'Know a fair amount', 'Know just a little', 'Know almost nothing') and asked, for each name they had heard of: 'Using one of the phrases on this card, how much would you say you know about . . .?' The first two positions give a measure of 'High Familiarity'. Finally, people were asked: 'Some of these companies are British owned, others aren't. So is . . . British owned, or what country does it come from?' This gives a measure of 'Correct Nationality'.

Results for these five measures of awareness and familiarity are given in the Table 1.1.

It will be seen that the largest manufacturing company in the world with substantial investment in the UK occupied fifth to seventh place out of eight on all of the measures of awareness and familiarity. In all cases too, it is behind the other motor manufacturers in the list (BL and VW).

TABLE 1.1 **Awareness and Familiarity for GM and Other Companies**

Company	Initial recognition (%)	Correct identification (%)	Prompted recognition (%)	High familiarity (%)	Correct nationality (%)
BP	98	90	98	32	92
BL	95	92	97	42	97
GEC	86	63	94	22	66
VW	80	75	91	27	82
TWA	76	52	89	12	50
IBM	68	16	66	12	27
GM	58(7th)	51(6th)	87(6th)	16(5th)	46(6th)
TI	28	12	35	5	21

Base: All respondents, 1232

At a later point in the questionnaire, the focus was turned more directly onto the motor industry, though the client's identity was cloaked by always asking questions about several motor companies. Two other results are of interest here. Firstly, questions to examine knowledge of GM's links with operating companies asked: 'Can you tell me what makes of cars, vans or trucks are part of the General Motors group?' In response, 31% said Vauxhall, 16% Opel, and 13% Bedford. A similar question about companies that make 'parts, tyres, spares, and so on' revealed 2% aware of the GM/AC Delco association.

A somewhat different approach asked respondents separately for BL, Ford and GM a series of questions designed to establish spontaneous associations, e.g.: 'When I mention the company Ford to you, what is the first thing that comes to your mind?' Interviewers probed for further associations until the respondent could think of no more. Table 1.2 shows the proportion who could think of no associations and the average number of associations for each company.

TABLE 1.2 **Extent of Spontaneous Associations**

	Ford	BL	GM
Proportion who could think of *no associations at all*	1%	4%	33%
Average number of associations	2.28	2.14	1.23

Base: All respondents, 1232

Thus impressions of GM were at a much lower level. Moreover the type of comment made was qualitatively different. The main spontaneous associations for GM were 'motor manufacturer' (26%), 'American' (20%) and 'big' (8%). Whilst some comments for Ford and BL were also of a similar general nature, there were many others which were more detailed e.g. the name of a model, and also more imagery, e.g. 'make reliable cars', 'have workforce problems'.

The conclusion from all of these questions and others was that GM had a *very low profile* indeed, with low awareness and knowledge and few impressions other than that of being 'a big American motor manufacturer'. In the circumstances it could be argued that GM would tend to have the generalised image of all large American multi-nationals operating in Britain. In relation to the question of whether GM should adopt a higher profile it was therefore necessary to understand attitudes to large American companies operating here in the UK.

Step 2: Attitudes to Large American Companies

Before respondents knew that the focus of our enquiry was the motor industry, they were asked a battery of attitude questions relating to the activities of large American companies in Britain. The technique involved a sorting board and shuffle pack. The sorting board had five boxes: 'Agree strongly', 'Tend to agree', 'Neither agree nor disagree', 'Tend to disagree', 'Disagree strongly'. The interviewer handed a pack of ten cards to the respondent and the question ran:

> Now I'd like you to think about large American-owned companies. Each of these cards shows something which somebody else has said to us about large American-owned companies which operate in this country, and I'd like you to show me how much you agree or disagree with each statement by placing the card in one of the five boxes on this sheet.

The statements used were based on the qualitative work. Table 1.3 shows the statements and the balance of opinion (i.e. the proportion choosing a *favourable* position on the scale *minus* the proportion choosing an *unfavourable* position).

Despite the obvious concern about their profit orientation, these results show that the British public's attitudes to large American companies is *very favourable* and people seem to be realistic in recognising their contribution, particularly in relation to investment and employment. Thus it would appear that, in relation to Step 2 in the construction of the argument, promulgation of American parentage, properly handled, would be likely to be a plus rather than a minus factor for operating companies in Britain. This leads us to examine the special subsection of the population who are already in that position, i.e. they already know about GM's links with their UK principal

TABLE 1.3   Attitudes to Large American-Owned Companies Operating in Britain

	Balance of opinion
It's a good thing to have American-owned companies having factories in Britain because they provide a lot of jobs	+60
One of the advantages of having American-owned companies here is that they have bigger financial resources for new development	+59
We should not stop American investment in factories in this country	+55
American-owned companies in this country do take care of their workforce	+41
American-owned companies do no more damage to the environment than equivalent British companies	+36
American-owned companies operating in this country tend to have more modern technology than British companies	+31
American-owned companies generally have fewer strikes among their workforce in this country than do British companies	+25
American-owned companies really do understand the British public and what it wants	+14
There should be a tax on American-owned companies because they send all their profit out of the country	−17
American-owned companies will move their jobs out of Britain to other countries if they think they can make more money	−57

Base: All respondents, 1232

operating companies, Vauxhall and Bedford, to see if their existing attitudes are more or less favourable.

Step 3: The Attitudes of the Currently Knowledgeable Population

The hypothesis under examination here is that a higher profile for GM in the UK in the future would be indicated if the currently knowledgeable have attitudes that are more favourable than average. Two other sets of questions we asked are of help in this assessment.

All those who spontaneously knew of the link between GM and its principal operating companies in the UK were asked two questions. First: 'Do you think it's a good or bad thing *for the Vauxhall company* that it is linked with General Motors?' Second: 'Do you think it's a good or bad thing *for the customer* that Vauxhall is linked with General Motors?' A similar pair of questions were asked about the GM/Bedford link. Results are shown in Table 1.4.

Among those who are aware of the links and who express an opinion, an overwhelming majority believe that the link is a good thing both for the

TABLE 1.4   Opinions of Link between GM and Operating Companies

	GM/Vauxhall		GM/Bedford	
	For company 446 (%)	For customer 446 (%)	For company 191 (%)	For customer 191 (%)
Good thing	71	57	66	52
Bad thing	6	4	3	4
Neither	12	10	10	19
Don't know	12	17	21	26

Base: All aware of links

Vauxhall and Bedford companies and for the customer. The reasons people gave in relation to the companies centred around a feeling that GM backing has been important to their survival and other 'parent-type' roles. In relation to the customer, reasons revolved around improved products and service, due to substantial GM backing.

Another set of results which proved of major importance in relation to this aspect concerned a special analysis of image data. Two image batteries were included towards the end of the questionnaire when respondents knew our focus of enquiry was the British motor industry. In each, Vauxhall was compared with Ford, BL and Talbot, firstly in relation to eight dimensions on 'the cars they make' and secondly in relation to eight dimensions on the 'companies themselves'.

The dimensions covered were as follows:

Cars they make	Companies themselves
Reliability	Efficiency
Range	Strong management
Sort of car I'd like to own	Care for neighbourhood
Durability	Reductions in workforce
Design	Fewer strikes
Re-sale value	Importing parts
Individuality	Media presence
Getting model right before launch	Contribution to country's economy

The method used to collect image data on the four companies was an associative technique. Interviewers handed respondents a card listing the four companies and the question then ran:

I'm going to read out a number of statements and I'd like you to tell me to which companies, if any, you think each statement applies. You may mention as many or as few companies as you like for each statement. So thinking firstly about the cars they make, which of these companies do you think . . .

The interviewer then read out for each battery a series of eight pairs of statements each representing the positive and negative side of an image dimension, e.g.:

'Make long-lasting and durable cars'	(Positive)
'Make cars which are not so long-lasting and durable'	(Negative)

The technique allows respondents three basic options in relation to each company on each dimension. They can either associate the company with the positive statement, or they can name the company in relation to the negative statement, or they can refrain from mentioning the company at all. This allows very flexible analysis because it is possible to calculate both the *strength* of the image among the public at large and the *character* of the image among those who have an impression.

The first measure, *image strength*, is quite simply the total proportion of people who have any impression at all of the company on the dimension. For example, 18% of our sample of the general public said that Vauxhall make cars that are 'long-lasting and durable' and 13% said that they make cars which are 'not so long-lasting and durable'. Thus:

Positive image strength is	18%
Negative image strength is	13%
Total image strength is	31%

The second measure, *image character*, is calculated as the proportion of all those who have an impression who are favourable. It is thus:

$$\frac{\text{positive image strength} \times 100}{\text{Total image strength}}$$

In our example, the image character of Vauxhall in relation to the dimension of 'make cars that are long-lasting and durable' is:

$$\frac{18 \times 100}{31} = 58$$

It is important to have this second measure as it standardises the comparison between companies which can be very difficult if they have very different levels of strength of image. Every company is examined only amongst those who have an impression.

These data are of course of considerable interest and were analysed by many different subgroupings. The one that is of particular relevance to our present discussion was one which looked at two groups 'the knowledgeable' and 'the ignorant', defined as follows:

> *The knowledgeable* Those who earlier in the questionnaire knew GM and that it was American, and also knew that Vauxhall was owned by GM (24% of the sample)
>
> *The ignorant* Those who did not know of the GM/Vauxhall link and did not know GM was American (47% of the sample)

Figure 1.1 shows the image character for Vauxhall among these two groups for the eight dimensions in the 'cars they make' battery.

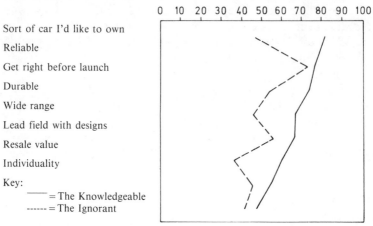

Figure.1.1 Image Character of Vauxhall

A similar but less marked result emerged in the 'companies themselves' battery. Thus it was clear that acquaintance with the Vauxhall company's American parentage was strongly associated with holding a better view both of the company and of its products.

There was of course the possibility that the knowledgeable group were more favourable in their views of *all* car companies. However, when this was checked this proved not to be the case as the Table 1.5 shows:

Thus it seemed that knowledge of Vauxhall's parentage does have a genuine favourable impact on perceptions of the company and its products. Taken with the previous information on perceptions of whether the GM links with its operating companies were a good or bad thing, there appeared to be strong evidence for the conclusion that 'Familiarity breeds approbation and not contempt'.

Although results pointed towards an upweighting in awareness of the local operating companies' links with GM, there remained one further potential obstacle, which might be termed the 'Britishness' issue in car buying.

TABLE 1.5   Summary of Image Character among the Knowledgeable and the Ignorant

	Vauxhall	Ford	BL	Talbot
(a) Number of dimensions out of eight for which the knowledgeable have a better image character than the ignorant:				
— 'Cars they make	8	2	1	0
— 'Companies themselves'	6	3	3	1
(b) Percentage difference in average image character between knowledgeable and ignorant:				
— 'Cars they make'	+ 17%	− 1%	− 8%	− 15%
— 'Companies themselves'	+ 2%	− 5%	0	− 4%

Step 4: The Britishness Issue

The qualitative work drew attention to the importance of the 'Britishness' dimension in car buying in Britain. It came spontaneously to the fore in all discussions. Two separate issues were distinguished:

1. Firstly, there was a perceived ambivalence between the generally expressed view that 'buying British' was important (because of its effect on the economy, stemming unemployment, etc.) and the specific importance of this factor in the actual purchase decision where it was hypothesised that other considerations (especially value for money) would overtake the general principle.
2. The second issue concerned the growing realisation among the public that car manufacture in the 1980s is increasingly a hybrid process with parts being made in one country, assembly taking place elsewhere, American ownership and traditional British names. People held differing views on just what they would regard as 'British'.

Given the relatively low awareness of and acquaintance with General Motors in Britain, but given the basically propitious platform for the company to take a higher profile in corporate communication terms, it became crucial to provide reliable data on these two 'Britishness' aspects.

Information on the first issue was obtained early in the questionnaire via the use of the question: 'If *you* were going to buy a car tomorrow, could you tell me from this card how important it would be to you that it was *British made*?'. Five options were presented and the results are given in the Table 1.6.

We see that there is, in fact, some element of a 'British-factor' in car purchase for about half the motorists in Britain.

Up to this point, people had been reacting to the words 'British made'. It clearly was important to address the second issue of what individuals

TABLE 1.6 Importance of Buying British in Car Purchase

	General Public 1232 (%)		Motorists 903 (%)	
I would only buy a British car	12%		10%	
It would be very important to me	20%	53%	19%	50%
It would be quite important to me	21%		21%	
It would not matter to me	44%	47%	45%	49%
I would not buy a British car	3%		4%	

understand by this term, given the involved nature of modern-day car manufacture.

In order to tackle this difficult area, a set of shuffle cards was produced each of which listed a possible combination of ways of manufacture. The interviewer then asked the following question:

> Nowadays, even with well-known makes, some cars are made partly in Britain and partly abroad. I'd like to find out what *you would count as a British-made car*. Each of these cards gives a description of a different way in which a car might be manufactured. I'd like you to sort them into two sets for me: those which you would count as British made, and those which you wouldn't count as British made.

She then shuffled the cards and handed them to the respondent.

A card looked like this:

> A well-known British-named car (like Ford, Austin or Vauxhall) where:
>
> All of the PARTS are made . . . . IN BRITAIN
> The car is ASSEMBLED . . . . IN BRITAIN
> The company producing the car is . . . . . . AMERICAN

On each card, the sentence at the top ('A well-known British-named car . . .') was the same; similarly, the phrases to the left of the card ('All of the parts . . .', etc.) remained constant. However, in rotation, 'Abroad' was substituted for 'In Britain' in either or both of the top two spaces on the right, and 'British' was substituted for 'American' in the bottom space.

The analysis demonstrated that the key dimension is *assembly in Britain*, followed by manufacture of the parts in Britain. The ownership of the company proved of less importance. This series of results held equally for those with a British factor in their car purchasing as it did for those who did not. For example, 79% of the most extreme group who claimed they would only buy a British car, said that a car with a British name with parts made and assembled in Britain but with American ownership would be regarded by them as 'British made'.

There were obviously commercially important messages for GM in relation to its manufacturing policies which is why no more detailed results can be given. However, for the issue currently under discussion, namely whether the perception of American ownership would *per se* be an inhibiting factor to car purchase, it was possible to conclude that for the vast majority this would not be the case.

Thus, in relation to the particular key issue which this whole series of analyses had been intended to address, it seemed fair to conclude that a higher GM profile in the UK and a more strongly perceived relationship between Vauxhall and Bedford and their American parentage would be beneficial to the companies. Of course there remained many decisions to be made in relation to the manner and nature of the promotion of a high GM profile and the research project had a great deal more to contribute towards the detailed tactics.

Other 'Publics'

These results from the General Public Survey are illustrative of the way the project was tackled. Without going into the detail of the results from the specialist and opinion-forming audiences, two generalised observations can be made:

1. The major conclusion that familiarity breeds approbation is reinforced by results from other publics. In general, opinion-forming groups have a more favourable impression than others. Thus such groups as dealers, fleet managers, local audiences living near GM plant and so on, who all know much more than average about GM and its links, also have a distinctly more favourable impression of the UK operating companies than the public as a whole.
2. Whilst all of the special groups designated for this investigation proved of interest, some provided information that was of genuinely major benefit to GM. In this category would come trades union leaders, Civil Servants and Members of Parliament, and motoring journalists. This is highlighted by the groups being proposed for re-investigation. The proposal is that, in due course, the General Public and the Trade (dealers and fleet buyers) surveys will be repeated. There will be *increased emphasis* on certain types of local audience and GM suppliers, and attempts will be made to *actually re-interview key individuals* from some

of the specialist categories like trades unionists, government personnel and journalists.

The discussions on (and the eventual commissioning of) a second research project in 1985 are evidence that the 1983 project was valuable and valued. In the next section we discuss some of the activity and thinking in the year or so following the research.

THE CONTRIBUTION OF THE RESEARCH PROGRAMME

The research findings were *very widely disseminated* in the UK.

Initial presentations of the full research findings were made by Charles Barker and BMRB to the working party that had commissioned the project and to the full Public Affairs Council. The PAC was determined that the findings should be acted upon and concluded that the best way of achieving this was to ensure that senior managers throughout the Corporation's UK companies should have the findings presented to them. A very large number of presentations were made round the country, each specially tailored to the needs and interests of particular operating companies or management groups.

The aim of this wide dissemination of findings was to ensure that right across GM's UK operations there was a real understanding of what the research had revealed about the attitudes of the Corporation's various publics in the UK. In consequence, the two years since the project have seen *real action and change* in the way the Corporation presents itself in the UK. The PAC or some other arm of senior management has not had to dictate that change must occur and what the detail should be. Rather the individual companies have been able to devise relevant strategies based on a proper understanding at the operational level of the opportunities and problems confronting the Corporation in the UK. The PAC has been able to monitor the changes that have taken place.

Some examples of the action that has been taken are as follows:

(a) As indicated in the previous section, the research showed very clearly that there were major benefits to be reaped from being known as a GM company. Membership of the GM international family of companies provides important reassurance to potential customers. Since this key finding emerged, *determined efforts have been made to get across the facts of the GM association* — in advertising, in promotion, in branding and countless other ways.

(b) The research showed the PAC that it had a big job to do, with major benefits available. It also gave key points as to how the job should be tackled. There is no single corporate communications programme through which GM is attempting to build on the survey findings. Rather, as a result of the strenuous efforts made to disseminate the survey findings and implications throughout the Corporation, *every piece of communications produced throughout the operating companies is created with an awareness of the strengths* that are there to be built on, and what weaknesses need, as the occasion arises, to be corrected.

(c) There have also been *several specific new central initiatives*. One example is the sponsorship programme for the Football Association, with a substantial sum being provided over a period of years to assist the Association in the training of the young and talented. Another example derives from GM's connections with Merseyside. GM has two prosperous factories near Liverpool providing much-needed jobs in an area of high unemployment. It was therefore seen as natural for there to be joint sponsorship of part of the large-scale and successful Liverpool Garden Festival in 1984.

(d) At the same time, the Corporation's signage and identity generally has taken note of the findings, and there was careful study of how a *corporate advertising campaign* might most usefully be conducted (and such a campaign actually began in the press in the UK in the autumn of 1985). Similarly, as a result of this greater awareness, we have seen a *significant change in the tone* of our *product* advertising within the Corporation in the UK. There is now a readiness to look to the reassurance that comes from the GM resource and strengths that stand behind the individual companies, while retaining the individual companies' identities as manufacturing and marketing organisations in their own right.

(e) In parallel with this, the Corporation has established an *extensive internal communications programme* for benefiting from the findings of the survey. Internal communications co-ordinators have been appointed at each plant, and their input is being backed up by video to keep employees, at all levels, informed of what is going on within the corporation, whilst a daily electronic news service, called 'Newsdesk' is being established to keep everyone in touch.

(f) In general, the major impact of the research has not been to fashion these new tools of communication, but in recasting the tone and approach of communications programmes that were already taking place, including not only product advertising as stated above, but the whole gamut of brochures, exhibitions, press and public relations activity and so on.

Viewed overall, this research programme has made a significant contribution to the thinking about and subsequent development of GM's corporate strategy in the UK. It has been presented to and acted upon by the highest levels of senior management in making longer term strategic decisions. It was always envisaged that the 1983 survey would establish a benchmark against which future progress would be measured. In Autumn 1985 the PAC, aided again by Charles Barker and BMRB, will be conducting a second survey in order to see what has been achieved and what changes have taken place in the perceptions the various publics have of the British companies which are operating as part of the GM international family of companies. The results will be awaited in eager and confident anticipation that there will be significant signs of progress in the long-term task of building the corporate standing of GM in the UK.

FURTHER READING

Drake, P. H., Penny, J. C. and Samuels, J. A., 'Britain at its Best: Researching the Effectiveness of a Major Corporate Image Advertising Campaign', *ESOMAR Congress (1981) Proceedings.*

ACKNOWLEDGMENT

This paper was first presented by Eric Fountain, Ian Parker and John Samuels at the 38th ESOMAR Congress, Wiesbaden, September 1985, 'Broadening the Uses of Research'. Permission for reprinting has been granted by the European Society for Opinion and Marketing Research, ESOMAR, J. J. Viottastraat 29, 1071 JP Amsterdam, The Netherlands, from whom the papers of this Congress (2 volumes) may be obtained.

APPENDIX 1.1   QUESTIONNAIRE CONTENT AND ORDER

For reasons of confidentiality it is not possible to include a copy of the actual questionnaire used. However, in order to understand more fully the problems facing the researchers in designing the questionnaire order so as to eliminate possibilities of contamination and education of responses by earlier questions, the listing below gives a clear idea of the questionnaire content and order.

INTRODUCTION	What people think about large companies
Q. 1	Initials recognition
Q. 2	Correct initials identification
Q. 3	Prompted company recognition
Q. 4	Familiarity with companies
Q. 5	Country of ownership of companies
Q. 6	Attitudes to large American-owned companies operating in Britain

Q. 7–16	Spontaneous associations for Ford, GM, BL
Q. 17	Importance of Britishness in car buying
Q. 18	Perceptions of what is British
Q. 19–20	Awareness of cars, vans and trucks made by BL and GM
Q. 21–28	Perceptions of value of link between GM and Vauxhall and Bedford from customer and company point of view
Q. 29–31	Awareness of components companies owned by Ford, BL, GM
Q. 32	Prompted awareness of components companies
Q. 33	Prompted knowledge of ownership of components companies
Q. 34–49	Classification details *re* motoring:
Q. 34–35	Whether driver and whether car available nowadays
Q. 36–39	Details of car available
Q. 40–43	Servicing and maintenance of car available
Q. 44–45	Details of other cars in household
Q. 46	Annual mileage
Q. 47	'Degree of interest in motoring' scale
Q. 48–49	Readership of specialist motoring press
Q. 50	Knowledge of connection between British motor companies and foreign motor companies
Q. 51	Image battery: 'Cars they make'
Q. 52	Image battery: 'Companies themselves'
Q. 53–54	Which companies are increasing market share and why
Q. 55–56	Awareness of Vauxhall models
Q. 57–58	Awareness of Opel models
Q. 59–62	Perceptions of value of Vauxhall-Opel link
Q. 63–68	Classification details on driving in the course of work
Q. 69	Image battery for vans and trucks (among those who drive van or truck)
Q. 70–71	Image battery for components companies (among those who change own spark plugs)
Q. 72	Awareness of other GM operating companies
Q. 73	Familiarity with GM operating companies
Q. 74	ITV viewing
Q. 75–76	Press readership questions
Classification	Demographics

Applied Marketing and Social Research 2nd Edition
Edited by Ute Bradley
©Copyright John Wiley 1987

2. The Fresh Cream Cakes Market: The Use of Qualitative Research as Part of a Consumer Research Programme

Jackie Dickens   *Leo Burnett Ltd.*

The research programme described here deals with *qualitative* research. This type of research has a language and craftsmanship different from that which applies to quantitative research. This contribution has therefore the double merit of describing a more typical case and setting it within the wider context of the basic techniques available to the qualitative researcher. As the author points out, the choice of basic techniques and variants upon these will be chosen to suit the problem at hand. The student can expect only guidance, therefore, and not hard rules.

This case appeared in the first edition of this book and has stood the test of time. The Fresh Cream Cake campaign was simply a good vehicle for demonstrating the use and value of qualitative research. The case has therefore been retained for this edition, but in the discussion sections it has been updated in line with new methodological approaches. Further references have been added.

INTRODUCTION

What is Qualitative Research?

Qualitative research is generally differentiated from quantitative research in terms of methodology. The differences are twofold. Firstly, qualitative research involves unstructured or semi-structured methods of data collection, group discussions and individual interviews being the most commonly used tools. It is *response*-orientated rather than *question* orientated, as the flow of any given individual or group interview will be at least partly, and often largely, determined by the respondent(s), rather than by the format of a prestructured questionnaire. Secondly, qualitative research involves relatively small samples which, whilst they may have been carefully selected to reflect the known characteristics of a target group, cannot necessarily be assumed to be *representative* of larger populations.

These two broad methodological differences between quantitative and qualitative research have led to differences in the criteria upon which each type of research is evaluated, and bought in the commercial context. With quantitative research, the technical knowledge and skills of the individual researcher and the reputation and resources of the research company appear to be critical factors. With qualitative research, the personal skills of the individual researcher are what the client is primarily buying. A paper published by the Market Research Society R & D Subcommittee on Qualitative Research suggests: '. . . it is agreed that the skill and experience of the interviewer/researcher conducting the group is the most important determinant of the value of the results of the study'.[1]

The same writers also suggest that the qualitative researcher is more like the artist: part of his stock in trade is his personal capacity for empathy, sensitivity, imagination and creativity, as well as his capacity for logical analysis'.

The nature of qualitative research methods, and, in particular, the heavy reliance placed upon the skills of the individual qualitative researcher have led to serious questions about the validity and reliability of qualitative research. Twyman[2] conducted an experiment which indicated that different individual researchers reached different conclusions on the basis of studies they had separately conducted on the same creative material. May (Qualitative Advertising Research, JMRS 1978) questions the extent to which an individual researcher's knowledge of his/her client's needs and expectations may, albeit unwittingly, influence the interpretation of qualitative data.

However, it seems to the writer that most criticisms of qualitative research stem from attempts to compare it directly with quantitative survey methods, and to employ criteria for evaluation based on the principles of survey research methodology. Such comparisons are on the whole, relatively meaningless, since the two types of methodology are designed, and largely used to tackle, *different types of problem*. The problems qualitative research is most frequently required to address are those of *understanding*, as opposed to *assessment*. Whilst the proper methodological response to *assessment* questions is the methodology of a *test*, the proper response to *understanding* questions is that of a *search*. Most problems of human social behaviour involve complex variables, where the relationship is not reflex or self-explanatory. Hence, questions such as how do consumers perceive the inter-relationships between brands in a given market? or how might a given advertising campaign be working? are essentially *qualitative* questions for which the methodology of *search* is often most appropriate. If we are searching for understanding, there can be no strict procedure. Furthermore, a given pattern of 'results' has no one necessary interpretation, and it is counter-effective to suggest that it should.

Hence it is important to evaluate qualitative research within the context of the problems to which the techniques are best suited. To employ qualitative techniques to predict which of a range of new product ideas might achieve the highest level of sales is clearly a nonsense. Thus the main criterion to employ when evaluating the worth of qualitative research is that of whether it can provide an *understanding* of a market, brand or service, which can help contribute towards making right decisions. We must *accept* that the unstructured way in which the data are collected means that they cannot be aggregated. Qualitative research can identify the *range* of behaviour and attitudes, but it cannot provide a basis for saying *how many* people behave in a certain way or hold particular views. Trust in the results must inevitably be largely derived from subjective judgemental criteria, and becomes heavily dependent upon trust in the individual researchers conducting a given study.

To look at it from the opposite viewpoint, the standardised way in which quantitative date are collected also has limitations. The questions to be asked and the ground to be covered must be determined in advance; question wording cannot be adapted to suit particular respondents, since everyone must be asked for the same sort of information in the same sort of way. Thus, we cannot capture the depth and detail of the individual case. Furthermore, as Stephen King points out, 'people do not go around with ready packaged views on everything—they often need to talk a topic out to discover what they really think'.[3]

The essential point is that we should judge the two methods of enquiry in relation to the problems for which each is appropriate, rather than seek to compare them solely on the basis of technical merit.

Uses of Qualitative Research

The types of problem qualitative research is mainly used to tackle are described below. These applications mainly reflect the commercial uses of qualitative research in the UK.

Broad Market Exploratory Studies

Qualitative research is frequently commissioned to examine consumer attitudes and behaviour in relation to a broad product field or service. This may constitute an initial examination of a potential new market for a client, or a fresh look at a developing or changing market. Such studies will often seek to understand:

— how consumers perceive the parameters of 'the market' and subsections within it;
— motivations for purchase of the product category, and brands within it;
— images of different brands and dimensions which seem key-to brand discrimination;
— underlying attitudes, aspirations and needs which may affect behaviour.

Goodyear in 1978 suggested that 'strategic studies aimed at giving a detailed understanding of the dynamics of a market have been on the increase in the qualitative sector for a number of years'. While such studies frequently constitute initial, exploratory research to be subsequently quantified, they can also be used to help understand and explain behaviour which has already been identified and described by quantitative surveys.

More Focused Exploratory Studies

Qualitative research is sometimes used to examine in depth the attitudes of a particular group within the population, attitudes towards one specific brand, or one facet of the brand mix.

For example, the perceived need to reconsider a brand's positioning may suggest the need for an intensive brand image study; the desire to expand a brand's franchise in a certain direction (e.g. to pull in more young, single users) may suggest a qualitative project specifically designed to examine the attitudes of this group; lack of understanding of a specific segment of the market (e.g. rejectors of a brand) may indicate the need to explore their motives in depth, and so on.

New Product Development

Qualitative research can prove especially useful in new product development at a number of stages, e.g. it can help to:

— provide an understanding of the structure of the market into which a new product is to be launched;
— examine the nature of strengths and weaknesses of new product concepts, thus helping to develop early ideas;
— provide an understanding of the contribution of various elements in the brand mix;
— explore positioning concepts for new products.

Examples of the use of qualitative research in new product development (e.g. see Essex and Knox[4]) tend to stress the importance of research as an integral *part* of a development programme, rather than simply a means of assessing a range of alternatives at various stages of the development process.

Creative Development

Again, qualitative research can contribute to various stages of the process of developing advertising.

Firstly, the most important contribution qualitative, and indeed all forms of research can make is that of helping to guide the advertising strategy. The strategy sets out the advertising intentions, and will encompass the advertising objectives, the target audience the advertising should address, and the key thought or feeling about the brand we want the target to take out of the advertising. A thorough analysis of available quantitative market and consumer data will be essential at this stage to understand the brand or service's current position within the market and determine competitive strengths and weaknesses. However, the special contribution qualitative research can make is that of providing an understanding of how different consumers relate to the brand or service concerned, on psychological as well as rational levels. Using qualitative research to explore the relative appeal of different positionings for a brand, using stimuli in concept form, can be helpful at this stage, as in the research programme for Fresh Cream Cakes.

Secondly, qualitative research can aid the development of the creative brief, which will be based on the advertising strategy. Because qualitative research can examine relationships between consumers and brands at an individual level this can help 'bring the target group to life' for creative people.[7]

Thirdly, qualitative research is frequently used to explore the potential of advertising ideas before finished advertisements have been produced. Typically, rough representations of advertising executions will be researched (e.g. drawn storyboards, animatics, rough press layouts) and consumer responses used to help guide further development. Whilst neither this type of research, nor indeed any form of quantitative pre-test using rough material, could reliably predict the sales-effectiveness of finished advertising, qualitative research used at this stage can help indicate whether, and how, advertising may achieve the objectives set, and provide guidelines for further development.

Fourthly, qualitative research can be used to help direct future development of campaigns where one or more ads have already run. Researching these to discover how they work with consumers can help guide the direction of subsequent executions. Such research cannot, of course, determine whether or not previous advertising has been sales effective. We would use different methods to understand *whether* advertising has worked; qualitative research can help us to explain *how* it has worked, and help us to do better in the future.

The preceding summary seeks only to provide an indication of the nature and uses of qualitative research. The main body of this chapter attempts to demonstrate how qualitative research was used at two stages of a research programme for fresh cream cakes. It has been written assuming that the reader is unfamiliar with the basic practices and processes involved. Hence descriptions of the basic techniques and how they can be applied are given at each stage of this case study. Clearly, the picture of 'how to do it' conveyed in this chapter reflects the methods of approach favoured by the writer, and should not be assumed to reflect the beliefs and practices of all qualitative research practitioners or companies.

THE FRESH CREAM CAKES MARKET: A CONSUMER RESEARCH PROGRAMME

The qualitative research studies described here constituted two parts of a consumer research programme conducted for the Milk Marketing Board to examine consumer attitudes and behaviour in relation to fresh cream cakes. The series of studies commenced in the early part of 1977 and was completed by the end of that year.

This research programme was not commissioned in response to any specific marketing or advertising problem, but rather to fulfil a need for up-to-date consumer information on which to base the direction of future marketing and advertising strategies. Qualitative and quantitative market studies had been conducted in 1972, but since that time consumers had experienced recession, and it has not known how this might have changed attitudes and purchasing patterns. Furthermore, developments in other markets which might be considered competitive to fresh cream cakes had occurred (e.g. frozen cream cakes/gateaux, packet cake mixes, chilled desserts). In any event, ascertaining sales trends over time is difficult in this market. Whilst the Milk Marketing Board was in possession of trend data relating to supplies of *fresh cream to bakers*, this could not in itself provide any reliable indication of trends in *unit sales*.

The appointed advertising agency on this account, Ogilvy and Mather, were heavily involved in the conception and design of this research programme. As with any account, a regular review of advertising strategy had led the agency to question whether the advertising objectives needed revision, and information was needed on which to base any rethinking. Hence the first two stages of the research programme were planned with the agency's needs very much in mind, whilst the third stage was specifically designed to aid the development of future advertising.

During 1977, three separate studies were conducted by Research Bureau Ltd. (RBL is one of the largest UK research companies, and part of the Research International group):

(i) *A preliminary qualitative study* designed to explore consumer attitudes and behaviour within the product field, and help guide the design of a subsequent quantitative survey.

(ii) *A quantitative survey* designed to produce reliable data about purchasing and eating behaviour, product image, and related consumer attitudes.

(iii) *A qualitative creative development study* designed to guide the creation of a new advertising campaign for fresh cream cakes.

The first and third, qualitative stages of this research programme are discussed in some detail, whilst the second, quantitative survey stage is referred to only briefly. This is simply because it is the purpose of this chapter to concentrate upon qualitative rather than quantitative research techniques. The reader should not assume any underestimation of the importance of the quantitative survey in establishing reliable information about the (then) current status of the market.

Two further points should be made prior to a detailed consideration of the research itself. Firstly, this was in many ways a 'typical' research programme. At no stages of research were novel approaches adopted, or experimental techniques employed. Studies very similar to those described will have been conducted on countless occasions, in a wide range of different markets by other qualitative research practitioners. However, it is not to the latter that this chapter is addressed, but to the student of market research, for whom a 'typical' case history may be more useful than an exceptional one. Secondly, there was very close co-operation between the client, research agency and the account planner from Ogilvy and Mather at all stages. This teamwork undoubtedly contributed in no small measure to the quality and actionability of the research.

PROJECT 1: A QUALITATIVE STUDY OF CONSUMER ATTITUDES AND BEHAVIOUR IN RELATION TO FRESH CREAM CAKES

When this study was commissioned, a follow-up quantitative survey was planned. Hence the specific objectives of this stage of research were defined in the light of this knowledge. In summary, they were *to provide a qualitative understanding of consumer attitudes and behaviour in this market which would*:

—help to guide the design of the quantitative survey; and
—help guide the subsequent interpretation of the results of the latter study.

It is important to remember that the subsequent quantification of qualitative research findings does not always occur, and the design of a qualitative study which would be required to 'stand on its own' might be differently conceived.

The reader will be taken through the various stages of this study, from inception to birth. Figure 2.1 attempts to illustrate a typical step-by-step approach to a qualitative consumer research project. As with all process models, it represents a simplification of the dynamics involved, but it will hopefully serve as a useful framework for a discussion of each stage in the process.

Stage 1: Planning

Planning a qualitative research study involves finding what seems, on the basis of inspection and judgement, to be 'the best' of many possible solutions. There is never any one right way of doing things, no ideally appropriate sample size and structure. Furthermore, a research design which seems, judgementally, to be the best solution may not prove feasible because of timing or budgetary constraints.

There are four main questions to be addressed at this stage:

(i) *To whom do we want to talk*; which market and consumer characteristics will primarily guide sample design?

(ii) *Which basic qualitative techniques do we want to employ*; shall we interview people individually, or in groups, and what sort of interviews or group discussions would be most appropriate?

(iii) In relation to both the above, *what should the size and structure of the sample be*?

(iv) *What question areas do we want to cover*?

In the case of this study, the main contribution to the solution of these problems was made by the advertising agency planner working on the account. She prepared a preliminary proposal for this study, which was discussed and agreed with the client and subsequently submitted to two research agencies. These in turn prepared detailed proposals for this first stage of research, building upon, and modifying, the initial advertising agency proposal, and preparing cost estimates. Research Bureau Ltd., the research agency selected to conduct the project, then finalised the research design for this first stage of the research programme, in consultation with the client and advertising agency. Hence all the questions listed were addressed, separately and severally, by each of those involved in the project. Each will be discussed in turn, indicating what the solutions were in this instance, and why they were selected.

Research need determined
by client and/or
↙ client's agent ↘

Client prepares	Client briefs one
detailed research	(or more) suppliers
proposal and may	and requests they
seek quotations from	submit detailed
one or more suppliers	research proposals
↘	↙

Stage 1: Planning

Work commissioned with selected
supplier; research design finalised
↓

Stage 2: Recruiting

Fieldwork controller briefed;
recruiting interviewers briefed
and commence recruitment
↓

Stage 3: Fieldwork

Qualitative researcher(s) conduct fieldwork
↓

Stage 4: Analysis

Tape recordings of interviews/
group discussions analysed by
researcher(s) and preparation
of verbal presentation of findings
takes place
↓

Stage 5: Presentation

Verbal presentation of findings to
client and client's representatives
(e.g. advertising agency)
↓

Stage 6: Report

Written report prepared and delivered
to client

Figure 2.1 Typical step-by-step approach to a qualitative consumer research study

To Whom do we Want to Talk?

Qualitative research studies are usually based on relatively small-scale quota samples. Such samples are not generally designed to be representative of a specific population, but to represent certain sectors of that population. Thus, when deciding whom we want to talk to, we need to try to answer two broad questions:

(i) What is the consumer profile of the market, or brand, with which we are concerned?

(ii) Given the nature of the research problem, which sectors of this population do we want to be represented in the sample?

In some cases, where the consumer profile for a product or brand is limited to a narrowly defined segment, or when the problem a study is required to tackle is in itself very specific, the decision about whom to talk to is relatively easy. For example, the writer has been involved in conducting studies to explore:

— how, and when, mothers of first babies make decisions about feeding solid foods;
— why credit card holders who use their cards for petrol, but not for other transactions, restrict usage in this way;
— how businessmen who regularly make transatlantic flights decide which airlines to use.

In other instances, the market for a product or brand may be very broad, possibly including the majority of men, women and children (e.g. chocolate bars), and the research problem may have broad-based objectives, which makes the task of designing a small-scale qualitative sample more difficult.

This first stage of the Fresh Cream Cakes research programme was a study with broad objectives, and the product *is* consumed by men and women of all ages, and by children. However, it was decided to restrict the sample to housewives, who were believed to be primary purchases of the product (based upon findings from the 1972 survey), and who would be the prime target for advertising. Representing different levels of product usage was thought to be of prime importance. Motives for purchase/consumption are often very different for heavy users of a product compared with infrequent users, and in this instance we ultimately needed to decide whether or not we could successfully appeal to all usership groups through a single advertising campaign. Given that the subsequent quantitative survey would represent *all* levels of usage, we believed that it would be most useful to represent the *extreme* groups within the qualitative sample; that is, heavy users and light plus non-users, ignoring the 'medium' group. This would, it was hoped, maximise our understanding of differences in motivation between those with greater and lesser involvement in the product field, and enable us to hypothesise which measures of attitude and motivation might discriminate between different user groups at the quantitative research stage.

We also believed that we needed to talk to both younger and older housewives, representing the upper and lower socio-economic groups. Furthermore, we wanted to make some attempt to spread our sample across different regions of the country. All these factors helped to determine our final sample structure, which is described subsequently.

Which Qualitative Techniques do we Want to Employ?

It is likely that the vast majority of qualitative research conducted in the UK is based on using group discussion or individual interview techniques, the former being considerably more popular than the latter, for reasons discussed later. For this project, group discussions were judged the most appropriate and cost-effective technique. However, this is not to say that a sample of individual interviews would not have produced equally useful results.

A 'typical' group discussion might consist of 8–9 respondents, recruited prior to the event, who attend a discussion which lasts for 1–1½ hours, chaired by a trained moderator. Similarly, a 'typical' qualitative interview might last for a similar time period, and again be conducted by a trained qualitative researcher, the interview appointment having been made beforehand by the recruiting interviewer.

However, exceptions to these norms do occur, although not, perhaps, as frequently as might be desired. The problem lies in the fact that these tools of the trade are too frequently perceived as defined 'techniques'. They can, and should, be adapted to suit the problem at hand. Qualitative 'interviews' can be conducted with any size and structure of group. The writer (and doubtless most other qualitative researchers) has conducted interviews with married couples (e.g. about cinema-going habits); with family groups (e.g. about television viewing); with peer groups (e.g. about pub going), and so on. Similarly, both group discussions and individual interviews can be planned to last for any reasonable time length, from a quarter of an hour to a whole day (with break periods). 'Sensitivity panels'[5], groups which reconvene on a regular basis over a period of time, have been reported to be particularly useful for some projects, for example, the development of new products.

We are currently witnessing more experimentation and innovation in the qualitative research field, in Europe more than the US. For an excellent review of the current 'state-of-the-art', readers are referred to Sampson's recent paper,[6] which in turn provides comprehensive references for further reading. The key point is that the techniques employed, and the subsequent analysis, should be designed to meet the needs of the task the research has been commissioned to tackle.

Nonetheless, there are some guiding principles which should help determine the choice between the two basic techniques, namely individual interviews and group discussions. *Individual interviews* are often more appropriate in the following instances:

1. *Where behaviour and attitudes may be very private*, and not admissable in a group situation. This may be true for research concerned with contraception, personal finance, certain types of patent medicine, etc. However, it is surprising how far membership of a temporary group can prove supportive, and often encourage, rather than discourage, discussion of 'personal' subject matter.
2. *Where research is required to explore relationships between attitudes and behaviour at an individual level.* For example, motives (or losing

weight vary from one individual to another (the desire to stay healthy, keep fit, be sexually desirable, fashionably dressed, etc.) These underlying motives may govern attitudes towards dieting patterns, slimming food product fields and individual brands. It can prove difficult to disentangle these relationships at an *individual* level using group discussions.

3. *Where research seeks to understand the sequence of events which leads towards a complex decision process.* For example, the choice of a career, the purchase of a car, the choice of a holiday all involve complex, multi-faceted decision processes. Individual interviews might be the better approach for providing an understanding of the segmented nature of such decisions.

Group discussions seem to be far more widely used for commercial research than individual interviews. This is partly for reasons of expediency. Conducting and analysing 30 individual tape-recorded interviews is considerably more time-consuming, and hence more costly, than conducting and analysing four group discussions with eight respondents in each. It may also be that research suppliers tend to avoid individual interviews because they can be less stimulating, and more tedious, to conduct and analyse. However, apart from reasons of time, cost and possible tedium, group discussions can be a preferable choice in the following situations:

1. Generally, where attitudes and behaviour are admissable and readily discussed in front of others, *the group discussion is an effective tool for generating a wide range of attitude and behaviour pattern examples.* The interaction between group members allows individuals to compare and contrast their views with those of others, stimulating them to articulate thoughts and feelings which might not otherwise have emerged.

2. *Group discussions are especially useful for eliciting brand image dimensions, both product orientated and emotive,* for the reasons outlined above. However, other methods have been claimed to be as, or more, successful in this respect.[8]

3. *Group discussions provide a quick and effective means of exploring advertising ideas in the early stages of development*, where a 'consumer input' to the development process is required. Here we are using consumers, in groups, as 'consultants', to provide views which, taken together with judgement, may help guide and modify future development.

For this project, we decided to use group discussions for a number of reasons. Firstly, the product field seemed unlikely to be one which would involve private behaviour not admissible in front of others. Secondly, motives for purchase seemed unlikely to be very complex: a fresh cream cake is, after all, a fairly frivolous buy. Thirdly, we knew the qualitative study would be followed by a quantitative survey; hence we wanted to generate a wide range of descriptive attitude and image data to help guide the design of a quantitative questionnaire. Group discussions are ideal for this purpose.

 In the event, we may have slightly misjudged the market and consumer attitudes relating to the product field. Precisely because fresh cream cakes are a frivolous product, they represent a sheer self-indulgence, not easily justified on rational grounds. The research results, discussed more fully later, suggested that attitudes towards personal self-indulgence seemed to differ between heavy and light buyers of the product. Had we included a proportion of individual interviews, we might have been able to explore the self-indulgence motive in more depth. However, this greater depth of understanding might not have affected the broad direction of our thinking, or proved actionable in marketing or advertising terms. As with many qualitative studies, we did not end up feeling we had lost out, but simply that we could have selected a slightly different approach.

What Should the Size and Structure of the Sample be?

Having decided whom we wanted to talk to, and which qualitative techniques seemed appropriate, we then had to decide upon the exact size and structure of our sample. This is never an easy task, as there is no one obvious solution. Decisions tend to be based upon the following factors:

1. *The extent to which different sample subgroups are hypothesised to hold different attitudes.* For example, attitudes towards skin care amongst women differ considerably according to age; thus in a study on this topic one might structure the sample carefully to ensure *separate* consideration of all age groups, from teens upwards. A study on dog foods might need to consider separately views of owners of different sizes of dog; research into motor oil would need to take account of the extent to which motorists undertake their own car maintenance, and so on. For this study, we believed it would be useful to *separate heavy and light users* of the product within the sample structure.

2. *The amount of reliance one wishes to place on the results.* Whilst one does not usually treat a qualitative research study as reliable in the statistical sense, one does not want to run the risk of the results being wholly misleading. The much-quoted Twyman study[2] indicated that qualitative 'results' based on a two-group discussion sample size may indeed be misleading. Some work has been done to examine the reliability of qualitative research data[9] but concern remains that research users all

too frequently place too much reliance upon data generated from small, unrepresentative samples.

3. *Time and cost restraints.* In the writer's experience, time considerations are often more pressing than cost restraints. Research buyers will often be prepared (or may be persuaded by their suppliers) to tailor their spending to the nature and importance of their problem. Time constraints are, in practice, often based upon 'paper' time schedules which can in reality be changed. However, where they *are* real, it is a question of weighing up whether *some* research would be better than none. Providing that a very small research project is not required to *make* a decision, the former may often be the preferable course. A few 'examples' of consumer opinion may, at the very least, help those who have to make a decision to see the variables they are considering in a fresh light.

This first stage of the Fresh Cream Cakes research programme was not hampered by unrealistic time or cost constraints, and there was concern to ensure that this study would provide a firm basis for both guiding the development and subsequent interpretation of the quantitative study. Hence we based our sample size and structure upon the hypotheses we had formed about whom we wanted to talk to, and upon which subgroups should be treated separately. The latter point is especially important to bear in mind where it is felt that people with disparate views, or patterns of behaviour, may conflict with each other in a group situation in an unproductive way. (For example, research designed to examine motives for cigarette smoking which included smokers and non-smokers in the same group might produce a very real conflict, but reveal little about individual smokers' motives.) We had already decided that we wanted to talk to:

—heavy and light/non-buyers of fresh cream cakes (light and non-buyers were not thought to be very different, since few people *never* buy fresh cream cakes; we did exclude those who simply disliked the product, since we felt it unlikely that any attempt to convert this group would be cost effective;
—housewives representing higher and lower socio-economic groups;
—older and younger housewives;
—people living in different regions of the country.

We also felt it would be useful to focus specifically upon a small sample of freezer owners, who bought frozen cream cakes, in order to understand their behaviour patterns in more detail, although freezer owners were not, of course, excluded from the rest of the sample.

Our final sample structure was as follows:

Total: 14 group discussions, all conducted amongst housewives:

   6 groups: 'Heavy' buyers of fresh cream cakes (once a week or more often):

       3 groups: BC1 class housewives (1 South, 1 Midlands and 1 North)

       3 groups: C2D class housewives (1 South, 1 Midlands and 1 North)

   6 groups: 'Light' and 'non-buyers' (the former were defined as those buying less often than once a month but at least once every three months, and the latter as those buying less often than once every three months — each group discussion included roughly equal proportions of each category):

       3 groups: BC1 class housewives (1 South, 1 Midlands and 1 North)

       3 groups: C2D class housewives (1 South, 1 Midlands and 1 North)

   2 groups: Freezer owners who bought frozen cream cakes at least once a month:

       1 group: BC1 class housewives

       1 group: C2D class housewives

Within each group, roughly half of the respondents had children aged under 12 years, and roughly half had children aged between 12–18. Additionally, 3–4 respondents out of a total of 8–9 in each group were working full or part-time.

What Question Areas do we Want to Cover?

For most qualitative studies, a brief, or 'topic guide' as it is sometimes called, is prepared in advance, setting out the subject areas to be covered by research. This may be prepared by the client researcher when he/she is quite clear about what is needed, or by the research agency when ideas and input are required from this source. In any event, both parties usually contribute to the content of the topic guide, and it will generally be discussed between them at a briefing meeting. In this case, the final topic guide was written by the research agency, based on the preliminary proposal prepared by the advertising agency planner.

The topic guide serves two broad functions. Firstly, it acts as a formal statement of what the research *is expected* to cover. Secondly, it forms, as the name suggests, a guide for the researchers conducting fieldwork, with which they will become very familiar before commencing research, and to which they can refer between individual fieldwork experiences to ensure that they are covering the ground set out. Thus whilst the content of the topic guide will be determined by the needs of the client, the *form* in which it is written should be geared towards the needs of researchers. The writer favours the use of broad questions which research should tackle (although these will not, of course, be questions asked of respondents in the form in which they are written).

An important thing to decide at this stage is the context within which the product field or brand will be approached — in other words, the starting point for group discussions or interviews. It will often be one objective of research to understand how a product is perceived within the broader context of a market, in order to hypothesise which characteristics differentiate it from competition.

In this instance we needed to understand how fresh cream cakes were compared with other types of cake, and whether there was any overlap between fresh cream cakes and other product fields (i.e. dessert products, confectionery products). Hence the topic guide suggested that discussion commence with a general exploration of how different types of cake are perceived and used, later homing in on fresh cream cakes in particular. Arguably, one could have commenced with a general discussion of family eating patterns, to ascertain how fresh cream cakes fit into this broader context. However, there is the danger there that too much of the discussion time will be spent on broader issues not appertaining to the problem at hand.

Nonetheless, there are occasions when the starting point of group discussions or interviews must be one stage removed from the product category being examined. For example, to understand why a woman chooses a particular brand of shampoo, one may need firstly to ascertain what type of hair she feels she has, and how she wants it to look. To understand why someone applies certain criteria to the choice of a lawnmower, one needs firstly to ascertain the extent and nature of his/her involvement in gardening, and so on.

The brief used for this study is appended to this chapter (Appendix 2.1) and shows how the development of discussion from broad through to more specific topic areas was envisaged. Also appended (Appendix 2.2) are a series of specific advertising positioning concepts which were introduced to respondents towards the end of the group discussions. These took the form of very simple, descriptive statements about the product, which were printed on cards. The objective of including these positioning concepts was not to see which 'won', but rather to help provide more understanding of the relative importance of different consumer motivations in this market.

Stage 2: Recruitment

Having planned the study, the next stage is that of recruitment, namely finding and making appointments with individuals who meet the quota requirements specified. Recruitment is not usually carried out by the researchers who conduct the qualitative fieldwork, but by trained field interviewers. (These may also conduct other types of survey research interviewing, especially if they work for research companies or fieldwork agencies who undertake qualitative *and* quantitative research projects.) However, it is desirable that some specialist training in qualitative research recruitment methods be given to interviewers, over and above 'standard' fieldwork training. The recruitment task and skills required, are rather different from those needed for survey research.

By far the most common method of approach to recruitment in the UK is for interviewers' homes to be used as interview or group discussion venues, with the interviewer acting as a 'hostess' to those she has recruited. The selection of respondents will be made on the basis of door-to-door interviewing conducted within the vicinity of the interviewer's home. A recruitment questionnaire will normally be provided, which may cover classification factors, product usership and/or any other detail of attitude or behaviour required to determine eligibility. For security reasons, recruitment questionnaires usually contain filter questions designed to exclude individuals who are employed (or whose close relatives are employed) in manufacturing or service industries connected with the product field under investigation, in market research companies, advertising agencies, or by the media. Increasingly, questioning will also seek to determine previous involvement in market research, especially qualitative studies, in an attempt to discourage the claimed tendency for some interviewers to recruit the same respondents too frequently.

Having ascertained that a respondent is eligible, the interviewer will then invite him or her to attend the group discussion or interview venue at the allotted time. Respondents are usually promised a small gift, often cash, as recognition for giving their time, and to help cover any associated expenses (e.g. local travel, babysitting).

With this first stage of the Fresh Cream Cakes project, this broad method of approach was followed. Interviewers from the RBL Qualitative Research Unit specialist fieldforce recruited respondents and held the discussions in their homes. The total sample of 14 group discussions was divided into seven pairs of groups, one recruiter being allocated to cover each pair. The recruitment questionnaire covered the following information areas:

(i) *Demographic classification*: age; social class; presence of children in household; working status;

(ii) *Screening questions*, to exclude any respondent who had attended a group discussion within the previous 12 months, and to exclude any who were associated with the manufacture or sale of cakes or with advertising, market research or the media;

(iii) *Usership questions*, designed to ascertain frequency of purchase of fresh cream cakes and frozen cream cakes: these questions referred to other types of cake as well (i.e. packet cakes, bakers' synthetic cream cakes, other bakers' cakes) as we did not wish to reveal the specific focus of our interest prior to group discussions.

Respondents were told we were holding group discussions and interviews about cakes in general, including both bought and home-made.

This practice of holding group discussions and interviews in recruiters' homes has both advantages and disadvantages. The main advantages are as follows:

1. Private homes provide informal and comfortable venues, conducive to informal, relaxed discussions, whereas hired halls and hotel meeting rooms are less likely to do so.
2. Interviewers experience a sense of continuity between the recruiting task and the 'end result' (for them), namely the *event* of the group discussions or interviews. This helps to motivate them, and, in particular, seems to help ensure high attendance levels. The agreement made between interviewer and respondent is personal rather than purely official — the former invites the latter to her home.
3. This form of approach is more easily organised, and less costly, than hiring accommodation in which to hold group discussions, and paying the recruiting interviewer to attend and act as hostess.

However, this method of recruitment has inherent disadvantages, only some of which can be surmounted by careful supervision and quality control:

1. Catchment areas tend to be small, and samples drawn from them may be unrepresentative. For example, respondents' experiences of grocery and other retail outlets may be limited to the selection available locally.
2. Even if they are individually recruited, respondents may well know each other socially. Whilst this can aid the conviviality of a group discussion, it may lead to concealment or distortion of reported behaviour and attitudes which might not have occurred in front of strangers.
3. Relatively small catchment areas also mean that recruiting interviewers can 'exhaust' their areas, literally running out of doors upon which to knock. (Unfortunately this may be especially true for interviewers who specialise exclusively in qualitative research recruitment, who may be the most skilled in other ways.)

Qualitative recruitment standards had become a subject of concern by the mid 1970s, and in the late 1970s a working party of the Market Research Society Study Group was set up to examine this issue. It is the writer's observation that standards have since improved considerably. Controls over recruitment procedures have been tightened by suppliers', and reports are usually obtained from group moderators to ensure that respondents recruited meet the criteria set.

Stage 3: Fieldwork

One could easily devote a whole chapter to a discussion of how qualitative interviews and group discussions are conducted. This is not least because there are no simple rules; every qualitative researcher develops his or her own style. Hence, this section will be limited to a discussion of procedures, inevitably at a fairly superficial level. Learning how to conduct qualitative interviews and group discussions effectively is best achieved initially by observing skilled practitioners, and ultimately by personal trial and error. The following step-by-step description of an approach to fieldwork is limited to the group discussion technique used for this study, and will inevitably reflect the writer's personal predilections and experiences.

Who Conducts the Fieldwork?

In the UK the majority of qualitative fieldwork is undertaken by researchers who specialise in this type of work. There are some researchers who are skilled in undertaking both qualitative and quantitative research projects, but these are in the minority. Qualitative researchers may be employed by companies who specialise in this type of research (many are quite small-sized organisations), or by specialist groups within larger research agencies. A number work on an independent freelance basis, often subcontracting the recruitment function to fieldwork agencies.

It is important to remember that the qualitative researcher(s) who conduct the fieldwork will usually also be responsible for data analysis, preparing and delivering a verbal presentation, and writing the final report. Thus a range of skills is required at each stage of the process. One attempt to describe the qualities which a qualitative researcher should ideally possess reads as follows.[1]

> They must have intellectual ability yet show common sense and be 'down to earth'! They must show imagination, yet be logical. While an eye for detail is essential they must have conceptual ability. They must show 'instant' empathy yet project themselves neutrally. They must be able to identify the typical yet think beyond stereotypes. They must be articulate but also good listeners. The ability to summarise concisely is essential but a literary flair or style is needed. While thinking analytically they must tolerate disorder.

The same writers go on to suggest that academic training in the behavioural sciences, whilst not essential, can be a distinct advantage. Certainly there is a tendency for qualitative researchers to have a qualification in psychology or an allied discipline, but there are many skilled practitioners with very different basic qualifications, and some who have none.

There seem to be more female than male qualitative researchers; there are a number of possible explanations for this, which will not be discussed here. However, the important point to bear in mind is that there are few occasions when the sex of the researcher need become a choice consideration. Clearly some subject matters virtually demand that interviewer and respondents be of the same sex (e.g. sanitary protection). In other instances, a researcher of the opposite sex to respondents may have some advantages. For example, a man can more credibly ask housewives to describe how pastry is made in some detail by pleading personal ignorance; similarly, a woman can elicit detailed descriptions of perceived differences between motor oils, or draught beers. However, in general it is the qualities and abilities of an individual researcher which will determine his/her suitability for a given study, rather than gender. For the Fresh Cream Cakes study, there was certainly no feeling that either male or female interviewers would be the more appropriate; in the event both researchers working on the project were female.

This brings us to the next question, that of *how many* researchers should be involved in a given project. Opinions on this subject differ, but the decision will in most instances be dependent on the size of the study concerned and the time available. Some researchers believe that, where feasible, a single researcher should be responsible for conducting and analysing all fieldwork. The advantages of this are that one individual can compare and contrast the findings which emerge from different sample subgroups, while retaining a concept of the overall results.

However, others favour dividing the fieldwork on a project among two or more researchers, arguing that this will reduce 'interviewer bias' and enrich the interpretation of the findings through the application of more than one head to this task. Certainly, with a large-scale project, interviewer fatigue may become a problem if one individual conducts all the fieldwork. 'Fatigue' here means the boredom that can result from going over the same ground again and again in interviews or group discussions when differences between individual attitudes and patterns of behaviour are minimal. (The writer generally prefers to conduct no more than half a dozen or so group discussions, unless a research project covers a series of rather different sample subgroups.) With the project discussed here, the total sample of 14 group discussions was, as mentioned, equally divided between the writer and one other female qualitative researcher. Each undertook some fieldwork in two out of the three geographical regions selected, and both worked closely together on the analysis and interpretation of findings.

The Group Discussion Venue

Let us now assume that recruiting has been completed and the researcher has arrived at a group discussion venue, in this instance one of the interviewer's homes used for this purpose. What needs to be done before the actual group commences? The interviewer/hostess should, as part of her training, have the necessary administrative arrangements in hand, in short:

(i) She should have prepared the room, ensuring that adequate chairs/settees are arranged in an informal circle, usually considered the most conducive pattern for relaxed discussion.

(ii) She should have made sure that occasional tables are provided for coffee cups, that ashtrays are available, and that the room will be adequately heated and lit.

(iii) She should be ready to serve tea/coffee and biscuits or other light refreshments as soon as respondents arrive in order to avoid any interruptions during the group discussion itself.

The researcher will usually arrive at least a quarter of an hour before the group discussion commences. He/she will check that the administrative arrangements are in order, and make personal preparations for the event. These may involve:

(i) Testing the tape recorder *in situ* and checking recording levels.

(ii) Deciding where to sit, and ensuring that a little distance is left between the researcher and respondents at either side so that the researcher can readily have eye contact with all participants.

(iii) Testing the video equipment (if this is being used to show commercials, for example) and ensuring that any other materials to be shown are to hand (e.g. concept boards, packs).

(iv) Checking the exact composition of the group with the interviewer (there may have been last minute cancellations and replacements); if there has not been time for recruiting questionnaires to be returned to the researcher before the group date, these will have to be quickly checked to ensure that sample requirements have been met.

(v) Taking a last look at the topic guide (which will have been carefully studied beforehand) to refresh one's memory.

The writer prefers each respondent to be shown into the room, and introduced by the hostess, on arrival. In this way an informal atmosphere can be established from the outset, and shyer respondents can hopefully be encouraged to chat a little before the group discussion starts. However, some researchers prefer respondents to assemble in an adjoining room, and to be shown in and introduced when all have arrived.

Introducing the Group Discussion

The form of introduction used is very much a matter of personal style. Some researchers prefer to avoid any sort of formal 'beginning' to a group, and might in this instance have simply commenced by saying 'we're here to talk about cakes—tell me about the sorts of cakes you like'. Others prefer to tell respondents something of what is required of them, why they have been selected to attend, and how the information they provide will be used. Despite the fact that the public is becoming increasingly familiar with market research practices, a group discussion may be an unfamiliar concept to most, and respondents may be uneasy about how they will be expected to perform. Additionally, it is desirable to explain why the proceedings are being tape recorded, despite the fact that increasing familiarity with tape recording equipment means that this rarely seems to be an inhibiting factor. (Indeed, qualitative group discussions and interviews are video recorded more frequently these days; some advertising agencies and research suppliers have special facilities for video-recording research sessions).

The form of introduction usually adopted by the writer is paraphrased below. However, this is not set up as a 'model', but simply as an example of one individual's approach:

> I come from an independent research company, and we conduct research on behalf of all types of different manufacturer and organisation. A lot of this research is trying to find out what people think about the different products they buy, and with discussion groups like this we get the chance to hear about your views in a little more detail than we could if we just asked you very specific questions. We usually tape record discussion groups because it is a lot easier than trying to write down everything you say at the time. We listen to the tapes later, and try to summarise what was said, but we don't use your names, so it is all quite confidential. We obviously want you to give your own personal views, and we don't imagine that everyone here has the same opinions, so do say if you disagree with something that has been said.
>
> Now today we want to talk about cakes, and, to start, could you tell me a bit about what sorts of cakes you buy, whether you ever make cakes, and so on.

Following the introduction, some researchers prefer to go round the room, seeking an initial contribution from each respondent. This both enables the researcher to gain an impression of group members, and breaks the ice by ensuring that each has contributed at the outset. However, the potential disadvantage of this approach is that it may establish an expectation amongst respondents of an ordered structure where each must speak in turn. Other researchers prefer to let the group 'take off' by throwing out a fairly general question at the beginning (as at the end of the introduction above) and simply letting an unstructured discussion occur. In either case, it is important to try to establish a pattern of discussion *amongst* group members at an early stage, rather than a series of interchanges between given individuals and the group moderator.

Running the Group Discussion

Running a group discussion effectively is much more difficult that it might seem. It is stimulating, but demanding, requiring total concentration throughout. The predominant function of the group moderator is that of listening and thinking, and deciding *when* to interject with a question, or probe. It is only when the techniques of *how* to pose non-directive questions and probes become second nature that the group moderator can concentrate upon listening to, and interpreting, what he/she hears. It is rather like driving a car. The learner will be preoccupied with grasping the mechanical skills; 'What should I do if they don't talk?'; 'How shall I stop them all talking at once?'; 'Have I covered all the question areas?' It is only when these basic skills have become instinctive that the group moderator can concentrate upon the complex navigational task, that of trying to understand consumer behaviour and attitudes in relation to the problem at hand. Thus it is not within the scope of this chapter to teach the student how to run a group discussion, or indeed to provide a detailed description of how these particular group discussions were conducted. This section will, therefore, be limited to describing the role of the group moderator, and providing a few basic guidelines.

Firstly, the group moderator must control the group. It is not simply a question of letting respondents chatter on, but of ensuring that the required ground is covered in adequate depth, and that all respondents are given a reasonable chance to participate. Thus the moderator will, from the outset, be trying to assess the group, ascertaining which are the more dominant and which the more submissive respondents, whether there are different levels of product experience amongst group members, or whether attitudes are polarised and likely to produce conflict within a group. Being aware of the dynamics within a group will guide the strategy for running that group. Some of the questions frequently asked at Market Research Society qualitative research courses and seminars are as follows:

1. *What do I do if people won't talk*? Firstly, don't worry! Your nervousness will be contagious. An initial period of silence is common, but someone will invariably step in to break it. Sit back and relax at the beginning of a group, thus helping to indicate that you are expecting

the group members to discuss things amongst themselves, and not address comments to 'the chair'. If respondents do run out of steam, change the subject, and if need be, come back to it later, using a slightly different approach.

2. *What do I do about a dominant group member who hogs the conversation*? Play the speaker of the house, and *avoid* catching her eye; indeed, try to use your eyes to encourage others to participate. When he, or she, has just made a contribution, ask what the other group members think about it, and fend off further interruptions by saying you want the views of everyone. Often other group members will recognise that you are trying to stem the flow from a dominant or aggressive respondent, and will start to help you with that task.

3. *How do I cope with conflict within a group*? Conflict is not necessarily detrimental. Indeed, when respondents are trying to defend, say, their preference for a particular product or brand faced with others who hold different preferences, they may articulate their reasons for preference more comprehensively. Conflict is potentially a problem where some group members claim a behaviour pattern or attitude which is more socially acceptable than that voiced by others. In these fresh cream cakes group discussions, some respondents, especially light or non-users of the product category, extolled the virtues of home baking at length, which could intimidate those who were neither skilled nor interested in cake making. In such instances, the group moderator can try to adjust the balance by suggesting, directly or indirectly, that the apparently less acceptable form of behaviour is both normal and acceptable. In this instance the moderator could (truthfully) claim that she was hopeless at making cakes, which encouraged those similarly disadvantaged to feel such behaviour was admissible.

There are other types of potential problem which cannot be discussed in detail here, and again the reader is recommended to observe groups in action, noting how group moderators deal with difficult situations.

Secondly, the group moderator inevitably has a considerable influence upon both the scope and the depth of the data collected. He/she will constantly be seeking to understand and interpret responses in order to decide whether, and how, to probe for more detail; whether to approach a subject from a different angle; when to cut conversation short and when to prolong it, and so on. With this Fresh Cream Cakes study, whether or not respondents indulged in solus eating, and how they felt about this, seemed to encapsulate more general attitudes towards self indulgence. Hence, this aspect of behaviour was probed in more detail than had been anticipated at the outset.

Thus it is not simply a question of leading the group in order to cover the required ground, but of deciding where the group is leading you; of being prepared, on some occasions, to adapt one's plans radically in order to pursue a line of thought which one had not anticipated. Within any given research project, individual groups may, therefore, follow very different formats, and this study was no exception. For example, light and non-users of fresh cream cakes spent more time discussing the perceived value for money of the product compared with home-baked cakes, whilst heavy users rarely compared these two types of cake on any dimension. Thus the writer can only give an indication of the *types* of questioning and probing technique employed in this study.

The group moderator will need to pose *non-directive questions* at various intervals during the group discussion, to change the direction of discussion where this is becoming stagnant and unproductive, and/or introduce completely new topics. For example, at an early stage in these group discussions, moderators asked respondents whether they perceived cakes in terms of various broad 'types', in order to ascertain the consumer view of the structure of this market. Consumers could indeed talk about different categories of cake; those made once a week, and kept in the cake tin to cut into; those made or bought primarily for children's teas; special occasion cakes; cakes which could be used as desserts, and so on. From this baseline, it became easier to comprehend how fresh cream cakes fitted into consumers' perceptions of the market. The experienced group moderator will fall into the habit of asking such questions in a non-directive manner. Even very specific topics can be introduced without leading respondents; for example, if one wants to turn attention towards frozen cream cakes, simply asking 'What about frozen cream cakes?' is enough to provoke discussion.

In addition to non-directive questions, the group moderator will also introduce *non-directive probes* to encourage elaboration , or further explanation of a point which has been made. For example, it became clear during group discussions that respondents considered fresh cream cakes to be rather 'special'. Clearly it is important to understand which dimensions contribute most to this 'special' image. To what extent do the appearance of the cakes, the price, the cream content, the shops in which they are sold, the eating occasions with which they are associated each make them 'special'? Simply asking 'In what way are they special?', or 'What is it that makes them special?' will provide the required detail. It is an important part of the group moderator's task to follow up broad judgemental descriptors: epithets such as 'good quality', 'good value for money', and 'nice taste' mean very different things in relation to different products.

Within group discussions or individual interviews, *projective techniques* may be used to explore motives for using a product, or attitudes towards it, which respondents may find difficult to articulate or of which they may not be wholly aware. Where choice of a particular product or brand reflects an individual's ideal self-image (e.g. perfume and other toiletry products, alcoholic drinks, cars), projective techniques can be especially useful in helping to elicit the less rational, but often highly motivating dimensions of brand imagery. (It is not within the scope of this chapter to describe the range of projective techniques available; interested students are advised to read about these elsewhere (see Sampson;[6, 10] Oppenheim;[11])).

However, in this study we were not dealing with a product field in which motives for purchase were likely to be emotionally complex, or related to ideal self-image projection. Hence the only projective technique employed as the very commonly used one of asking respondents to imagine a 'stereotype user', a typical cream cake buyer and eater, and describe their images in terms of perceived appearance, personality, lifestyle, and so on. The images thus obtained helped provide an understanding of differences between heavy and light users in terms of attitudes towards the product and motives for purchase (see 'Findings').

Finally, it must be reiterated that this limited description of the practice of leading group discussions can give very little indication of the complexities of the process. The group discussion leader must constantly be aware, and interested in this process; sensitive to the dynamics of the group, and to the needs of individual respondents; considering, interpreting, and following up data as it emerges. He/she must control the group, without being authoritarian; be supportive, while remaining detached. It is a demanding, but stimulating task, and not to be underrated.

Stage 4: Analysis

Let us now assume that all the fieldwork is complete. How does one start to tackle the analysis of what often amounts to many hours of tape-recorded conversation? Broadly speaking, there are two basic processes involved, which usually occur concurrently rather than consecutively:

1. *A systematic analysis* of the tape recorded conversation is undertaken, involving initial transcription and subsequent organisation of the data.
2. *A conceptual analysis* of the data: this occurs throughout the process, namely whilst one is conducting the fieldwork, whilst transcribing the tapes, and when drawing together the material. Here the researcher's experience, possibly within the same or allied markets, will be instrumental in helping to *explain* the data. Where more than one researcher is involved in a project, this conceptual analysis will also entail discussion between them.

When it comes to detailed patterns of working, individual researchers have their own favoured methods. This section will simply describe, step-by-step, how the two researchers involved undertook the analysis on this project, which reflects the procedures normally adopted within RBL at that time. Most reputable qualitative researchers probably adopt similar procedures on most projects.

Tape Transcription

The physical task of transcribing the tape-recorded material can be undertaken by an audio-typist, leaving the researcher to analyse the typed transcripts. This saves the researcher's time, and can prove especially desirable where large individual interview samples are involved, when personal transcription can prove both tedious and time-consuming. The increasing sophistication of portable tape-recording equipment means that even group discussion recording can be of a sufficiently high quality to be transcribed virtually word for word by an audio-typist. However, on this project, the researchers involved produced edited transcripts of their own group discussions. This entailed transcribing the majority of each group discussion verbatim, omitting only conversation judged irrelevant, and in some instances summarising repetitive comment.

There are advantages to be gained from personally transcribing one's own discussions and interviews, especially for the relatively inexperienced researcher. Firstly, a typed transcript cannot replicate the atmosphere of a group discussion; the pauses, the laughter, the levels of enthusiasm generated in discussion cannot be experienced by reading a transcript. Secondly, when listening to the original recording, one can recall better the contributions of individual members, and hence distinguish differences of opinion which may have emerged at various points during the group. (Stereo recording equipment facilitates one's ability to recall individual members of a group in relation to where they were sitting in the room.) Thirdly, one can more readily gain an impression of the extent to which there was group accord or dissension on a given point. Murmured agreements and disagreements may not be transcribed as such.

To some degree, the material can be organised during the transcribing process. For example, notes can be made in the margin indicating the relevant topic area; reaction to different stimuli (e.g. ads) can be written on different pages, and so on. Furthermore, thoughts and ideas relating to data interpretation can be noted down within the body of the transcript or in the margin.

Finding a Conceptual Framework

Before becoming involved in the detailed organisation of the transcribed data, the two researchers working on the project had a lengthy discussion of the findings and, with the aid of a flip chart, worked out a preliminary framework for structuring the presentation. Words and phrases indicating their impressions of the detailed findings were jotted down under various section headings, and points of interpretation discussed. Differences between findings which emerged from different sample subgroups were mulled over, and reasons for such differences hypothesised. Intuitive thoughts were aired, and personal hunches discussed. This interchange of views about the interpretation of the findings, and their implications for marketing and advertising decisions, is especially important as this encourages consideration of *different* explanations of consumer responses, thus helping to avoid any tendency to try to make the findings 'fit' an overall 'story'.

However, the two researchers involved had been in regular contact throughout the fieldwork process, discussing findings as they emerged, and comparing views. Hence, a hypothesis put forward by one researcher would be probed by the other in later groups. As dicussed earlier, the analysis and interpretation of qualitative research findings occurs throughout the fieldwork. Nonetheless, a more formal discussion of findings can be particularly useful at this point in time, when, following the transcription of the data, researchers can become lost in the detail.

Organising the Data

Armed with the 14 edited group transcripts and the conceptual framework resulting from the interim meeting, one of the two researchers then set about drawing the material together. Using separate sheets of paper for each main subject area, and different coloured pens to represent different sample subgroups, the comment emerging from each group was summarised. Whilst with individual interviews it is possible to attempt some quantification (e.g. noting the extent to which a particular descriptive term is used), with group discussions this is less feasible, and one must be limited to noting where opinion seemed to be conflicting or otherwise within any one group. Some practitioners prefer to write out individual verbatim quotes to illustrate particular points on these analysis sheets, whilst others may note down references to these, based upon transcript page numbers, so that they can be readily found for use to illustrate the written report commentary.

This researcher then prepared draft presentation charts based upon the conceptual framework and the detailed analysis, which were discussed with, and modified by, the second researcher prior to the formal presentation of findings.

Stage 5: Verbal Presentation

As with most qualitative research projects, a verbal presentation of the findings of this research was given to the Milk Marketing Board and their advertising agency prior to the production of the written report. The verbal presentation often assumes considerable importance, partly because time constraints may mean that action is based upon this. Furthermore, senior marketing and advertising personnel who often attend verbal presentations of research findings may be unlikely to read the written report. The presentation may also serve as a forum for discussion of the research findings amongst all interested parties.

As with any form of verbal communication, careful structuring of content, clarity of expression and an interesting delivery are all important. Qualitative researchers are, rightly or wrongly, often judged upon the 'quality' of their presentation, and in this context the concept of quality includes both presentation content and communication abilities. Again, this section cannot provide instruction to the novice. Each individual will adopt his or her own style of presentation, and indeed will adapt this to the needs of the audience. The following paragraphs will simply set out how this presentation was organised, and suggest a few guidelines for consideration.

The structure of this presentation followed the following, fairly typical format:

(i) *Research objectives* were outlined to remind the audience of the main purpose of the research.

(ii) *The research method* was briefly described, indicating the achieved sample size and structure.

(iii) *Main findings* were presented step-by-step, commencing with a summary of consumer perceptions of the cake market as a whole, and focusing in to a more detailed consideration of fresh cream cakes in particular.

(iv) *A final summary* outlined what seemed to be the most important hypotheses to emerge from this research.

The content of the presentation was tabled at the outset; this indicates to the audience exactly what will be covered, and helps to avoid premature questions. The entire presentation lasted for about an hour and a quarter, and was followed by general questions and discussion.

The writer generally prefers to chart presentations, using summary words or phrases to represent each point one wants to make about a particular topic area. Sometimes a diagrammatical form of presenting a concept of market structure, or a decision process model, will help communication. Wherever possible, summary words or phrases used on charts should represent consumer language, and the verbal presentation itself can be brought to life by illustrating points that are made with verbatim quotations from group discussions or interviews.

The advantages of using charts are that these provide a structure to the presentation, both for the presenter and the audience, and also place specific points within their broader context. This helps to avoid the danger of individual audience members latching on to the specific hypotheses which support their own views, and ignoring those which do not! However, some researchers dislike using charts, feeling that they render qualitative findings into 'tablets of stone'.

The *content* of the main findings section covered the following broad areas, and the final report echoed this structure, although the latter was, of course, more detailed:

(a) *Broad perceptions of the cake market,* and consumer-defined 'segments' within it.
(b) *Choice and preference dimensions in relation to bought vs. home-made cakes,* and how these dimensions operate within different market segments.
(c) *Perceptions of fresh cream cakes,* including:
   — product characteristics;
   — eating experiences and satisfactions;
   — roles of fresh cream cakes, including physical, social and psychological roles;
   — serving occasions and product suitability for each;
   — perceptions of different types of fresh cream cake, especially individual vs. large.
(d) *Frozen cream cakes,* in comparison with 'fresh'.
(e) *Purchasing patterns,* especially impulse vs. planned decisions.
(f) *Retail outlets,* concentrating particularly on perceived cost and quality differences.
(g) *Projected images* of stereotype fresh cream cake eaters.
(h) *Reactions to a series of positioning statements,* prepared by the advertising agency, which had been introduced at the end of the group discussions to help guide the direction of advertising strategy development.

Finally, the importance of an effective verbal presentation canot be over-stressed. Data which are not adequately communicated to those who will use them are data wasted. There are many traps for the unwary, and this section will conclude by offering a few suggestions for avoiding these.

1. Resist the temptation to present *all* the data. When planning the presentation, go back to the research objectives, and ensure that both content and structure are geared towards meeting these. This research project represented the first stage of a basic market study; hence there was a requirement to cover broader attitudes to the cake market in general, at least in summary form. However, many projects have very

specific objectives, and in these instances it may be a mistake to present broad attitudes towards a market which, while they might have been covered in research to ascertain opinions of a specific brand within a broader context, may simply tell the audience what they already know from other research.

2. Do indicate where *differences* in attitude between sample subgroups seem to be evident, or where findings seem unclear. Trying to mould qualitative results into one 'story', in which the various parts hang together, may well distort the true picture.

3. As far as possible, do try to make it clear when you are reporting consumer statements of behaviour and attitudes, and when you are discussing your *interpretations* of this reported data. Additionally, it is important to consider, and present, alternative possible explanations for a particular research finding.

4. Try to convey a real flavour of the people you talked to by *using their language*, and conveying how, and when, their enthusiasm was expressed. Creative people in advertising agencies will be particularly receptive towards a research presentation which helps them to envisage their target audience, and understand how the consumer feels and thinks. If groups have been video recorded, edited highlights can prove an interesting way of illustrating specific research findings.

5. Try to resist the attempts sometimes made by research users to 'quantify' the findings. 'How many people said that?' is a frequent form of question in a research presentation, and while one can reasonably indicate whether the point in question seemed to be a majority view, or a lone voice in the wilderness, *one should discourage the tendency to try and place numbers on qualitative findings*. With group discussions in particular, it is often open to conjecture whether an opinion voiced by one respondent was also held by others who were silent at the time.

Stage 6: Written Report

Qualitative research reports usually consist of a descriptive commentary on the findings of the research, which is illustrated by verbatim quotations from the group or interview transcripts. As with the verbal presentation, the main findings should be organised under a series of subject headings, although the report will usually contain more detailed comment. This report was in no-way atypical, and contained the following main sections:

— overall summary;
— background and objectives;
— method and sample;
— main findings (organised under subject headings in a similar fashion to the verbal presentation);

—appendices (recruitment questionnaire, topic guide, and copies of stimuli used, i.e. advertising positioning statements).

As this report dealt with a basic market study, it was fairly lengthy (65 pages of typescript). Projects dealing with more specific problems can often be effectively reported more briefly. Indeed, the writer questions the extent to which full reports of qualitative research studies are needed, or indeed used. In many instances where decisions are taken on the basis of verbal presentation and subsequent discussion of implications, lengthy written reports which arrive some weeks later are often redundant. In such instances, swiftly produced summary reports, together with copies of presentation charts, are often of more real value.

Once again, this section cannot aim to teach the novice, but can merely offer some guidance. Individual companies and individual researchers develop their own particular styles of structuring and writing reports, and different styles suit different buyers. The following observations are offered:

1. *The summary* of a qualitative research report is extremely important, as this may be the only part read by some. It is preferable to restrict the summary to key findings, rather than attempt a synopsis of all results.
2. The report should be illustrated with *apt verbatims*, which will add colour and life to the text. The writer has seen reports which read as if the verbal quotes are simply linked together with text, or, as Mary Tuck once commented, where they are scattered indiscriminately 'like currants in a bun'. Illustrations should add to the overall communication, rather than simply labour the point being made or pad out the report.
3. *Interpretations* of findings and recommendations arising out of the research should be clearly referred to as such, so that the reader can be clear when he is considering consumer comment or 'researcher' comment. However, as discussed earlier, interpretation is an integral part of the qualitative research process. Hence one can never wholly separate 'findings' from 'interpretation'.

It is not within the scope of this chapter to provide a comprehensive summary of the findings of this research. However, some flavour of the results can be given by indicating the nature of selected findings, and illustrating these with verbatim comments.

(a) Fresh cream cakes were perceived to be a *discrete market segment*. They were not directly compared to or contrasted with other cakes, or indeed with other food products:

'You think of them in a class of their own. You can't really compare them
with anything else. If I wanted a fresh cream cake, and they didn't have any,
I've no idea what I would choose instead.'

(b) Unlike most other cakes (and, indeed, many other food products) the
bought variety were generally considered the best. Few respondents
attempted to make fresh cream cakes themselves:

'Some of them look so gorgeous, and no matter how hard you try, you can't
get them looking like that yourself. I suppose it's the professional touch.'

(c) The *appearance* of fresh cream cakes was highly motivating, often
contributing to impulse purchase decisions. It was hypothesised that
appetising product shots would be all important in advertising:

'If you're standing in a long queue for bread at Hobbley's (local bakers)
you're drooling by the time you're served, you can't help buying them.'

(d) The *fresh cream* content obviously constitutes a strong part of the eating
pleasure. However, the overall eating experience is sensually gratifying,
and in some ways unique. Fresh cream cakes are sweet, but not sticky;
'gooey', but not heavy; creamy, but not cloying:

'It's just the thought of putting your teeth into all that cream.'

'They're pure self-indulgence, but they're not sickly like most sweet things.
They must be fattening . . . but they're not heavy like some cakes.'

(f) Fresh cream cakes are very definitely seen as a *treat*. Their purchase
cannot be rationalised on the grounds of nutrition value, filling
properties or economy. In this way they are more akin to chocolate
and confectionery than to other cakes. They represent a small
extravagance, which can only be justified on the grounds of pleasure:

'If you're feeling a bit daft one Saturday, you might say "we'll have one
each, as a big treat".'

'I think it's the only luxury we've got left!'

'I buy them when I'm feeling thin and my pocket's feeling fat!'

(g) Fresh cream cakes were perceived to be more of an *adult* than a child
indulgence. Indeed, it was sometimes claimed that children are not
especially fond of fresh cream, or that they don't appreciate fresh cream
cakes, preferring sicklier less delicate confections:

'Children have all sorts of extras. You buy them to treat yourself.'

(h) However, it was in relation to the *personal self-indulgence* motive that frequent buyers differed most from infrequent buyers. The former seemed happy to admit to self-treating behaviour, indeed even to sneaky, solus eating of fresh cream cakes. Any feelings of guilt experienced were quickly brushed aside:

'You stand outside the shop, and think "I shouldn't really, but I deserve it".'

'We sometimes have one each later on in the evening when the children have gone to bed. It's frightfully mean!'

'Sometimes I buy one just for myself, and I feel I've got to eat it before anyone sees me. You're making me feel guilty, all you sharers of cakes (addressing other group members). I'm a secret cream cake eater.'

'I always feel a bit wicked when I'm having anything luxurious. I think that's part of the pleasure really.'

In contrast, infrequent buyers found it more difficult to rationalise 'selfish' behaviour. They seemed to need more rational motives for buying fresh cream cakes, such as a treat for guests, a surprise for all the family:

'I would feel guilty if I only bought one. I would feel the money could buy another loaf.'

'I couldn't just go and buy a cake for myself without buying some for the family as well. I just couldn't do it.'

(i) When projecting the 'stereotype cream cake eater', there were again differences between the sample subgroups. Frequent buyers seemed more likely to project a warm, happy person, who enjoyed her food and enjoyed life. 'Someone who would spread a lot of butter on her bread and really enjoy it.' Infrequent buyers often projected an image of someone rich, and rather selfish, sitting in an elegant teashop eating cream cakes on her own.

Overall, therefore, these findings suggested that, above all, advertising should concentrate upon conveying the sheer pleasure obtained from eating fresh cream cakes. Positioning statements which reflected more rational product benefits, such as 'goodness', 'quality' or 'value for money' seemed irrelevant to purchasing motivations. However, quantitative data were needed in order to define more precisely the core target for advertising in terms of demographic profiles, eating behaviour and product attitudes. Furthermore, we needed to check out both broad and specific hypotheses which had emerged at this qualitative stage of research, especially those relating to differences between frequent and infrequent buyers of fresh cream cakes.

PROJECT 2: A QUANTITATIVE STUDY OF CONSUMER ATTITUDES AND BEHAVIOUR IN THE FRESH CREAM CAKES MARKET

As discussed at the outset of this chapter, the objectives of this quantitative study were broad. The research was required to provide reliable data about fresh cream cake purchasing and eating behaviour, product image and related consumer attitudes. To provide some indications of changing market trends, the survey needed to be comparable in terms of design and content to the previous market study conducted in 1972. Nonetheless, the findings of the qualitative research described suggested some additions to the questionnaire, particularly in relation to product image and consumer attitude dimensions.

It is not intended to describe the design of this survey in any detail, or to provide a comprehensive summary of the findings. However, some reference will be made to the ways in which this quantitative survey contributed towards our understanding of the market, and in particular how it helped to define the advertising objectives and advertising strategy for fresh cream cakes.

A national sample of 1250 housewives was interviewed, within which five different fresh cream cake usership groups were equally represented (250 each of very heavy, heavy, medium, light, and non-buyers). Whilst non-buyers had not been included at the qualitative stage, for reasons discussed earlier, it was decided to include these at the quantitative stage in order to contrast their beliefs and attitudes with those held by the different buyer groups. This effective sample was drawn from a contact quota sample which had been designed to represent demographic characteristics of housewives at a regional level. The survey data were weighted to restore the real proportions of the five usership groups, based on random sample omnibus readings taken immediately prior to the fieldwork for this project. The overall design replicated that used for the 1972 survey, which had been conducted by a different supplier.

The key findings, which were instrumental in directing advertising objectives and advertising strategy, were as follows:

1. The data we had suggested that the market for fresh cream cakes was probably static at best, and certainly did not appear to be growing. The proportion of the buyers classified as 'heavy' purchasers (once a week

or more often) appeared to have declined since 1972 and housewives claimed to have cut down on the quantity bought on any one occasion. However, there was a compensating increase in the number of family size (vs. individual) cream cakes bought, probably reflecting a concern for economy. Given the uncertain economic climate at that time, it was felt that the objectives of advertising should be to *maintain consumption* of fresh cream cakes rather than to attempt to expand the market.

2. A growing proportion of respondents seemed to feel that fresh cream cakes were a luxury they could no longer afford. Since the 1972 survey, consumers seemed to have become more knowledgeable about prices, more inclined to claim that the price of fresh cream cakes can be an offputting factor, and less likely to claim that the product is 'worth' the outlay. Hence it seemed essential that advertising concentrate upon *improving the status* of the product to help the housewife justify purchase.

3. Based upon claimed purchasing frequency, it seemed that heavy buyers accounted for a disproportionate amount of total purchase volume. 'Light' buyers (once a month–every three months) appeared to account for an insignificant proportion of purchases. Hence it was felt that advertising should concentrate upon communicating messages likely to be of prime importance in *maintaining the allegiance of relatively 'heavy' buyers.*

4. As in 1972, the delicious appearance and pleasure derived from eating fresh cream cakes remained the most important product benefits, and these were more likely to be endorsed by heavy buyers. Claimed impulse purchase decisions, occurring on the spur of the moment when in the shop, still appeared to account for nearly a half of all purchase decisions. Certainly the quantitative research confirmed the qualitative finding that the *pleasurable* rather than functional properties of fresh cream cakes were the most motivating. However, light and non-users were more likely to claim that fresh cream cakes were fattening, and that their consumption is guilt-inducing, again confirming the hypotheses which emerged from the qualitative study.

5. Marked differences between the 1972 and 1977 findings occurred in relation to the perception of fresh cream cakes as a 'personal' vs. 'family' treat. Firstly, the proportion of housewives with young children who were heavy buyers had decreased. Secondly, the tendency to claim that fresh cream cakes represent a personal vs. a family treat had increased considerably. Given the decrease in the quantity of cakes bought on any one occasion, and the perception that fresh cream cakes are primarily an adult treat, it seemed that *personal self-indulgence motives* were the most important for the advertising target, again confirming our earlier hypothesis.

Overall, therefore, the quantitative survey results helped to redefine the advertising objectives, namely to maintain the allegiance of current (and frequent) buyers. They also indicated that the role of advertising should be to enhance the special appeal and eating pleasures obtained from fresh cream cakes, concentrating upon personal self-indulgence, vs. family treat, motives.

PROJECT 3: A QUALITATIVE CREATIVE DEVELOPMENT STUDY

The objectives of this third study were specifically to guide the development of a new advertising campaign for fresh cream cakes. Based on the findings of the qualitative and quantitative research projects described, the advertising objectives and advertising strategy had been defined, and the generation of a range of preliminary creative ideas had occurred. Indeed, the writer had been involved with the advertising agency planner in an informal discussion of these preliminary ideas with the creative team working on the account.

Prior to this development research, the initial ideas had been sifted, and the most promising developed, resulting in three candidate 'routes' which had been made into photomatics (i.e. 'rough' TV advertisements, utilising still photographs, linked together on videotape together with a soundtrack). This qualitative study was required to suggest potential strengths and weaknesses of these different routes, to guide the decision as to which might be most effective in meeting the strategy, and to indicate possible modifications to scripts and executional guidelines which might improve the finished product.

This research will be discussed under similar section headings to those used for describing the first stage study, but will be confined to indicating features specific to this particular study.

Stage 1: Planning

Again, group discussions were judged the most appropriate tool for providing the type of guidance needed. We were not looking for any 'measures' of advertising visibility, branding or communication. Indeed, we were dealing with material which was still a long way from finished advertising, and hence were not in a position to predict advertising effectiveness on any criteria.

In terms of sample design, it was felt we should concentrate upon the prime target for advertising, namely heavy users of fresh cream cakes (buying once a week or more often). A total of six group discussions was conducted, amongst the following sample:

Total: 6 groups, all consisting of housewives; class C1C2:

3 groups: housewives with children aged under 12: (1 South, 1 Midlands, 1 North)

3 groups: housewives with children aged 12–18: (1 South, 1 Midlands, 1 North)

Again, fieldwork was conducted by two researchers from the RBL Qualitative Research Unit, and was completed during October 1977.

Stage 2: Recruiting

Recruiting was conducted in exactly the same fashion as that described for the first stage of research, using a similar recruiting questionnaire. Again, respondents were told they would be discussing cakes in general.

Stage 3: Fieldwork

The approach to conducting group discussions was very different from that adopted at the first stage of research. Both the objectives and the ground we needed to cover were more tightly defined, hence general discussion of the product field was kept to a minimum, serving mainly as a 'warm-up' process. Indeed, in the writer's opinion, lengthy discussion of a product field prior to exposure to advertising for that product can lead to over-rational responses to and evaluation of, the advertising material. We do not normally discuss the merits of a product at great length before we are exposed to advertising for that product.

Respondents were shown each of the three photomatics in turn, having been told that these represented rough ads. The order of showing was rotated across the six groups. Initial, unprompted reactions were obtained, following which probing sought to elicit:

— initial reactions to, and involvement with, each execution;
— comprehension of visual and verbal elements;
— communication and relevance;
— reactions to executional elements.

Non-verbal cues were also noted by interviewers, in particular the ways in which respondents reacted to the advertising stimuli (i.e. with apparent pleasure, amusement, boredom). As with the previous study, the group discussions were tape recorded, and transcribed prior to presentation and reporting.

Stage 4: The Findings

This section will aim simply to discuss the key findings, indicating in particular how these helped to guide advertising development.

Of the three candidate advertising routes, one seemed to be far less promising that the other two, and will thus not be discussed here. The other two were rather different, in terms of both the role of the product within the advertising and the consumer motivations tapped by the advertising. These two approaches can be summarised as follows:

(a) *Lovely Day*. This approach indicated how a fresh cream cake can brighten up the day. The photomatic depicted a young woman returning from a shopping trip, in the rain. She removes her wet clothing, takes some fresh cream cakes out of her shopping bag, and sits down to enjoy them with two friends. The enjoyment of the cakes is shown in the women's facial expressions as they bite into them. A male voice over says:

> What a lovely day! . . . for a fresh cream cake.
>
> Just a little light choux pastry, a lick of chocolate, and a load of fresh whipped dairy cream . . .
>
> And suddenly everything's fine.
>
> Fresh cream cakes.
>
> Have a lovely day.

(b) *Naughty Cakes*. This approach sought to present the sheer self-indulgence associated with eating fresh cream cakes in an amusing manner. A male presenter firstly talks disparagingly about a heavy piece of fruitcake, then picks up a chocolate eclair oozing with fresh cream, which he bites into with evident delight. The soundtrack was as follows:

> I'd like to talk to you today about naughty cakes.
>
> This garden fête effort by Mrs. Pettigrew, for instance, is *not* a naughty cake.
>
> In fact it's a thoroughly *sensible* cake
>
> On the other hand, this eclair covered with thick dark chocolate and positively oozing with delicious fresh cream is a very naughty cake indeed . . .
>
> Fresh cream cakes: Naughty . . . but nice!

The results suggested that 'Lovely Day' seemed to be the 'safer' of the two routes. It represented a situation with which most respondents could identify, and presented some justification for treating oneself. The product was 'deserved' (after shopping in the rain) and was also filling an entertainment role (i.e. shared amongst friends):

'That's typical of what a lot of women do. You come home after a morning's shopping with something nice.'

'If I go for a cup of coffee with my best friend, I always take along a couple of fresh cream cakes.'

This approach allowed respondents to rationalise any guilt associated with buying fresh cream cakes by suggesting the 'morale boost' properties of the product. However, a potential disadvantage was that the approach was *about* fresh cream cakes, suggesting when and why one might eat them, and did not convey *feelings for* the product as strongly as the second approach.

'Naughty Cakes' encapsulated for many the irrational, sensual enjoyment of the product; the suggestion of illicit pleasure represented their feelings about fresh cream cakes, in that they are an extravagant, but delicious, indulgence.

'That sums it all up for me.'

'That's exactly what they are really.'

'You do think "Naughty but nice" yourself, especially when you're on a diet.'

'That immediately makes me want one.'

'Everything that is nice is naughty.'

The cake was central to the advertising idea, and the overall message seemed to be focused upon the sheer pleasure obtained from indulgence in the product. The 'slogan' was judged apt and catchy, and most respondents reacted warmly to the humorous style of the advertising.

However, there were one or two potential problems. Firstly, a few respondents argued that this approach might be more likely to induce guilt than pleasure. This perception was exacerbated by the fact that the male presenter used seemed slightly too authoritarian; a presenter with more obvious 'naughty boy' qualities was deemed more appropriate. Secondly, there was some feeling that the humour seemed slightly 'silly', which again seemed to be a problem associated with the rather 'manic' actions and facial expressions of the presenter.

Overall, therefore, this research suggested that the 'Lovely Day' route might be the safer of the two candidates, but that it seemed to have less potential for achieving the strategic objectives, namely enhancing the status of fresh cream cakes by conveying the self-indulgent pleasure they can uniquely deliver. It seemed that the 'Naughty Cakes' route could potentially fulfil the strategic objectives more fully, and, with carefully chosen presenters, could be developed to create an involving and entertaining campaign. Furthermore the line 'Naughty . . . but nice' seemed to be potentially memorable.

CONCLUSIONS

Following deliberation between the client and the advertising agency, and subsequent to a further research study which examined these two approaches in a slightly more developed form, the 'Naughty . . . but nice' route was developed to form a new Fresh Cream Cakes advertising campaign.

The campaign ran for some eight years and, whilst it was impossible to measure sales effectiveness given the complexity of distribution channels, appeared to be successful in achieving the objectives set. Advertising awareness levels were very high, and the theme line 'Naughty . . . but nice' was exceptionally well recalled in association with fresh cream cakes. Quantitative campaign monitoring also indicated that attitudes we had desired to influence continued to shift in a positive direction, and consumers retained enthusiasm for the advertising, exhibiting very low levels of 'getting fed-up' with the campaign.

The creative teams who conceived the advertising idea and who have since developed the theme must take credit for the work. However, the research undoubtedly contributed towards our understanding of the market, and the development of the strategy, and subsequent advertising. The research programme also proved to be an excellent example of good teamwork, with the client, advertising agency and research agency working closely together to achieve common goals.

REFERENCES

1. R&D Subcommittee on Qualitative Research, 'Qualitative Research—a Summary of the Concepts Involved', *Journal of the Market Research Society* **21** (1979) 2
2. TWYMAN, W.A. 'Designing Advertising Research for Marketing Decisions', *Journal of the Market Research Society* **15** (1973) 2
3. KING, S., 'Public vs. Private Opinion', *ESOMAR Congress Proceedings* (1979)

4. ESSEX, P. and KNOX, R., 'Researching Marketing Needs and Action Approaches for New Products — 'To Russchian with Love', *Market Research Society Annual Conference Proceedings* (1979)
5. SCHLACKMAN, W. 'A Discussion of the Use of Sensitivity Panels in Market Research', *Journal of the Market Research Society* **26** (1984) 3
6. SAMPSON, P., 'Qualitative Research in Europe — The State of the Art and Art of the State', *ESOMAR Congress Proceedings* (1985)
7. BURNS, C., SIDDALL, J. and STEVENS, R., 'Translating Research into Product Advertising — 'do you speak L'Aimant?', *Market Research Society Annual Conference Proceedings* (1979)
8. COWLING, A. B., 'Use of Elicitation Technique for Producing Dimensions of Brand Choice', *Market Research Society Annual Conference Proceedings* (1973)
9. COOPER, P. and BRANTHWAITE, A., 'Qualitative Technology: New Perspectives on Measurement and Meaning through Qualitative Research', *Market Research Society Annual Conference Proceedings* (1977)
10. SAMPSON, P., 'Qualitative Research and Motivation Research', in *Consumer Market Research Handbook, 3rd ed.*, Worcester, R. M. and Downham, J. (Eds), North Holland 1986
11. OPPENHEIM, A. M., *Questionnaire Design and Attitude Measurement*, Heinemann (1965)
12. WALKER, R. *Applied Qualitative Research*, Gower (1985)

APPENDIX 2.1 RESEARCH BRIEF

General Attitudes towards Cakes

It is suggested that discussion commence by encouraging respondents to discuss cake purchasing and consumption in general. Establish the extent to which respondents seem orientated towards home baking, and if so what types of cake, and the extent to which they purchase cakes of various types/for what types of eating occasion/with which family members in mind, etc.

At this stage try to build up a picture of how respondents subdivide 'the cake market', and the extent to which this overlaps with other markets. For example, do respondents tend to have a 'cut into' fruit cake or similar always in the house, and is this differently perceived from impulse buy small cakes? Are cakes for Sunday tea differently perceived from cakes/chocolate biscuit count lines, etc., bought for everyday? Does there appear to be any pattern in the way in which cakes are bought/served over the course of a week?

Situations in which Different Cakes are Served

Following on from the above discussion it will be interesting to dwell more specifically upon the suitability of different cakes for different eating occasions to meet different needs, etc. Are any particular types of cake thought more suitable for giving to a friend with coffee/giving children's friends for tea/serving to guests for Sunday tea, etc., and if so why? Is a range of cakes ever served, and expected to fulfil different types of role (e.g. fruit/sponge cake as a filler, plus cream cakes as something 'special')? Are cakes of any type ever served as a dessert, and if so which types, and why? It will be important at this stage to understand how fresh cream cakes fit in with other cakes/sweet snacks/desserts.

General Attitudes towards Cream Cakes

By this stage, you should be beginning to establish broadly how people perceive fresh cream cakes. Previous research has suggested that they are rather 'special' and 'unique'. Does this still seem to hold true? Are they in fact outside any perceptions of regular/basic cake making/purchase/ consumption, tending to be a regular or occasional 'treat' (e.g. buying a new lipstick vs. buying a new pot of cleansing cream)? To what extent do heavy buyers differ from light buyers in this respect?

Previous research has suggested that heavy buyers of cream cakes tend to use more cakes generally, to buy rather than make cakes, and to be more likely to serve fancy cakes than plain. For light/non-users, are cream cakes representative of the *type* of cake they don't care for particularly? Are they a 'pinnacle' of cake eating that they do not aim to reach?

Fresh Cream Cakes—Product Perceptions

What do respondents actually like (or dislike) about fresh cream cakes? What is the nature of their special qualities? How do respondents view them compared with other things which may be 'special'—e.g. perfume, champagne, steak, etc.

How important is the cream itself? Is it crucial? How do they compare similar cakes which do not contain fresh cream? How would they feel if a new sort of artificial cream cake were introduced, which really tasted as good as fresh cream? Are fresh cream cakes good in all ways? Are some cream cakes (from some stores) better than others, and if so in what ways?

Are fresh cream cakes special in a way that can be discussed in terms of other 'special' cakes? Encourage respondents to think of other cakes they would describe as special (e.g. Christmas cake, Dundee cake, chocolate gateau) and define the ways in which these afford gratifications in comparison with fresh cream cakes.

What are the most important features of the eating experience? Do respondents like them because they are gooey and 'squelchy'? Previous research has suggested that heavy users do not perceive cream cakes to be particularly fattening. Does this still hold true, and to what extent do heavy users' views differ from those of light users/non-users? Are cream cakes thought of in terms of 'goodness' or 'lack of badness'? Are they thought to be rather purer/more natural than other 'shop' cakes?

Fresh Cream Cakes—Situations/Occasions

To some extent this will have been probed in the early part of the discussion. When do respondents serve fresh cream cakes, on which meal/snack occasions, and to fulfil which needs? For light users in particular, are they reserved for 'special' occasions, and if so why? What sort of role do they play in the context of morning coffee/tea and cake/tea as a meal, etc? Are they used as a dessert, and if so are they considered more or less suitable for this purpose than other types of cake?

Are they considered to be particularly suitable for guests, and if so what types of guest—when would they serve cream cakes and when something else?

Purchasing

How do respondents set about purchasing cream cakes? To what extent do they comprise impulse purchases? Can they describe an impulse purchase— how do they feel when they are looking at the cakes; what is going through their minds; what finally leads them to buy them or not to buy them on any given occasion? How do respondents feel about buying cream cakes in different types of outlet (e.g. baker, supermarket)? Is the quality/freshness thought to differ according to the outlet, or is there a feeling that fresh cream cakes are made in some central depot/bakery and distributed to retail outlets? If there are thought to be differences between outlets, what are these? Do they affect the cake/pastry taste and texture, the cream itself (amount/thickness)?

How do respondents assess cream cakes in terms of price/value? Do they feel they are reasonably priced, or expensive, and what criteria are used in assessing value? To what extent is the presence of fresh cream justification for a higher price than other cakes? There may be some feeling that, because they are 'special', they are *per se* a 'luxury price'. Try to check out whether this is so. Do respondents compare the price of fresh cream cakes with other cakes, with desserts, with the price of fresh cream (double or single) or what?

Imagery

What types of people do respondents imagine buy a lot of cream cakes? Probe for appearance, personality, lifestyle, eating habits, etc. What types of people do they imagine most enjoy fresh cream cakes—probe similarly. What types of people do they imagine would not buy fresh cream cakes, and what types of people would not enjoy them? Probe as above. It will be particularly important to look at the *nature* of self-indulgent associations, and also to isolate how far cream cakes have feminine rather than masculine connotations.

Advertising Recall/Advertising Concepts

Respondents will be asked whether they can remember any advertising for fresh cream cakes, and reactions to this will be sought. For each concept, it will be useful to encourage respondents to project advertising development — what sort of commercial do they feel could be made for each — what type of cast, etc?

Frozen Cream Cakes

Obviously this section will be more fully developed with the specialist freezer groups, although awareness and use of frozen cream cakes will be covered in all groups.

How do respondents view frozen cream cakes, and how are they compared with the fresh equivalent? To what extent is quality thought to differ in terms of both the cakes themselves and the cream filling? What effect do respondents feel freezing has on cream, if any?

How do respondents compare branded cakes (e.g. Birds Eye) with non-branded varieties sold at freezer centres? Are there thought to be differences in quality/price?

In what sizes do respondents normally buy frozen cakes, and why do they choose these sizes? How do they feel about different size packs in terms of value?

How are frozen cream cakes used? Are they used in much the same way as fresh cream cakes or not? Is there more tendency to use them for pre-planned meal occasions (because of the need to defrost) such as Sunday tea, dessert, etc? Do respondents feel some types of cream cakes freeze better than others, and if so which?

Do respondents ever freeze cream cakes themselves, and if so what do they feel about this?

APPENDIX 2.2   FRESH CREAM CAKES—CONCEPTS EXPLORED DURING THE GROUP DISCUSSIONS

Natural Goodness

Fresh cream cakes are good for you, because they're made with the natural goodness of fresh dairy cream.

Family Treat

There's nothing a mother can treat her family to that will delight them as much as fresh cream cakes.

Good Value

It's worth paying a little extra for fresh cream cakes because they're made with the finest of ingredients—fresh dairy cream.

Quality

There's only one kind of cake that gives you the very best in quality—a fresh cream cake.

A Little Luxury

These days when you have to think twice about every extra you spend, thank goodness you can still afford the real luxury of fresh cream cakes.

Self-Indulgence

It's not really wicked to spoil yourself a little—with something as gorgeously mouthwatering as a fresh cream cake oozing with real dairy cream.

ACKNOWLEDGMENT

This research programme was commissioned by the Milk Marketing Board in conjunction with their advertising agents, Ogilvy and Mather. The research was conducted by Research Bureau Ltd., by whom Jackie Dickens was then employed as head of the Qualitative Research Unit.

This chapter is reproduced by permission of the Milk Marketing Board.

Applied Marketing and Social Research 2nd Edition
Edited by Ute Bradley
©Copyright John Wiley 1987

3. *Clover New Product Development*

Sarah Day *Dairy Crest Foods*

A detailed case history is presented here from the development of the new product idea to the launch of Clover covering eight stages. Each research exercise covers:
—the marketing problem,
—the research method used to solve it in detail,
—complete questionnaires or extracts where appropriate,
—analyses, results and interpretations.
The full research programme for the new brand is given in a chart which indicates the time taken for each stage.
The case also demonstrates the value of desk research, plus qualitative and quantitative research at particular stages of the research programme. It will be especially useful for the student of new product research.

INTRODUCTION

Dairy Crest Foods is a major UK producer of dairy products such as butter and cheese. When the Company was set up in the late 1970s, one of its main objectives was to maximise the return on dairy product manufacture: to do this, Dairy Crest needed to develop and launch branded dairy products with 'added value'. A number of new brands have been launched since 1979, the most successful of which has been the dairy spread, Clover.

The development of Clover began at a time when there was great concern over declining butter sales. It became evident that Dairy Crest needed to create a product that would both stem the decline of butter consumption and, if possible, win back business from margarine, thus ensuring long-term profits for English and Welsh butter fat producers: the product had two constraints:

(i) its major ingredient should be butter fat;
(ii) it should be produced using dairy production expertise and resources.

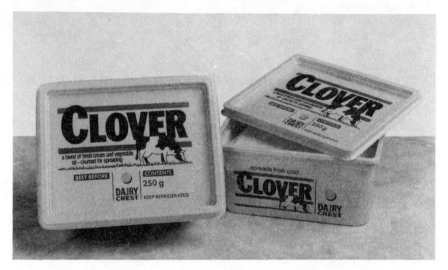

A research programme was drawn up, designed to isolate a real opportunity for a unique new product within the limitations of the above two constraints. The research programme covered the development and testing of each of the following elements of the marketing mix:

— positioning and strategy;
— product;
— packaging (type, shape, design);
— name;
— advertising and promotions;
— price.

The research was not necessarily conducted in the above order (see Fig. 3.3.); rather, the elements were developed in isolation using the overall strategy as guidance, and gradually pieced together to form a coherent mix— which was then tested via a simulated test market prior to the launch of Clover.

Before any development could take place, however, desk research was carried out which included the study of usage and attitude data.

STAGE 1 — DESK RESEARCH (1979)

The marketing department within Dairy Crest needed to determine, 'where are we now?' before they could assess, 'where do we want to be?'. A detailed review of the yellow fats market was conducted using all the relevant pieces of research information that were available. These included:

— Mintel
— National Food Survey
— TCA
— TGI

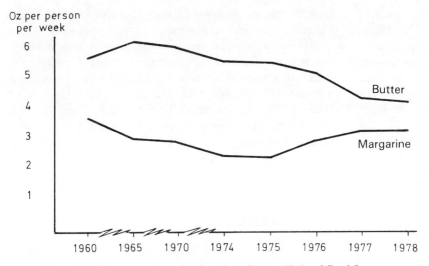

Figure 3.1 UK consumption of Yellow Fats. Source: National Food Survey

—Usage and Attitude Study
—Industry Statistics (including foreign markets).

The data revealed not only *what* was happening in the yellow fats market but also *why* it was happening. Some of the key findings are outlined below.

The decline in butter consumption in the UK really began in 1975, when margarine consumption began to increase (see Fig. 3.1). The main reason for this disparity was the significantly higher price increases on butter compared to margarine.

The successful product innovation and marketing by the margarine manufacturers of brands such as Krona and Flora also contributed to the decline of butter: they capitalised on certain key benefits these brands had over butter, namely price, perceived health and spreadability. Margarine manufacturers first identified the desirability of a more spreadable product in the early '70s when they launched softer, more spreadable products in tubs. The consumption of soft margarine grew steadily over the years as its usage became more acceptable and extended into cooking as well as spreading purposes.

A *Usage and Attitude Study* conducted for the Butter Information Council (BIC) by Taylor Nelson and Associates in 1979 revealed many of the reasons behind the switching away from butter to margarine by consumers. (The methodology used for this survey is appended in Appendix 3.1). It confirmed that price, perceived health and convenience were the main benefits margarine had over butter, but that a real butter taste was still the gold standard for most consumers.

One of the conclusions Dairy Crest derived from the study was that a need existed for 'a spreadable butter'. Thus, a product which offered the taste of butter, protected the emotional appeal of butter, but spread straight from the refrigerator, became the target requirement. Target consumers became housewives who had switched or were about to switch away from butter to margarine, motivated by the need for convenience and spreadability; these tended to be younger, downmarket women, while butter loyalists tended to be older women in the AB socio-economic group.

As part of the desk research, a worldwide 'trawl' of new products was carried out: this discovered a dairy spread in Sweden which had a high butter fat content and was selling well.

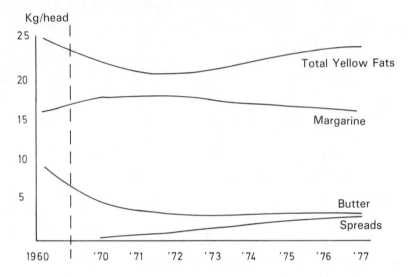

Figure 3.2 Sweden: consumption per capita of spreads

Indeed, the Swedish dairy spread was achieving precisely what Dairy Crest hoped to achieve with its new product in the UK: it had reversed the upward trend of margarine by stealing volume share from the margarine sector, (see Fig. 3.2) and had increased overall butter fat consumption. Product samples were obtained by agreement with the Swedish manufacturer.

The development of Clover was underway.

STAGE 2—PRODUCT RESEARCH

Before any brand development could take place, the product had to be tested 'blind' to establish its strengths and weaknesses vs. the competition.

2a. Exploratory Product Research (March 1979)

Two initial exploratory group discussions were conducted amongst C1C2 housewives aged 20–45 before the product was tested quantitatively. The aim of the exploratory research was to establish consumer vocabulary in this area of the yellow fats market, and to assess the ability of consumers to discriminate between butter and butter-type products. Following the research, it was decided to test the new product against soft margarine (the main competition) and butter (the benchmark).

2b. *Quantitative Blind Product Test (July 1979)*

A hall test was conducted by RSGB to assess quantitatively the performance of the new product against soft margarine and butter.

Method—the hall tests were conducted in Croydon amongst three matched samples of 200 housewives; quotas on age, social class, presence of children and butter/soft margarine usage controlled each matched sample. Products were tested at 5°C, and 'blind' in blank packs: they were coded G4—soft margarine, D7—test product, and L3—butter. The research was a sequential monadic test followed at the end of the interview by a paired comparison. The test design was that of a 'round-robin'.

Conclusions—the test product performed well. It retained the positive attributes of butter in terms of appearance and taste, and it spread almost as well as soft margarine. Respondents expected the product to be cheaper than butter, but more expensive than margarine. With no price mentioned, however, respondents expressed more interest in buying the test product than either the butter or soft margarine products: this result was clearly unrealistic (since no price was mentioned) but was, nevertheless, encouraging.

STAGE 3—CONCEPT RESEARCH

By the second half of 1979, Clover's project team had found a gap in the market for 'a spreadable butter', and a product which satisfied the Company criteria.

At this point in the programme, the need was to begin developing a brand with 'added value', a brand that could justify a butter price. A brief was written and the advertising agency, Young and Rubican, was commissioned to help create the new brand.

Using the central proposition of 'a butter that spreads straight from the refrigerator', the advertising agency needed to develop a platform in terms of name, pack and advertising which correctly interpreted the consumer need. A major constraint, however, was that the word 'butter' could not be used to describe the product to the consumer: this was because the product contained vegetable oil and had a lower butter fat content than butter.

The agency created five concepts which were theoretical approaches to positioning the central proposition: these covered:

   (i) Modern butter (a butter for today's demands).
   (ii) Convenience (butter plus).
   (iii) Traditional/natural (butter that spreads).
   (iv) Taste (a spread that really tastes like butter).
   (v) Quality (butter pedigree, value for money).

These were put into an initial stage of concept research: only copy was used without pictures or names.

3a. Concept Research I (August 1979)

NOP was commissioned to conduct the research, the main objective of which was to help in the development of the new product's positioning.

Method—five matched samples of housewives were interviewed using a semi-structured questionnaire comprising mainly open-ended questions. (The questionnaire used is appended in Appendix 3.2). Each sample consisted of 50 housewives, C1C2D social class, aged under 55, who 'buy butter nowadays'; quotas controlled age and class and the fieldwork was divided between London, Newcastle, Bristol, Birmingham and Leeds.

Each sample considered one concept only in terms of communication, interest, uniqueness, credibility and likelihood of purchase at a 'cost the same as Country Life butter which is a little more expensive than the cheapest butter'.

Conclusions—a straightforward 'butter that spreads' concept was the most appealing, although there was some scepticism surrounding this claim: the word 'spread' was suggestive of margarine rather than butter. Unless the margarine associations could be overcome, commanding a butter price would be impossible.

3b. Concept Research II (October 1979)

Further concepts were developed which aimed to maximise butter imagery. This time pictures, brand names and the Company name were used in addition to copy. The concepts in summary were:

    (i) 'Swift'—convenience.
    (ii) 'Better'—not butter/not marge—it's better.
    (iii) 'Butterley'—traditional butter taste.
    (iv) 'Dairy Soft'—traditional butter taste.

The concepts were developed in the light of the earlier research, and were tested to see whether they successfully gave an impression of butter, of spreadability and of a product which could justify a butter price.

Method—qualitative research was carried out due to the need for exploratory, developmental information at this stage. NOP conducted four group discussions in London, with C1C2 housewives who 'buy butter nowadays', aged 35–45 years, with children under 15 in the family. Each group considered one concept in detail to begin with and then the others in rather less detail.

Conclusions—the research again confirmed the dichotomy between margarine and butter:

	Butter	Margarine
Positives	Tastes good	Spreads
Negatives	Doesn't spread	Poor taste

The attitude seemed to be 'if it spreads, it can't be butter'. None of the concepts was ideal, although their shortcomings provided guidance for further development. In essence, the correct impression was derived from a *combination* of supportive elements rather than specific ones. Thus, every element had to reinforce the proposition: one single weak link could destroy it.

The two stages of concept research demonstrated the need to:

—maximise butter imagery and emphasise butter taste;
—demonstrate, but not over-emphasise, spreading;
—avoid margarine cues in order to justify price.

The preferred name at this stage was 'Dairy Soft'.

STAGE 4—PACKAGING AND NAME RESEARCH

One potentially weak link in the mix might have been the packaging because a spreadable product had to be in a tub—but a tub was suggestive of margarine.

Initial qualitative exploratory research suggested the need to avoid round or flimsy packaging, and thus to use a firm, brick-shaped pack. Various pack shapes were created, and two were short-listed for research.

4a. Pack Shape Test (November 1979)

The aim of the research was to decide between two types of pack—an oblong tub and a square-shaped tub. Both had the 'Dairy Soft' design and name. NOP conducted the research.

Method—interviews were conducted in home amongst a sample in London of 50 C1C2D housewives, aged under 55, who 'buy butter nowadays'. Housewives were shown a description of the new product, 'a butter-like spread which has all the characteristics of butter—for example, texture, appearance, flavour—but which spreads direct from the fridge'. They were invited to choose between the two pack shapes for 'going best with the product', advantages, disadvantages, ease of storing in fridge, impression of quantity, ease of use and impression of butter. The order of showing the packs was rotated. (The questionnaire is appended in Appendix 3.3).

Conclusions—the square-shaped pack performed significantly better than the oblong pack, because it was easier to store and use, and was seen as more attractive.

4b. Pack Design Test I (January 1980)

Using the square-shaped tub, three pack designs were created using the 'Dairy Soft' name. Research was conducted by NOP to evaluate the performance of the three pack designs in terms of visibility, legibility, impression given of the product, and consumer preference. Quantitative research was required.

Method—a hall test was conducted, where respondents were recruited from passers-by in the streets surrounding the halls: they were shown a display of butter and margarine brands including one of the 'Dairy Soft' packs (always in the same position in the display) and then interviewed individually. Three matched samples each of around 100 housewives were used—all 'buying butter nowadays', C1C2D, aged under 55, with quota controls on age and class. The interview format was as follows:

—recall of brands/products from display;
—consideration of test pack shown in display (but now in front of respondent) in terms of impression of product and of pack, and interest in buying at 'Country Life' price;
—consideration of all three test packs against the concept for 'which goes best'.

Conclusions—the impact of all three pack designs was low, although they performed fairly well in terms of impressions of the product.

Recommendations based on the research included improving the butter imagery, and branding more strongly by simplifying the packs and possibly changing the name.

4c. Name and Pack Exploratory Groups (March 1980)

Two new designs were produced on the basis of the above recommendations in an attempt to improve both the impact and the dairy imagery: a new brand name, 'Clover', was also introduced as it was felt to be more emotive. Of the two new pack designs, one followed a premium butter route, the other a standard butter route. The following test packs were thus available for further research:

Design	Name
Premium butter	'Clover'
Premium butter	'Dairy Soft'
Standard butter	'Clover'
Standard butter	'Dairy Soft'

Prior to testing these quantitatively in the same way as before, it was decided to carry out two group discussions to explore housewives reactions to the pack design and names. The purpose of this small scale exploratory research was to give indications of the relative strengths and weaknesses of the different designs and names so that any improvements could be made to the packs prior to the quantitative stage.

Method—two group discussions were conducted by NOP in London, with housewives who 'buy butter nowadays', C1C2, aged 35–44. A concept statement was shown at the start of the groups to set the scene for the discussion. The four packs noted above were considered along with the 'cow in field' pack from the earlier research as a point of reference.

Conclusions—the results of the two groups were used to improve the four packs prior to the quantitative test, and confirmed the strong dairy connotations of the four packs.

4d. Pack Design Test II (April 1980)

The objectives of this test were to evaluate the performance of the four packs (two designs/two names) developed for the previous research in terms of visibility, legibility, impression given of the product and consumer preference.

Method—this was basically the same as the earlier pack design test with matched samples of around 100 testing each name and each design (200 in total). There was a change in the interview format, however, to cover the different names.

Conclusions—the name 'Clover' achieved higher recall levels and stronger dairy imagery than 'Dairy Soft'. The yellow standard butter pack was preferred to the premium butter design, and it achieved stronger butter imagery.

The 'Clover' name and the yellow, standard butter pack design were chosen on the basis of the research. The product designation on pack was also agreed: 'A blend of full cream milk and vegetable oil churned in a butter-maker'.

STAGE 5—MIX ASSESSMENT (MAY 1980)

At this stage of Clover's development, most elements of the marketing mix had been finalised, namely the product, positioning, pack, name and advertising approach. These elements needed to be tested as a 'complete package' to ensure that they were working together towards the overall strategy of positioning the product as a 'genuine and totally acceptable alternative to butter which provides the advantage of spreading, without sacrificing quality and taste'. The stimuli used in the mix assessment included a rough commercial (storyboards and narrative tape), a poster, a coupon, the pack and the product. (The advertising script is appended in Appendix 3.4.)

Method — ten depth interviews were conducted by The Consumer Connection with main target housewives — butter users under 55 years in the C1C2D class. Respondents were shown the stimulus material — rough TV commercial, poster and coupon, followed by the pack: they then tried the product. The product was also left for in-home use and a recall interview was made after seven days to ask the housewives' opinion of it. The research was conducted in the south of England.

Conclusions — results from the depth interviews showed that the individual elements of the marketing mix were working well together to endorse the strategic positioning of Clover. There was some scepticism regarding a spreadable product tasting like butter, but this was largely overcome by reassurance given by individual elements such as the name, 'Clover', the use of farm visuals, the pack shape and colouring, and the expression 'churned in a butter-maker'. Indeed, the concept was both intriguing and appealing, and thought likely to achieve trial through curiosity.

Some concerns, however, arose after the respondents had tried the product in-home following the depth interviews. Whilst the product obtained good reactions in terms of its taste, appearance and smell, it did not live up to the respondents expectations in terms of spreadability. Indeed, although 'a price similar to Country Life butter' was thought reasonable, there was little interest in buying the product because it did not perform in spreading as expected so it had no real product benefit over ordinary butter.

Following the research, R & D were briefed to improve the spreadability of the product. Unfortunately, the problem was difficult to solve because the addition of more vegetable oil to improve spreadability reduced the taste and texture performance of the product, and made it less similar to butter than was intended. The vegetable oil produced an unpleasant 'greasiness' especially at room temperature. The problem was eventually solved, however, using the expertise of oil/fat technologists within Dairy Crest.

Interim Report

By the end of 1980, the research programme for Clover had been virtually completed. A final product test was planned on the new product before a brand-share prediction was due to be carried out in which an indication of the volume potential for the brand would be given.

The project team working on Clover was now preparing for its launch. The advertising approach tested in the mix assessment research was modified slightly by Young and Rubican, and a test market launch package was developed.

But by 1981, the project team hit a major problem—the product was inherently unprofitable without an EEC butter fat subsidy applied to its butter fat content. A case for the subsidy was written and submitted in 1981—but it was rejected. The launch of Clover had to be postponed as a result.

A stronger, revised case for the subsidy was prepared, which stated: 'Dairy Crest strongly believes that (Clover) will increase net consumption of butter fat'. This revised case was re-submitted at the end of 1982. The subsidy was finally agreed, which meant Clover could be launched.

STAGE 6—IN-HOME CONCEPT/PRODUCT PLACEMENT (SEPTEMBER 1982)

Whilst waiting for the subsidy agreement, the final stages of research were being carried out. Because the product specification had changed, the product should have been tested 'blind' against butter and soft margarine using the same method as the 1979 product test by RSGB: this would have served to check the product's performance against the benchmark and the competition. This research was recommended, but was prevented by R & D who felt the new product was not sufficiently developed to enable a fair comparison with established butter and margarine products to be made.

Instead, the product was tested in the in-home concept/product placement which had been planned from the beginning. Because the yellow fats market had changed in that margarine consumption had increased since the original research was done in 1980, two concepts were tested: one compared the product to butter in line with the original strategy, and the other compared Clover to margarine—aimed at 'margarine users who still hanker after the taste of butter'. The objectives of the research were to assess which concept generated the desired impression of the product and to assess the product's performance in a realistic in-home situation.

Method—AMRS Market Research Ltd. conducted the in-home placement in the south of England. Two matched samples of around 125 housewives aged 20–54 were recruited, each sample seeing one concept only. The samples were controlled by quotas on age, social class, presence of children, and butter/margarine usage.

The product was placed for eight to ten days in plain 250 gram packs. (Copies of the questionnaire and the two concepts used are appended in Appendices 3.5, 3.5a, and 3.5b.)

Conclusions—of the two concepts, the butter positioning gave a significantly more accurate impression of the product:

	Sample seeing 'Butter concept' (%)	Sample seeing 'Margarine concept' (%)
Product was as expected	50	34
Product was different to expected	50	66

In addition, the sample seeing the butter concept were more likely to think Clover was butter than the other sample. The product itself performed well overall in-home: there were one or two slight negatives, such as the salt level, which were later addressed by R & D. Various price points were mentioned at the end of the interview: propensity to buy figures at the envisaged price—42p—were encouraging.

STAGE 7—BRAND-SHARE PREDICTION

A mini-test market was necessary before Clover was launched so that the Company could make market predictions and assess where the business would come from. A major concern at this time was that Clover should not cannibalise butter. Several research agencies were approached, with the result that John Parfitt—creator of the Parfitt-Collins model—was commissioned to conduct the brand-share prediction. At that time, he was running the Mass Observation 'Sharescale' technique.

Method—the test was conducted using a panel of 150 housewives who were recruited in Woking and Wolverhampton. Half of the sample regularly used premium margarine for spreading and half regularly used butter for spreading. The research, which took a total of 12 weeks, began with the recruitment of the panel. Panel members were introduced to the test via briefing sessions held in central locations. Here, they were shown a representative display of yellow fat products and a reel of commercials showing advertised yellow fat brands: both the display and the reel contained the test product, Clover. Respondents were told at this stage that their purchasing of the product sector was to be measured, and their recent purchasing was recorded prior to the test. Following this introductory stage, a brochure was given to panel members which contained all the main yellow fat brands: each page depicted a brand, its current advertising slogan, the lowest local price, and an order form on which they could order that product if they so wished. Completed order forms were given to the interviewers who then delivered the ordered products the following day. In the first week of the research, Clover's page in the brochure included a substantial money-off coupon: this was intended to promote high trial initially so that the all-important repeat purchase levels could be measured using a meaningful sample. Panel members filled in their order forms once weekly for 12 weeks. Whilst the price of the competitive products was largely constant over that time, Clover's price moved every two weeks in order that the price sensitivity of the new product could be measured. (Note: Some of the 'Sharescale' results for Clover were adversely affected by an unforeseen drop in butter prices over part of the test period).

Calculations—the brand share was estimated by multiplying the expected cumulative penetration level with the repeat purchase rate and the buying rate index (see Parfitt and Collins[1]).

Conclusions—the main conclusion from the research was that Clover would be highly successful, the main evidence being the substantial repeat purchasing rates the brand produced. Whether it would gain from butter or margarine depended very much on its price point, a lower price achieving greater steal from margarine, a higher price greater butter share. At the proposed price of 42½p (2p below the cheapest butter price when butter prices were at normal levels), Clover's estimated brand share of the butter and margarine market was 3.3% at a 20% cumulative penetration level and 16% repeat purchase rate.

STAGE 8—LAUNCH OF CLOVER

Clover was launched into test market in the Midlands during 1983. The 30 second commercial used in the launch was entitled 'Small Expectations'— but the awareness of Clover was high even before the advertising started due to a successful piece of PR in which Clover was compared favourably with butter during a feature shown on BBC's 'Breakfast Time' in the Midlands. As a result, Clover achieved great success in its test market, reaching good trial and repeat purchase level in a fairly short space of time.

Clover was rolled out nationally during 1984, and quickly achieved company objectives:

(i) It had taken a substantial share of business from margarine.
(ii) It generated a net increase in butter fat consumption over and above the expected level.
(iii) It substantially increased Dairy Crest's yellow fat sales.

A new variant—Clover Slightly Salted—was launched in 1985 following an RBL 'Sensor' test to assess its volume potential. (For RBL Sensor, see Appendix 3.6)

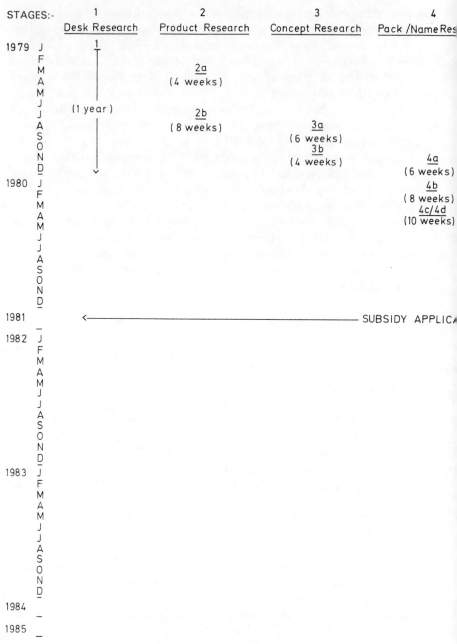

Time in brackets denotes estimated time taken from commencement of project to results

Figure 3.3 Clover NPD Research Programme.

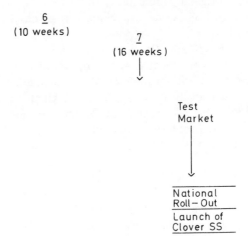

5	6	7	8
Mix Assessment	In–Home Placement	Brand (-Share) Prediction	LAUNCH!

$\underline{5}$
(6 weeks)

$\underline{6}$
(10 weeks)

$\underline{7}$
(16 weeks)

Test
Market

National
Roll–Out

Launch of
Clover SS

Figure 3.3 Clover NPD Research Programme.
Time in brackets denotes estimated time taken from commencement of project to results

Thus, the new brand, Clover, has been an unprecedented success for Dairy Crest Foods and illustrates the value of a thorough, effective research programme.

REFERENCE

1. Parfitt, J. H., and Collins, B. J. K., Use of Consumer Panels for Brand-Share Prediction. *Journal of Marketing Research*, **5** (1968) 131–145.

APPENDIX 3.1 *USAGE AND ATTITUDE STUDY: 1979*
(Stage 1 of case)
This Appendix is published by kind permission of Taylor Nelson Research.

Methodology

The data in this study was based on interviews with a representative sample of housewives aged 16 or over in Great Britain.

Housewives were selected for interview according to a quota representative within TV area in terms of age, working status and social class. This representative sample produced 1,986 interviews with housewives.

Since housewives who claim that they were using less butter and more margarine were of particular interest, and since it was not known precisely what proportion of the housewife population in Great Britain would be in this group, a booster sample of 91 housewives of this kind was recruited.

From the original representative contact sample, TNA were able to tabulate the profile of housewives who claimed that they were using *less* butter *and more* margarine.

TNA then weighted the booster sample so that its profile was the same as that of the equivalent group in the representative sample.

The weighted booster interviews were then added into the representative sample in such a way as to preserve the original incidence of housewives who claimed that they were using *less* butter *and more* margarine. In this way the un-weighted total of (1,990 plus 91, equals) 2,081, was up-weighted to 2,561. Not all of these went on to give a full interview. Only those who said that of the items on the list shown to them they bought either butter or 'margarine in packets' or 'margarine in tubs' qualified for full interview. Only four (0.2%) did not qualify as yellow fat users.

Interviewing was done in the period 22 October — 2 November 1979, by fully trained TNA interviews working under the supervision of area organisers.

The usual standards of quality control were applied to the interviewing in terms of both postal and follow-up interview checks with sub-samples of respondents.

APPENDIX 3.2   CONCEPT RESEARCH I

(Stage 3 of case)

This Appendix is published by kind permission of NOP Market Research Ltd.

SERIAL NO: _____

INTERVIEWER NO: _____

NAME: _____

ADDRESS: _____ _____

_____ TEL. NO: _____

OCCUPATION OF HEAD OF HOUSEHOLD: _____

Class:		*Presence of children in household:*		
	(15)		(18)	(18)
C1	1	(15)	Yes—0–15 years 1	
C2	2		No children under 15 years .. 2	
D	3			
Age:	(16)	*Number in household:* (including respondent)		
Under 35	1	(16)	Children (WRITE IN): _____	(19)
35–44	2			
45–54	3		Adults (WRITE IN): _____	(20)
			Total: _____	(21)
Town/City:	(17)			
London	1	(17)		
Newcastle/Durham	2			
Bristol/Plymouth/				
Exeter..............	3			
Birmingham/Coventry ..	4			
Leeds/Sheffield	5			

Ask all housewives:

Q. A   Do you buy butter at all nowadays?   (22)   (22)

Yes.................... 1

No.................... 2 *Close interview*

Show concept statement and say:
'This is how a new product is being described. Would you just read through it and then I'd like to ask you some questions about it.'

Leave concept statement for respondent to look at throughout the interview.

Q.1a What is the main thing that's telling you about the new product?

(23)

1	2	3
4	5	6
7	8	9
0	X	Y

(24)

1	2	3
4	5	6
7	8	9
0	X	Y

Q.1b What else is it telling you? *Probe:* Anything else?

(25)

1	2	3
4	5	6
7	8	9
0	X	Y

(26)

1	2	3
4	5	6
7	8	9
0	X	Y

(Show card A)

Q.2a Which of the phrases on this card comes closest to how likely you would be to try a product described like that?

(27)   (27)

If respondent says: 'Depends on the price' *CODE HERE* 1
and say: 'Well if the price was right, how likely would you be to try the product?

I would definitely try it   2
I would probably try it   3
I might or might not try it   4
I would probably not try it   5
I would definitely not try it   6

Q.2b Why in particular do you say you . . . (*quote rating given above*)? *Probe:* Any other reason? *Continuing probe:* Anything else?

(28)

1	2	3
4	5	6
7	8	9
0	X	Y

(29)

1	2	3
4	5	6
7	8	9
0	X	Y

Q.3a Does this product, as it's described here, remind you of any others
you've tried or seen, or is it completely new?

	(30)	(30)
Reminds me of others	1 ASK Q.3b	
Completely new	2 GO TO Q.4.	

Q.3b Which others does it remind you of? *Probe:* Any others?

(31)
1 2 3
4 5 6
7 8 9
0 X Y

(32)
1 2 3
4 5 6
7 8 9
0 X Y

Q.4a Is there anything you find hard to believe in this description?

	(33)	(33)
Yes	1 ASK Q.4b	
No	2 GO TO Q.5.	

Q.4b What do you find hard to believe? *Continuing probe*: Anything else?

(34)
1 2 3
4 5 6
7 8 9
0 X Y

(35)
1 2 3
4 5 6
7 8 9
0 X Y

Q.5a Would you expect a product described like this to cost about the same
as the butter you normally buy or more or less than the butter you
normally buy?

	(36)	(36)
Same as the butter I normally buy	1	
More than the butter I normally buy ...	2	
Less than the butter I normally buy	3	

Q.5b *If more ask*: How much more?
A lot more......................... 5
A bit more......................... 6

If less ask: How much less?
A lot less 7
A bit less 8

Q.5c Why do you think it would cost . . . (*Quote answer at Q.5a)?*
Continuing probe: Anything else?

```
                                                    (37)
                                                   1  2  3
                                                   4  5  6
                                                   7  8  9
                                                   0  X  Y
                                                    (38)
                                                   1  2  3
                                                   4  5  6
                                                   7  8  9
                                                   0  X  Y
```

Q.6a It will actually cost the same as Country Life butter which is a little
      more expensive than the cheapest butter. Which of the phrases on
      this card comes closest to how likely you would be to buy at that price?
      (*Show card B*)   (39)   (39)

      I would definitely buy it   1
      I would probably buy it   2
      I might or might not buy it   3
      I would probably not buy it   4
      I would definitely not buy it   5

Q.6b Why do you say that? *Probe:* Anything else?

```
                                                    (40)
                                                   1  2  3
                                                   4  5  6
                                                   7  8  9
                                                   0  X  Y
                                                    (41)
                                                   1  2  3
                                                   4  5  6
                                                   7  8  9
                                                   0  X  Y
```

Q.7a About how often do you buy butter?   (42)   (42)
      Every week   1
      Less often   2

Q.7b Which brand do you normally buy?
      Anchor 3
      Country Life   4
      Danelea. 5
      Kerrygold   6
      Lurpak 7
      Wheelbarrow   8
      Others (*write in & ring*).   9

Q.8a Do you buy soft margarine nowadays?   (43)   (43)
      Yes . . . . 1 ASK Q.8b

      No   2

Q.8b About how often do you buy soft margarine?
      Every week   3
      Less often   4
      Thank you for your help!
      Interviewers signature: _____

Note: in the reproduction of this questionnaire the original question layout has been retained
as far as possible, but not the page layout.

APPENDIX 3.3 PACK SHAPE TEST

(Stage 4 of case)

This Appendix is published by kind permission of NOP Market Research

SERIAL NO. _____
(6–9)

INTERVIEWER NO. | | | | |

(10)   (11)   (12)   (13)

NAME OF RESPONDENT: _____

ADDRESS: _____

_____

TEL. NO. (IF ANY): _____

OCCUPATION OF HEAD OF HOUSEHOLD: _____

Age:	(15)	*Group:*	(16)
16–34	1	C1	1
35–44	2	C2	2
45–54	3	D	3

Good morning/afternoon/evening. I am from NOP Market Research and we are conducting a survey in the area. To ensure we talk to a cross-section of people, would you tell me if you or any of your relatives or friends work in any of the areas on this card. (*Show card A*)

Accountancy	1	Advertising	N
Banking	2	Marketing	N
Building	3	Market Research	N
Catering	4	Foodstuff Manufacturer	N
Confectionery	5	Foodstuff retailer,	
Iron and Steel	6	wholesaler	N
Law	7	Politics	N
Mining	8	Journalism	N

If *any* coded 'N' rung *do not recruit.*

Q.A (*Show card B*) Would you tell me which of the products on this list do you buy nowadays?

(17)

Butter	1 *
Cream	2
Cheese (hard/soft)	3
Eggs	4
Lard	5
Margarine	6
Soft margarine	7
Milk	8
Yoghurt	9

Only continue if code 1* rung.
If respondent does NOT buy butter close interview.
I would like to talk to you about packaging for a new product. This is how the new product is described . . . *Show concept and read out.*
Place the SQUARE pack on the LEFT and the OBLONG one on the RIGHT in front of the respondent.
I would like to know what you think about these two packs — this *square* one with the design all round, and this *oblong* one with the design just on the top. They would each contain the same amount of Dairy Soft and would both cost the same.

Q.1a Which of these two packs do you like best for a product described like this (*Point to concept board*)?

	(18)
Oblong	1
Square.	2
No difference	3

Q.1b Why do you say that? Any other reason? *Probe for full and clear answers.*

(19)
1 2 3 4
5 6 7 8
9 0 X Y

(20)
1 2 3 4
5 6 7 8
9 0 X Y

Q.2a *Point to SQUARE pack.* Thinking about this pack, what advantages do you think this pack has for a product like that? *Probe:* Any other advantages?

(21)
1 2 3 4
5 6 7 8
9 0 X Y

(22)
1 2 3 4
5 6 7 8
9 0 X Y

Q.2b And what disadvantages does this pack have? *Probe:* Any other disadvantages?

(23)
1 2 3 4
5 6 7 8
9 0 X Y

(24)
1 2 3 4
5 6 7 8
9 0 X Y

Q.3a *Now point to OBLONG pack.* Now thinking about this pack, what advantages do you think this pack has for a product like that? *Probe:* Any other advantages?

(25)
1 2 3 4
5 6 7 8
9 0 X Y

(26)
1 2 3 4
5 6 7 8
9 0 X Y

Q.3b And what disadvantages does this pack have? *Probe:* Any other disadvantages?

	(27)
_____	1 2 3 4
_____	5 6 7 8
_____	9 0 X Y
_____	(28)
_____	1 2 3 4
_____	5 6 7 8
	9 0 X Y

Q.4a Which one, if either, of the two packs do you think would be easier to store in the fridge?

	(29)
Oblong	1
Square.	2
No difference	3

Q.5 Which, if either, looks as though it would contain more of the product?

	(30)
Oblong	1
Square.	2
No difference	3

Q.6 And which, if either, looks easier to use?

	(31)
Oblong	1
Square.	2
No difference	3

Q.7 Finally, does one make you think of butter more than the other? *If yes ask:* Which one? *Write in spontaneous comment:*

	(32)
Oblong	1
Square.	2
No difference	3

Q.8 On average how often do you buy butter?

	(33)
Once a week or more often	1
About once a fortnight	2
About once every three weeks	3
About once a month	4
Less often	5

Q.9 And which brand do you normally buy? *If more than one ask*: Which one brand do you buy *most* of?

	(34)
Anchor	1
Country Life	2
Danelea.	3
Kerrygold	4
Lurpak	5
Wheelbarrow	6
Other (*write in & ring*)	7
Don't know	8

Check back to Q.A to see if soft margarine bought. If yes ask Q.10, others go to personal details.

Q.10 On average how often do you buy soft margarine?

                                                          (35)
       About once a week or more often 1
       About once a fortnight 2
       About once every 3 weeks 3
       About once a month 4
       Less often 5

Q.11 And which brand do you normally buy? *If more than one ask*: Which do you buy *most* of?

                                                          (36)
       Stork SB........................... 1
       Blueband 2
       Flora.............................. 3
       Outline 4
       Summer County 5
       Fresh Fields 6
       St. Ivel Gold 7
       Other (*write in & ring*) 8

APPENDIX 3.4   CLOVER LAUNCH SCRIPT
(Narrative tape used in Mix Assessment—Stage 5 of case.)

Imagine the sun's just rising on a frosty morning, down on a Devon dairy farm. A number of cows are walking towards the farmhouse. To all the world it looks like they're exchanging a few words. Not to be seen or heard, we follow them to a warmly-lit doorway, where peering over their shoulders we see they are looking into the farmhouse kitchen.

Here just as usual a farmer is preparing his breakfast before he takes his cows to the milking parlour. He's a no-nonsense farmer, not given to taking up new-fangled ideas, but friendly enough. There's bacon cooking in the pan, a kettle whistling, the early news on the wireless. But today one senses something special is about to happen.

Instead of the butter, our farmer takes a tub from the refrigerator. It's a new product called Clover. Now we know why the cows are so intrigued. Slightly suspiciously, our discriminating butter user looks up at his cows as he removes the lid from the tub of Clover. There's an air of anticipation as he tastes a little on a crust of bread. Still, a slight nod of approval relieves the apprehensive looks on the cows faces as only the rapport between man and beast can. We learn that Clover tastes of traditional butter because, naturally enough, it comes from the milk of English cows—churned with vegetable oil. But will it spread when it's really cold, straight from the 'fridge'? We're about to find out. Tentatively our farmer spreads a little Clover onto his freshly sliced, crusty bread. As he sees how easily it spreads, he smiles knowingly to the cows.

Then continues enthusiastically to spread Clover on his bread . . . suddenly he pauses. We cut to a look of bewilderment on the cows faces, then back to our farmer who lets out a side splitting raucous 'Mooooo'. He laughs heartily to himself, continuing to enjoy his bread and Clover. Turning to our cows, one says to the other in a voice as plain as day, 'He says it spreads!' They can't retain their excitement any longer and proceed to frolic in the backyard. And between chuckles, spread the news that new Clover spreads, 'It spreads'.

Young and Rubicam Ltd.
21st April, 1980.

APPENDIX 3.5
'BUTTER CONCEPT' IN IN-HOME PLACEMENT

Fresh Bread Refrigerated Butter. Fresh Bread Refrigerated Clover.

Introducing new Clover from the Dairy Crest Creameries of the Milk Marketing Board.

It tastes of traditional English butter. Because like butter it comes full cream milk.

But to make Clover unique, its churned with some vegetable oil.

So it spreads straight from the fridge. No more having to leave the butter out.

Try some Clover for yourself. You won't believe it until you do.

CLOVER — Milk Marketing Board
CLOVER — Milk Marketing Board

It spreads, It spreads!

(Young and Rubicam Ltd.)

APPENDIX 3.5a 'MARGARINE CONCEPT' USED IN IN-HOME PLACEMENT

THEY MAY SPREAD THE SAME, BUT THEY CERTAINLY DON'T TASTE THE SAME.

At first glance, new Clover may not seem much different from margarine.

After all, it spreads straight from the fridge, just like margarine.

But you'll notice a world of difference when you taste it.

Because Clover is made with lashings of English full cream milk, to give it a real butter flavour

With just a little vegetable oil added to help it spread.

So now you don't have to sacrifice taste for convenience.

MADE IN THE DAIRY CREST CREAMERIES OF THE MILK MARKETING BOARD

(Young and Rubicam Ltd.)

APPENDIX 3.5b   IN-HOME CONCEPT/PRODUCT PLACEMENT
(Stage 6 of case)

This Appendix is published by kind permission of
AMRS Market Research Ltd.

Only interview housewives aged 20–54 years according to quota

Exclude those connected (personally or through family or close friends) with any of the occupations listed on card X.

Q.A   We are carrying out a survey about butter and margarine. Please would you look at this card (*show card A*) and tell me which one of these phrases best describes what you use for spreading on bread?

	C8	Quota
I only use butter	1	B
I mainly use butter	2	
I use butter & margarine equally	3	B & M
I mainly use margarine	4	
I only use margarine	5	M
I don't use butter or margarine for spreading		Close

If housewife fits quota, continue. Others close.

Q.B   *If butter used at all, ask*:

Which brand of butter do you usually use for spreading?

	C9
Anchor	1
Country Life	2
Danelea	3
Kerrygold	4
Lurpak	5
Others (write in)	6

Q.C *If margarine used at all, ask*:
Which brand of margarine do you usually use for spreading?

		C10
Blue Band	....	1
Echo	....	2
Flora	....	3
Krona	....	4
Outline	....	5
(St. Ivel) Gold	....	6
Stork S.B.	....	7
Summer County	....	8
Others (write in)	....	9

Classification:

Name:_____

Address:_____

_____

_____

_____

Occupation (Self): _____

Occupation (H/H): _____

Interviewer: _____

Date: _____

Age:		C11
	20–34	V
	35–54	X

Social	AB	1
Class:	C1	2
	C2	3
	DE	4

Children under 16 yrs at home:

	Yes	6
	No	7

Q.1 *Show concept board.* Could you look at this for a moment and then tell me what you think about the product shown there (*Record all spontaneous comment*)

_____
_____
_____
_____
_____
_____

C13
V X 0
1 2 3
4 5 6
7 8 9
C14
V X 0
1 2 3
4 5 6
7 8 9

Q.2 What type of product do you think it is? *Continuing probe:*

_____
_____
_____
_____
_____
_____

C15
V X 0
1 2 3
4 5 6
7 8 9
C16
V X 0
1 2 3
4 5 6
7 8 9

Q.3a Does it seem to you to be different from other products you have seen in the shops, or not?

	C17
Different...........................	1
Not different/Don't know	2

Q.3b *If different, ask:* In what way? *Continuing probe:* Any other way?

C18		
V	X	0
1	2	3
4	5	6
7	8	9

C19		
V	X	0
1	2	3
4	5	6
7	8	9

Q.3c *If not different, ask*: Which is it like among products you have seen?

C20		
V	X	0
1	2	3
4	5	6
7	8	9

C21		
V	X	0
1	2	3
4	5	6
7	8	9

Q.4a *Ask all*: How would you expect it to be used—in addition to what is used already or instead of something?

	C22
In addition........................	1
Instead of something	2

Q.4b *If instead of, ask*: What would it be instead of?

C23		
V	X	0
1	2	3
4	5	6
7	8	9

Q.5a As you can see, this product comes from the Dairy Crest creameries. Have you ever heard of Dairy Crest before?

	C25
Yes	1
No.................................	2
Not sure	3

Q.5b What other products do you think that they make (from the name)?
Probe: Anything else?

C26		
V	X	0
1	2	3
4	5	6
7	8	9

C27		
V	X	0
1	2	3
4	5	6
7	8	9

Q.6a Which of the phrases on this card best describes how you feel about trying this product shown here? (*show card B*)

	C28
I certainly would like to try this product	1
I might like to try this product	2
*I am not sure whether I would like to try this product	3
*I don't think I would like to try this product	4
I certainly would not like to try this product	5

Q.6b *If not sure/would not like, ask:* Why do you say that? *Probe:* Any other reason?

C29		
V	X	0
1	2	3
4	5	6
7	8	9

C30		
V	X	0
1	2	3
4	5	6
7	8	9

Close interview and return questionnaire. Do not count towards quota but classify.

Q.7 *If certainly would/might like to try, ask:* The manufacturer is interested in finding out what housewives think about this product. Would you be prepared to help us by trying it over the next week?
If yes: Ask Q8 and Q9
If no: Close and return questionnaire to head office. Do not count towards quota but classify.

Q.8 *Ask those who have accepted the placement* (*show blank pack*) About how much would you expect the product (you have just read about) to cost in a 250 gram pack this size?

C31		
V	X	0
1	2	3
4	5	6
7	8	9

(32)		
V	X	0
1	2	3
4	5	6
7	8	9

Narrow down any range

Q.9 Before I go I am going to read out a list of possible prices at which this product would be on sale for this size pack. From what you know about the product from this description (*point to concept board*), I would like you to tell me for each price I read out whether you would or would not buy at that price. *Prices will be read out as follows, varying the starting point.*

	44p	38p	46p	40p	50p	42p	36p	48p	
Would buy	2	X	3	0	5	1	V	4	C33
Would not buy	N	N	N	N	N	N	N	N	

===

*Recall interview for Mrs*_____

Good morning/afternoon/evening, I have come back to find out what you think of the product I left with you a week ago.

R.1a Have you tried the product at all?

          C8

     Yes   1

     No   2

R.1b *If no, ask*: Why have you not tried it? May I have the product to take away — *Collect product and close interview*

		C9
V	X	0
1	2	3
4	5	6
7	8	9
		C10
V	X	0
1	2	3
4	5	6
7	8	9

R.2 How much of it have you used? *Read out pre-codes*

          C11

     All   1

     ¾   2

     ½   3

     ¼   4

     Less than ¼   5

R.3 What did you think of it overall? *Probe:* Anything else?

		C12
V	X	0
1	2	3
4	5	6
7	8	9
		C13
V	X	0
1	2	3
4	5	6
7	8	9

R.4a And was the product as you expected it would be, or was it different?

          C14

     As expected   1

          Route R5

     Different..........................   2 R4b

Q.4b *If different, ask:* In what ways was it different? *Probe:* Any other ways?

C15		
V	X	0
1	2	3
4	5	6
7	8	9

C16		
V	X	0
1	2	3
4	5	6
7	8	9

Q.4c And was it better or worse than you expected?

C17

Much better   1
A little better   2
A little worse   3
Much worse   4

R.5 *Ask all:* What if anything did you particularly *like* about the product? *Probe:* Anything else?

C18		
V	X	0
1	2	3
4	5	6
7	8	9

C19		
V	X	0
1	2	3
4	5	6
7	8	9

R.6 What, if anything, did you particularly *dislike* about it? *Probe:* Anything else?

C20		
V	X	0
1	2	3
4	5	6
7	8	9

C21		
V	X	Y
1	2	3
4	5	6
7	8	9

R.7 Thinking about the rest of your family, what did they think of the product? (*Record for each family member*)

Husband

C22

Liked it   1
Did not like it   2
Did not try   3
(no husband)   4

Children: (0–15 Yrs)

C23

Liked it   1
Did not like it   2
They were divided   3
Did not try   4
(no children)   5

Other adult family members:	C24
Liked it...............................	1
Did not like it........................	2
They were divided	3
Did not try	4
(no other adults).....................	5

R.8a How did you use this product — did you use it in any of these ways?
      (*Show card C*)

	C25
Spreading on its own (on toast/ biscuits/bread).....................	1
Spreading with other things on top (on toast/biscuits/bread)............	2
In sandwiches/rolls with other filling	3
In mashed potatoes	4
On vegetables	5
In cooking	6
Other ways to be recorded:	7

(*Probe for other uses and write in*)

	C26
_____	V X 0
_____	1 2 3
_____	4 5 6
_____	7 8 9

R.8b *For each type of use recorded in R.8a, ask:* What would you normally
      have used for.....................if you had not had this product to test?

Spreading on its own (on toast, biscuits, bread)

	C27
_____	V X 0
_____	1 2 3
_____	4 5 6
_____	7 8 9

Spreading with other things on top (on toast/biscuits/bread)

	C28
_____	V X 0
_____	1 2 3
_____	4 5 6
_____	7 8 9

In sandwiches, rolls with other filling

	C29
_____	V X 0
_____	1 2 3
_____	4 5 6
_____	7 8 9

In mashed potatoes

	C30
_____	V X 0
_____	1 2 3
_____	4 5 6
_____	7 8 9

On vegetables

C31		
V	X	Y
1	2	3
4	5	6
7	8	9

In cooking

C32		
V	X	0
1	2	3
4	5	6
7	8	9

Other uses — specify again and show what would have been used for each

C33		
V	X	0
1	2	3
4	5	6
7	8	9

C34		
V	X	0
1	2	3
4	5	6
7	8	9

R.8c *For each type of use recorded in R.8a, Ask*: How did you like the product I left you, compared with what you normally use for............ did you like the product I left you better or about the same or not as much?

Spreading on its own (on toast/biscuits/bread)

C35

Test product better (than product
    normally used)   1
About the same   2
Test product not as good   3

Spreading with other things on top (on toast/biscuits/bread)

C36

Test product better (than product
    normally used)   1
About the same   2
Test product not as good   3

In sandwiches, rolls with other filling

C37

Test product better (than product
    normally used)   1
About the same   2
Test product not as good   3

In mashed potatoes

	C38
Test product better (than product	
normally used)	1
About the same	2
Test product not as good	3

On vegetables

	C39
Test product better (than product	
normally used)	1
About the same	2
Test product not as good	3

In cooking

	C40
Test product better (than product	
normally used)	1
About the same	2
Test product not as good	3

Other uses — specify again

	C41
Test product better (than product	
normally used)	1
About the same	2
Test product not as good	3
	C42
Test product better (than product	
normally used)	1
About the same	2
Test product not as good	3

R.9 *If the test product was not used for cooking, ask*: Why didn't you use it in your cooking? *(Probe)*

C43		
V	X	0
1	2	3
4	5	6
7	8	9

C44		
V	X	0
1	2	3
4	5	6
7	8	9

R.10 *Ask all*: Where did you keep this product?

C45		
V	X	0
1	2	3
4	5	6
7	8	9

R.11 Which of the phrases on this card (*show card D*) best describes your opinion of this product for EASE OF SPREADING?

	C46
Very easy to spread	1
Easy to spread	2
Neither easy nor difficult	3
Difficult to spread	4
Very difficult to spread..............	5

R.12 And which of the phrases on this card (*show card E*) best describes your opinion of the APPEARANCE of this product?

	C47
I like the appearance very much	1
I quite like the appearance	2
I neither like nor dislike the appearance......................	3
I dislike the appearance..............	4
I strongly dislike the appearance	5

R.13a And which of the phrases on this card (*show card F*) best describes your opinion of the TASTE of this product?

	C48
I like the taste very much	1
I quite like the taste.................	2
I neither like nor dislike the taste	3
I dislike the taste	4
I strongly dislike the taste............	5

R.13b *If dislike/strongly dislike, ask:* What did you dislike about the taste? *Probe:* Anything else?

C49		
V	X	0
1	2	3
4	5	6
7	8	9

C50		
V	X	0
1	2	3
4	5	6
7	8	9

R.14 *Ask all:* Having tried it what *type* of product do you think it is? *Probe:* What type of product is it most like?

C51		
V	X	0
1	2	3
4	5	6
7	8	9

C52		
V	X	0
1	2	3
4	5	6
7	8	9

R.15a These are some things that might be said about the product you tried (*offer shuffle cards G*). Please would you tell me which of these, if any, *you* think apply to this product.

C53

Only code the statements thought to apply

Too smooth........................	1
An appealing colour	2
Too thin..........................	3
Tastes like butter	4
Tastes like margarine................	5
Too creamy in texture	6

C54

Too salty	1
Too oily	2
An unappealing colour	3
Not salty enough	4
Too watery	5
Looks like butter	6
Looks like margarine................	7

R.15b *If tastes like margarine, ask*: You say it tastes like margarine — why do you think that? *Probe:*

C55

V X 0
1 2 3
4 5 6
7 8 9

_____

C56

V X 0
1 2 3
4 5 6
7 8 9

R.15c *If neither tastes like butter, nor tastes like margarine, ask:* You don't think it tastes like butter or margarine — what does it taste like to you? *Probe:*

C57

V X 0
1 2 3
4 5 6
7 8 9

_____

C58

V X 0
1 2 3
4 5 6
7 8 9

R.16 *Ask all:* Which of the phrases on this card (*show card H*) best describes how likely you feel you would be to want to try this product again if you saw it in the shops?

C59

I certainly would like to try this product again	1
I might like to try this product again.............................	2
I am not sure whether I would like to try the product again	3
I don't think I would like to try this product again	4
I certainly would not like to try this product again	5

R.17 Now that you have tried this product how much would you expect a 250 gram pack like the one you tried to cost?

C60		
V	X	0
1	2	3
4	5	6
7	8	9

Narrow down any range

C61		
V	X	0
1	2	3
4	5	6
7	8	9

R.18a I am going to read out a list of possible prices at which this product would be on sale for the size of pack you tested. For each price I read out I would like you to tell me if you would or would not buy at that price. (*Prices will be read out as follows, varying the starting point*).

Prices	44p	38p	46p	40p	50p	42p	36p	48p	
Would buy	2	X	3	0	5	1	V	4	C62
Would not buy	N	N	N	N	N	N	N	N	

R.18b Actually this product will be on sale at 42p for a pack the size you tried. Which of the phrases on this card (*show card J*) best describes how you feel about including this product amongst the foods you regularly buy?

C63

I would certainly include this in the foods I regularly buy 1

I might include this in the foods I regularly buy 2

I am not sure if I would include this in the foods I regularly buy 3

I don't think I would include this in the foods I regularly buy 4

I certainly would not include this in the foods I regularly buy 5

R.18c *If don't think I would/certainly would not include, ask*: Why do you think you would not include this product in the foods you regularly buy?

C64		
V	X	0
1	2	3
4	5	6
7	8	9

C65		
V	X	0
1	2	3
4	5	6
7	8	9

R.18d *If would certainly/might/not sure include, ask*: If you did buy this product, would it be in addition to what you buy now or instead of something?

	C66
In addition to	1
Instead of..........................	2

R.18e *If instead of, ask*: What would it be instead of?

C67		
V	X	0
1	2	3
4	5	6
7	8	9

C68		
V	X	0
1	2	3
4	5	6
7	8	9

Thank respondent and close interview

Note: in the reproduction of this questionnaire the original question layout has been retained as far as possible, but not the page layout.

APPENDIX 3.6   SENSOR MODELS

This Appendix is published by kind permission of Research Bureau Ltd. It provides technical details for Sensor models used in the calculation of volume potential (Stage 8 of case).

1. The Trial/Repeat Model
2. The Brand Preference Model
3. The Brand/Price Trade-off Model
4. The Nature of Market Shares

1. The Trial/Repeat Model

As its name implies, this model measures the rates of Trial and Repeat Purchase for a new brand. The model is based on observation of the behaviour of respondents at the initial contact in the central location and, following usage of the new brand in their homes, at a subsequent recall interview.

In the central location, respondents are shown advertising both for the new brand and for its principal competitors. They are then shown a shelf display of products within the product field including the new brand. Each product is priced as it would be in a normal shop. The respondents are all given a shopping coupon, generally valued slightly above the price of the new brand, and are invited to make a purchase from the display. Each respondent is free to purchase the new brand or its competitors singly or in whatever combination and quantity she chooses. If the value of the coupon is greater than the value of a purchase, the respondent is refunded the appropriate amount in cash. If her purchases exceed the value of the coupon, she must make up the difference with her own money. If a respondent chooses not to make any purchases, she can cash in her coupon for its full face value.

At the recall interview the respondent is given the opportunity to repurchase the brand at its full market price which she must pay for with her own money. The money is handed over to the interviewer in exchange for the product but—respecting the market research code of practice—this money is refunded in full at the close of the contact.

Trial is measured at the first and Repeat Purchase at the second contact as follows:

Trial in Shop

The percentage of respondents choosing the new brand with their coupon from the central location shelf display. It includes both those taking the new brand on its own and those selecting it together with another brand. The percentage is based on all respondents contacted for the central location research regardless of whether they are recontacted or not.

The level of trial observed for the new brand is maximised since the brand, by definition, has perfect — 100% — distribution in the shelf display and, as a result of the advertising, has perfect awareness among respondents. Estimates therefore need to be made of the levels of distribution and awareness the new brand will in fact achieve in the market place and to use these to downweight the observed level of trial to one that will be effectively achieved in the market place.

Estimated Distribution

This is an estimate provided by the Company of the effective level of value distribution (Value Weighted Shops Handling less Out of Stock) expected for the new brand after 9 to 12 months on the market. Usually the estimate will be in the form of a range of possibilities from pessimistic to optimistic rather than a single figure.

Estimated Brand Awareness

This is an estimate provided by the Company of the level of total awareness (spontaneous plus prompted) that the new brand is expected to achieve after 9 to 12 months on the market. As with the Distribution estimate this will usually be given as a range of possibilities from low to high.

Effective Market Trial

This is a straightforward multiplication of:
Trial in Shop $\times$ Distribution $\times$ Awareness $=$ Effective Market Trial.

Repeat Purchase R1

This is the percentage of all those purchasing the new brand with the coupon from the shelf display who, when recontacted at the recall interview, agree to purchase it again with their own money. The percentage is based on all effective recontacts, i.e. all shelf display purchasers who are recontacted at home and who have tried the new brand.

Repeat Purchase R2

This is the estimate of the repeat purchase rate among triers (i.e. purchasers from the shelf display) who do not wish to buy the new brand again at the recall interview with their own money. It is taken from the preference share of this group for the new brand from the Preference Allocation model.

Long-Term Repeat Purchase

R1 and R2 are combined using the Markov formula:

$$\frac{R2}{(1-R1)+R2}$$

to arrive at a long-term repeat purchase rate.

Estimated Market Share

This is a straightforward multiplication of:

Effective Market Trial × Long-Term Repeat Purchase = Long-Term Market Share. The share represents what the brand will achieve after 9–12 months in the market.

2. The Brand Preference Model

This model measures the probability of purchase for a new brand among those consumers who will include it within their individual repertoire of brands. Experience has shown these probabilities to be closely correlated with actual repeat purchase rates and so allows market shares to be estimated.

The probabilities are assessed from the preferences given by respondents for the brands that come with their repertoire of brands (referred to as the 'Salient Set of brands'). The 'Salient Set' is established for each respondent at the first contact from answers given spontaneously to a series of questions like 'brands in-home now', 'brand last purchased', 'brands ever used', 'brands would not consider buying'. Then each respondent's preferences are measured from a series of paired comparisons among all brands within her salient set by asking her to allocate a total of 11 points between each pair in accordance with how much she likes each of the two brands.

Preferences are measured twice, first at the initial contact and then at the recall when the new brand is included in the set of each respondent. The purchase probabilities obtained at the initial contact are fine-tuned using a B factors to align them more closely with current market share estimates amongst the target group.

The preference shares obtained at the recall interview show the estimated repeat purchase rate for the new brand among consumers including it within their salient set of brands. A comparison between preference shares for the existing brands on the market obtained at the two contacts indicates from where within the market the new brand will gain its sales.

Market shares from the model are calculated as follows:

Preference Share

This is the share of the new brand from the Preference Allocation model among all Triers of the brand (i.e. purchasers of the test brand from the shop display who are recontacted at the recall and includes both repeat and non-repeat buyers).

Estimate of Market Level of Saliency

In order to derive a market share for the new brand from this model, it is necessary to estimate the percentage of consumers who will include the brand in their salient set of brands after the brand has been on the market for 9–12 months. This is because in the Sensor test the new brand has a saliency level of 100% as the brand for test purposes has been 'forced' into the salient set of all respondents.

The procedure used to arrive at this estimate is as follows:

   (i) The penetration of the existing brands included in the test is calculated, derived from some of the early Sensor salient set questions.
  (ii) Calculate for the same brands their percentage inclusion in the salient set of respondents.
 (iii) Conduct a regression analysis between the two sets of figures.
 (iv) The market level of trial (i.e. the penetration) of the new brand derived from the Trial/Repeat model is then fed into the regression to arrive at the new brand's estimate of marked saliency.

Estimated Market Share

This is a straightforward multiplication of:
Preference Share × Level of Saliency = Long-Term Market Share

3. The Price Trade-Off Model

This model, developed by Research International and now validated over a large number of projects, measures the probability of purchase for the new brand at a series of different pricing situations. As such it provides invaluable information on the new brand's likely market place performance at other pricing situations in addition to the particular one at which it was tested.

At the recall interview, following the opportunity to repurchase the new brand, the respondent is presented with her salient brands including the new one with each brand clearly priced. She is asked to indicate the brand she would purchase at that particular pricing situation. The brand chosen then has its price altered and a further decision is asked for. This procedure continues until at least one brand has been presented to the respondent at all its planned prices.

Market shares from the model are calculated thus:

Market Share at Test Prices

This is the market share of purchases of the new brand among Triers of the brand from the shelf display from the Price Trade-Off Model when the prices of all brands are set at those used in the shelf display at the central location.

Estimate of Market Level of Saliency/Market Share

As with the Brand Preference model, in order to arrive at a market share from the Price Trade-Off model it is necessary to take account of the fact that all respondents in the test have the new brand by definition in their salient set. The market share is derived by multiplying the new brand's share by the estimate of market saliency previously calculated:

   i.e. Brand Price Trade-Off Share × Level of Saliency = Long-Term Market Share.

Other pricing situations can be simulated with this model by simply changing the prices to be applied to particular brands. Thus the effect on the new brand of either increasing or decreasing its own price or from changing the prices of competitors can be gauged.

4. Nature of Market Shares

All the market shares provided by the models for the new brand are in the form of share of purchase occasions. These can be converted to quantity or value shares by the appropriate weighting for pack size, relative speed of consumption of the new brand compared with other brands in the field and unit price.

   Weighting procedures are also included in each model to allow for individual respondent's consumption rates of the product field.

Applied Marketing and Social Research 2nd Edition
Edited by Ute Bradley
©Copyright John Wiley 1987

4. The Contribution of Research in the Development of the BBC's Computer Literacy Project

Vivien Marles *British Broadcasting Corporation*
Pam Mills *British Broadcasting Corporation*

Marketing and advertising managers are used to the idea of researching new products from the development stage to market evaluation. Therefore research is applied to advertisements, but it seems it is used less in the development of TV programmes. Why? This case lists many of the reasons and also concentrates on the factors which make TV programme development work so interesting:

(i) Establishing the true nature of the problem requiring research.

(ii) Defining the appropriate target group.

(iii) Drawing the right implications (from i. and ii.) for alternative possible production approaches.

These three points could form the basis of a number of interesting classroom exercises.

In addition to these broad questions the researcher will also be interested in:

— sample definitions (e.g. using stage 1 of the research to help define the sample for stage 2),

— qualitative research being used to elicit reactions to a pilot film of the proposed programme series; and

— the use of on-going quantitative BBC research exercises to provide background material, etc.

The article is well supported by documentary evidence (Appendices) and references.

ORIGINS

Difficult as it may be to believe, as recently as 1980 the home computer boom was still very much in the future. But even by 1980 it was already recognised that advances in microprocessor technology were going to have a big impact on individuals and society over the next 20 years. A 1978 BBC television documentary in the 'Horizon' series — 'Now the Chips are Down' — showed some of the changes which were coming. The television audience was fascinated by this new perspective. The audience of 2.8 million was the highest for any 'Horizon' programme that season, and the Appreciation Index score of 84 — the highest for 'Horizon' that year — indicated a great deal of interest in the subject.

Following extensive internal discussion, the BBC's Continuing Education Television Department decided to give priority to increasing the public's understanding of microprocessor technology, its applications and its implications for society. 'The Silicon Factor', three 40-minute programmes for a general audience, was first transmitted in early 1979, followed by a five-part series, 'Managing the Micro', aimed at decision-makers in business and industry.

Computer awareness was increasing also in education and in government circles — particularly in the Department of Industry, the Department of Education and Science, and the Manpower Services Commission. Furthermore, 1982 was designated 'Information Technology Year'. To coincide with this event the BBC planned to launch a major new project in the field of computer literacy. Previous series and programmes had concentrated on the impact of the microcomputer as a major social force to which people would have to adjust, but reactions indicated a major gap in the public's awareness of and knowledge about micros. The overall aims of the BBC's Computer Literacy Project were, therefore: first to introduce interested adults to the world of computers and computing; and, second, to provide the opportunity for people to learn, through direct experience, how to use a microcomputer. This task required answers to fundamental questions about what is meant by computers, computer language, and computer memory, and how the individual can harness the potential of the computer. Ten TV programmes were planned in the series, but it was recognised that a television series in isolation could have little impact. The series would, therefore, be supported by a range of other materials which ultimately included a book, a linked microcomputer system, a user guide, a range of applications programs, and an associated course in programming in one computer language — BASIC — provided by the National Extension College, and a national referral service.

A highly experienced production team was allocated to the project, with extensive support. A large number of production decisions had to be made about the new series, and, inevitably, many of these would be made on the basis of experience, expediency or creative institution. From an early stage, BBC's in-house Broadcasting Research Department was called in to discuss key production decisions and to help determine the potential contribution of consumer research.

RESEARCH AND PRODUCTION

Compared with the care and the detail with which advertising campaigns are researched to fill the spaces between broadcast programmes, virtually no developmental research is carried out on the programmes themselves. Most of the research resources in British broadcasting organisations are spent on retrospective research — measuring how many people watched (or listened to) a programme or a spot, and, in very simple terms, what they thought of it. Many factors contribute to this avoidance of developmental research, some based on hard reality and experience — the sheer magnitude of TV output, the limited risk for much of the output, the lack of clear-cut criteria for testing ideas or programmes — other reasons based on misconception or prejudice — the fear that research might in some way undermine creativity or even kill a good idea, the wealth of experience which has produced consistent winners over the years, fears about the cost and time implications, and a fundamental lack of awareness of the potential contribution of research to at least some of the many questions that arise during the development of a programme idea and its execution.

Fortunately for this project, the Executive Producer, John Radcliffe, and his team were sufficiently concerned to ensure that they optimised the proposed series and at a fairly early stage they contacted BBC Broadcasting Research Department to discuss the ways in which research might help the production process. (See also Mills[1]; Marles and Radcliffe[2]; Laking and Rhodes[3]; Laking and Jackson[4]).

PRODUCTION QUESTIONS

Each stage of research will be discussed in detail below. At this point an overview is given of the main issues facing the production team.

The *aims* of the series were clearly defined:

1. To provide for a TV audience an introduction to the microcomputer.
2. Through the TV series and the associated support material and activities, to provide an opportunity for those interested to learn how to use microcomputers.

The *constraints* were clear from the start:

1. The series was to be produced by the BBC's Continuing Education Department. It would, therefore, be shown at times traditionally allocated to the output of that Department, none of them peak viewing times: Sunday morning, with repeats on a weekday afternoon (for educational use) and late at night.

Then there were two important constraints, well established from research on television viewing (see Goodhardt; Ehrenberg and Collins[5]):

2. The audience would inevitably contain a cross-section of the population, including casual viewers as well as the motivated. This is true of all TV output. No programme is only watched by the highly motivated.
3. Most viewers would only watch one or two out of the series of ten programmes. This generalisation applies to all TV series: most of the viewers who see any part of a series miss most programmes in the series. One implication is that each programme would have to be effective as a one-off, and not be inextricably linked to preceding programmes.

And, finally, there is the fact of life that:

4. Most of the viewers who saw any of the series would not take advantage of any of the support material or facilities. Again, this meant that each programme had to stand on its own merits, but also be capable of being enriched by the support material.

Arising from this background were basic questions concerned with the targeting of the series:

(i) Was there a real need for such a series?
(ii) Who should be the target — a specialist audience or a more general audience?
(iii) What was their existing level of knowledge about and attitudes to computing?

Once the target audience had been defined, a wide range of questions would arise concerning content and presentation, for example:

(i) What should be the balance between theory and example, or between studio and location work?
(ii) Should the series aim to teach by detailed communication or to capture interest and leave the educational task to other support materials?

(iii) Should the tone be exploratory and very accessible, or more didactic and explanatory?
(iv) How should the presenters reflect these aims?

Following transmission, there would, of course, arise the key question:

—*Did it work?*

And as part of this:

(i) How many and who watched it?
(ii) What did they think of it?
(iii) What did they learn?
(iv) What did they do?—Did they use the support material and/or activities? And, if so, did *they* work?

And, importantly:

(v) *What do we do next?*

The following sections will outline the research approach and describe and comment on some of the findings.

POSTSCRIPT ON THE APPROACH

The development and evaluation of 'The Computer Programme' is characteristic of the approach of BBC Broadcasting Research Department in the 1980s. The relationship between the BBC's Research Department and production staff had had a patchy history since the Department was founded in 1937. By 1980, however, efforts were being made to apply some of the research approaches familiar in advertising and new product development research to the development of programmes. As can be seen from this project, the emphasis was on providing creative and qualitative feedback, on helping production staff to a greater understanding of their potential audience and its needs, using a flexible, pragmatic approach to the particular problems posed, rather than on the establishment of a quantitative system of evaluation which would provide the basis for a 'Go/No Go' decision by producers, their heads of department or channel controllers.

Important elements in this approach are:

(a) The demonstrable gulf between production staff and the audience in their assumptions, knowledge and beliefs about the subject—a gulf resulting from background, education, and professional values, which is constantly reinforced by peer group values. And a recognition by the production team of the need to bridge that gulf.

(b) Starting the research early in the process so that relevant information about existing attitudes, beliefs, knowledge and interests can be taken into account, rather than collecting this type of information merely to confirm production decisions already made.

(c) Partial integration of the researcher into the production team in order to overcome the inevitable initial reservations about the role of research. In cases such as this the broadcasting researcher, like a planner in an advertising agency, shares the producer's interest in developing the best possible programme by working with, not against, the production process.

(d) Involving the production staff as much as possible in the research process — by detailed discussion of the briefs, and of the questionnaires, by extending invitations to attend interviews and group discussions, or to read transcripts or verbatim quotations, and by lengthy personal debriefs, allowing sufficient time for adequate discussion about and understanding of the results and, perhaps more importantly, for exploration of the implications they might have for the programme. All this can easily seem a waste of time and effort to a researcher, but in our experience it pays off handsomely.

(e) A co-operative and constructive stance on the part of the researcher rather than the traditional critical, analytical approach so dear to the academic researcher. This includes understanding, and working from the basis of, the producer's framework of assumptions, and setting up research to test these. This certainly does not imply that research should seek to reinforce the producer's prejudices. The development of 'The Computer Programme' demonstrates how research can modify and mould the approach of a sensitive and receptive production team. This co-operative research orientation also implies the acceptance of material that is already available or, at least, easy to produce and at an acceptable and realistic cost. Production cost, and considerations of timing generally, preclude preparation of materials which the rigorous analytical researcher would ideally require to isolate and identify the key influences on viewer response. Compromises are needed to convince the production client that research can be an integrated and not merely a disruptive part of the process. The pilot film used in this developmental research, although not ideal, provided an adequate basis for investigating production approaches.

(f) The development of such relationships *within* the organisation has tremendous benefits. Experience can be cumulated across a range of projects. That elusive but essential chemistry between researcher and producer can be developed in on-going relationships. Without the pressure of gaining future contracts, the internal researcher can perhaps be bolder and more searching than an external researcher, and is certainly more likely to recommend that research can make no contribution to a particular problem, and should, therefore, not be undertaken; or, as in this project, the researcher may tailor the research to facilities readily available (such as existing measurement surveys) rather than recommending expensive new research.

PREPRODUCTION RESEARCH

Defining the Target Audience

There were many questions in the minds of the production team about the nature of the likely target audience for the series. As noted above, the series was planned for transmission late-night on BBC-1 for the general audience, with repeats on Sunday mornings on BBC-1, and on weekday afternoons on BBC-2 for use in schools and colleges. Previous research and experience indicated that the audience would certainly include both strongly motivated and more casual viewers, with few watching many of the programmes in the series and most watching only one or two. But who would the viewers be? What would be the balance between motivated and more casual viewers? How much would they already know about computing? What would be their attitude to the subject, and how far would this influence their propensity to learn? How far would they be willing or able to accept technical explanations? The needs and interest of the audience would be varied, what should the priorities be as between one group and another? It was clear that, before a number of basic crucial production decisions could be made, information about the likely audience was needed. In collaboration with the production team a two stage research strategy was proposed. The first stage was designed to establish whether or not there was any demand for such a series. The second study was designed to provide guidance on the content, style and format of the series.

Characteristics of the Likely Target Audience

The prime objectives of the first stage of the research were to establish:

(i) The profile of people who might be interested in watching a television series on computers and computing.
(ii) The level of interest and the profile of likely purchasers of a home microcomputer priced at about £180.

In order to answer these questions with an acceptable degree of precision, a large-scale national sample survey was required. A series of questions were added to the BBC's routine national Daily Survey of Listening and Viewing. In 1981, this survey was carried out throughout the United Kingdom every day of the year on the basis of a quota sample within a stratified random selection of local authority areas. Each day 2000 individuals aged four or over were interviewed in the street by fully-trained interviewers. Questions were asked to establish what listening and viewing had taken place on the preceding day, i.e. 24-hour recall. (In April 1982, the methodology of the survey was changed to an in-home interview with 1000 individuals aged four or over. The main purpose of the survey is now to establish audiences to radio and to provide a sampling frame for the selection of a panel for the measurement of audience reaction to television programmes.)

In the 1981 survey, quota controls were set on sex, age, social grade and working status in order to ensure a balanced sample. In order to provide an adequate subsample for separate analysis, Scotland, Wales and Northern Ireland were over-sampled, and weighted at the analysis stage to produce results representative of the United Kingdom as a whole. In addition to yielding information about television and radio, the Daily Survey of Listening and Viewing provided an efficient vehicle for asking a limited number of straightforward additional questions to a large, nationally representative sample, in much the same way as a commercial omnibus survey. The questionnaire about the computing programme (Appendix 4.1) was asked of all informants aged 12 and over. Fieldwork was conducted over three days—from 5th–7th January, 1981, and 4573 successful interviews were achieved. All those interviewed were handed the following description of the proposed series, which was also read out to them, and asked to say how interested they would be in watching it:

> The series introduces the basic ideas behind computing in order to increase peoples' understanding of how computers work. It will explain the principles of computer programing and show how people with no technical experience can use computers.

Interest was measured on a four point scale: very interested, fairly interested, not particularly interested, not at all interested.

Questions were also asked about respondents' own computing experience and their interest in buying a home microcomputer, priced about £180. Details of the respondent's age, sex, social class and educational qualifications are routinely collected on this survey. This stage of the research enabled us to identify the types of people who were most interested in viewing, and revealed various differences as between different subgroups of the population.

The analysis of the responses was carried out on the BBC ICL mainframe computer. The scope of the analysis was limited by the range of variables routinely included in the interview—sex, age, social grade, area, and working status—and by a limitation imposed by the analysis program then in use on cross-analysis of results within the questionnaire.

In response to the description of the proposed series (see Table 4.1) just over half (52%) the sample said they would be interested in watching the proposed television series on computing and computers. However, the number who were *moderately* enthusiastic (30%) outweighed those who were *very* interested (22%) in the series, perhaps indicating some reservations about the idea rather than outright enthusiasm. However, less than a third (29%) rejected the idea and said they would not be at all interested in seeing the series.

TABLE 4.1   Levels of Interest in watching a New Series on Computing

Interest	Total sample 4573 (%)
Very interested	22
Fairly interested	30
Not particularly interested	17
Not at all interested	29
(don't know)	2

The key tabulation is shown in Table 4.2. The pattern of responses confirmed preconceptions about interest levels. More men than women were *very* interested in seeing the series, although similar proportions were *fairly* interested. The level of interest was consistent across the different age groups up to the 50–64 age group, who were less interested than younger people. Interest fell off even more markedly amongst those aged 65 and over. Amongst the younger respondents, the 30–49 year olds were most enthusiastic—more people in this age group than in any other said they would be *very* interested in seeing the series.

Middle class respondents were far more likely to express interest in the series than working class people. This might have been related in part to a middle class tendency to express interest in things generally, particularly those things they think people *ought* to know about. Related to this social class bias was the higher level of interest amongst those who had been in full-time education after the age of 19 or had some educational qualifications compared to those who had less educational experience or no qualifications at all.

Respondents were asked how interested they would be in having a small desk-top computer for their own personal use, and how likely they would be to buy one (see Tables 4.3 and 4.4).

A quarter of those interviewed were interested in having their own microcomputer, slightly more expressing moderate (14%) than keen (11%) interest. All respondents apart from those who said they were not interested

TABLE 4.2   Levels of Interest within Subgroups

		Population 1981 (%)	Very and fairly interested 2378 (%)	Very interested 1995 (%)
Sex:	Male	48	59	(29)
	Female	52	46	(16)
Age:	12–15	8	58	(18)
	16–19	8	58	(21)
	20–29	17	58	(21)
	30–49	30	59	(28)
	50–64	20	50	(25)
	65 +	17	35	(14)
Class*:	A } *	5	64	(34)
	B }	25	64	(30)
	Cx } **		52	(22)
	Cy }	70	40	(14)
Terminal age	15 or under	60	42	(17)
of education	16	18	55	(20)
	17–18	10	61	(27)
	19–20		74	(26)
	21 +	13	69	(38)
Formal	None	N/A	41	(15)
educational				
qualifications	Some	N/A	63	(29)

* *Roughly equivalent to NRS ABC_1 grouping*
***Roughly equivalent to NRS C_2DE grouping*

in owning a micro, were then asked how interested they would be to buy one at £180. A quarter of those asked claimed that they would be very (8%) or fairly (17%) likely to buy. These findings *cannot* of course, be extrapolated to estimate sales, because such questions tend to elicit overclaiming and would need to be validated against sales data for other microcomputers before they could be used for forecasting. Nevertheless, they could indicate, for the

TABLE 4.3   Level of Interest in Owning and Buying a Small Desk-Top Computer for £180

Interest in having own desk-top computer		Likelihood of buying at £180	
Base: Total (100%)	4573	Those at all interested in having one	1919
	(%)		(%)
Very interested	11 ⎫ ⎡	Very likely to buy	8
Fairly interested	14 ⎬→	Fairly likely	17
Not particularly interested	11 ⎭	Not very likely	33
Not at all interested	58	Not at all likely	33
Don't know/No reply	6 ⎣	Don't know/No reply	10

TABLE 4.4   Level of Interest and Likelihood of Buying within Subgroups

		Very or fairly interested in having a desk-top computer (Base 4573 (total)) (%)	Very or fairly likely to buy at £180 Base 1919 (those at all interested in having one) (%)
Sex:	Male	31	30
	Female	20	19
Age:	12-15	68	17
	16-19	38	25
	20-29	34	28
	30-49	27	30
	50-64	14	23
	65+	5	11
Class:	A ⎫ *	36	31
	B ⎭	33	30
	Cx ⎫ **	25	24
	Cy ⎭	16	18
Terminal age	15	13	22
of education:	16	31	23
	17-18	36	28
	19-20	38	24
	21+	42	31

* Roughly equivalent to NRS ABC_1 grouping
**Roughly equivalent to NRS C_2DE grouping

short term, the likely *upper* limit of purchasing for personal use (i.e. excluding institutional use).

At the very early planning stages of the project research was useful in indicating a high level of interest in the series, fairly broad appeal, but slightly greater interest amongst males, younger people and the better educated.

Refining the Target Audience and the Production Approach

The decisions about the appropriate production approach presented much more difficult research problems than had the description of the target audience. Matters of content, style and tone are notoriously difficult to research effectively. The production team, however, planned to produce a pilot film and such a film would provide an excellent stimulus for respondents in order to elicit relevant reactions to the proposed series. It was not possible to produce a specially designed film which would permit a controlled experiment. We, therefore, had to be content with researching those aspects of presentation included in the film. Nonetheless, this provided a significantly better basis for research than asking entirely hypothetical questions, or dealing with still photographs.

The second study therefore designed to refine the target audience and to test detailed reactions to a pilot programme to establish:

—levels of interest in the programme;
—reactions to the content, style and format of the programme;
—reactions to the balance between informing and entertaining;
—reactions to the presenters;
—comprehensibility of the terminology used.

This was achieved by inviting selected groups of people to respond to a range of possible production approaches as shown in the 'pilot' television programme. This approach is known as group testing and is particularly well suited for detailed reactions to television programmes or pilot material.

The Sample

The profile of the sample recruited to see the pilot programme was determined by two criteria. Firstly, based on the results from the survey of the general public, the sample was designed to over-represent those groups where the percentage saying they would be 'very interested' in viewing the series was particularly high. Thus more men than women and more in the middle class than in the working class groups were recruited. The second criterion was the need to recruit fairly homogenous subgroups of respondents to take part in group discussions, since a wealth of research experience has shown that in order to generate the most useful and uninhibited range of discussion in a group setting it is helpful if members are of the same sex, from similar social class groups and not too widely different age groups, particularly if there are likely to be differences in knowledge and experience of the subject under discussion. Such differences generally arise in relation to technology. For the purpose of this research, 120 people were specially recruited in two locations, London and Manchester. There were two sessions at BBC premises in each location, each session divided into three subgroups:

London
    Session A: 30 Middle Class:
        Group 1: 10 men aged 20–39
        Group 2: 10 men aged 40–60
        Group 3: 10 women aged 40–60

    Session B: 30 Working class:
        Group 4: 10 men aged 20–39
        Group 5: 10 men aged 40–60
        Group 6: 10 women aged 20–39

Manchester
  Session C: 30 Middle class:
    Group 7: 10 men aged 20–29
    Group 8: 10 men aged 40–60
    Group 9: 10 women aged 20–39

  Session D: 30 Working class:
    Group 10: 10 men aged 20–39
    Group 11: 10 men aged 40–60
    Group 12: 10 women aged 40–60

In the event, 104 recruits were able to attend between 17th and 20th March 1981. At recruitment, respondents were asked how interested they would be in watching a television series on computing.

Only those people who said they would be 'very interested' in watching such a series were recruited because it was felt that to seek reaction from a group of respondents who had little or no interest in the subject matter would not provide the sort of diagnostic information that would help the producers refine the material or the style of the programme. In addition, professional computer programmers and those working in broadcasting were deliberately excluded from the sample.

Respondents were recruited from the 20–60 age group because older people had shown considerably less interest in seeing a television series on computing, whereas people under 20 were excluded both on the grounds that the series was not primarily intended for use in schools and colleges and that, within the scope of available research resources, the whole spectrum of age could not be adequately covered.

Recruitment

All recruitment was undertaken by BBC Broadcasting Research interviewers in London and Manchester, using a specially designed recruitment questionnaire (see Appendix 4.2).

The four sessions were held in the evenings and lasted for about 2½ hours. Respondents were given a small cash incentive for attending and to cover their travelling expenses and light refreshments were provided.

The Procedure Employed for the Group Tests

An introduction to the session was given by a researcher from the Broadcasting Research Department and the following points were stressed:

—that the pilot programme was not a finished television programme.
—that comments on the content were required;

—that criticisms were welcome; and
—that it contained a selection of ideas and examples of the sort of the things could be included in the series.

Before viewing the 'pilot' programme, respondents were asked to fill in a short questionnaire (Appendix 4.3) on their knowledge of computers and their attitudes towards the technology, since these were likely to influence their reactions to the series. They were also asked specific questions about what they wanted to see in a television series on computing. The pilot programme, which was specially produced, lasted about 40 minutes and included examples of various production techniques, such as the use of analogies, the use of humour, alternative styles of presentation, alternative levels of explanation, and the balance between different types of item. It was made very clear to those attending the viewing groups that the programme was a 'pilot' and not a finished programme designed for transmission. The film was divided into four sections. Respondents filled in the appropriate part of a self-completion questionnaire after seeing each section. (Appendix 4.30)

Immediately after the pilot programme finished the recruits completed a further questionnaire (Appendix 4.3a part 5) along very similar lines to the first one, in order to assess whether the programme had modified their opinion or attitudes. They were, then divided into smaller groups (each of about ten) for more informal, spontaneous discussion. These groups were led by experienced researchers and tape recorded, and the main areas covered were:

—attitudes in general towards computers;
—overall reactions to the idea of a series on computing;
—content of pilot programme;
—reactions to presenters;
—the level of interest the programme generated in encouraging people to try out a microcomputer for themselves.

The Nature of the Data

The group discussion technique involved dividing the audience at each session into groups of about ten members. The discussion was allowed to develop spontaneously with, at first, minimum intervention from the researcher present. Thus, a relaxed atmosphere in which people could feel free to talk frankly with each other was fostered. Towards the end of the discussion, the researcher steered the group towards topics not yet raised in order to ensure that a similar range of subjects was covered in each group.

The main advantage of this qualitative approach was that a wide range of detailed information was elicited which allowed some insight into *why* people reacted to the programme as they did. The limitation of such data is that it is by its very nature interpretative and based on the views of only 104 people, and therefore population estimates cannot be made.

The data derived from the self-completion questionnaires provide a measured response to the pilot programme which complemented the more interpretative qualitative data. It also represented the views of the individuals interviewed as opposed to the group view represented by the qualitative findings.

The Results

In April 1981 the results of the research were presented to the project team. Reflecting the findings of the initial study (Table 4.5), they showed that people's general attitudes towards computing were very positive. Respondents felt that the advantages of computers outweighted the disadvantages, that computers were an increasingly important aspect of their lives, which could not be ignored, and that it would be a good thing to know more about how they worked and what they could do. There was a lively interest in computer applications, then and in the future. There was also a certain fear about the impact of the technology, particularly in terms of depersonalisation and the storing of personal details on computer data-banks. There was a good deal of anxiety among the less 'computer literate' about their capacity to come to grips with these ideas. This was strongest among older people. But the study suggested that, despite this, a great many people were willing to make a determined effort to do so.

The production team had expected the series to appeal strongly to people who were more technically minded, like the readers of the computer magazines, or to people with an interest in the subject because of their jobs, like businessmen or managers or teachers. The research confirmed this,

TABLE 4.5 General Attitudes towards Computers

		Agree	Undecided	Disagree
I do not think you could learn a lot about computers from television	% pre-	23	16	60
	% post-	23	6	69
The advantages of computers outweigh the disadvantages	% pre-	14	18	67
	% post-	13	13	70
I don't think I'll ever understand computers	% pre-	10	22	66
	% post-	13	16	68
I would very much like to have a small computer of my own	% pre-	46	24	26
	% post-	52	19	25
I am very keen to learn more about computers	% pre-	85	11	5
	% post-	85	8	8

indicating that interest would be strongest among men, among middle class or skilled working class viewers, among the better educated, and among people under 50. It seemed that the production team had a number of options open to them and that one of these would be to aim to satisfy this more committed, knowledgeable audience, rather than trying to appeal to the population at large. The study indicated that this first group would want a serious approach, which set out — above all — to be clear and informative to those who already had an interest in the subject. The audience on Sunday mornings would be more likely to consist of motivated viewers, and the daytime audience in institutions would be largely watching in classrooms for whom the need would probably be similar.

However, the national survey had also suggested that there was a general interest among people at large in the idea of learning about computing and computers, and this was also borne out by the group sessions. These confirmed a strong potential interest in the subject among women as well as men, among working class viewers as well as middle class viewers, among older age groups as well as younger. The needs of this wider audience were different from the needs of the more motivated. They wanted plenty of practical examples, and not too much theory; they were apprehensive about being given too much technical information; they wanted simple, straightforward explanations, they were not afraid of a little humour from time to time. They liked a varied and non-didactic style of presentation. In particular, they were anxious about their capacity to understand the subject. The approach demanded by the more motivated section of the audience would almost certainly alienate them.

The Choice of the Target Audience

After much discussion the production team decided to go for the wider audience, for three main reasons. First, there was clearly a real desire to learn about the subject among the population at large. Secondly, television is, after all, a mass medium. The late-night showings gave the production team the chance to reach millions of people, who were better reached through television than by any other means. Thirdly, television is good at capturing people's interest, demystifying, and showing practical examples. Communication of detailed straight explanation is perhaps better left to books and other support resources. Here again, it was felt to be well suited to the needs of the wider audience, rather than the committed minority.

Production Approaches

The production team therefore redefined the main objective of the television series. The aim was now to act as a 'gateway' into the subject for the casually interested people, by introducing some elementary principles of computing in a way that made them accessible to large numbers of people, and to communicate a number of key ideas namely:

—that this was an extremely important subject because of its future influence on everyone's lives;
—that it was intrinsically fascinating;
—that it was possible for everyone to learn a good deal about it;
—that there was no need for anxiety about one's capacity to understand it;
—that there were available a great many ways of pursuing one's interest further.

The research suggested that the more technically-minded members of the audience might be left rather unsatisfied, but a calculated decision was made to accept this. It was thought that if the programmes were well made, with interesting examples, this group would learn something and the other elements of the project offered many opportunities for more advanced study.

Decisions on content and presentation flowed naturally from the decision to go for a wide audience. The series would include a large number of practical examples on film and would make extensive use of illustrations through analogy, and use a good deal of repetition. The programmes would need to look attractive and varied, and there needed to be a friendly relaxed style of presentation. Generally the material would have to be chosen so as to appeal deliberately to those sections of the audience which had been identified by the research as being less strongly motivated.

EVALUATING THE PROJECT

In January 1982 the BBC formally launched the Computer Literacy Project. It was an integrated project focusing around the ten part television series, 'The Computer Programme', and comprising a BBC microcomputer system, applications software programmes, a book, *The Computer Book*, computing courses and a network of advice and information centres up and down the country. To complete the research programme required an evaluation of each element of the project and the extent to which the package operated as a whole. The purpose of this detailed and complex evaluation was to contribute to the planning of the second television series and to assist with strategic decision making on the future direction of some of the other elements of the project.

Audience Size

The BBC's routine audience measurement system—the Daily Survey of Listening and Viewing (see Tables 4.6, 4.7 and 4.8)—showed that the audience

TABLE 4.6   Audience Size

Mondays 3.00 pm		Sunday mornings		Monday late-night	
1982	Millions	1982	Millions	1982	Millions
11th January	0.4	14th February	0.4	22nd March	1.2
18th January	0.2	21st February	0.3	29th March	1.2
25th January	0.2	28th February	0.3	5th April	0.9
1st February	0.2	7th March	0.2	19th April	0.7
8th February	0.3	14th March	0.3	26th April	1.3
15th February	0.2	21st March	0.2	10th May	0.4
22nd February	0.3	28th March	0.2	17th May	0.9
1st March	0.1	4th April	0.2	24th May	0.6
8th March	0.3	18th April	0.1	7th June	0.9
15th March	0.2	25th April	0.1	14th June	0.5

Source: BARB

for the Monday night transmission (March-June 1982) was typical for the time of day and averaged about one million for each of the programmes in the series. The audience did, of course, vary from week to week depending on seasonal factors and competitive offerings of the other three TV channels. As had been predicted, most viewers saw one or two programmes in the series, with hardly any seeing more than three out of the ten programmes. This is a fairly typical pattern of loyalty for a series of this type. The series, which was designed to appeal to a general, non-specialised, non-technical audience was watched by a good cross-section of the viewing public. Men were slightly over-represented in the audience, as were people aged between 25 and 54 and those in the skilled working class social groups. This is, on the whole, a good reflection of the kinds of people who are available to watch television at around 11.30 p.m. on weekday evenings.

TABLE 4.7   Audience Composition for the Monday Late-Night Transmission

Audience Composition(%)		UK Population (aged 16+)(%)
Male	53	48
Female	47	52
16–24	10	18
25–34	22	18
35–44	19	15
45–44	24	15
55–64	15	34
65+	9	
AB	13	15
C1	21	20
C2	42	33
DE	24	33

Source: BARB

TABLE 4.8 Series Loyalty

Number of programmes seen in the Monday late night transmission	Proportion of the adult population who had watched any part of:
One	16%
Two	5%
Three	2%
Four	1%
Five	*
Six	*
Seven	*
Eight	*
Nine	*
Ten	*
Average number of programmes viewed	1.5

* Less than 1%

Audience Reaction

Detailed reactions to the series were collected on the BBC's routine Audience Reaction Service. This survey was designed to establish viewers' reactions to all the television programmes they watch. It was conducted nationally, based on a representative quota of the population. Approximately 800 adults (16 +) were contacted each day on the Daily Survey of Listening and Viewing and given a five-day self-completion viewing diary (Appendix 4.4) covering all the television programmes broadcast in their area over the five days immediately following the interview. Questions about viewers' opinions of 'The Computer Programme' were included in the survey over a three-week period immediately after the end of the series, starting on June 15th 1982. Opinions of just over 500 viewers were collected.

Overall reactions from amongst the general audience were extremely favourable (Table 4.9). The vast majority of viewers (80%) thought it provided a good basic introduction to the subject of computing and that it explained some of the basic principles of computing very clearly.

The programmes were seen as interesting, informative and stimulating. By and large the general viewers felt that the level at which the information had been pitched was 'about right'. Those most satisfied in the series were men, older people and those in the middle and skilled working class groups. The more computer literate sections of the audience, predictably, found the programmes too elementary for them. Unlike the general audience they claimed not to have learned much from the series but found it useful in clarifying points and stimulating interest. They recognised the series as having been aimed largely at a non-computer literate viewing public and as such

TABLE 4.9   Overall Opinions of 'The Computer Programme'

| | Total | Sex | | Age | | | | | Class | | |
| | | Male | Female | Under 24 | 25–34 | 35–44 | 55+ | AB | C1 | C2DE |
People who have watched any part of the series and Agree with each statement	510 (%)	317 (%)	193 (%)	166 (%)	112 (%)	146 (%)	86 (%)	116 (%)	141 (%)	253 (%)
It was a very good introduction to the subject of computing	80	82	76	78	75	83	83	86	86	76
It explained some of the basic principles of computing very clearly	77	79	73	78	74	80	77	84	79	73
It was very interesting	68	73	62	68	63	71	75	75	70	68
I thought the explanations were too brief	31	33	29	30	27	32	36	26	39	28
It was too elementary for me	26	31	19	33	25	25	13	42	22	21
I found it difficult to understand	15	10	23	16	13	14	22	7	12	20

thought it was pitched at the right level and contained the right information for beginners. These viewers were positive about watching future series on computing and suggested several specialised topics which may be of interest to the small but growing number of computer literate viewers.

Encouragingly the series seemed to have appealed to a wide range of viewers from the computer illiterate through to the more knowledgeable and from BBC microcomputer users through to users of other, more sophisticated and less sophisticated, makes of micro. Research had indicated a growing public interest and awareness in computing of an increasingly sophisticated nature which would have an impact upon the content, style and level of sophistication for future television series in the project. Information from the evaluation of the first series made a significant contribution to the decisions behind the second series, 'Making the Most of the Micro'.

The Rest of the Package

In addition to an evaluation of the television series, the Broadcasting Research Department was also asked to assess detailed reactions to the other components of the project. The research methods were selected in the light of severe restrictions on budgets and very small target groups to be surveyed. These components and an outline of the research approach are set out below:

Summary of Evaluative Research

1. Television series: 'The Computer Programme'	Evaluation using BARB/ARS Telephone survey. (Appendix 4.5, 4.5a) provide an example)
2. The computer system	Postal survey amongst BBC micro purchasers (Appendix 4.6 provides a standard example).
3. The software ('Welcome Pack' — introductory software to the system):	Postal survey amongst BBC micro users and recipients of the pack.
4. The user guide	Postal survey amongst recipients of the provisional user guide.
5. The Computer Book	Postal survey amongst purchasers of the book.
6. The Liaison network (information flow of local contacts and computing courses)	Estimates of the numbers of contacts
7. IMPACT OF THE COMPLETE PACKAGE	Estimates of take-up and overlap. Postal surveys and lists at contact points.

The Computer System

Detailed information on the computer system was required to indicate:

—who was buying/using the system;
—what people were using it for;
—what they thought of the actual hardware; and
—why they had chosen a BBC machine.

It was important, therefore, to make contact with individuals who had bought and who were using a BBC micro. A postal survey approach was adopted since, in the early days, purchasers were relatively few and were inevitably far between. It was felt that those contacted would be sufficiently motivated to complete a questionnaire and this was borne out by the eventual response rate of 80%, which guaranteed that the results were representative of all buyers. The sample was drawn from the lists of names and addresses of purchasers provided by the company responsible for dispatching the systems and a total of 1000 questionnaires were mailed out in June 1982. The lists of names were arranged in surname alphabetical order and after removing all the institutional users, 1000 of the remaining names and addresses were systematically selected.

The User Guide and Welcome Pack

Reactions to these two elements of the package were required to establish how useful they were in helping people use their micros in order to assist with the production of future hardware manuals and guides to computer programming. As these items were integral to the computer system, specific questions were added to the postal survey on the computer system.

The Computer Book

Research into readership and opinions of '*The Computer Book*' was required to assist with the writing and development of future books on the subject. The areas under investigation were:

—what prompted people to buy the book;
—how much of it was read or looked at;
—how it matched up to expectations;
—readers' overall impressions;
—strengths and weaknesses.

A survey of book purchasers was required. This was achieved by inserting reply paid postcards into the first 15 000 books which went on sale in

January 1982 seeking volunteers to take part in a survey of readers opinions. The limitations of this approach were recognised, but limited funds and the problems of contacting a sample representative of all buyers of the book necessitated the adoption of this approach involving a highly self-selecting sample. Approximately 2500 postcards were returned during the first three months of 1982, representing about 17% of purchasers during that time. Next, 500 names and addresses were systematically selected and sent a self-completion questionnaire in June 1982. A response rate of 87% was achieved, which went some way to allaying fears about the representativeness of this sample.

The Overall Impact of the Project

This was measured by an estimate of the numbers of people who participated in one or more of the individual elements.

A total of about seven million of the adult population had seen some part of 'The Computer Programme' at all over its third transmission. Demand for *The Computer Book*, which was published to coincide with the launch of the series, was high (approximately 60 000) in the first nine months of 1982. The NEC's introductory course on programming in BASIC *30 Hour BASIC*, which was planned as part of the project for the more committed student of the computing, sold around 100 000 copies in the first nine months of 1982. The computer Referral Service, which provided information about the project and put people in touch with local learning opportunities, received 120 000 enquiries in the first year of the project. About 1000 institutions and organisations have agreed to become referral points. Demand for the microcomputer system exceeded all expectations in its first year, and over 40 000 systems had been delivered by the end of 1982.

REFERENCES

1. MILLS, P. 1986: 'Improving the Programmes — concept and pilot research' in, *Media in Education Development* March 1986
2. MARLES, V. and RADCLIFFE, J., 'The Computer Programme — a Case Study', in *BBC Broadcasting Research Findings 1981-2* (BBC Publication), (1983)
3. LAKING, A. and RHODES, M., 'QED: Research for a Second Series', in *BBC Broadcasting Research Findings 1983* (BBC Publication), (1984)
4. LAKING, A. and JACKSON, A., 'Can You Avoid Cancer?', in *BBC Broadcasting Research Findings 1985* (BBC Publication), (1986)
5. GOODHARDT, G. J., EHRENBERG, A. S. C. and COLLINS, M. A., *The Television Audience: Patterns of Viewing*, Saxon House (1975)

APPENDIX 4.1   BRITISH BROADCASTING CORPORATION
'HANDS ON MICRO ELECTRONICS'

Extra questions to be asked of all adult and child (aged 12–15 years only) respondents to the Daily Survey on:

6th January 1981 — Logs dated 5th January
7th January 1981 — Logs dated 6th January
8th January 1981 — Logs dated 7th January

	FOR OFFICE USE ONLY
Q.1 I am going to read out a short description of a new television series. It introduces the basic ideas behind computing in order to increase peoples' understanding of how computers work. It will explain the principles of computer programming and show how people with no technical experience can themselves use computers. Please would you tell me from this list how interested you would be in watching it — if it were shown at a convenient time.	

Very interested 1
Fairly interested 2
SHOW   Not particularly interested 3   RING ONE
CARD A   Not at all interested 4   CODE
Don't know 5

6

Q.2 Have you personally ever used a computer, either by operating the machine or dealing with computer output, in your work or study?

Yes 1   RING ONE
No 2   CODE
Don't know 3

7

Q.3 Please tell me from this list how interested you would be in having a small, desk-top computer for your own personal use?

Very interested 1
Fairly interested 2   RING ONE
SHOW   Not particularly interested 3   CODE
CARD A   Not at all interested 4   →skip to Q.5
Don't know 5

8

Q.4 How likely would you be to *buy* a small desk-top computer if you could get one for about £180? Would you be:

Very likely to buy one 1
Fairly likely to buy one 2   RING ONE
READ   Not very likely to buy one 3   CODE
OUT   or Not at all likely to buy one 4
Don't know 5

9

Q.5 During the past six months or so, have *you personally* used . . .? (RING ONE CODE ON EACH LINE)

	YES	NO	DON'T KNOW	
a) A pocket or desk calculator	1	2	3	10
b) A video-cassette recorder	1	2	3	11
c) Teletext, that is Ceefax, Oracle or Prestel	1	2	3	12
d) Television games equipment	1	2	3	13

And finally a few questions about yourself:

Q.6   How old were you (or do you expect to be) at the end
of your full-time education?

15 years or under	1		
16	2		
17–18	3	RING ONE	14
19–20	4	CODE	
21 +	5		
Don't remember	6		

Q.7   Could you read through this list of qualifications and tell me
which, if any, you have at the moment? Please read out the
appropriate letters from the card. (SHOW CARD B).

A. None	1	15
B. School Certificate passes	1	16
C. C.S.E. passes	1	17
D. G.C.E. 'O' level passes	1	18
E. G.C.E. 'A' level passes	1	19
F. O.N.C. or O.N.D. passes	1	20
G. B.E.C. or T.E.C.	1	21
H. H.N.C. or H.N.D. passes	1	22
I. City and Guilds	1	23
J. Teaching Diploma	1	24
K. Degree	1	25
L. Others (*Write in*)	1	26

....

PLEASE TRANSFER THE FOLLOWING
INFORMATION FROM THE MAIN LOG

			(27)
	SEX	Male	1
		Female	2
			(28)
	AGE	12–15	3
		16–19	4
		20–29	5
		30–49	6
		50–64	7
		65 +	8
	(51)		(29)
	CLASS	A	1
IN EMPLOYMENT	5	B	2
IN FULL-TIME EDUCATION	6	Cx	3
NOT IN EMPLOYMENT	7	Cy	4

OCCUPATION 30, 31
OCCUPATION OF HEAD OF HOUSEHOLD 32, 33

....
INTERVIEWERS NO:-   34–37
LOG NO:-   38, 39
LOG DATE:-   40–44
AREA CODE   45–50

APPENDIX 4.2

FEBRUARY, 1981
(Project 80/24)

BRITISH BROADCASTING CORPORATION
BROADCASTING RESEARCH DEPARTMENT
RECRUITMENT QUESTIONNAIRE: 'HANDS-ON MICROELECTRONICS'

CODE   ROUTE

COLS:	2	3	4	5
QUESTIONNAIRE NO:				

Good Morning/Afternoon/Evening. I am conducting a survey about a new television series for the BBC.

Q.1   First of all I am going to read out a short description of a new television series: 'The series introduces the basic ideas behind computing in order to increase people's understanding of how computers work. It will explain the principles of computer programming and show how people with no technical experience can use computers.' Please tell me from this list how interested you would be in watching it — if it were shown at a convenient time.

Col. 6

SHOW CARD A

RING ONE CODE

ONLY

Very interested	1	→ASK Q.2
Fairly interested	2	CLOSE INTERVIEW
Not particularly		RECORD AS 'NOT
interested	3	ELIGIBLE AT Q.2 ON
Not at all interested .	4	CALL SHEET. NO
Don't know	5	Q'NNAIRE REQUIRED

Col 7

Q.2   Do you or does anyone in your household work in the following . . .?

READ OUT—

Q'NNAIRE REQUIRED

Car manufacturing	1	IF CODE 3 OR 4
Retail trade	2	CLOSE INTERVIEW
Broadcasting (Radio		RECORD AS 'NOT
or Television)	3	ELIGIBLE AT Q.2 ON
Computer		CALL SHEET. NO
programming	4	
None of these	5	OTHERWISE ASK Q.3
		OTHERWISE ASK Q.3

Q.3   As part of our research we are inviting people to attend an informal meeting to help develop a new television series. The meeting will be held at:

AT   7.30 p.m.
ON
AT

and will last for between 2 and 2½ hours. We are giving each person invited £7 to cover their expenses. Would you be willing to come along?

Col 8

Yes	1→	ASK Q.4
No	2→	CLOSE INTERVIEW RECORD AS REFUSED UNABLE TO ATTEND ON CALL SHEET. NO Q'NNAIRE REQUIRED

	CODE	ROUTE
PLEASE NOTE: Q.4, 5, 6 AND 7 ARE ALL QUOTA CONTROLS		

So that we can be sure that we have talked to all kinds of people I'd like to ask you a few questions about yourself.

		CODE	ROUTE
Q.4	Which of these age groups are you in?	*Col. 9*	CLOSE INTERVIEW RECORD AS 'NOT ELIGIBLE AT Q.4 ON CALL SHEET, NO Q'NNAIRE REQUIRED
	Under 20	1 →	
	20–29 years	2 ⎫	
READ OUT	30–39 years	3 ⎪	→ ASK Q.5
	40–49 years	4 ⎬	
	50–60 (incl.) years .	5 ⎭	CLOSE INTERVIEW RECORD AS 'NOT ELIGIBLE AT Q.4' ON CALL SHEET NO Q'NNAIRE REQUIRED
	61+ years	6 ↗	

				CODE
Q.5	Do you have a full-time or a part-time job?			*Col. 10*
	"In Employment"	⎧	Working full-time (over 30 hours per week)	1
		⎨	Working part-time (9–30 hours per week)	2
		⎩	Student (school or college)	3
	"Not in Employment"	⎧	Retired	4
		⎪	Unemployed worker	5
		⎨	Housewife (not doing any part-time work or working 8 or less hours per week) ...	6

		CODE
Q.6	What is the occupation of your head of household? (WRITE IN)	
	RECORD GRADE	*Col. 11*
	A	1
	B	2
	Cx	3
	Cy	4

		CODE
Q.7	Record sex	*Col. 12*
	Male	1
	Female	2

IF INFORMANT FILLS YOUR QUOTA, RECORD THEIR DETAILS ON QUOTA AND CALL SHEETS, HAND OVER INVITATION. REMIND RESPONDENT TO BRING SPECTACLES IF NECESSARY. COMPLETE DETAILS BELOW:

Name of Informant ....
Address ....
....

	CODE
(Tel. Number) .... *AREA*	*Col. 13*
INTERVIEWER'S NAME .. LONDON	1
INTERVIEWER'S NO. ...... MANCHESTER ...	2

APPENDIX 4.3   BBC BROADCASTING RESEARCH
PRE QUESTIONNAIRE: PROJECT NO. 80/24

A
Confidential

Col. 14	Col. 15–18				FOR OFFICE USE ONLY

Q.1   Have you *personally* ever used a computer in any of the following ways?
(PLEASE TICK ALL THAT APPLY TO YOU)

i.   Written or specified computer programmes .... ☐   1   19

ii.   Actually operated a computer .... ☐   1   20

iii.   Used a computer terminal .... ☐   1   21

iv.   Punched computer tape or cards .... ☐   1   22

v.   Used a computer printout or output .... ☐   1   23

vi.   Any other ways (TICK BOX AND WRITE IN) .... ☐
.... ☐   1

v.   Never used a computer   1   29

Q.2   How much would you say you know about computers and computing?

Absolutely nothing   ☐   1
A little   ☐   2   PLEASE TICK   30
Quite a lot   ☐   3   ONE BOX
A great deal   ☐   4

Q.3   Please would you indicate how much you agree or disagree with each of the following statements by ticking ONE BOX ON EACH LINE:

	Agree a lot 1	Agree a little 2	Undecided 3	Disagree a little 4	Disagree a lot 5	
i. The disadvantages of computers outweigh the advantages	☐	☐	☐	☐	☐	31
ii. I am very keen to learn more about computers	☐	☐	☐	☐	☐	32
iii. I do not think you could learn a lot about computers from television	☐	☐	☐	☐	☐	33
iv. I would very much like to have a small computer of my own	☐	☐	☐	☐	☐	34
v. I don't think I'll ever understand computers	☐	☐	☐	☐	☐	35

Q.4   Based on what you've been told about the series   FOR OFFICE
       which of the following things, if any: USE ONLY
       a) do you think are likely to be covered in the
          series and
       b) would you like to see covered in the series?

PLEASE TICK AS MANY OR AS FEW AS YOU LIKE IN EACH COLUMN	(a) Likely to be covered	(b) You would like to see covered	
The users of computers in business and industry			36, 37
How to write computer programs	☐	☐	38, 39
Recent advances in computer technology	☐	☐	40, 41
Building your own computer	☐	☐	42, 43
The effects of computers on our everyday lives			44, 45
Explanation of the electronic workings of computers			46, 47
The ways that computers will change our lives in the future	☐	☐	48, 49
None of these	☐	☐	50, 51
Any other things (TICK IN BOX AND WRITE IN) ..			52, 55
....	☐	☐	56-60

Q.5   And what do you think the series will be like?

PLEASE TICK ONE BOX IN EACH LINE	Agree a lot	Agree a little	Undecided	Disagree a little	Disagree a lot	
	1	2	3	4	5	
Entertaining	☐	☐	☐	☐	☐	61
Difficult to understand.........	☐	☐	☐	☐	☐	62
Informative	☐	☐	☐	☐	☐	63
A series I will learn from	☐	☐	☐	☐	☐	64
Boring	☐	☐	☐	☐	☐	65
My sort of series ...	☐	☐	☐	☐	☐	66

Q.6   And finally, can you describe the sort of person you think
       the series is intended for?

       (PLEASE WRITE IN) ....
                           67-76
                         ....

APPENDIX 4.3a BBC BROADCASTING RESEARCH
POST QUESTIONNAIRE: PROJECT NO. 80/24

B
Confidential

Col.1	Col. 2-5		FOR OFFICE
2			USE ONLY

Part 1.

Q.1 What do you think were the main things that part of the film was trying to tell you?
(PLEASE WRITE IN)   6–15
....

Q.2 a) And was there anything that you felt was not explained clearly enough?

YES ¹ ☐   NO ² ☐   PLEASE GO TO QUESTION 3

Q.2 b) What was that?
(PLEASE WRITE IN)   17–21
....

Q.3 Thinking of that sequence as a whole please indicate what you thought of it by ticking *ONE* BOX ON EACH LINE:

	Agree a lot 1	Agree a little 2	Disagree a little 3	Disagree a lot 4	
Entertaining	☐	☐	☐	☐	22
Difficult to understand	☐	☐	☐	☐	23
Informative	☐	☐	☐	☐	24
Boring	☐	☐	☐	☐	25
My sort of series	☐	☐	☐	☐	26
Clearly explained	☐	☐	☐	☐	27
Badly presented	☐	☐	☐	☐	28

Q.4 Would you say that you:

Learnt a lot from   ☐ 1 ⎫ PLEASE GO
the sequence   ⎬ TO
Learnt a little   ☐ 2 ⎭ QUESTION 5 PLEASE
                                           TICK   29
Learnt almost   ☐ 3 ⎫ PLEASE GO ONE BOX
nothing   ⎬ TO
Learnt nothing at all ☐ 4 ⎭ QUESTION 6

Q.5 And what were the main things you learnt?
(PLEASE WRITE IN) ....
....   30–39

Q.6 Are there any other comments you would like to make? If so, please write them in the space below.   40–49

FOR OFFICE
USE ONLY

Part 2.

Q.1   What do you think were the main things that part of the
film was trying to tell you?
(PLEASE WRITE IN)   50–58
....
....
....
....

Q.2   a) And was there anything that you felt was not explained
clearly enough?

          1   2
YES ☐   NO ☐   PLEASE GO TO QUESTION 3   59

Q.2   b) What was that?
(PLEASE WRITE IN) ....
....

Q.3   Thinking just of that sequence please indicate what you
thought of it by ticking *ONE* BOX ON EACH LINE:

	Agree a lot 1	Agree a little 2	Disagree a little 3	Disagree a lot 4	
Entertaining	☐	☐	☐	☐	66
Difficult to understand	☐	☐	☐	☐	67
Informative	☐	☐	☐	☐	68
Boring	☐	☐	☐	☐	69
My sort of series	☐	☐	☐	☐	70
Clearly explained	☐	☐	☐	☐	71
Badly presented	☐	☐	☐	☐	72

Q.4   Would you say that you: Card 3

Learnt a lot from   ☐ 1 ⎤ PLEASE GO
  the sequence   TO
Learnt a little   ☐ 2 ⎦ QUESTION 5 PLEASE
                               TICK   6
Learnt almost   ☐ 3 ⎤ PLEASE GO ONE BOX
  nothing   TO
Learnt nothing at all   ☐ 4 ⎦ QUESTION 6

Q.5   And what were the main things you learnt?
(PLEASE WRITE IN) ....
....   7–16
....

Q.6   Are there any other comments you would like to make? If
so, please write them in the space below.   17–26

FOR OFFICE
USE ONLY

Part 3.

Q.1 a) What do you think were the main things that part of the film was trying to tell you?
(PLEASE WRITE IN)   27–35
....
....
....
....

Q.1 b) Please indicate what you thought of the 'Treasure Island' part of the sequence by ticking ONE BOX ON EACH LINE:

	Agree a lot	Agree a little	Disagree a little	Disagree a lot	
	1	2	3	4	
Entertaining	☐	☐	☐	☐	36
Difficult to understand	☐	☐	☐	☐	37
Informative	☐	☐	☐	☐	38
Boring	☐	☐	☐	☐	39
Too long	☐	☐	☐	☐	40
Clearly explained	☐	☐	☐	☐	41
Well presented	☐	☐	☐	☐	42

Q.2 Now thinking of the lesson on how to write a computer program, can you tell us what they said the following were?

   i. A syntax error:
      was it (a) A typing error.. ☐ 1
      or (b) A grammatical
        mistake .... ☐ 2   PLEASE   43
      or (c) Forgetting to tell   TICK
        the computer   ONE BOX
        when you've
        finished a line . ☐ 3

  ii. What did the Dollar sign ($) mean to the computer?

      was it (a) To expect an
        answer in the
        form of words ☐ 1
      or (b) To expect an   PLEASE
        answer in the   TICK
        form of numbers ☐ 2 ONE BOX
      or (c) To expect an
        answer in the
        form of words
        or numbers ... ☐ 3   44

FOR OFFICE
USE ONLY

iii. Why did each line in the computer program have a
number?
was it (a) To ensure that the
lines are typed in
the right order ☐ 1 PLEASE
or (b) To store the TICK 45
program in the ONE BOX
right order .... ☐ 2
or (c) For counting how
many lines the
program has .. ☐ 3

iv. What did the instruction INPUT mean to the
computer?
it told
it to (a) Print out the line
numbers ...... ☐ 1 PLEASE
or (b) Expect an answer TICK 46
to be typed in at ONE BOX
the terminal ... ☐ 2
or (c) It made the
program oper-
ational .... ☐ 3

Q.3 Please indicate what you thought of the lesson on how to
write a computer program by ticking ONE BOX ON EACH
LINE

	Agree a lot 1	Agree a little 2	Disagree a little 3	Disagree a lot 4	
Entertaining	☐	☐	☐	☐	47
Difficult to understand	☐	☐	☐	☐	48
Informative	☐	☐	☐	☐	49
Boring	☐	☐	☐	☐	50
My sort of series	☐	☐	☐	☐	51
Too long	☐	☐	☐	☐	52
Clearly explained	☐	☐	☐	☐	53
Well presented	☐	☐	☐	☐	54

Q.4 Now, thinking of the sequence
as a whole, was there anything
that you felt was not explained
clearly enough?

1 2
YES ☐ NO ☐
PLEASE GO TO QUESTION 5 55

What was that? 30
(PLEASE WRITE IN) ....
.... 56–61

FOR OFFICE
USE ONLY
Card 3

Q.5   Would you say that you:

Learnt a lot from   ☐   1 ⎞ PLEASE GO
  the sequence   ⎟   TO
Learnt a little   ☐   2 ⎠ QUESTION 6 PLEASE
                                                  TICK

62

Learnt almost   ☐   3 ⎞ PLEASE GO ONE BOX
  nothing   ⎟   TO
Learnt nothing at all ☐   4 ⎠ QUESTION 7

Q.6   And what were the main things you learnt?
      (PLEASE WRITE IN) ....
                        ....
                        ....

63–72
card 4

Q.7   Are there any other comments you would like to make? If
      so, please write them in the space below.

6–15

FOR OFFICE
USE ONLY

Part 4.

Q.1   What do you think were the main things that part of the
film was trying to tell you?
(PLEASE WRITE IN)   16–25
....
....
....
....

Q.2   a) And was there anything that you felt was not explained
clearly enough?

       1   2

YES ☐   NO ☐   PLEASE GO TO QUESTION 3   26

Q.2   b) What was that?
(PLEASE WRITE IN)   17–30
....

Q.3   Thinking of that sequence as a whole, please indicate what
you thought of it by ticking ONE BOX ON EACH LINE:

	Agree a lot 1	Agree a little 2	Disagree a little 3	Disagree a lot 4	
Entertaining	☐	☐	☐	☐	37
Difficult to understand	☐	☐	☐	☐	38
Informative	☐	☐	☐	☐	39
Boring	☐	☐	☐	☐	40
My sort of series	☐	☐	☐	☐	41
Clearly explained	☐	☐	☐	☐	42
Well presented	☐	☐	☐	☐	43

Q.4   Would you say that you:

Learnt a lot from   ☐ 1 ⎫ PLEASE GO
  the sequence   ⎪   TO
Learnt a little   ☐ 2 ⎭ QUESTION 5 PLEASE
                                            TICK   44

Learnt almost   ☐ 3 ⎫ PLEASE GO ONE BOX
  nothing   ⎪   TO
Learnt nothing at all   ☐ 4 ⎭ QUESTION 6

Q.5   And what were the main things you learnt?
(PLEASE WRITE IN) ....
....   45–54
....

Q.6   Are there any other comments you would like to make? If
so, please write them in the space below.   55–64

FOR OFFICE
USE ONLY

Part 5.

Q.1   Please indicate what you thought of the people taking part
      in the film by agreeing or disagreeing with each comment
      below:

a) Chris Serle (The main Presenter)

	Agree a lot 1	Agree a little 2	Disagree a little 3	Disagree a lot 4	
Easy to follow	☐	☐	☐	☐	65
Pleasant manner............	☐	☐	☐	☐	66
Knows a lot about computers	☐	☐	☐	☐	67
Enthusiastic................	☐	☐	☐	☐	68
Wrong for the series	☐	☐	☐	☐	69
Boring	☐	☐	☐	☐	70
I liked him	☐	☐	☐	☐	71

PLEASE WRITE IN ANY OTHER COMMENTS .....
....   72–75

b) Jonathan Baldachin (The
   Teacher)

	Agree a lot 1	Agree a little 2	Disagree a little 3	Disagree a lot 4	
Easy to follow	☐	☐	☐	☐	6
Pleasant manner............	☐	☐	☐	☐	7
Knows a lot about computers	☐	☐	☐	☐	8
Enthusiastic................	☐	☐	☐	☐	9
Wrong for the series	☐	☐	☐	☐	10
Boring	☐	☐	☐	☐	11
I liked him	☐	☐	☐	☐	12

PLEASE WRITE IN ANY OTHER COMMENTS .....
....   13, 14

c) Jane Corbin (The Presenter
   in the first part of the film)

	Agree a lot 1	Agree a little 2	Disagree a little 3	Disagree a lot 4	Card 5
Easy to follow	☐	☐	☐	☐	15
Pleasant manner............	☐	☐	☐	☐	16
Knows a lot about computers	☐	☐	☐	☐	17
Enthusiastic................	☐	☐	☐	☐	18
Wrong for the series	☐	☐	☐	☐	19
Boring	☐	☐	☐	☐	20
I liked her	☐	☐	☐	☐	21

PLEASE WRITE IN ANY OTHER COMMENTS .....
....   22, 23

d) Serena Macbeth (The presenter of the last sequence)

	Agree a lot 1	Agree a little 2	Disagree a little 3	Disagree a lot 4	
Easy to follow	☐	☐	☐	☐	24
Pleasant manner............	☐	☐	☐	☐	25
Knows a lot about computers	☐	☐	☐	☐	26
Enthusiastic................	☐	☐	☐	☐	27
Wrong for the series	☐	☐	☐	☐	28
Boring	☐	☐	☐	☐	29
I liked her	☐	☐	☐	☐	30

PLEASE WRITE IN ANY OTHER COMMENTS .....

.... 31, 32

Q.2 Having seen an example of what the series may be like, which
of the following things, if any:
a) do you think are likely to be covered in the series and
b) would you like to see covered in the series?

PLEASE TICK AS MANY OR AS FEW AS YOU LIKE IN EACH COLUMN	(a) Likely to be covered	(b) You would like to see covered	
The uses of computers in business and industry	☐	☐	33, 34
How to write computer programs	☐	☐	35, 36
Recent advances in computer technology	☐	☐	37, 38
Building your own computer ..	☐	☐	39, 40
The effects of computers on our everyday lives	☐	☐	41, 42
Explanation of the electronic working of computers	☐	☐	43, 44
The ways that computers will change our lives	☐	☐	45, 46
None of these	☐	☐	47, 48
Any other things (TICK BOX AND WRITE IN	☐	☐	49–52
....			53–56

....

Q.3 For each of the following words or phrases, please indicate
whether or not the film was as you had expected.

PLEASE TICK ONE BOX ON EACH LINE	MORE THAN I HAD EXPECTED 1	LESS THAN I HAD EXPECTED 2	ABOUT THE SAME 3	
Entertaining	☐	☐	☐	57
Difficult to understand.......	☐	☐	☐	58
Informative	☐	☐	☐	59
Boring	☐	☐	☐	60
My sort of series ...	☐	☐	☐	61

FOR OFFICE
USE ONLY

Q.4   Please would you indicate how much you agree or disagree
      with each of the following statements. PLEASE TICK ONE
      BOX ON EACH LINE.

	Agree a lot 1	Agree a little 2	Undecided 3	Disagree a little 4	Disagree a lot 5	
The disadvantages of computers outweigh the advantages -------------	☐	☐	☐	☐	☐	62
I am very keen to learn more about computers --------------	☐	☐	☐	☐	☐	63
I do not think you could learn a lot about computers from television -------	☐	☐	☐	☐	☐	64
I would very much like to have a small computer of my own	☐	☐	☐	☐	☐	65
I don't think I'll ever understand computers --------------	☐	☐	☐	☐	☐	66

Q.5   a) Now that you have seen the pilot programme, how much
         would you say you know about computers and computing?

Absolutely nothing   ☐ 1
A little   ☐ 2   PLEASE TICK
Quite a lot   ☐ 3   ONE BOX   67
A great deal   ☐ 4

b) Would you say that you:

Know a lot more than
you did before .... ☐ 1
Know a little more than   PLEASE TICK
you did before .... ☐ 2   ONE BOX   68
Know about the same as
you did before .... ☐ 3

Q.6   How likely do you think you will be to watch the series if
      it is shown at a convenient time?

Not at all likely .... ☐ 1
Not very likely .... ☐ 2   PLEASE TICK
Fairly likely............ ☐ 3   ONE BOX   69

FOR OFFICE
USE ONLY

Q.7   Please indicate from the list below how interested you would
be in having a small, desk-top computer for your own
personal use:

Very interested   ☐ 1 ⎫ PLEASE GO
                             ⎬   TO   PLEASE
Fairly interested   ☐ 2 ⎭ QUESTION 8 TICK   70
Not particularly   ☐ 3 ⎫ PLEASE GO   ONE
   interested   ⎬   TO   BOX
Not at all interested ☐ 4 ⎭ QUESTION 9

Q.8   How likely would you be to *buy* a small, desk-top computer
if you could get one for about £180?

Very likely to buy one   ☐ 1 PLEASE
Fairly likely to buy one   ☐ 2 TICK ONE   71
Not very likely to buy one   ☐ 3 BOX
Not at all likely to buy one ☐ 4

Q.9   Having seen an example of what the series may be like can
you describe the sort of person you think it is intended for?

(PLEASE WRITE IN) ....
....

Q.10 When would you:
a) Expect the series to be transmitted and
b) Like the series to be transmitted

	a) When you would expect it to be transmitted	b) When you would like it to be transmitted		
Weekday mornings	☐	☐		10, 11
Weekday afternoons	☐	☐		12, 13
Weekday evenings	☐	☐	PLEASE	14, 15
Saturday mornings	☐	☐	TICK AS	16, 17
Saturday afternoons	☐	☐	MANY OR	18, 19
Saturday evenings	☐	☐	AS FEW AS	20, 21
Sunday mornings	☐	☐	YOU LIKE	22, 23
Sunday afternoons	☐	☐		24, 25
Sunday evenings	☐	☐		26, 27

Q.11 And finally, a few questions about yourself:

a) Have you ever studied any computing subjects?
                        YES ☐ 1
                        NO   ☐ 2   35

b) If 'Yes', and was that at:
School	☐		36
Evening classes	☐	PLEASE	37
Day classes	☐	TICK ALL	38
College	☐	THAT	39
University	☐	APPLY	40
Lecture courses	☐	TO YOU	41

FOR OFFICE
USE ONLY

Q.12 How old were you when you finished your
full-time-education?

15 years or under	☐	1
16 years	☐	2
17–18	☐	3
19–20	☐	4
21 +	☐	5

42

Q.13 And do you have any qualifications?

YES ☐ 1

NO ☐ 2

43

If 'Yes' which of the following, if any, do you have:

School Certificate passes	☐	44
C.S.E. passes	☐	45
G.C.E. 'O' level passes	☐	46
G.C.E. 'A' level passes	☐	47
O.N.C. or O.N.D. passes	☐	48
B.E.C. or T.E.C.	☐	49
H.N.C. or H.N.D. passes	☐	50
City and Guilds	☐	51
Teaching Diploma	☐	52
Degree	☐	53
Others (PLEASE WRITE IN)		54

....

PLEASE TICK

Q.14   MALE   ☐ 1
        FEMALE   ☐ 2

Q.15 AND YOUR AGE-GROUP

20–29	☐	1
30–39	☐	2
40–49	☐	3
50–60	☐	4
61 +	☐	5

Thank you for your help,

Your name ....

Q.16 Would you be prepared to take part in an experiment in learning how to use a microcomputer?
This would involve:
   i. Attending an evening meeting where you will be given a microcomputer to borrow for about ten days and given some basic instruction on how to program it.
   ii. Using the microcomputer in your home for about ten days — learning how to use it on your own and keeping a careful diary of your progress.
   iii. Attending a second evening meeting to discuss the difficulties and successes of the experiment.

YES ☐   NO ☐

Please could we have your name, address and telephone number

Name . . . .

Address . . . .

Tel No. . . . .

Thank you for helping us.

Note: in the reproduction of questionnaires in Appendix 4.3a the original question layout has been retained as far as possible, but not the page layout.

APPENDIX 4.4

'THE COMPUTER PROGRAMME' (021)
Mondays, 22nd March—14th June,
about 11.30 pm—BBC-1

Q.1   How many of the ten programmes in the series did you see?

NONE 0	ONE 1	TWO TO FIVE 2

SIX TO TEN 3	NOT SURE 4

IF YOU SAW *ANY PART* OF *ANY* OF THE PROGRAMMES IN THE
SERIES, PLEASE ANSWER THE FOLLOWING QUESTIONS:

. . . .

Q.2   OPINION OF THE SERIES

(Please ring one code on each line)

		Agree	Disagree	Don't Know
(a)	It was a good introduction to the subject of computing	1	2	3
(b)	I found it difficult to understand	1	2	3
(c)	It was very interesting	1	2	3
(d)	I thought the explanations were too brief	1	2	3
(e)	It was too elementary for me	1	2	3
(f)	It explained some of the basic principles of computing very clearly	1	2	3

. . . .

Q.3   Overall did you find the programme(s) that you watched:

extremely interesting and/or enjoyable	very interesting and/or enjoyable	fairly interesting and/or enjoyable	neither one thing nor the other	not very interesting and/or enjoyable	not at all interesting and/or enjoyable
6	5	4	3	2	1

Q.4 Here are some general questions about the BBC-1 Computer Literacy Project. Please answer them, even if you have never heard of it.

PLEASE RING ONE

Within the last nine months have you: CODE ON EACH LINE

(a) Watched any programmes in the television series 'The Computer Programme'   YES 1   NO 2

(b) Bought the BBC book which accompanies the television series called *The Computer Book*   YES 1   NO 2

(c) Bought the National Extension College (NEC) book called *30 Hour Basic*   YES 1   NO 2

(d) Contacted a local computer club, group or sombody locally for advice or information about computers   YES 1   NO 2

(e) Applied for the National Extension College (NEC) Computing course   YES 1   NO 2

(f) Applied to any other course on Computers and Computing   YES 1   NO 2

(g) Ordered or purchased any BBC computer software programs   YES 1   NO 2

(h) Bought the BBC Microcomputer System   YES 1   NO 2

Finally please write any further comments you wish to make below and on the back cover of the booklet.

APPENDIX 4.5

CARD 2 RESPONDENT NUMBER

'THE COMPUTER PROGRAMME' SURVEY

Programme 3

Hello, I'm calling from Audience Selection, the independent market research company. Please may I speak to ....?

Hallo, Mr/Mrs/Ms .... I'm calling from Audience Selection, the independent market research company. We spoke to you a few days ago and asked if you would watch a programme in the BBC television series 'The Computer Programme'.

Q.1 Did you watch 'The Computer Programme' at all last night? It was shown on BBC-1 at 11.40 pm last night?   *Col. 14* | *ROUTE*

Yes — did watch it	1	Q.2
No — did not watch it	2	Q.3b

ASK ALL WHO VIEWED

Q.2 Did you watch: *Col. 15*

	All of it	1
READ	Most of it	2	Q.3
OUT	Only part of it	3

ASK ALL

Q.3 Was that the first time you had seen that particular programme?   *Col. 16*

Yes	1
No	1	Q.4
Don't know	3

Q.4 What did you particularly like about last night's programme?
(PROMPT: What else did you like? What did you like about it? (UNTIL NO MORE RESPONSES)
WRITE IN:

_____

_____

_____

_____

_____   Q.5

ASK ALL |ROUTE

Q.5   And what did you not particularly like about the
      programme?
      (PROMPT: What other criticisms do you have? What
         did you not like about it? (UNTIL NO MORE
         RESPONSES))
      WRITE IN:

      _____

      _____

      _____

      _____
                                                                      Q.6
      _____
ASK ALL

Q.6   Thinking of the programme as a whole, what would you
      say you learnt from it? (PROMPT: What else? UNTIL
      NO MORE RESPONSES)
      WRITE IN:

      _____

      _____

      _____

      _____
                                                                      Q.7
      _____
Q.7   Did you expect to learn anything?   *Col. 17*
                                  Yes   1   Q.8
                                  No   2   Q.9

Q.8   *IF YES TO Q.7*
      How much did you expect to learn?   <u>READ OUT</u>   *Col. 18*
                                  A lot   1   ⎫ Q.9
                                  A little   2   ⎭
      ASK ALL

Q.9   How much would you say you knew about how computer
      languages work *before* you watched last night's
      programme?   <u>READ OUT</u>   *Col. 19*

                          ☐   A lot   1   ⎫
                                A little   2   ⎬ Q.10
                          ☐   Not very much   3   ⎭
                                Nothing at all   4

Q.10 And do you think you know more about it now?   *Col. 20*
                                  Yes   1   Q.11
                                  No   2   Q.12

Q.11 *IF YES TO Q.10*
      How much more do you   *Col. 21*
      know now? <u>READ OUT</u>   A lot more   1   ⎫
                                    A little more   2   ⎭ Q.12

ROUTE

ASK ALL

Q.12 How much would you say you knew about subroutines
in computer programmes before you watched last night's
programme?   *Col. 22*
TICK START   READ OUT

☐   A lot   1
               A little   2   } Q.13
☐   Not very much   3
               Nothing at all   4

Q.13 And do you think you know more about it now?   *Col. 23*
                              Yes   1   Q.14
                              No   2   Q.15

Q.14 *IF YES TO Q.13*
How much more do you know now?   READ OUT   *Col. 24*
                    A lot more   1   } Q.15
                    A little more   2
ASK ALL

Q.15 I am going to read out some comments that people have
made about last night's programme. Please tell me
whether you agree or disagree with each one.
                    CIRCLE ONE CODE PER LINE

	AGREE	DISAGREE	DON'T KNOW	
☐ It was a good introduction to the subject of computing	1	2	3	*Col. 25*
I found it difficult to understand	1	2	3	*Col. 26*
It helped me understand more about how to use my microcomputer	1	2	3	*Col. 27*
It was very interesting	1	2	3	*Col. 28*
I thought the explanations were too brief	1	2	3	*Col. 29*
It was too elementary for me	1	2	3	*Col. 30*
☐ It explained some of the basic principles of computing very clearly	1	2	3	*Col. 31*	Q.16

Q.16 Compared with what you had expected were you, on
balance, pleased or disappointed with the programme?   *Col. 32*
                              Pleased   1   Q.17
                              Disappointed   2   Q.19

ROUTE

Q.17 *IF 'PLEASED' AT Q.16* (CODE 1)
In what ways were you pleased with the programme?
(PROMPT: What other things were you pleased with?
In what ways were you pleased? UNTIL NO MORE
RESPONSES)
WRITE IN:

_____

_____

_____

_____   Q.18

Q.18 And what aspects of the programme were you
disappointed with?
(PROMPT: What other things were you disappointed
with? In what ways were you disappointed? UNTIL NO
MORE RESPONSES)
WRITE IN:

_____

_____

_____

_____   Q.21

Q.19 *IF 'DISAPPOINTED' AT Q.16.* (CODE 2)
In what ways were you disappointed with the programme?
(PROMPT: What other things were you disappointed
with? In what ways were you disappointed? UNTIL NO
MORE RESPONSES)
WRITE IN:

_____

_____

_____

_____   Q.20

Q.20 And what aspects of the programme were you please
with?
(PROMPT: What other things were you pleased with?
In what ways were you pleased? UNTIL NO MORE
RESPONSES)
WRITE IN:

_____

_____

_____

_____   Q.21

Q.21 Do you think you will watch the rest of the series?   *Col. 33*
                                             Yes   1   Q.22
                                             No   2   Q.23

		ROUTE

Q.22 *IF YES AT Q.21*
   Do you think you will: *Col. 34*
         <u>READ OUT</u>   Definitely watch   1
                          Probably watch   2   } Q25
                          Don't know   3

Q.23 *IF NO AT Q.21*
   Do you think you will: *Col. 35*
         <u>READ OUT</u>   Probably not watch   1
                          Definitely not watch   2   } Q.24
                          Don't know   3

Q.24 Why do you think you won't watch any more
   programmes?
   (PROMPT: What else? In what ways was it ....?
   UNTIL NO MORE RESPONSES
   WRITE IN:

   _____

   _____

   _____

   _____   Q.25

   ASK ALL
Q.25 Have you seen any of the other programmes in the series?   *Col. 36*
                          Yes   1   Q.26
                          No   2   Q.27

Q.26 *IF YES AT Q.25*
   How many programmes, including the one you watched
   last night, have you seen altogether? There are ten
   programmes in the series?   *Col. 37*
                          1   1
                          2–3   2
                          4–5   3
                          6–7   4
                          8–9   5
                          All 10   6
                          Don't know   7   Q.27

Q.27 What aspects of computing would you be most interested
   in seeing covered in the *next* series on computers and
   computing?

   (PROMPT: What else would you like to see? Can you
   explain that? UNTIL NO MORE RESPONSES)
   WRITE IN:

   _____

   _____

   _____

   _____   Q.28

ROUTE

Q.28 In a further television series on computers and computing, which of the following items would you be interested in seeing something about? Is that very interested or quite interested?

CIRCLE ONE CODE ON EACH LINE

TICK START	VERY INTERESTED	QUITE INTERESTED	NOT INTERESTED	DON'T KNOW		
The uses of microcomputers in the home	1	2	3	4	*Col. 38*	
How computers work electronically	1	2	3	4	*Col.39*	
How to write programmes in advanced programming languages	1	2	3	4	*Col. 40*	
The use of microcomputers in business and industry	1	2	3	4	*Col. 41*	
How to use your microcomputer	1	2	3	4	*Col. 42*	
The theory of computer programming	1	2	3	4	*Col. 43*	
The social implications of microtechnology	1	2	3	4	*Col. 44*	Q.29

Q.29 What do you hope to use your BBC microcomputer for? (PROMPT: What else? Can you explain that? UNTIL NO MORE: RESPONSES) WRITE IN:

_____

_____

_____

_____   Q.30

Q.30 Within the last nine months have you.

a) Bought the BBC book which accompanies the series, called 'The Computer Book'?

		Col. 45
Yes	1	Q.30(c)
No	2	Q.30(b)

ROUTE

Q.30 b) *IF NO TO Q.30a*
Do you intend to buy it?

		Col. 46	
Yes		1	Q.30c
No		2	

c) Bought the NEC (National Extension College)
30 Hour Basic?

		Col. 47	
Yes		1	Q.30e
No		2	Q.30d

d) *IF NO Q.3c*
Do you intend to buy it?

		Col. 48	
Yes		1	Q.30e
No		2	

e) Contacted a local computer club or referral point?

		Col. 49	
Yes		1	Q.30g
No		2	Q.30f

f) *IF NO TO Q.30e*
Do you intend to?

		Col. 50	
Yes		1	Q.30g
No		2	

g) Applied for the NEC (National Extension College)
computing course?

		Col. 51	
Yes		1	Q.30i
No		2	Q.30h

h) *IF NOT TO Q.30c*
Do you intend to?

		Col. 52	
Yes		1	
No		2	Q.30i

i) Within the last nine months have you:
Applied to attend any other course on computing or
computers?

		Col. 53	
Yes		1	Q.30k
No		2	Q.30j

j) *IF NO TO Q.30i*
Do you intend to?

		Col. 54	
Yes		1	Q.30k
No		2	

Ordered or purchased any BBC software programs?

		Col. 55	
Yes		1	Q.31
No		2	Q.30l

l) *IF NO Q.30k*
Do you intend to?

		Col.56	
Yes		1	Q.31
No		2	

|ROUTE

Q.31 And now I'd like to ask you a few questions about yourself?
What is your highest qualification?   *Col. 57*

READ OUT & CIRCLE ONE ONLY

Degree, diploma, teaching certificate	1
'A' levels, HND/HNC	2
'O' levels, OND/ONC	3
OTHER (WRITE IN)	4

DO NOT READ OUT   _____

_____

NONE OF THESE   5   Q.32

Q.32 What was your age last birthday?

WRITE IN AND   Col. 58   Col. 59
CODE BELOW   [   ]   [   ]

Col. 60

Under 16	1
16–19	2
20–29	3
30–44	4
45–64	5
65 +	6 Q.33

Q.33 What do you do for a living? (IF A STUDENT WRITE IN DETAILS OF COURSE) RECORD FULL DETAILS   *Cols. 61–62*

_____

_____

_____

_____   Q.34

Q.34 Are you your own head of household?   *Col. 63*

Yes   1   RECORD CLASS

No   2   AT Q.35

Q.35 What does your head of household do for a living?
RECORD FULL DETAILS   *Cols. 64–65*

_____

_____

_____

_____

		ROUTE
RECORD CLASS	*Col. 66*	
Higher managerial/administrative/professional A	1	
Intermediate managerial/administrative/professionalB	2	
White collar clerical/junior managerial C1	3	
Skilled blue collar C2	4	
Unskilled blue collar/Unemployed/State pension DE	5	Q.36

Q.36 When we spoke to you earlier you said you would be prepared to watch 'The Computer Programme' on 19th April at about 11.30 p.m. Are you still prepared to watch it?

	Col. 67	
Yes	1	
No	1	CLOSE

THANK RESPONDENT—REMIND THEM TO WATCH PROGRAMME ON 19th APRIL AT ABOUT 11.30 pm FOR INTERVIEW ON 20th APRIL. FILL IN CLASSIFICATION DATA OVERLEAF.

Note: in the reproduction of this questionnaire (Appendix 4.5) the original question layout has been retained as far as possible, but not the page layout.

APPENDIX 4.5a

7	8	9	10	11

CARD 3 RESPONDENT NUMBER
CARD No. COLS 12 + 13 (03)
(BASE: 167)

'THE COMPUTER PROGRAMME' SURVEY—PART II

Programme 4

Hello, I'm calling from Audience Selection, the independent market research company. Please may I speak to ....?

Hallo, Mr/Mrs/Ms .... I'm calling from Audience Selection, the independent market research company. We spoke to you a few days ago and asked if you would watch a programme in the BBC television series 'The Computer Programme'.

Q.1 Did you watch 'The Computer Programme' at all last night? It was shown on BBC-1 at 11.40 pm last night?

Col. 14 ROUTE

Yes—did watch it	1	Q.2
No—did not watch it	2	CLOSE

ASK ALL WHO VIEWED

Q.2 Did you watch:

Col. 15

	All of it	1
READ	Most of it	2
OUT	Only part of it	3

Q.3

ASK ALL

Q.3 Was that the first time you had seen that particular programme?

Col. 16

Yes	1	
No	1	Q.4
Don't know	3	

Q.4 What did you particularly like about last night's programme?
(PROMPT: What else did you like? What did you like about it? (UNTIL NO MORE RESPONSES)
WRITE IN:

_____

_____

_____

_____

_____

Q.5

|*ROUTE*

Q.5   And what did you not particularly like about the
      programme?
      (PROMPT: What other criticisms do you have? What
          did you not like about it? (UNTIL NO MORE
          RESPONSES))
      WRITE IN:

      _____

      _____

      _____

      _____

      _____   Q.6

ASK ALL

Q.6   Thinking of the programme as a whole, what would you
      say you learnt from it? (PROMPT: What else? UNTIL
      NO MORE RESPONSES)
      WRITE IN:

      _____

      _____

      _____

      _____   Q.7

Q.7   Did you expect to learn anything?   *Col. 17*
                                       Yes   1 →   Q.8
                                       No   2 →   Q.9

Q.8   *IF YES TO Q.7*
      How much did you expect to learn?   <u>READ OUT</u>   *Call. 18*
                                       A lot   1⎫
                                       A little   2⎭   Q.9
      ASK ALL

Q.9   How much would you say you knew about how computer
      languages work *before* you watched last night's
      programme?   <u>READ OUT</u>   *Col. 19*

                       ☐   A lot   1⎫
                             A little   2⎪   Q.10
                       ☐   Not very much   3⎪
                             Nothing at all   4⎭

Q.10 And do you think you know more about it now?   *Col. 20*
                                       Yes   1   Q.11
                                       No   2   Q.12

Q.11 *IF YES TO Q.10*
      How much more do you
      know now? <u>READ OUT</u>   A lot more   *Col. 21*
                                    A little more   2   Q.12

ROUTE

Q.12 *ASK ALL*

In the programme they outlined the difference between a RANDOM ACCESS MEMORY CHIP (RAM) AND A READ ONLY CHIP (ROM). Can you tell me which of the following describes either a RAM, a ROM or neither?

☐ TICK START.

	A RAM	A ROM	NEITHER	DON'T KNOW	
It identifies the memory memory location	1	2	3	4	*Col. 22*
A memory into which information can be put	1	2	3	4	*Col. 23*
It is the boundary between 2 parts of a computer system	1	2	3	4	*Col. 24*
A memory circuit which stores permanent information which can not be changed	1	2	3	4	*Col. 25*
It keeps the operation in time sequence	1	2	3	4	*Col. 26*

ASK ALL

Q.13 How much would you say you knew about RAMS and ROMS *before* you saw last night's programme?

			Col. 27	
TICK START	☐	A lot	1	
		A little	2	Q.14
	☐	Not very much	3	
		Nothing at all	4	

Q.14 And do you think you know more about them now?

	Col. 28	
Yes	1	Q.15
No	2	Q.16

IF YES AT Q.14

Q.15 How much more do you know now?

	Col. 29
A lot more	2
A little more	2

ROUTE

Q.16 *ASK ALL*
I am going to read out some comments that people have made about last night's programme. please tell me whether you agree or disagree with each one.

CIRCLE ONE CODE PER LINE

TICK START	AGREE	DISAGREE	DON'T KNOW		
☐ It was a good introduction to the subject of computing	1	2	3	*Col. 30*	
I found it difficult to understand	1	2	3	*Col. 31*	
It helped me understand more about how to use my microcomputer	1	2	3	*Col. 32*	
It was very interesting	1	2	3	*Col. 33*	
I thought the explanations were too brief	1	2	3	*Col. 34*	
It was too elementary for me	1	2	3	*Col. 35*	
☐ It explained some of the basic principles of computing very clearly	1	2	3	*Col. 36*	Q.17

Q.17 Compared with what you had expected were you, on balance, pleased or disappointed with the programme?　　*Col. 37*

Pleased	1	Q.18
Disappointed	2	Q.20

IF 'PLEASED' AT Q.17 (CODE 1)
Q.18 In what ways were you pleased with the programme? (PROMPT: What other things were you pleased with? In what ways were you pleased? UNTIL NO MORE RESPONSES)
WRITE IN:

_____

_____

_____

_____

_____

_____

Q.19

|ROUTE

Q.19 And what aspects of the programme were you disappointed with?
(PROMPT: What other things were you disappointed with?
In what ways were you disappointed? UNTIL NO MORE RESPONSES)
WRITE IN:

_____

_____

_____

_____

_____   Q.22

IF 'DISAPPOINTED' AT Q.17 (CODE 2)
Q.20 In what ways were you disappointed with the programme?
(PROMPT: What other things were you disappointed with? In what ways were you disappointed? UNTIL NO MORE RESPONSES)
WRITE IN:

_____

_____

_____

_____   Q.21

Q.21 And what aspects of the programme were you please with?
(PROMPT: What other things were you pleased? UNTIL NO MORE RESPONSES)
WRITE IN:

_____

_____

_____

_____

Q.22 Do you think you will watch the rest of the series?	*Col.38*	
Yes	1	Q.23
No	2	Q.24

IF YES AT Q.22

Q.23 Do you think you will:		*Col. 39*
READ OUT Definitely watch		1
Probably watch		2
Don't Know		3

IF NO AT Q.22   *Col.40* |*ROUTE*

Q.24 Do you think you will:

        <u>READ OUT</u>   Probably not
                        watch   1
                      Definitely not
                        watch   2
                      Don't know   3   Q.25

Q.25 Why do you think you won't watch any more
      programmes?
      (PROMPT: What else? In what ways was it ....?
      UNTIL NO MORE RESPONSES)
      WRITE IN:

_____

_____

_____

_____

_____   Q.26

Q.26 Now I would like to ask you a few questions about the
      main presenters. Please tell me whether you agree or
      disagree with each comment I read out.

     ☐   TICK START

     a) Firstly Ian Macnaught-Davies — he was the
        presenter with glasses.

	AGREE	DISAGREE	DON'T KNOW	
He explained things clearly	1	2	3	*Col. 41*
He was knowledgeable about computers	1	2	3	*Col. 42*
He was boring	1	2	3	*Col. 43*
He was right for the series	1	2	3	*Col. 44*

What other comments would you like to make?
(PROMPT — What else?)

_____

_____

_____

_____

b)   Now Chris Serle, the main presenter.

	AGREE	DISAGREE	DON'T KNOW	
He explained things clearly	1	2	3	*Col. 45*
He was knowledgeable about computers	1	2	3	*Col. 46*
He was boring	1	2	3	*Col. 47*
He was right for the series	1	2	' 3	*Col. 48*

What other comments would you like to make?
(PROMPT—What else?)

_____

_____

_____

_____

c) And now Gill Neville—the reporter

	AGREE	DISAGREE	DON'T KNOW	
She explained things clearly	1	2	3	*Col. 49*
She was knowledgeable about computers	1	2	3	*Col. 50*
She was boring	1	2	3	*Col. 51*
She was right for the series	1	2	3	*Col. 52*

What other comments would you like to make?
(PROMPT)—What else?)

_____

_____

_____

IF RESPONDENT WAS SUCCESSFULLY
INTERVIEWED ON 6th OR 7th APRIL, GO TO
TIME OF INTERVIEW ON LAST PAGE AND
CLOSE.

IF RESPONDENT WAS NOT INTERVIEWED ON
6TH OR 7TH APRIL CONTINUE TO END OF
QUESTIONNAIRE.

ASK ALL WHO WERE NOT INTERVIEWED ON 6th OR 7TH APRIL

Col. 53 |ROUTE

Q.27 Have you seen any of the other programmes in the series?

Yes	1
No	2

IF YES AT Q.27

Q.28 How many programmes, including the one you watched last night, have you seen altogether? There are ten programmes in the series?

Col. 54

1	1
2–3	2
4–5	3
6–7	4
8–9	5
All 10	6
Don't Know	7

Q.29 What aspects of computing would you be most interested in seeing covered in the *next* series on computers and computing?
(PROMPT: What else would you like to see? Can you explain that? UNTIL NO MORE RESPONSES)
WRITE IN:

_____

_____

_____

_____

_____

Q.30 In a further television series on computers and computing, which of the following items would you be interested in seeing something about? Is that very interested or quite interested?

CIRCLE ONE CODE ON EACH LINE

TICK START	VERY INTERESTED	QUITE INTERESTED	NOT INTERESTED	DON'T KNOW	
The uses of microcomputers in the home	1	2	3	4	Col. 55
How computers work electronically	1	2	3	4	Col.56
How to write programmes in advanced programming languages	1	2	3	4	Col. 57

continued _____

CIRCLE ONE CODE ON EACH LINE

|ROUTE

TICK START _continued_	VERY INTERESTED	QUITE INTERESTED	NOT INTERESTED	DON'T KNOW		
The use of microcomputers in business and industry	1	2	3	4	*Col. 58*	
How to use your microcomputer	1	2	3	4	*Col. 59*	
The theory of computer programming	1	2	3	4	*Col. 60*	
The social implications of microtechnology	1	2	3	4	*Col. 61*	Q.31

Q.31 What do you hope to use your BBC microcomputer for?
(PROMPT: What else? Can you explain that? UNTIL
NO MORE: RESPONSES)
WRITE IN:

_____

_____

_____

_____   Q.32

Within the last nine months have you:

Q.32 a) Bought the BBC book which accompanies the series,
called 'The Computer Book'?   *Col. 62*
                                   Yes   1   Q.32b
                                   No   2

Do you intend to buy it?   *Col. 63*
                                   Yes   1
                                   No   2   Q.32b

b) Bought the NEC (National Extension College)   *Col. 64*
30 hour Basic?
                                   Yes   1   Q.32c
                                   No   2

Do you intend to buy it?   *Col. 65*
                                   Yes   1
                                   No   2   Q.32c

|ROUTE

Q.32 c) Contacted a local computer club or referral point: *Col. 66*

Yes	1	Q.32d
No	2	

Do you intend to?   *Col. 67*

Yes	1	
No	2	Q.32d

d) Applied for the NEC (National Extension College) computing course?   *Col. 68*

Yes	1	Q.32e
No	2	

Do you intend to?   *Col. 69*

Yes	1	
No	2	Q.32e

e) Applied to attend any other course on computing or computers?   *Col. 70*

Yes	1	Q.32f
No	2	

Do you intend to?   *Col. 71*

Yes	1	
No	2	Q.32f

f) Ordered or purchased any BBC software programs?   *Col. 72*

Yes	1	Q.33
No	2	

Do you intend to?   *Col. 73*

Yes	1
No	2

Q.33 And now I'd like to ask you a few questions about yourself?
What is your highest qualification?   *Col. 74*

READ OUT AND CIRCLE ONLY ONLY

Degree, diploma, teaching certificate	1
'A' levels, HND/HNC	2
'O' levels, OND/ONC	3
OTHER (WRITE IN)	4

DO NOT READ OUT {

_____

_____

_____

NONE OF THESE	5

ROUTE

What was your age last birthday?
WRITE IN AND CODE BELOW
        Col.75   *Col.76*
┌──────┐ ┌──────┐
│   │ │   │
└──────┘ └──────┘
                                    Col. 77
            16–19   1
            20–29   2
            30–44   3
            45–64   4
            65 +   5

What do you do for a living? (IF A STUDENT WRITE
IN DETAILS OF COURSE) RECORD FULL DETAILS

_____

_____

_____

_____

Are you your own head of household?   *Col. 78*
                          Yes   1   RECORD
                          No   2   CLASS
What does your head of household do for a living?
RECORD FULL DETAILS

_____

_____

_____

_____

_____

RECORD CLASS   *Col. 14* CARD 4

Higher managerial/administrative/professional   A   1
Intermediate managerial/administrative/
    professional   B   2
White collar clerical/junior managerial   C1   3
Skilled blue collar   C2   4
Unskilled blue collar/Unemployed/State pension   DE   5   Q.36

THANK RESPONDENT—FILL IN
CLASSIFICATION DATA OVERLEAF.

ROUTE

CLASSIFICATION

SEX:		*Col. 15*
	Male	1
	Female	2

AREA:		*Col. 16*
	North	1
	Midlands	2
	South	3

DATE OF INTERVIEW:		*Col. 17*
	20 April 1982	1
	21 April 1982	2

TIME OF INTERVIEW:		*Col. 18*
	9.00 — 10.00 am	1
	10.00 — 11.00 am	2
	11.00 — 12.00 am	3
	12.00 — 1.00 pm	4
	1.00 — 2.00 pm	5
	2.00 — 3.00 pm	6
	3.00 — 4.00 pm	7
	4.00 — 5.00 pm	8
	5.00 — 6.00 pm	9

		Col. 19
	6.00 — 7.00 pm	1
	7.00 — 8.00 pm	2
	8.00 — 9.00 pm	3
	9.00 — 10.00 pm	4
	10.00 — 11.00 pm	5
	After 11.00 pm	6

LENGTH OF INTERVIEW:

Col.20   Col.21

INTERVIEWERS NAME: _____

Note: in the reproduction of this questionnaire (Appendix 4.5a) the original question layout has been retained as far as possible, but not the page layout.

APPENDIX 4.6

BBC MICROCOMPUTER SYSTEM

Cols 1–12

1					

It is important that
everyone who has
received a questionnaire
should return it so that
we can get a broad cross
section of views about
the BBC microcomputer

How to fill in your answers

1. Please answer all the questions that apply

2. For most of the questions you need only put a tick (☑)
    in one of the boxes. Some questions have extra space for
    you to write in your comments. If you find there is not
    enough room, please use the back of this page.

OFFICE USE
ONLY

(Col. 13)

Q.1 Are you the main user of the BBC Microcomputer?

YES ☐   1

NO ☐   2

Q.2 *IF NOT*: Who is the main user? (*tick one box*) (Col. 14)

Wife/Husband ☐   1

Son/daughter ☐   2

Parents ☐   3

Someone else ☐   4

(*please give details*)   5

_____   (Col. 15)

_____

_____

We are interested in the views of the *Main User* of the
BBC Micro. If you yourself are not the main user please
pass this questionnaire to the person who is, so that they
can fill in their answers and return it to us.

Q.3 Do you use your BBC Micro for ....?

(Col. 16)

tick all that apply

a) Teaching purposes ☐ (Col. 17)
(*please give details*) (Col. 18)

.... (Col. 19)

.... (Col. 20)

....

b) Business or work ☐ (Col. 21)
purposes (Col. 22)
(*please give details*) (Col. 23)

.... (Col. 24)

.... (Col. 25)

....

c) Study related ☐ (Col. 26)
purposes (Col. 27)
(*please give details*) (Col. 28)

.... (Col. 29)

.... (Col. 30)

....

d) Other purposes ☐ (Col. 31)
(*please give details*) (Col. 32)

.... (Col. 33)

.... (Col. 34)

.... (Col. 35)

Q.4 And what else do you hope to use your BBC Micro for?
(*please give details*) (Col. 36)

.... (Col. 37)

.... (Col. 38)

.... (Col. 39)

Q.5 Do you use your BBC Micro more, less or about the
same as you thought you would? (*tick one box*) (Col. 40)

More ☐ 1

Less ☐ 2

About the same ☐ 3

Don't know ☐ 4

Q.6 Since you started using your BBC Micro have you
personally felt the need for help, either with the machine
itself or with programming? (Col. 41)

YES ☐ 1

NO ☐ 2

OFFICE USE
ONLY

Q.7   Which of the following if any, have you got advice from?
                              (*tick all that apply*)

Books	☐	(Col. 42)
Computer clubs	☐	(Col. 43)
Family members	☐	(Col. 44)
Friends/colleagues	☐	(Col. 45)
Specialist press	☐	(Col. 46)
Other (*please describe*)	☐	(Col. 47)

_____

_____

_____

none of these	☐	(Col. 48)

Q.8   Please tell us about any problems or difficulties you have
        had in getting started with your BBC Micro:

_____   (Col. 49)

_____   (Col. 50)

_____   (Col. 51)

_____   (Col. 52)

Q.9   Here are some comments people have made about using
        the BBC Micro, please say whether you agree or disagree
        with each one.
                              (*tick one box on each line*)

	AGREE (1)	DISAGREE (2)	DON'T KNOW (3)	
I had difficulties in getting started.	☐	☐	☐	(Col. 53)
I am able to do more with my Micro than I first thought I could.	☐	☐	☐	(Col. 54)
I would have liked information included with my Micro on how to write programs.	☐	☐	☐	(Col. 55)
I shall mainly use software programs I buy.	☐	☐	☐	(Col. 56)
I don't use my BBC Micro very often nowadays.	☐	☐	☐	(Col. 57)
I can't use my BBC Micro for what I had planned to.	☐	☐	☐	(Col. 58)
It's an easy machine to use.	☐	☐	☐	(Col. 59)
I shall mainly write my own programs.	☐	☐	☐	(Col. 60)

OFFICE USE
ONLY

Q.10 Compare with what you had expected, what do you think of the BBC Micro computer overall? Are you ....(*tick one box only*)

(Col. 61)

Very pleased with it	☐	1
Quite pleased with it	☐	2
A little disappointed with it	☐	3
Very disappointed with it	☐	4

Q.11 If you are all pleased, in what ways are you pleased with your BBC Micro? (*please give full details*)

_____   (Col. 62)
_____   (Col. 63)
_____   (Col. 64)
_____   (Col. 65)

Q.12 If you are at all disappointed, in what ways are you disappointed with your BBC Micro? (*please give full details*)

_____   (Col. 66)
_____   (Col. 67)
_____   (Col. 68)
_____   (Col. 69)

Q.13 One of the features of the BBC Micro is the high resolution graphics feature. How important is this feature for you? (*tick one box only*)

(Col. 70)

Very important	☐	1
Quite important	☐	2
Not very important	☐	3
Not at all important	☐	4
Don't know	☐	5

Q.14 Which of the following items of computer hardware do you .... a) already have?
b) would you be likely to buy?
(*tick all that apply to you*)

	(a) Already have	(b) Likely to buy	
A disc-drive	☐	☐	(Col. 17, 72)
A printer	☐	☐	(Col. 73, 74)
A teletext receiver	☐	☐	(Col. 75, 76)
A second processor	☐	☐	(Col. 77, 78)
Another Micro computer (*please give details*)	☐	☐	(Col. 79, 80)

_____
_____
_____

Q.15 Included with your BBC Micro was a copy of the provisional *User Guide*. So that we can improve the Guide we would like your views on it.

2 | | | | | |

Have you looked at the provisional *User Guide* at all?

(Col. 7)

YES ☐ (please answer 1

NO ☐ Q.17 next) 2

Q.16 IF NO: Why have you not looked at it?
(please give details)

_____ (Col. 8)
_____ (Col. 9)
_____ (Col. 10)
_____ (Col. 11)

(Please turn to Q.24)

Q.17 How much of the provisional *User Guide* have you yourself read or looked at? *tick one box only* (Col. 12)

all if it ☐ 1
most of it ☐ 2
some of it ☐ 3

Q.18 Here is a list of the sections contained in the provisional *User Guide*, please indicate which ones you found particularly useful in helping you use your BBC Micro. *(tick all that apply)*

Section Title:		*Particularly useful in helping to use your Micro*
1. Getting going	(Col.13)	☐
2. Giving the computer instructions	(Col. 14)	☐
3. Variables	(Col. 14)	☐
4. Computer programs	(Col. 15)	☐
5. Recording programs on cassette	(Col. 16)	☐
6. BASIC Keywords	(Col. 17)	☐
7. VDU Drivers	(Col. 18)	☐
8. Printer control	(Col. 19)	☐
9. Changing filing systems	(Col. 20)	☐
10. User defined keys	(Col. 21)	☐
11. Cassette files	(Col. 22)	☐
12. Machine operating systems	(Col. 23)	☐
13. Minimum abbreviations	(Col. 24)	☐
14. Error messages	(Col. 25)	☐

OFFICE USE
ONLY

Q.19 So overall, how useful did you find the provisional *User Guide* in helping you use your BBC Micro?

(*tick one box only*)

Very useful	☐	1
Quite useful	☐	2
Not very useful	☐	3
Not at all useful	☐	4

Q.20 In what ways did you find it ....
—useful?   .... (Col. 28)

.... (Col. 29)

.... (Col. 30)

.... (Col. 31)

....

Q.21 —not useful?   .... (Col. 32)

.... (Col. 33)

.... (Col. 34)

.... (Col. 35)

....

Q.22 Here are some comments people have made about the provisional *User Guide*. Please indicate whether you agree or disagree with each one. (*tick one box on each line*)

	Agree	Disagree	Don't Know	
	(1)	(2)	(3)	
I found the lay out clear and easy to follow	☐	☐	☐	(Col. 36)
The demonstration programs were very helpful.	☐	☐	☐	(Col. 37)
It told me nothing about how to write programs	☐	☐	☐	(Col. 38)
It was too complicated for me	☐	☐	☐	(Col. 39)
It is only useful for people who know how to program	☐	☐	☐	(Col. 40)

Q.23 What else would you have liked to see included in the provisional *User Guide*? (*please give details*)

.... (Col. 41)
.... (Col. 42)
.... (Col. 43)
.... (Col. 44)

OFFICE USE
ONLY

Q.24 Have you received your copy of the revised *User Guide* yet?

(Col. 45)

yes	☐	1
no	☐	2
don't know	☐	3

Q.25 Besides yourself, who else uses the BBC Micro?
(*please tick all that apply*)

my wife/husband	☐	(Col. 46)
my parents	☐	(Col. 47)
my son(s) (aged 15 or under	☐	(Col. 48)
my son(s) (aged over 15)	☐	(Col. 49)
my daughter(s) (aged 15 or under)	☐	(Col. 50)
my daughter(s) (aged over 15)	☐	(Col. 51)
Others (please say whom)	☐	(Col. 52)

. . . .   (Col. 53)

. . . .   (Col. 54)

. . . .   (Col. 55)
(Col. 56–80v)
(Cols 1–6)

3					

Col. 7–80v)
Cols 1–6)

4					

Q.26 During the last nine months have you ..?

a) Bought the BBC Book which
accompanies the television series, called   (Col. 7)

The Computer Book	YES	☐	1
	NO	☐	2

(Col. 8)

And do you intend to buy

it?	YES	☐	1
	NO	☐	2

(Col. 9)

Q.26 b) Bought the National Extension College
(NEC) book called *30 Hour*

31 *Basic* . . . . .YES	☐	
NO	☐	2

(Col. 10)

And do you intend to buy

it?	YES	☐	1
	NO	☐	2

OFFICE USE
ONLY

Q.26

(Col. 11)

c) Contacted a local computer club or
referral point .... YES ☐   1

┌───────NO ☐   2
▼   (Col. 12)
And do you intend to? .... YES ☐   1

NO ☐   2
                                                        (Col. 13)
d) Applied for the National Extension
College (NEC) computing
course .... YES ☐   1

┌───────NO ☐   2
▼   (Col. 14)
And do you intend to apply? YES ☐   1

NO ☐   2
                                                        (Col. 15)
e) Applied to attend any other course on
computing .... YES ☐   1

┌───────NO ☐   2
▼   (Col. 16)
And do you intend to apply? YES ☐   1

NO ☐   2
                                                        (Col. 17)
f) Ordered or purchased any BBC
software programs ..... YES ☐   1

┌───────NO ☐   2
▼   (Col. 18)
And do you intend to? .... YES ☐   1

NO ☐   2
                                                        (Col. 19)
g) Seen any of the BBC television series 'The
Computer Programme' . YES ☐   1

NO ☐   2
                                                        (Col. 20)
Have you bought any other books to help
you with your BBC Micro? ....

┌───────YES ☐   1
▼
NO ☐   2
Which ones have you bought?

....   (Col. 21)
....   (Col. 22)
....   (Col. 23)
....   (Col. 24)

Note: in the reproduction of this questionnaire (Appendix 4.6) the original
question layout has been retained as far as possible, but not the page
layout.

Applied Marketing and Social Research 2nd Edition
Edited by Ute Bradley
©Copyright John Wiley 1987

5. Assessing What Is Being Measured by a Readership Survey

H. A. Smith   *IPC Magazines Ltd.*

A great deal of time and effort is expended on media research: to find out who reads or watches which print media, TV or radio programme. The National Readership Survey is a well established perennial in this field and this chapter concentrates on its main features. It also emphasises the 'thinking' input required for checking its continued usefulness, balancing the need for continuous data with the wish for accommodating change. The issues involved can be complex, but once understood, the student will be able to study a specific issue of the NRS with real interest.

The case can draw out many interesting discussions:

—defining a reader;
—the principles involved in designing and wording a readership survey,
—its likely results, how to interpret and use them;

as well as lead to detailed studies of the NRS.

INTRODUCTION

Readership surveys, that is, surveys conducted to establish the number and types of people reading one or more publications, are carried out primarily to help advertisers and agencies decide where to spend advertising money. Such surveys are also of some value to publishers when they are trying to identifying the types of people buying their publications, but when used in this way the data must be interpreted with care. This is because there are often many more readers of a publication than buyers and they can be very different types of people. For example, the number of readers per copy of a newspaper will average around three, increasing in the case of some magazines to an average of 12 or more. The number of different readers attracted to a publication will be determined by many different considerations, including the frequency of publication, the nature of the editorial, the types of people buying the title in the first place and the extent to which the title is likely to end up in a public place such as a waiting room, where a great deal of reading takes place.

Under these circumstances publishers would be wrong to assume that readers and buyers are similar types of people. In some cases the relationship is fairly straightforward and there is little risk that the publisher will be mislead, but judgement always needs to be used. For example, 80% of the readers of the magazine *Look Now* are young women aged 15–24 so it is reasonable to expect that overwhelmingly this magazine will be bought by the same type of person (a fact which is self-evident from the editorial), but would it be equally reasonable to assume that because 47% of the readers of *The Sun* are women a similar proportion of copies of the paper are also bought by women? Almost certainly not.

Readership surveys, therefore, are primarily carried out to aid the buying and selling of advertising space.

THE NEEDS OF THE ADVERTISER

An advertiser will look upon his advertising expenditure as one of a number of ways in which he can encourage people to buy his product. Advertising should be seen as a marketing input alongside such alternatives as the quality of the packaging, point of sale display material, competitions, coupons, money-off promotions, bonuses to wholesalers and retailers to take extra stock and the sales force itself. One of the most difficult tasks facing a manufacturer is to decide how to spend his money between such alternatives. Much reliance is placed on past experience, but even so a great deal rests on the judgement of the executives involved. They will take into account the position of the brand or service in the marketplace, the benefits which they think each of the marketing alternatives will give them, the activities of their competitors and many other factors.

Once a budget for advertising has been agreed the next step is to decide which media should be used. Television, newspapers, magazines, radio, cinema or posters? Again the crucial decisions tend to be made on the basis of past experience and subjective judgement. The research which the different media carry out to measure the size and nature of the audiences which they offer advertisers plays little part in influencing the choice *between* media.

It is true that more and more research is now being carried out with the aim of evaluating the performance of an advertising campaign, but in the main such work concentrates on measuring different creative treatments and other variations within a medium (primarily television), rather than measuring the performance of one medium against another.

That is, readership surveys are mainly used to help in the choice of the actual publications (known as the schedule) to be used for an advertising campaign, once it has been decided to advertise in newspapers or magazines.

The next step for an advertiser is to decide what type of publication should be used. Normally this is a fairly easy decision. If the advertiser wants immediate response or is making an advertising claim which dates rapidly, such as a supermarket chain advertising special offers, daily newspapers or sometimes weekly magazines with a rapid production cycle are the only possibilities, while if an advertiser wants good quality colour then he must be in magazines.

Once such decisions have been made the choice of titles to be used within a group of publications is mainly determined by the number and types of readers attracted to each one. That is, with the exception of direct response advertisers. Such advertisers do not need readership surveys because they are in the fortunate position of being able to judge the value of different publications by counting the number of replies they receive. For example, when a mail order advertiser in the *Sunday Times* Colour Supplement codes his coupon ST4, or invites readers to write to Dept. ST4, he is identifying the response to a particular advertisement. The measure of the response obtained in this way is not necessarily the full story, but it goes a long way to measuring the worth of an advertisement.

COMPARATIVE DATA ESSENTIAL

As explained, readership surveys are carried out to enable advertisers to identify which publications would be most suitable for their advertising. For this purpose all likely or 'candidate' publications need to be measured in a comparative manner, the advertiser wanting to know how many people read each of the publications on his candidate list and their demographic, product purchasing or personality/lifestyle characteristics.

There are many different surveys carried out to provide this information, some being sponsored by individual publications but most carried out on a joint basis by groups of publishers. For example, there is a survey which covers the readership of farming publications by farmers, another concerned with the readership of medical journals by doctors and a third covering the electronic press. In all such cases problems may arise not only in collecting accurate readership information, but in identifying the appropriate universe to be sampled. For doctors this is relatively easy because lists of doctors exist, while area sampling for farmers is also relatively simple to organise, but the problems of identifying those executives in industry who are involved in electronics and who are in a position to influence decisions about electronic products are easy to visualise.

The best known of all readership surveys, however, is the National Readership Survey, or NRS. This survey has been running continuously since 1956, but with many improvements introduced over the years. It is controlled by a body known as the Joint Industry Committee for National Readership Surveys (JICNARS) and is currently designed to measure the readership of over 200 national and regional newspapers and magazines.

The NRS occupies a central position for those concerned with the design and execution of readership surveys, not just in this country, but worldwide. It is by far the oldest and best established of all readership surveys, with many other surveys being modelled on its design and procedures. The NRS sample is also very strictly controlled and as a consequence many survey organisations use results taken from it to set quotas for their samples, especially those relating to social class.

THE NATIONAL READERSHIP SURVEY

The objective of the NRS, given at the front of every report is stated to be as follows:

THE NRS OBJECTIVE

The general objective of the National Readership Survey is to provide such information, acceptable to both publishers of print media and buyers of space, as will be most relevant to the assessment and efficient use of the medium. Among possible measures, this requires providing a basis for estimating the numbers and kinds of people likely to receive different patterns of potential exposure to advertisements inserted in individual publications or combinations of publications.

To meet this objective personal interviews are conducted with a randomly selected sample of adults aged 15 + selected from the Electoral Registers. Currently around 27 000 successful interviews are carried out every year, achieved from an original sample of 40 000 individuals, giving a success rate of 70%.

The main part of the interview is concerned with the collection of readership information. Later questions cover the types of information which advertisers need to identify their target markets, such as the sex and age of the respondent, the size of the household, social class, whether or not there are children in the household, car ownership, types of holidays taken, and so on.

(a)

'Sunday'*magazine with the*   News of the World
      News of the World

      Sunday Mirror   The People
                                           (Sunday People)

(b)

SUNDAY NEWSPAPERS
AND COLOUR MAGAZINES

'Sunday'*magazine with the*   News of the World
      News of the World

      Sunday Mirror   The People
                                           (Sunday People)

ALMOST ALWAYS	QUITE OFTEN	ONLY OCCASIONALLY	NOT IN THE PAST YEAR
At least 3 issues out of 4	At least 1 issue out of 4	Less than 1 issue out of 4	

Figure 5.1 Front (a) and reverse (b) of NRS prompt card

The completed NRS questionnaire is 21 pages long, but for illustrative purposes a copy of the readership questions is given as Appendix 5.1, while Appendix 5.2 shows the page of the questionnaire on which the information relating to Sunday newspapers and their colour supplements is recorded. Figure 5.7 shows one of the 40 prompt aid cards which are used, again relating to a selection of Sunday newspapers and their colour supplements.

It will be seen from Appendices 5.1 and 5.2 that three sets of questions are asked:

Question 1

These questions are designed to separate all publications covered by the survey into those which have been read or looked at for two minutes or more in the year before the interview and the remainder. This is a very coarse filter. It is designed to exclude only those cards which the respondent is quite sure contain no titles he or she has seen in the past year. The interviewer stresses to the respondent that it doesn't matter where the publication was seen, whose copy it was nor how old.

The fronts of the prompt cards are used to assist in this task. If the respondent has read or looked at any title on a prompt card that prompt card goes through to the next set of questions.

Question 2

This set of questions is designed to establish the frequency with which every title on an 'accepted' prompt card is read. The range of response options given to the respondent is as follows:

— almost always;
— quite often;
— only occasionally;
— not in the past year.

The reverse side of the prompt card is used to assist the respondent in this task. As will be seen from Figure 5.1, a numerical scale is added to the verbal scale to help the respondent decide which frequency position is most appropriate for each of the titles on the prompt card.

There are three points to note about this scale:

1. It is very short, with only three frequency options for any title read or looked at in the past year. The choice of such a short scale was quite deliberate. It was known from previous work that claims on any frequency scale will tend to bunch at either end of the scale, with few

respondents wanting to make a mid-frequency claim. It was also known that it was quite unrealistic to expect great precision from respondents when they are trying to estimate how often they read a newspaper or magazine. Someone might be expected to know whether it was a few or many copies out of ten, but not whether it was seven copies rather than eight out of ten.

Hence a short scale simplifies the respondent's task and is quite adequate for the purposes to which the data is put (see below).

2. The scale is worded so that it is equally relevent to all publications, no matter their frequency of issue. This is a very important point since the design of the survey sometimes requires publications with similar editorial content, but with different publication frequencies, to be grouped on the same card. For example, all gardening publications are put on the same card, some being published weekly and some monthly. If different frequency scales had been used this would have been very confusing for respondents, even though it might have been the case that a specific frequency scale was better for a particular publishing frequency group. Thus a scale:

—every day;
—most days;
—once or twice a week;
—less often;

might seem to be more appropriate for daily newspapers, but clearly it would not fit monthly magazines.

3 A response option 'Not in the past year' is incorporated in the scale. This option is necessary because the respondent may well have never read some of the titles included on an 'accepted' prompt card. Remember, a respondent was required to have read or looked at only one title on a card in the last year for it to be placed on the 'Yes' pile.

Question 3

For all publications read in the last year this question establishes when the last reading event took place. If this was within the issue period of the publication (yesterday for dailies, last week for weeklies, last month for monthlies, etc., the respondent is counted as an Average Issue Reader (AIR). When a readership figure for a publication is given it is this figure which is quoted.

The responses to the frequency questions, when used in conjunction with the basic AIR measures, enable schedule planners to compare alternative schedules on the basis of the coverage of the target market which each will achieve and the frequency of 'Opportunities To See' (OTS). The calculations necessary to obtain such coverage and frequency estimates are only possible with the aid of computers, with a number of computer bureaux in London specialising in such work.

What is a Reading Event

It will be seen from this description of the NRS that the only definitions of a reading event which are given to respondents are that:

(i) It must involve reading or looking at a publication for two minutes or more.

(ii) It doesn't matter who bought the publication, where it was seen or how old it was.

These are good working definitions which in practice do not seem to present any major problems in interpretation in the field. Nevertheless, many users of the data were worried because little was known about the way in which the respondents interpreted the questions they were asked. Were literally all reading events being included or did some respondents filter out events which they considered to be trivial? Was there a tendency for different types of events to be recalled with varying accuracy and, if so, which types of events benefitted and which ones suffered?

Were some respondents able to answer the questions more accurately than others and, if so, how did the accuracy vary (by sex, age and class, for example)?

Such considerations may not appear to be all that significant, until it is remembered that the results from the NRS are the main planning tool used when determining how the £1282 million spent in 1985 on display advertising in national and main regional newspapers and magazines should be allocated *between* publications, once the choice to use print has been made. This means that the results from media research studies are used very differently from the way other research studies are used. They very directly influence how large sums of money are spent (for example, an advertisement page in a magazine like *Woman* costs £11 000, in *Sunday* £24 000 or in the *Daily Telegraph* £22 000). For this reason the demands for accuracy in media research are far greater than is normally the case.

This concern as to what was being measured by the NRS lead JICNARS to establish a Study Group, under my chairmanship, to investigate the situation[1]. Initially the Group decided to tackle the task in the manner of a classic textbook research study. That is, we thought the best approach was to find out as much as possible about the nature of the activity which the NRS was intended to measure and, in the light of the knowledge so gained, design a set of questions which it was hoped would minimise inaccuracies in response.

In fact, if a study as important as the NRS was being designed today such work would almost certainly be done first, but the reality is that when the NRS was planned 30 years ago there was no appreciation of the need for such careful preparation in the wording of questions.

Since those early days of the NRS many aspects of the Survey have been investigated, especially in a study in 1960 by Dr W. Belson [2], but no enquiry has been undertaken which concentrated on the *nature* of the reading events being counted and, perhaps, missed.

The first action of the Study Group was to prepare a very loose brief for research companies, describing the objectives of a readership survey and asking them to put forward initial design proposals for a 'green-fields' project. As far as possible the researchers were asked to free their minds of any constraints which they might feel were imposed by the existing study.

Four very good submissions were received. One, though not really relevant to the brief, led directly to other improvements in the design of the NRS, so the exercise was certainly worthwhile for this alone, while the other three gave rise to much debate. However, in the end the reviews and evidence that were submitted, together with our own common sense, forced us to conclude that it would not be possible to devise a set of questions which could be expected to have a consistent interpretation across all types of publication covered by the Survey and for all individuals, no matter their age, sex, class, education level or where they live.

PRAGMATIC APPROACH PREFERRED

This being the case it was decided to turn the problem inside out. Instead of talking to people about their reading habits, in a small-scale qualitative way, and using this knowledge to attempt to improve the wording of the questions asked, we decided to take two separate measures of reading from NRS respondents, one using the standard approach and one using methods which were thought more accurate but impractical for the main Survey (called the yardstick measure), and to compare results. We could then attempt to identify discrepancies and examine their nature.

Though apparently straightforward this approach was by no means simple. There were three main problems which had to be resolved before we felt we had an acceptable design:

1. We had to satisfy ourselves that the separate yardstick measure was going to be as accurate as possible. We knew we could be more demanding than would be possible in the on-going survey, but we had to have confidence that there was no way in which it could be significantly improved. We strove for the 'ultimate' measure. After

considerable debate we decided that the best approach was the simplest one. We would invite all respondents, irrespective of their responses during the NRS interview, to go through a publication page by page until they could be certain whether or not they had seen it previously. Further, a positive claim had to be supported by the respondent being able to provide background information about whose copy was being read, where, when and for how long. About 5% of initial positive claims were subsequently rejected because the reading event was too vague in the respondent's mind for him or her to be able to answer these further questions.

2 We had to decide which publication groups should be covered by the research. Greatest doubt about the accuracy and meaning of the NRS results centred on the monthly and less frequently issued publications, because of the longer time periods covered by the questions and because of the greater importance of casual reading, but for the same reasons we knew that such publications would give us the greatest problems in the conduct and interpretation of the yardstick questions. It would have meant tackling the most difficult task first.

On the other hand, few doubts were expressed about the results for the daily newspapers, so although they would have been the easiest group to research the benefit was likely to be least. Hence it was decided that the first study should cover the Sunday newspapers and their colour supplements.

This decision was also influenced by cost considerations. We knew that if it was possible to carry out the research by asking a limited number of additional questions at the end of the main NRS interview this would be considerably cheaper than the alternative of conducting a separate follow-up interview two or three days after the main one. Sunday newspapers and their colour supplements fitted this requirement.

3. With most publication groups, a third problem area is to decide the age of the issues to be used to provide the yardstick measure. If they are too young some tail-end reading will be lost, while if they are too old some of the early contacts will have been forgotten. However, by working with Sunday newspapers and their colour supplements we would minimise this problem since other research[3] had shown that the reading life of these publications was very short. This meant that we could use issues that were around one week old without the risk of losing any significant level of reading.

DESIGN OF STUDY

The additional yardstick questions were asked at the end of all NRS interviews carried out in England and Wales throughout the month of May 1984.

Scotland was omitted because the Sunday publications in that area are very different from the rest of the country.

The follow-up questions covered either three or four publications. Each interviewer carried one issue of the appropriate set of titles published on the Sunday eight days before the start of the interviewing period, which ran for six days Monday to Saturday. (See Bar 1 in Figure 5.2).

The interview started by handing the respondent the three or four issues being checked, asking them to take time and sort the issues into two groups, those that had been seen previously and those not seen. For each title seen four further questions, as already listed, were asked to establish further details about the reading event. They sought to establish whose copy was being read, where the reading took place, when and for how long it lasted.

These questions had two purposes. They acted to verify the claim made at the start of the follow-up interview that an issue had been seen and they provided information on the nature of the reading event which had taken place. If they could not be satisfactorily answered it was decided that the initial claim to have read the issue had been in error and the claim was rejected.

In addition to these further questions, a spread traffic check was carried out on up to two issues which the respondent claimed to have read or looked at. It was intended that this information would further help to calibrate the reading events recorded and missed by the NRS.

Around 400 interviews were carried out for each of the eight newspapers and six supplements covered by the research. The supplements were always covered at the same time as their parent newspaper.

ALLOWING FOR GENUINE DIFFERENCES IN RESPONSE

The two sets of questions described in the previous section produced two measure of readership, namely:

(i) *AIR—Average Issue Readership*. The main measure produced by the NRS, as already described.

(ii) *SIR—Specific Issue Readership*. The measure resulting from the additional questions.

These two measures are clearly measuring different things, but because the reading life for the publications chosen for this research is short and because of the careful balancing of the age of the issues being used against the timing of the interviews it was expected that the majority of responses would be in agreement. Either both an AIR and SIR claim would be made, or neither.

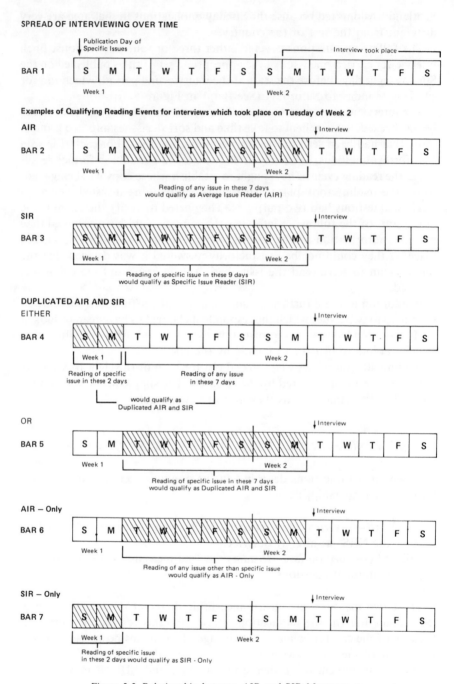

Figure 5.2 Relationship between AIR and SIR Measures

There would, however, be some instances where the claims would be in conflict, as is shown in Figure 5.2.

In this illustration:

—*Bar 1* shows the relationship between the period of interviewing and the publication day of the issues being checked.

—*Bar 2* shows how a respondent would qualify as an AIR reader (Average Issue Reader)—that is, a reader as normally measured by the NRS.

—*Bar 3* shows how a respondent would qualify as an SIR reader (Specific Issue Reader)—that is, they had read the specific issue being used for the yardstick measure.

—*Bar 4 and 5* show how a respondent could qualify as a reader from both the standard NRS and yardstick questions.

—*Bar 6* shows how a respondent could qualify as an AIR reader, but not as a SIR one. In the tables they are identified as AIR-only.

—*Bar 7* shows the opposite case, i.e. how a respondent could qualify as having read the specific issue more than a week before the interview and had not read the subsequent issue—that is, they qualify as a SIR— only reader.

Apart from the genuine differences in response, which will occur for the reasons described in Bars 6 and 7, there will be other discrepancies revealed which are due to inaccurate reporting during the first NRS interview. Reading events which should have been reported will have been overlooked or reading claims will be made which should not have been made.

The purpose of the study was to deduce the size and nature of these inaccuracies.

SUMMARY OF RESULTS

The nature of the study meant that no conclusions could be drawn with total certainty. However, the Study Group was able to make judgements with what was felt to be a high level of accuracy, especially when the analyses by frequency of reading were taken into account. (There is no absolute truth in any form of readership research.) Their findings were as follows:

(a) The NRS succeeds in providing good measures of the readerships of Sunday newspapers and their colour supplements, neither including a significant number of trivial contacts, nor missing many worthwhile ones.

(b) If anything, the study underestimates the true readership levels, by 3%, on average, for Sunday newspapers and 6% for the supplements.

(c) This last point is illustrated in Table 5.1. Theoretically the SIR figure should always be lower than (or equal to) the AIR one, because the SIR estimate will miss any reading which takes place later in the reading tail than the age of the copy being checked. However, it will be seen from Table 5.1 that the actual position is the reverse. In total, the SIR claims exceeds AIR.

Since we are working on the assumption that the SIR measure provides the best possible yardstick the conclusion must be that the AIR measure, that is, the one which is published in the NRS reports, is an under-estimate.

(d) When the result is analysed for the two reading frequency groups it will be seen that the patterns are quite different. For those respondents who claimed, during the main NRS interview, to read 'almost always' the AIR level exceeded the SIR one by an amount which was greater than we expected. Remember, these are claims being made by regular

TABLE 5.1   Relationship between AIR and SIR Claims

| | | NRS Frequency | | |
	Total	Almost always	Quite often/ Occasionally	Not in past year
Newspapers				
All potential claims(*)	3292	502	397	2393
All AIR claims	545	462	83	0
All SIR claims	564	419	89	56
Difference %	+3%	−9%	+7%	+10%**
Duplicated AIR and SIR claims	438	403	35	0
As % of AIR	80%	87%	42%	0%
AIR only claims	107	59	48	0
As % of AIR	20%	13%	58%	0%
SIR only claims	126	16	54	56
As % of AIR	23%	3%	65%	10%**
Colour Supplements				
All potential claims	2445	283	287	1875
All AIR claims	314	254	60	0
All SIR claims	332	221	69	42
Difference %	+6%	−13%	+15%	+13%**
Duplicated AIR and SIR claims	237	210	27	0
As % of AIR	75%	83%	45%	0%
AIR only claims	77	44	33	0
As % of AIR	25%	17%	55%	0%
SIR only claims	95	11	42	42
As % of AIR	30%	4%	70%	13%**

*May 1984 NRS sample, excluding Scotland; **Based on total AIR claims

readers and refer to newspapers; it is surely most unlikely that 9% of them would have delayed their Sunday newspaper reading for at least eight days after publication, which is what would have had to happen for this result to be right. A much more likely explanation is that a proportion of these regular readers were answering in terms of their normal behaviour, forgetting that the week before their NRS interview they had broken their pattern of normal behaviour and not read their Sunday newspaper and its supplement.

Hence the conclusion is that the NRS results contain an element of over-claiming by regular readers. Such a conclusion is in line with general market research experience that respondents will sometimes answer in terms of normal rather than actual behaviour.

(e) In contrast, the SIR results for occasional readers exceed the AIR claims. Theoretically this cannot occur, the most likely explanation, deduced from the detailed information on the reading events, being that the AIR level was an under-estimate because respondents had forgotten a proportion of their reading of non-household copies away from home. Typically this would be waiting room and similar casual reading.

(f) Table 5.2 shows the amount of reading carried out by these different groups of respondents, as measured by spread traffics. That is, the proportion of all spreads in the publication which the respondent claims to have read or looked at.

Such a measure is important to advertisers because it is directly related to the measure which particularly interests them, namely what is the probability that an advertisement will be seen.

Three interesting conclusions can be drawn from this table:

1. The levels are high. This is clearly important to advertisers. If they place an advertisement in a publication they clearly want to be sure that it will have a fair chance of being seen.
2. The levels for AIR claimants are higher than those for the SIR-only ones. This is important, since it means that the readerships which the NRS over-estimates are more important to advertisers than those which are under-estimated.
3. The levels for the regular readers are higher than those for the occasional ones. This means that, as a generalisation, regular readers are more valuable to advertisers than occasional ones because they will have a higher probability of seeing the advertisements in the publication.

As a result, the conclusion is that the NRS readership measure incorporates to a slight extent advertisement exposure probabilities, since we have already seen that reading by regular readers tends to be over-claimed and that by occasional readers under-claimed.

TABLE 5.2 Claimed Spread Traffic

	NRS Frequency											
	Total			Almost always			Quite often/ Occasionally			Not in past year		
Newspapers	(a)	(b)	(c)	(a)	(b)	(c)	(a)	(b)	(c)	(a)	(b)	(c)
	%	%	%	%	%	%	%	%	%	%	%	%
All SIR claims covered*	525	411	114	396	380	16	81	31	50	48		
Proportion of spreads seen %	70	74	57	74	75	63	60	65	57	54		
Colour Supplements												
	%	%	%	%	%	%	%	%	%	%	%	%
All SIR claims covered (*)	305	221	84	208	197	11	63	24	39	34		
Proportion of spreads seen (%)	71	74	63	75	75	63	64	66	62	62		

(a) Total SIR claims; (b) Duplicated AIR and SIR claims; (c) SIR-only claims
(*) To avoid overloading the respondent an upper limit was imposed upon the number of issues covered by the spread traffic check. Hence the difference between the 564 newspaper SIR claims and the 525 newspapers covered by the spread traffic check and the 332 and 305 supplement claims.

(g) The right-hand columns in Tables 5.1 and 5.2 show that a significant number of SIR claims were made by respondents who had reported during their NRS interview that they had not read that publication in the past year. Further, from Table 5.2, it can be seen that the actual amount of reading carried out by these respondents was not all that much lower than the average level. Clearly the filters at Question 1 or 2 in the NRS interview should not have excluded such respondents, thus highlighting the risks in any market research interview that early filters will wrongly exclude from subsequent questions a proportion of respondents who should have been included.

GENERAL IMPLICATIONS

1. These results can be taken to be good for market research in general. The JICNARS Meaning of Reading Study subjected the NRS results for two publication groups to a demanding and detailed scrutiny, but they emerged with a clean bill of health.
2. Some errors were revealed, but they were relatively small and tended to cancel out since they operated in different directions. In fact, it would appear that when the amount of a publication read is taken into account the NRS actually provides a better measure of what the users of the data want than had been appreciated in the first place.

   The problem of errors, which may well operate in different directions, is not, however, unique to readership research. The outcome of this study underlines the importance to all market researchers of minimising the risk of errors by paying careful attention to the wording of questions, the flow of the questionnaire and the instructions to the interviewer.

REFERENCES

1. *An Investigation into the Reading Behaviour Measured by the NRS.* 1985 JICNARS, 44 Belgrave Square, London SW1X 8QS.
2. Belson, W.A. Studies in Readership, Business Publications Ltd. (1962).
3. A Media Involvement Study, 1984 MMG Group of Publishers, PPA, 15–19 Kingsway, London, WC2B 6UN.

ACKNOWLEDGMENT

The author is grateful to the Joint Industry Committee for National Readership Surveys (JICNARS) for making available the material on which this article is based. This chapter is reproduced by permission of JICNARS.

APPENDIX 5.1 READERSHIP QUESTIONS FROM NRS READERSHIP SURVEY

NATIONAL READERSHIP SURVEY

SORT CARDS INTO NUMERICAL ORDER, NUMBERED FACE UPWARDS

Introduction

We want to find out about the newspapers and magazines you have read at all in the past year. I should like you to look through each of these cards in turn. As soon as you see any publication on a card that you can remember reading at all in the past year, please put that card on this pile. If you are sure you have not read any of the publications on a card in the past year, please put that card here. If you are not sure about a card, put it aside and we shall come back to it later.

EXPLAIN

It doesn't matter who bought the publication, where you saw it or how old it was. Just so long as you can remember spending a couple of minutes reading or looking at *any* of the publications on a card in the past year it goes on this pile.

HAND OVER FIRST CARD (CARD 1, DAILIES OR SUNDAYS DEPENDING ON ORDER SPECIFIED)

Q.1 Now, have you read or looked at any of these newspapers in the past 12 months?

IF 'YES' PUT ON "YES-PILE"

IF 'NO' PUT ON "NO-PILE"

IF 'NOT SURE' PUT ON 'NOT-SURE PILE'

HAND OVER ALL OTHER CARDS AND ALLOW INFORMANT TO SORT INTO 'YES—SEEN IN PAST YEAR', 'NO—NOT SEEN' AND 'NOT SURE'.

WHEN INFORMANT HAS SORTED ALL CARDS, HAND OVER 'NOT SURE' CARDS AND PROBE.

I should like you to look through these cards again — What is the problem?

EXPLAIN AS NECESSARY. IF STILL IN DOUBT, PUT ON 'YES' PILE

TAKE 'YES' CARDS (FOR CODING). HAND OVER 'NO' CARDS AGAIN

While I am recording these, would you make sure there aren't any other publications you have read or looked at in the past year on each of the other cards. Just to remind you, it doesn't matter who bought it, where you saw it or how old it was so long as you spent at least a couple of minutes reading or looking at it in the past year.

CODE ALL 'YES' CARDS (USE CODE '1') WHILE INFORMANT IS RE-CHECKING 'NO' CARDS. CODE ADDITIONAL 'YES' CARDS AS APPROPRIATE (USE CODE '2' FOR ADDITIONAL 'YES' CARDS)

BEFORE ASKING Q.2, SORT 'YES' CARDS BACK INTO NUMERICAL ORDER AND PUT 'NO' CARDS AWAY

Introduction

Now I should like you to tell me how often you read the papers and magazines you remember seeing in the past year and when you last read or looked at them.

HAND OVER FIRST 'YES' CARD TURNED OVER TO SHOW FREQUENCY

ASK Q.2 AND Q.3 FOR EACH 'YES' CARD BEFORE GOING TO NEXT CARD

Q.2a) Which of these newspapers/ magazines do you read or look at almost always? (FOR FIRST CARD AND OTHER CARDS AS APPROPRIATE—I mean at least 3 issues out of 4)

> CODE APPLICABLE
> PUBLICATIONS UNDER (a)

b) Which do you read or look at quite often?

> CODE APPLICABLE
> PUBLICATIONS UNDER (b)

c) And which have you read or looked at only occasionally in the past year?

> CODE APPLICABLE
> PUBLICATIONS UNDER (c)

> ASK FOR EACH OTHER TITLE
> ON 'YES' CARD NOT CODED
> UNDER Q.2a), b) or c).

d) Have you read or looked at any issue of . . . in the past year? And . . .?

> IF 'NO' CODE '0' UNDER d)

> IF 'YES' PROBE:

Would that be almost always . . . Quite often . . . Only occasionally?

> CODE AS APPROPRIATE
> UNDER a), b) OR c)

> ASK FOR SAME CARD

Q.3a) Which, if any, of these newspapers/magazines did you read or look at 'yesterday' ('Saturday' FOR MONDAY INTERVIEWS—BUT FOR SUNDAY NEWSPAPERS AND COLOUR MAGAZINES ALWAYS ASK "yesterday")

> EXPLAIN:

I mean you spent at least 2 minutes reading or looking at any copy.

> CODE APPLICABLE
> PUBLICATIONS UNDER a)

b) Which others have you read or looked at on or since: last . . . day? (NAME DAY OF INTERVIEW)

> IF 'TODAY' ASK 'Apart
> from today?'

> CODE APPLICABLE
> PUBLICATIONS UNDER b)

> FOR EACH OTHER TITLE CODED
> UNDER a), b) or c) AT Q.2 (i.e. not
> coded '0')

c) When did you last read or look at any copy of . . .?

> IF 'TODAY' ASK 'Apart
> from today?'

> PROBE AND CODE
> ACCORDINGLY UNDER c)
> OR b) IF APPLICABLE)

> WHEN FIRST 'YES' CARD
> IS COMPLETED FOR Q.2 AND
> Q.3 ETC. FOR ALL 'YES' CARDS
> IN TURN

APPENDIX 5.2   SPECIMEN ANSWER PAGE FROM NRS QUESTIONNAIRE

FOR EACH 'YES' CARD ASK Q.2 AND Q.3 BEFORE GOING TO NEXT 'YES' CARD

2(a) Which of these newspapers/magazines do you read or look at almost always?

CODE ACCORDINGLY

(b) Which do you read or look at quite often?

CODE ACCORDINGLY

(c) And which have you read or looked at only occasionally in the past year?

CODE ACCORDINGLY

FOR REMAINDER OF TITLES ON 'YES' CARD:

(d) Have you read or looked at any issue of . . . in the past year?

IF 'NO' CODE '0', IF 'YES' ASK:

Would that be almost always . . . quite often . . . only occasionally?

CODE ACCORDINGLY

Sundays/Colour Magazines

3(a) Which, if any, of these newspapers/magazines did you read or look at yesterday?

EXPLAIN: 'at least 2 minutes reading or looking at any copy'

CODE ACCORDINGLY

(b) Which others have you read or looked at on or since last . . . day? (NAME DAY) (apart from today)

CODE ACCORDINGLY

FOR REMAINDER OF TITLES ON 'YES' CARD (UNLESS CODED '0' AT Q.2):

(c) When did you last read or look at any copy . . .? (apart from today)

CODE ACCORDINGLY

BN(1–3   SN(4–9)   CC18(10–11)   3(12)

Q.1 'Yes' CARD seen in past year	Publications	Q.2 (a) Almost always	(b) Quite often	(c) Only occ.	(d) Not past year	Q.3 (a) Yest	(b) Past 7 days	Past 4 wks	(c) Past 3 mnths	Longer ago	
(33)	*Card 39*										
1	*Telegraph* Sunday Magazine..........	1	2	3	0	5	6	7	8	9	(37)
	Sunday Telegraph..................	1	2	3	0	5	6	7	8	9	(36)
2	*Sunday Express* Magazine...........	1	2	3	0	5	6	7	8	9	(35)
	Sunday Express....................	1	2	3	0	5	6	7	8	9	(34)

Q.1		Q.2				Q.3					
'Yes'		(a)	(b)	(c)	(d)	(a)	(b)	(c)			
CARD seen in past year	Publications	Almost always	Quite often	Only occ.	Not past year	Yest	Past 7 days	Past 4 wks	Past 3 mnths	Longer ago	
(27)	*Card 40*										
1	*Sunday Times* Magazine	1	2	3	0	5	6	7	8	9	(31)
	Sunday Times	1	2	3	0	5	6	7	8	9	(30)
2	*Observer* magazine	1	2	3	0	5	6	7	8	9	(29)
	The Observer	1	2	3	0	5	6	7	8	9	(28)
(20)	*Card 41*										
	Sunday Today	1	2	3	0	5	6	7	8	9	(25)
1	*You* (Mail on Sunday Magazine	1	2	3	0	5	6	7	8	9	(24)
	The Mail on Sunday	1	2	3	0	5	6	7	8	9	(23)
2	*Sunday Post* (Scotland)	1	2	3	0	5	6	7	8	9	(22)
	Sunday Mail (Scotland)	1	2	3	0	5	6	7	8	9	(21)
(13)	*Card 42*										
1	*Sunday* (NoW Magazine)	1	2	3	0	5	6	7	8	9	(17)
	News of the World	1	2	3	0	5	6	7	8	9	(16)
2	*The People* (Sunday People)	1	2	3	0	5	6	7	8	9	(15)
	Sunday Mirror	1	2	3	0	5	6	7	8	9	(14)
(40)	*Card 43*										
1	*Sunday Sun* (Newcastle)	1	2	3	0	5	6	7	8	9	(43)
	Sunday Mercury (Birmingham)	1	2	3	0	5	6	7	8	9	(42)
2	*Sunday Independent* (Plymouth)	1	2	3	0	5	6	7	8	9	(41)

Space to (76)   JN (77–80)

Applied Marketing and Social Research 2nd Edition
Edited by Ute Bradley
©Copyright John Wiley 1987

6. *Ad-Hoc Pricing Research*

Rory P. Morgan   *RBL (Research International) Ltd.*

Pricing has always been an important and difficult area for market research. Many developments in methodology have taken place and this chapter fully discusses the issues involved in *ad-hoc* pricing research. The detailed examples illustrate how knowledge of these issues translate to specific choices of methodology in particular market situations.

Detailed references are provided.

INTRODUCTION

The research techniques currently available for *ad hoc* pricing problems have come a long way since the early days of the 50s and 60s. Partly this is due to the growth of a number of significant trends in the marketing arena (e.g. the economic climate, 'consumerism', centralisation of the retail trade, to name but a few), but also to the growing sophistication of the market research industry, and a better knowledge of the ways in which consumers actually make purchasing decisions.

On the other hand, while *ad-hoc* techniques have become more sophisticated, so has the appreciation of the strengths and weaknesses of alternative approaches when applied to different marketing problems and markets. Even in the computer age, there is no methodology that can be taken 'off the shelf' and applied willy-nilly without some consideration of the issues involved. Nor is there (typically!) a perfect solution. The skill of the researcher, and the wisdom of the marketeer, lies in identifying the main features of the market and the problem in hand, and tailoring the methodology to suit the constraints imposed. Often, compromises must be made.

AVAILABLE TECHNIQUES

Broadly speaking, the techniques available for pricing research fall into distinct approaches, as summarised in Figure 6.1[1]. Two quite distinct schools of thought operate.

Monadic Tests

The first approach attempts to measure a consumer's reaction to price for an item (brand, service or whatever) in a monadic way, with no consideration made of alternatives at other prices. Thus the respondent task (from a psychological point of view) assumes the decision making process to be an absolute one, given certain pricing conditions applying.

In fact, the simplest (and oldest) price testing technique along these lines is a monadic 'Buy' rating scale (with labelled categories ranging from 'I would definitely buy' to 'I would definitely not buy'), on which a respondent faced with a product set at a single price indicates his or her likelihood of purchasing the product at that price. This method is often incorporated into many concept and product tests, where the stimulus product is fully branded. However, although adequate as a measure of overall acceptability, the scale on its own can hardly be regarded as a specific pricing measure, and many researchers regard it as suffering from a number of critical problems; of which the two most pressing are firstly, that it generally must be evaluated in the context of past normative data, and secondly, that it does not allow in its single scale form the testing of other prices both above and below the one explicitly presented. For this reason, other approaches evolved over time with the *specific* aim of researching price.

As an example, a technique devised originally by Gabor and Granger in 1965,[2] presents respondents with a set of randomised price cards, and asks them to consider a particular product at these prices. For each price, the respondent is asked to state whether he or she would purchase. From the aggregated data, the percentages claiming to purchase at each price can be displayed graphically, providing a 'demand curve' that is the *ad-hoc* analogy to that provided by classical econometric methods, and from which some estimate of the 'elasticity of demand' can be made. In economics, this 'elasticity' is usually calculated as the percentage change in demand — or the percentage claiming to buy — resulting from a single percentage point change in price. As will be appreciated, in a non-linear relationship between demand and price (or where the slope of the curve is not constant) this value will change according to the point on the curve where it is measured.

Case History 1 is illustrated in Figure 6.2, which was obtained by applying this technique to a toiletries market. For this study, 200 users of a certain

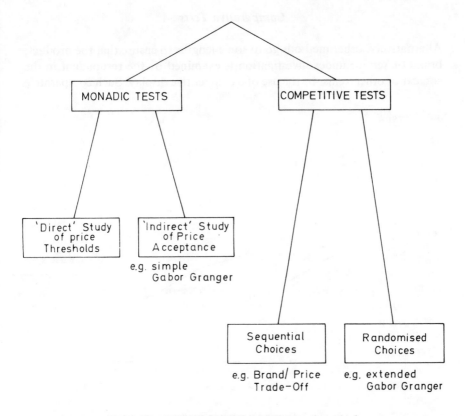

Figure 6.1 A classification of pricing research methods

toiletries product were recruited to take part in an in-hall test, the sample being subject to quota controls on demographics, as well as usual brand usage. For the pricing part of the study, respondents were shown the concept for a new product, together with a 'mock-up' of the pack. Following this, they were then presented with a sequence of randomised prices (ten prices were considered in total) and for each price, their likelihood of purchasing the product on a five-point 'I would buy' scale was recorded. Note that the order of presentation of prices was rotated between respondents.

Figure 6.2 therefore contains the percentages of this sample who replied in either of the top two 'buy' categories, analysed in total, and for users of two brands in the market, X and Y. (Note that the study included brands other than X and Y, therefore X and Y do not sum to the total sample in Figure 6.2). As can be seen, sub-analysis of different product user groups revealed marked differences in sensitivity to price, with users of X exhibiting considerably greater sensitivity to price in the lower end of the price spectrum compared to users of Y.

Comparative Tests

Alternatively, other methods go to some lengths to ensure that the product, brand or service under investigation is examined by the respondent in the context of other items, by the use of a competitive display. Such comparative

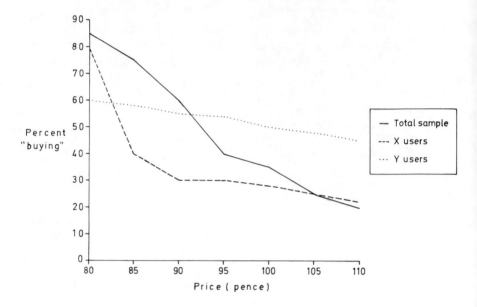

Figure 6.2 Demand curves for a toiletries product

approaches are often preferred by researchers, since they allow, to a greater degree, pricing judgements to be made by respondents with reference to alternative options, which is clearly nearer 'real-life' in many situations.

The simplest of these is an extension of the Gabor-Granger method described above—the only difference being that the randomised stimuli contain not one priced product, but a range of products.[3]

Another common technique using this approach is that of Brand/Price Trade-Off or BPTO.[4] In this, respondents are faced with a competitive display of products, each of which is priced. Given this display, the respondent is asked for his or her most likely purchase under those circumstances. This price for the chosen item is then raised by one level—the others remaining the same—and the question repeated. The process ends when the price range being evaluated is exhausted, or when the respondent refuses to 'buy' further.

Unlike the Gabor-Granger approach discussed earlier, the data is not analysed by simple aggregation of responses, but by the construction of a computer model, in which the most probable choice of every respondent under all possible combinations of product and price is stored. Demand curves are generated using this model by performing a series of sequential 'simulations', in which the price set for a target product is successively incremented, while all other products remain at fixed prices (usually current market values). Each simulation provides brand share estimates, so that the predicted shares for all products can be plotted, in addition to that for the product being researched. This analysis thus provides a means of establishing the likely switching patterns, or gains and losses, resulting from price movements. An account of the theory of this method and its derivation is given in Lunn and Morgan.[5]

Case History 2 is illustrated in Figure 6.3, which is a demand curve derived from a BPTO model for a relaunched alcoholic drink. For this study, a quota sample of 250 frequent buyers of the product field was recruited to take part in an in-hall pricing study. (In this case, purchasers of own-label spirit were excluded.) Each respondent was asked for his or her usual source of purchase, and only those brands known to be available at those places were shown to that respondent—thus controlling for variability of patterns of distribution. The standard BPTO elicitation procedure was adopted—that is, respondents were shown a priced display of their *evoked set* of brands (which always included the relaunched brand of interest), each of which was priced. Starting at a predefined pricing scenario, respondents were asked to specify the brand/price option they were most likely to buy under the pricing conditions displayed. After each choice, the price for *that item* was incremented, and the question repeated. The resulting data was analysed on RBL's FOCUS software, and a computer model constructed.

Figure 6.3 shows a series of simulations conducted on this model, with competitor brands A and B kept constant at their market price levels, while that for the relaunched brand was successively incremented. As can be seen, as the price rises, the share for the product falls. What is of interest however, are the gains made by competitors, since it is clear that one competitor (B) benefits more than the other (A).

SELECTING AND ADAPTING TECHNIQUES FOR MARKETS

In most cases and in practice, a researcher would need to tailor the methodologies described above to account for the particular features of his or her market. While in many situations this is straightforward, there exist pitfalls for the unwary, and it is generally worthwhile making a fundamental examination of the issues involved that could potentially determine the methodology chosen.

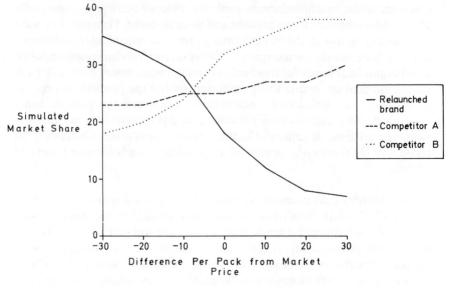

Figure 6.3 Relaunch of an alcoholic beverage

Problems Concerning the Market Context

Is the Market 'Diffuse' or 'Well-defined'?

Some markets are characterised by being 'well-defined', in the sense that the competition to any brand can easily be specified (e.g. washing powder, or the whisky market described earlier). These markets lend themselves to techniques using competitive displays, since the basic assumption is of a fixed-size market, where the major interest is potential changes in market share. Other markets (e.g. convenience foods) are much less easy to define in terms of competition, and different techniques (typically monadic) may have to be used. Moreover, in situations where price changes are expected to alter the *size* of the total market (either by forcing consumers to cease purchasing any product, or by encouraging new entrants), competitive methods are clearly inappropriate.

The Nature of the Competition

This is an extremely important issue for the research if the intention is to use competitive displays. In diffuse markets, it is worth starting out with a working definition of what is meant by the term. For example, many marketing companies have been misled into assuming that product X 'competes' with product Y because it is similar in respect of brand share, product image positioning, weight of advertising, quality, price, overall distribution levels, and so on. In fact, the manufacturer of product Y may agree with this assumption. However, this may not be the case. It may compete in industrial terms, but a better definition would examine to what extent the two (or more) products are likely to be seen by consumers as alternatives, given a need.

Another problem arising from this concerns patterns of retail distribution, since researchers intending to put two products together in a competitive display should first check that consumers typically do have the choice of either at their usual place of purchase. This, of course, is another definition of competition. One way of solving this problem for competitive methods is to adjust the display for each respondent, to replicate as far as possible for the purpose of the exercise those brands normally available.

The Extent of Brand Loyalty

In some markets, the concept of a 'usual user of brand X' is misleading, since consumers may move through a repertoire of acceptable brands, where purchasing is probabilistic, and this may reflect a search for novelty or change (e.g. confectionery). In others, consumers may exhibit less switching in the short run, and short-term brand loyalty may be more apparent (e.g. cigarettes).

Dependence on Occasion

Purchasing in some product fields is known to be very dependent on the underlying occasion, and products can be bought for a variety of occasions (e.g. foods for entertaining vs. normal family use, or perfumes for office vs. evening wear). These occasions are essentially then 'sub-markets', since the criteria for choice, brand preferences, and the price sensitivities exhibited, may differ. In these cases, it may be necessary to sample for particular occasions, and put the respondent very specifically in the purchasing context of those occasions. If the market is known to feature a significant amount of gift purchasing, separate sampling may again be needed to cover patterns of purchaser/recipient, possibly by occasion.

Awareness and Distribution

In some markets (and for some brands) it is unreasonable to expect respondents to deliver judgements on brands that they have never heard of, or even if they have, that are not available where they normally do their shopping. In most fast-moving grocery markets, adjustments must be made to the technique to take acount of this.

Case History 3   This aspect was considered earlier, in *Case History 2*. However, to further illustrate this, in a recent example of a BPTO conducted in the sauces and condiments market (*Case History 3*), it was known that distribution of brands varied enormously across retail outlets. In order that each respondent was not presented with brands that would not normally be present at the point of sale, an '*evoked set*' of brands was created specifically for each respondent, reflecting the pattern of distribution at her usual place of purchase. Thus, although the full BPTO model contained around 20 brands, each respondent only examined at most seven brands, which were the most relevant brands in her case.

Price Variation

In addition, substantial variation in actual prices according to outlet type can cause problems (especially for monadic tests), since the reaction of a consumer to a price will depend on the prices they are accustomed to at their usual source of purchase. In these cases, the Recommended Retailers Price (RRP) may be an unwise choice to use in research, since it will be used by the trade in different ways. Thus, for some respondents it will be expensive, and for others cheap.

In view of this, some researchers have experimented with the simple expedient of asking the respondent for the price he or she usually pays for a product, and presenting a monadic set of prices for the test product adjusted to a constant relative differential to this. Unfortunately, apart from the problems this presents to the interviewer, there is considerable evidence that respondents have (typically) poor recall of prices paid.

Consequently, a common solution to this problem is to recruit separate parallel samples of shoppers of different stores, whose price structure is known in advance. Thus, each sample can be presented with prices specifically adjusted to their retail environment.

Realism of Point of Sale

In the 'simulated buying' approaches typical of comparative methods, we ask respondents to consider a mock display of products. But how realistic should this be? Should we replicate pack facings? Should we use real packs or photographs? (Real packs are fine for, say, canned peas, but present logistical problems for washing machines). In short, have we really recreated the decision environment? Displays may be an acceptable approximation in many markets, but may be inadequate in situations where the purchasing context is all-important (e.g. draught beer in pubs, or soft drinks after sport) or where it is difficult for respondents to summon up the criteria that prompted an impulse purchase (e.g. ice-cream in cinemas).

Own Labels

In many markets, a decision must be taken whether to include 'Own labels' in the research. In some cases, own labels are virtually brands in their own right (e.g. packet teas). If they are to be included, however, potential problems arise. Not all consumers have the opportunity to purchase them, and where they do, they may have to be tailored to the respondent (i.e. show Sainsbury's own label to a Sainsbury shopper, Tesco's own label to a Tesco shopper, and so on). This is particularly important in markets where consumers discriminate between the quality or price of different own labels, but it makes the fieldwork and analysis more difficult.

Problems concerning the Product Field

Type of Decision

Some products tend to stimulate deliberation and more purposeful choice among consumers (e.g. margarine), whereas others are more at the mercy of impulse (e.g. snack foods). As has been suggested above, the very nature of a market research interview tends to make respondents more deliberative, and hence 'simulated shopping environments' tend to suit non-impulse areas.

Need for Information?

As an extension of the preceding point, some markets are characterised by a great deal of consideration (e.g. audio equipment, and consumer durables in general) before purchasing. In fact, many researchers recognise a period preceding the purchase in which the consumer collects information (such as from specialist magazines and colleagues/friends) in order to form an opinion. They are also often more receptive to advertising during this period.

In view of this, a common restriction is often placed on sampling, so that only those consumers who have actually made a purchase in the recent past are interviewed. However, it is also possible to 'recreate' the information-gathering process. For example, in a pricing study conducted in the motor car market, respondents were asked to read magazines and brochures containing reviews and price lists before the interview proper.

Multiple Purchases

In markets where multiple purchasing (i.e. the purchase of more than one pack at a purchasing occasion) is common, problems can arise, since it may not be the unit price that is relevant, but the total outlay over a number of packs. In this case, a common trade-off for the consumer may be between more packs of a cheaper product against fewer packs of a dearer one. The decision may also depend on the ultimate end-use of the product (e.g. DIY paints and the decorating task in hand) or different uses within the home (e.g. toilet tissue bought for more than one bathroom).

Clearly, the problem area suggests a comparative approach with a competitive display rather than a monadic approach. However, the BPTO method would have been inappropriate, since the models constructed do not typically take into account multiple purchasing. An extended Gabor-Granger method would be preferable, since for each pricing scenario presented to the respondent, it would be possible to ask not only for which brands would be purchased, but also how many of each.

Case History 4 is an example of how this approach can be used to measure likely changes in market volume for different product categories as prices change, using an extended Gabor-Granger approach in the hot drinks market. The problem centred around substantial increases in the cost of raw materials, and there was some fear that the inevitable price rises would cause consumers to opt out of the market.

In this case, given the lack of market definition, and the difficulty of employing quota sample controls, a representative sample of 300 housewives was recruited in-home. In the course of the questionnaire, respondents were asked to consider 25 price scenarios in turn, each containing a wide variety of product types (tea, coffee, malt drinks, chocolate and so on). For each scenario, they were asked to state their likely purchasing for each item, in terms of the number of packs likely to be bought over a month. From this, it was possible to tabulate and graph the volume implications of a number of pricing possibilities for the product field in question. This is shown in Figure 6.4, and as can be seen, the share of the product fell very little even with a 40% price rise. (On the other hand, it also gained very little as its price fell relative to competition.) This confirmed the view that the product field was characterised by strong product field loyalty, and that consumers were unlikely to opt out as prices rose.

Differential Use-Up Rates

It is common to find from consumer panel data that in many fast-moving grocery markets, the quantity of product purchased over time is independent of the brands chosen. This is because the product has a 'unitary use' — it can only be used so many times (e.g. foods). However, other markets are characterised by the fact that the rate at which repeat purchasing occurs will very much depend on the brand chosen, since brands differ in terms of usage life (e.g. radio batteries, or washing-up liquid). Here, the consumer must trade-off the price against the expected length of service. This can be a

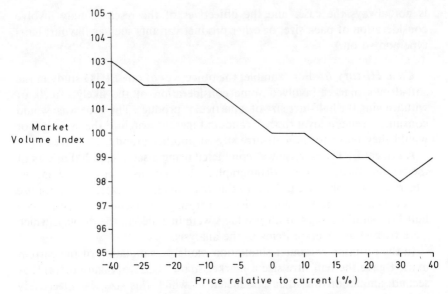

Figure 6.4 Market volume for a hot drink product

problem in *ad hoc* pricing models where a volume share prediction is required, and the model must be constructed accordingly.

Case History 5 As an example, to cater for this problem in a BPTO study conducted in the washing-up liquid market, it was necessary to adjust the simulation procedure by giving each brand an index of 'usage life', so that the brand share estimates generated by the model took account of differential use up rates. For the three major brands, these were as follows:

Brand A: 0.76
Brand B: 1.15
Brand C: 0.89

The effect of this was to alter the way in which the resulting computer simulation model operated. In any simulation, the brand 'chosen' contributed a weight to the total share outcome in proportion to its use-up rate. In this way, the final brand share estimates took some account of use-up, and the shares were more in line with volume.

Pack Sizes

In many markets, the 80/20 rule applies, and research can be conducted using the pack size accounting for the largest volume in the market. However, this is not always the case, and the objectives of the research may involve consideration of pack size, or other product variants such as flavour, hair-type and so on.

Case History 6   For example, the objectives of one BPTO study in the soft-drinks market involved some consideration of the likely effects of withdrawing the half-litre size of a particular product. The issue was: would consumers remain loyal to the brand and merely switch to the litre size, or would they move to the half-litre size of another brand?

A typical BPTO exercise was conducted using a sample of 300 buyers of the product field, subject to demographic and brand usership quota controls. The research took place in-hall. In this case, the BPTO exercise did not use an 'evoked set' but a common display for all respondents. However, both half-litre and litre sizes of all products were included in the display, which were treated as separate items in the analysis.

In the resulting computer simulation model, a simulation of the current market gave the half-litre size a market share of 22% [Figure 6.5(a)]. A second simulation was then conducted in which this size was effectively 'delisted' — i.e. it was not available in the model. Since the simulation examines each respondent in turn, it was possible to note the switching patterns of those respondents who were originally predicted to buy the half-litre size. As can be seen from Figure 6.5(b), only a small fraction of buyers in fact would be prepared to transfer to the litre size, and as a result, this course of action was reconsidered.

	(a) Original Shares	(b) Where did that 22% go?
Competitor X (litre)	10%	19%
Test Brand (half-litre)	22%	—
Test Brand (litre)	13%	14%
Competitor Y (half-litre)	19%	41%
Competitor Y (litre)	36%	26%

Figure 6.5

SOME FINAL CONSIDERATIONS

In many ways, the technique chosen should reflect the issues discussed earlier. However, there are still a few points to consider.

Venue

A variety of options exist for conducting pricing research. Telephone, in-hall and in-home interviewing methods are all offered, although some techniques are restricted in the ways the interview can be done. Telephone methods by and large can only deal with *current* markets (i.e. the respondent knows the products from his or her experience), and with monadic presentations of price (it would be difficult for a respondent to mentally envisage a competitive display of products, all priced). Hall and in-home testing can deal with New Product Development concepts, but it can be difficult with competitive displays to achieve the point of sale realism in the home that can be achieved in-hall. (For example: an interviewer could carry around enough real packs if the product field was toothpaste, but not if it was washing powder.) On the other hand, a well-dispersed in-home approach would lead to less sample clustering problems than the equivalent sample size conducted in three or four hall sites. This can be important where source of purchase is a recruitment criterion—hall sites are dependent on the custom generated by stores in the immediate vicinity.

Sample Quotas

The points discussed above have suggested sample constraints defined in terms of source of usual purchase, heaviness of consumption, occasion and so on. Clearly quotas for these can only be imposed in the light of knowledge of how these factors vary in the population. Consumer panel data or Usage and Attitude surveys are clearly vital help here, and in the absence of suitable data it may be necessary to conduct preliminary research (e.g. omnibus trailers) to establish incidence figures.

Sample Sizes

As ever, there is no 'right' answer here, and the techniques themselves generally do not impose *a priori* definitions of appropriate sample sizes. Most researchers would aim to determine beforehand the minimum cell size necessary for any subgroup analysis that might be conducted. This could depend on a number of factors. In competitive tests, a good rule is to consider the sampling criteria, and estimate the number of respondents in the sample who will represent the products under investigation. For example, a 'random' sample of 200 respondents might generate 100 users of a brand with a 50% share of the market, but only four of a brand with a 2% share. Hence selective sampling may be useful here.

A second consideration might be the objectives of the research. If a simulation model such as BPTO is being used, a smaller number of brand users present in the sample may be adequate if the intention was to reduce the price, since you would expect to attract switchers. On the other hand, a larger user base would be needed if the intention was to increase price, since one would expect to lose share. The golden rule here is to define the likely direction of brand switching, and ensure that there are sufficient likely switchers present in the sample. Generally speaking, these are the people of interest.

THE OUTCOME

It goes without saying that the chosen methodology should be capable of meeting the objectives set for it. However, there are a few issues that may require some consideration concerning the styles of analysis possible.

Description or Prediction?

Generally speaking, the objectives set for pricing research fall into two categories: on the one hand, a need for a good description of the character of the market place (e.g. price 'elasticities', brand overlap, repertoire patterns and so on); and on the other hand, a need for predicting the outcome of hypothesised price changes, generally in the form of brand share estimates. Bear in mind, however, that any form of prediction resulting from *ad-hoc* methods will be subject to sampling error.

Identification of Risk Groups

As noted above, changes in brand share can be achieved by relatively small numbers of 'switchers' in a marketplace. A key issue in pricing research, therefore, is akin to those in market segmentation: identify loyalists/switchers and profile them (not only in terms of demographics and brand usership — media activity questions could be included in the questionnaire in many cases). These groups could then be tracked over time, over a number of studies.

One model?

If a simulation model is desirable, there are cases where it is better to build a number of submodels corresponding to different sectors in the marketplace, rather than one 'global' model. There is no especial benefit in building 'grand' total market models, especially since most modellers would agree that a sort of inverse law applies to the scope of models: the wider the scope of the model, the less precise the answer given. In general, if your knowledge of the market suggests that consumers in one sector are most unlikely to stray to another sector, you might be justified in dividing the problem up. This may even apply to purchaser groups of particular pack sizes.

Ease of Access

Again, if the outcome of the research is a simulation mode, it is worth bearing in mind that this represents an investment in a corporate asset that may well be useful after the original problem has disappeared. It is generally worthwhile establishing how easy it would be to conduct further simulations on the model at a later date, and what the practical implications might be. Also, how is access obtained? It may be advantageous to enter the simulation specification (the pricing scenario) personally over a telephone link to a distant computer. Indeed, recent developments in software for pricing models have made it possible to set up data locally on in-house microcomputers, permitting instant access at negligible cost.

REFERENCES

1. FRAPPA, I. and MARBEAU, J. P., 'Pricing New Products at Better Value for Money: The Ultimate Challenge for Market Researchers', *ESOMAR Congress Proceedings, Vienna* (1982)
2. GABOR, A. and GRANGER, C., *The Attitude of the Consumer to Prices in Pricing Strategy*, Staple Press (1969)
3. MORGAN, R. and GODFREY, S., 'The Role of Pricing Research in New Product Development', *Market Research Society Annual Conference Proceedings*, Brighton (1985)
4. BLAMIRES, C., 'Pricing Research Techniques: A Review and a New Proposal', *Journal of the Market Research Society* **23** (1981) 3
5. LUNN, J. A. and MORGAN, R. P., 'Some Applications of the Trade-Off Approach', in *Applied Marketing and Social Research*, 1st ed., Bradley, Ute (Ed), Van Nostrand Reinhold (1982).

Applied Marketing and Social Research 2nd Edition
Edited by Ute Bradley
©Copyright John Wiley 1987

7.   *Product Testing*

K. T. Boyd   *Research Bureau Ltd.*

This chapter has been revised from the first edition of the book and two further appendices have been added, substantially expanding the arguments relating to comparative testing and the testing of new products. The last appendix will be useful to the student of new product research and its content can be related to the practical examples given by Day in Chapter 3.

The chapter deals with the main problems which confront the researcher when testing products:

problem definition;
deciding on the kind of assessor required for the test;
deciding on the task that the assessors will be asked to undertake;
the number of products that each assessor can handle;
test order;
assessment of the products by some overall measure and by attribute measures;
conditions under which tests should be carried out;
blind versus branded-testing; and
the determination of sample size.

The argument throughout is presented in a logical order and detailed examples are included to illustrate the text. These had to be disguised before they could be published. References for further reading are provided.

WHY TEST PRODUCTS?

One of the most important things that a manufacturing and marketing company has to decide is exactly what products it is going to make and sell.

This chapter is concerned with methods commonly used to gather information to help in making this decision when the products concerned are relatively cheap items purchased by the people who consume them—products such as soaps, toilet preparations, manufactured foods, and so on. We are not concerned here with more costly things such as machinery, motor cars or refrigerators.

The costs of getting a new product of the sort we are concerned with into the market are often very great, and it is worthwhile spending money to collect information which, as far as possible, will ensure that a new product is successful in the sense that enough of it is sold to ensure a profit to the seller. It is one of the functions of market research to collect this information. How should it be done?

The first, and probably the most important, thing that a market researcher needs to know is why a particular product, or set of products, is being considered for marketing and to whom it is hoped to sell. There are many possibilities:

(a) The product may be entirely new (say, a new breakfast cereal).

(b) A manufacturer may wish to improve a product he already sells (by, for instance, putting a better perfume in his toilet soap). There will be several ways of trying to achieve this kind of improvement, so he may wish to test several versions and pick the best one.

(c) The maker of a product may be considering a new manufacturing process, or a modification of his present one. He may hope that this will improve his product, or he may hope that it will make it cheaper but no worse. For example, a manufacturer of instant coffee might be considering a new drying process.

(d) A manufacturer may wish to reformulate a product to make it cheaper. His hope would be that the change made no difference to the product's sales.

(e) A manufacturer may wish to create, or augment, a range of similar products (say, canned soups).

(f) A manufacturer may be concerned with the development of a product, and his Research and Development people may wish to know the effect on consumers of changing various factors which can be controlled. For example, a maker of margarine might be interested in finding the effects of changing the amount of soya bean oil, the amount of flavour additive, the amount of salt, as well as the temperature at a stage in the manufacture. Knowledge of the effects of such changes might help him to produce a better or, perhaps, a cheaper product. This procedure is called Factorial Testing and is too complicated to go into in any detail here. However, for the benefit of any readers who might want to learn more of this method, a very brief outline of it is included in Appendix 7.1.

This list of possible reasons for product testing is not meant to be exhaustive, but it does give an idea of the range of problems that might confront a market researcher, and some of the questions he needs to ask if he is going to design a satisfactory test.

WHO SHOULD ASSESS THEM?

One reason why this sort of question must be asked and answered is that the information helps to determine the type of consumer who should be involved in the test. For instance, if the objective is to cheapen a product, the only relevant people are those who use the current version, because the only risk of introducing the new cheap version is that the current buyers will be alienated. However, if a product is supposed to have been improved, the question of finding a suitable group of people to assess it is more difficult. Clearly, what might generally be regarded as an improvement might not be seen as such by the current users — 'It's different, and I don't like change' might be their response — so one needs enough current users assessing the product to give assurance that this is not happening. On the other hand, one might judge that current users would not buy any more of the product even if they agreed that it had been improved — one would not wash more often with a brand of soap just because one believed it was better than it used to be — so a sample composed entirely of current users could not indicate a possibility of extra sales. But if non-users thought the product had been improved, some of them might be converted into users, which suggests that non-users should form part of the sample. One would only market the product if the evidence showed that users liked it at least as well as the current version, and that non-users liked it better.

There is another distinction worth making, because it affects the choice of assessors: if the supposed improvement is a functional one — a floor cleaner has been changed so that it does the same job with less effort, say, rather than a cosmetic improvement such as a perfume change in a toilet soap — then any assessor who can detect the difference is as useful as any other. It is not likely that, say, users would think it had been made worse while non-users thought the opposite. One must always be careful with arguments like this, though. It may be possible to improve the way a product performs its function, but to do this in a way which is acceptable to non-users but unacceptable to users. For example, front-loading washing machines will overflow unless a 'low suds' washing powder is used in them. Perhaps such a powder could be changed so that it removed stains more efficiently, but also lathered more. If the users of this brand all had front-loading machines, while a substantial proportion of non-users did not, a test of the changed product might well show users rejecting it and non-users thinking it improved.

Part of the problem is that some non-users of a brand are not potential users under any reasonable assumptions and are irrelevant to a test of the brand. They can only be identified with an intelligent understanding of the product field in which the test brand lies. Since there are few brands of the kind we are talking about which are regularly used by more than 10% of the population it is much more expensive to recruit a sample of users than a sample of non-users, and it is cheaper still to recruit a random sample of all people including users and non-users in the right proportions. In fact, placing any constraint on the type of person to be used for assessing a product is bound to increase the cost of the market research and so should always be avoided unless there seems to be a serious risk of producing misleading results by omitting constraints. If they are judged to be essential, they should always be kept to a minimum.

THE KINDS OF TEST AVAILABLE

Once the problem has been properly defined, and a decision made about the kinds of assessor required, the next matter to be settled is the exact task that the assessors are to be faced with. There are two fundamentally different sorts of task they might be given when, as often happens, several similar products need to be assessed.

Each person may be given just *one product* to use and then asked to assess it on a verbal scale, such as:

Excellent
Good
Fairly good
Average
Rather poor
Poor
Very poor

Typically, such scales contain five, seven or nine gradations with the middle gradation being 'average' or some similarly neutral word. Results from all the assessors are then combined by awarding scores to the words (e.g. Excellent scores 7; Good scores 6; and so on) and then calculating an average for each product. The products, if there are more than one, are compared by comparing their averages.

The average scores allow one to place the products in a rank order of excellence and so to determine which is the best. Moreover, the magnitude of the average can, if one has used the scale a number of times for similar types of product, be compared with a norm established by experience from the scores given to successful products. Thus, the average of scores on a 7–point scale given in market research tests to products which have been successfully marketed might be 4.8. If the average score for the best product in a test is greater than 4.8, one might decide that it was worth marketing, but a lower score would be taken to mean that it should be further improved and then tested again.

Example 1 illustrates this method. The sausages were formulated differently, and the object of the test was to find the one most likely to be successful in the market.

Example 1

Four different sausages were tested for acceptability.* 400 housewives were recruited to carry out the test, and each housewife was presented with 1 lb of one type of sausage to cook and eat in her home. Respondents were given no information about the sausages, and they were all identified by the codes, P4, Q3, R2, S1.

After a few days, each housewife was interviewed and asked to rate the product she tested on the following scale:

	Score
Excellent	5
Very good	4
Good	3
Rather poor	2
Very poor	1

Table 7.1 shows the numbers of people who gave each score.

TABLE 7.1

	P4 $n = 100$	Q3 $n = 100$	R2 $n = 100$	S1 $n = 100$
5	19	13	11	9
4	60	55	54	49
3	16	22	24	26
2	3	8	7	10
1	2	2	4	6
Mean	3.91	3.69	3.61	3.45

All the examples used in this chapter relate to the same four test sausages. The examples have been selected because they permit comparisons between different test methods and conditions.

The mean score for P4, for instance, is:

$$\frac{(5 \times 19) + (4 \times 60) + (3 \times 16) + (2 \times 3) + (1 \times 2)}{100} = 3.91$$

For each product, we may also estimate the variance of its mean from the formula:

$$\text{Var (mean)} = \frac{n\Sigma(f\chi^2) - (\Sigma f\chi)^2}{n^2(n-1)}$$

where n is the number testing each product (100 in this case), χ is the score and f is the number of people giving it. Thus $\Sigma(f\chi^2)$ for P4 is:

$$(5^2 \times 19) + (4^2 \times 60) + \ \ldots \ + (1^2 \times 2) = 1593$$

and $\Sigma f\chi$ is $100 \times 3.91 = 391$. Inserting this into the formula above gives 0.0065.

The variances of the means for P4, Q3, R2 and S1 are, respectively, 0.0065, 0.0076, 0.0085 and 0.0100, which have an average value of 0.0082.

We may now test the difference of two means for statistical significance. Thus, for P4 and R2:

$$t = \frac{3.91 - 3.61}{\sqrt{(0.0065 + 0.0085)}} = \frac{0.3}{\sqrt{0.015}} = 2.449$$

Reference to tables of the t-distribution shows this value to be significant at the 2% level.

We may also calculate the variance of the four means. This is 0.0366 with three degrees of freedom.

Dividing their variance by the average variance of the means gives:

$$F = \frac{0.0366}{0.0082} = 4.463$$

The calculation is as follows:

$$\Sigma\chi^2 = 3.91^2 + 3.69^2 + 3.61^2 + 3.45^2 = 53.8388$$
$$\Sigma\chi = 3.91 + 3.69 + 3.61 + 3.45 = 14.66$$

Substitution into the formula:

$$\frac{n\Sigma\chi^2 - (\Sigma\chi)^2}{n(n-1)} \text{ gives} \frac{4 \times 53.8388 - 14.66^2}{4 \times 3} = 0.0366$$

Reference to tables of the *F*-distribution shows this to be significant at the 1% level. That is, if the four products were really identical, the chance of getting mean scores as widely spread as, in fact, they were is less than 1 in 100. It is therefore reasonable to assume that the respondents to the test recognised that the products differ in 'excellence'. We may therefore reasonably assert that P4 is the best and that S1 is the worst.

It should be noted that an assessor can only use a verbal scale like the 'Excellent to very poor' one, above, by making a mental comparison, of the test product with some concept of similar products: a toilet soap can only be judged 'good' in relation to other toilet soaps the assessor may have experience of, and one of the objections to this kind of test is that one assessor may judge a product to be 'good' relative to his experience, while another judges it 'poor' relative to his different experience. Clearly, such changes in the bases of judgement can only cloud the issue of determining a meaningful average score. The objection can be mitigated by choosing assessors with, as far as possible, similar experiences: they might be chosen, for instance, as users of a particular brand, though this tends to be expensive, as has been said above.

The fact is that all assessments are relative ones. Hence, the object of assessment can only be to establish the relative goodness of test products amongst themselves, and possibly against some standard. In a test where each person assesses just one product, comparisons between products can only be made by comparing their average scores. An alternative method of testing is to ask assessors to make the comparison *directly*, and this can be done by giving each person *at least two products* and asking him to place them in a rank order of excellence. In practice, this rank ordering is usually done in terms of preference. Thus, an individual might be given product A and product B, and asked to use them and then say which, if either, he prefers. His answer would be 'Prefer A', 'Prefer B' or 'No preference'. Suppose 110 people have been asked to assess A and B in this way: we might find that 50 (45%) preferred A, 40 (36%) preferred B, and 20 (18%) said 'No preference'. A convenient way to summarise these results is to say 'The net preference in favour of A is $(45 - 36) = 9\%$, and 18% had no preference'. (Note that the net preference could equally well be expressed in favour of B. This would be -9%.)

The advantages of this method of testing are:

1. The necessary comparisons between products are made by individuals, rather than by arithmetic comparisons of mean scores obtained from different groups of people. The trouble with means is that part of the difference between them is attributable to differences between the groups that gave them: even if two groups were given the same product, they would not give identical means.

2. Each individual assesses two products rather than one, and this allows a smaller sample size to be used for the same degree of sensitivity.

A disadvantage is that comparisons are entirely internal among the products actually tested. Hence, if comparisons are required between experimental products and a product in the market, this must be included as an extra item in the test, as an internal comparison only, will not indicate how good (or bad) even the winner is.

EXTENSIONS OF COMPARATIVE TESTING

The simple comparative test of just two products can be extended in two ways. Firstly, more than two products can be tested by arranging that every possible pair is assessed by a group of people. Each group should be the same size. Thus, if products A, B and C are to be tested, one group could assess A and B another group B and C, and a third group A and C. (In general, if t products are to be tested, this can be done as $t(t-1)/2$ pairs.) Secondly, each individual can be asked to assess, by ranking them, more than two products. Thus, someone asked to assess products A, B and C might say he liked B best, C next and A least. Whichever method is used, it is possible to analyse the data so that a number is attached to each product, allowing them to be placed in a meaningful rank order. But before saying how this may be done, it is necessary to enumerate some conditions that must be fulfilled if ranking methods of testing are to be used:

1. There must be no carry-over effect from one product to another which would preclude a proper assessment of the second one. Ranking could not be used as a way of testing anti-dandruff shampoo, for example: two of them could not be assessed by one person over a short period because if the first one worked he could not properly assess the second one.
2. The task given to an assessor must not induce excessive sensory fatigue and, hence, confusion. For example, there must be a limit to the number of perfumes that can be successfully assessed by one person in a short period.

These conditions are often satisfied in practical cases, and we will now return to the problem of summarising data collected from a ranking test. The first thing to do is to award suitable numbers to each rank position, and the best way to do this is to award a 'score' of $(k-1)$ to the product ranked first by someone placing k products in rank order. The product ranked second should be given a score of $(k-3)$, and so on downwards in steps of 2.

The reasons for using this scoring system are purely arithmetic. There are three points to note:

1. If numerical scores are to be attached to objects whose rank order is known, but nothing more, it is reasonable to make the difference in scores the same for all pairs of objects with adjacent rankings.
2. If the numerical scores differ by two for objects ranked adjacent, then, regardless of how many objects are ranked and regardless of any tied rankings, each object can be given an integral score.
3. If k objects are ranked, we gain information about their standing relative to each other, but nothing about their standing relative to another object not among the k ranked. Thus the mean scores of k-ranked products cannot properly be used to indicate their absolute 'virtue', but only their relative 'virtues'. Hence, the mean score can be chosen, for convenience, to be zero. (Note that this statement does not deny that if one or more objects are common to two ranked sets of k objects, then the two sets, together, contain information about the relative standing of all the objects.)

Thus, if someone ranks A, B, C and D (there may be other products E, F, G, . . ., etc. in the test), and puts them in the order A (1st), C (2nd), D (3rd), B (4th), 'scores' would be $(4-1) = 3$ for A. $(4-3) = 1$ for C, $(4-5) = -1$ for D, and $(4-7) = -3$ for B. If he had put A and C equal first, these products would each get scores of 2, being the average of 3 and 1. Note that the total of the scores given must always be zero for each person, so $3 + 1 + (-1) + (-3) = 0$ and $2 + 2 + (-1) + (-3) = 0$, if two products are ranked equal 1st.

The next step is to find the total score for each product over the whole test. To find mean scores these totals are then multiplied by:

$$\frac{(t-1)}{n} \times \frac{100}{k(k-1)}$$

where t is the number of products in the test, k is the number of products ranked by each person, which must be the same for every person, and n is the total number of people in the test. It is assumed that every set of k is tested by the same number of people and that every pair of products occurs the same number of times in the sets of k. Otherwise, the mean scores found in this way are only approximate.

The result of these calculations is a number for each test product with the following properties:

(i) They sum to zero.
(ii) They allow the products to be placed in a hierarchical order of 'goodness', the product with the highest number being the 'best' and that with the lowest the 'worst'.

(iii) The differences between any pair of numbers is an estimate of the net preference % that would have been found if the corresponding products had been tested as a single pair.

To illustrate this method, consider the example of a simple net preference given earlier. Here, two products ($t = 2$) were tested as a pair ($k = 2$) by 110 people ($n = 110$). The results were:

(i)   50 people put A first (and, so, B second);
(ii) 40 people put B first (and, so, A second);
(iii) 20 gave no preference, i.e. ranked A and B equal.

Here, $(k - 1) = 1$, the score for products ranked first; $(k - 3) = -1$, the score for products ranked second; and the average of 1 and -1 is zero, which is therefore, the score for products ranked equal.

Hence, the total score for A is:

$$50 \times 1 \text{ [from (i)] } + 40 \times (-1) \text{ [from (ii)] } + 20 \times 0 \text{ [from (iii)] } = 10$$

The total score for B is:

$$50 \times (-1) \text{ [from (i)] } + 40 \times 1 \text{ [from (ii)] } + 20 \times 0 \text{ [from (iii)] } = -10$$

$$\frac{t-1}{k(k-1)} \times \frac{100}{n} = \frac{2-1}{2(2-1)} \times \frac{100}{110} = \frac{5}{11}$$

which is the multiplier of the total scores to give mean scores. Hence, the mean scores are $(10 \times 5/11)$ or $50/11\%$ for A, and $-10 \times 5/11)$ or $-50/11\%$ for B, and the net preference is $50/11 - (-50/11) = 100/11\%$ in favour of A.

Now suppose that A, B and C ($t = 3$) have been assessed in pairs ($k = 2$) by a total of $n = 300$. The results might be as in Table 7.2.

TABLE 7.2

Pair	Prefer A	Prefer B	Prefer C	No Pref.	Total
A, B	50	40	—	10	100
B, C	—	45	37	18	100
A, C	62	—	33	5	100

Total Scores
$A = 50 + 62 - 40 - 33 = 39$
$B = 40 + 45 - 50 - 37 = -2$
$C = 37 + 33 - 45 - 62 = -37$

$$\frac{t-1}{k(k-1)} \times \frac{100}{n} = \frac{2}{2} \times \frac{100}{300} = \frac{1}{3}$$

This, times total scores, gives mean scores:

$$A = 13\% \qquad B = -\tfrac{2}{3}\% \qquad C = -12\tfrac{1}{3}\%$$

Example 2 shows results for the sausage test carried out by this method.

Example 2

The same four products were tested, but this time 60 housewives were given P4 *and* Q3, 60 were given P4 *and* R2, and so on. Since there are six ways to pair four products, 360 housewives were involved. Of the 60 housewives testing a pair, say P4 and Q3, 30 were asked to try P4 first and 30 were asked to try Q3 first. Thus any bias in favour of the first product tested was cancelled. Each housewife was asked to say which product, if either, she preferred. Table 7.3 shows the numbers preferring each product. Each column of the table represents a different pair. Thus, of the 60 people who tested S1 and R2, 19 preferred S1, 29 preferred R2, and 12 expressed no preference. The right-hand column shows the row totals.

TABLE 7.3

S1	19	21	14	—	—	—	54
R2	29	—	—	26	20	—	75
Q3	—	27	—	23	—	18	68
P4	—	—	33	—	29	30	92
No preference	12	12	13	11	11	12	71

Consider S1. In all, 180 people tested it. 54 of them preferred it, while $(12 + 12 + 13) = 37$ gave no preference in pairs contained S1. Hence $180 - 54 - 37 = 89$ people ranked it second. Also, since $k = 2$, the score for a winning product is $(k - 1) = 1$, and for a losing product it is -1. Obviously, the score when a product has no preference recorded for it should be zero. Hence, we can produce Table 7.4.

TABLE 7.4

	1st	2nd	Total net score	Mean net preferences
S1	54	89	− 35	− 14.58
R2	75	71	4	1.67
Q3	68	77	− 9	− 3.75
P4	92	52	40	16.67
			0	0

The last column is derived from the previous one by multiplying by:

$$\frac{t-1}{k(k-1)} \times \frac{100}{n} = \frac{3 \times 100}{360 \times 1 \times 2} = \frac{5}{12}$$

The variance of the difference of two mean net preferences is $100\,P\,(t-1)/n$, where $P\%$ of the sample express a preference. Here:

$$P = \frac{360-71}{360} \times 100 = \frac{289}{360} \times 100$$

and $t = 4$. So the variance of a difference is:

$$\frac{100^2 \times 289 \times 3}{360^2} = (8.179)^2$$

Hence, a t-value may be found by dividing the difference between two mean net preferences by 8.179.

Also, if k products are ranked by each person, an F-value is:

$$\frac{3}{n(k+1)\,k(k-1)} \; \Sigma q_i^2$$

where q_i is total net score for the ith product in the range $(k-1)$ to $(1-k)$.

In the special case that $k = 2$, n in the above formula for F may be replaced by the number giving a preference, i.e. by $nP/100$, which in this case is 289:

$$F = \frac{3}{289 \times 3 \times 2 \times 1} (35^2 + 4^2 + 9^2 + 40^2)$$

$$= \frac{2922}{289 \times 2} = 5.055$$

This has three degrees of freedom and is highly significant. One can conclude, therefore, that the mean net preferences in Table 7.4 are not all estimates of zero, differing from zero only by chance. Hence, we may be confident that P4 is the best product, that S1 is the worst, and that R2 and Q3 are mid-way between the other two. We could not be confident that R2 was better than Q3, since the net preference (i.e. $1.667 - (-3.75)$) is only about 5.4%, which is much less than 8.179, the standard error of a net preference derived from the mean net preferences in Table 7.4.

HOW MANY PRODUCTS SHOULD EACH PERSON ASSESS?

The simple answer to this question is 'as many as possible'. (But this must be qualified by considerations of carry-over, fatigue, time and so on, as has been discussed above.) The reason for this answer is that it must be intuitively reasonable that the more information one can extract from each assessor, the more economical the job will be. So, it must be more economical to extract information about three products, say, than two. In detail, the problem is more complicated and requires a knowledge of statistics, but the result is simple enough — a decision to give each person $(k + 1)$ products to rank, rather than k, means that the sample size can be reduced by a factor of $(k + 2)$ $(k - 1)/(k + 1)^2$, *within any loss of precision in the final results.*

The effect is dramatic. Suppose seven products have to be tested; the table shows various possibilities for equal precision, i.e. 175 people each ranking sets of four products would determine the seven product mean scores just as precisely as 630 people would if they each ranked just two products:

k	2	3	4	5	6	7
n	630	280	175	126	98	80

In practice, it would be reasonable to have about 100 people testing each of the 21 possible pairs, giving a total sample of 2100, but this could be reduced to only $2100 \times 80/630 = 267$, as the table indicates, if everyone assessed all seven products. (630 people ranking two are equivalent to 80 people ranking seven. So one person ranking two is equivalent to 80/630 people ranking seven. Hence, 2100 people ranking two are equivalent to $2100 \times 80/630$ people ranking seven.)

Examples 3 and 4 show how tests might work if each person tested three products and four products. Note that these tests would hardly be practicable if carried out 'in home', because people might have forgotten which product was which by the time they had tested them all and tried to rank them. (Notice also that 360 people in Example 2, 240 people in Example 3 and 180 people in Example 4 all show about the same degree of significance between the products. This kind of result is to be expected, since the number of products each person ranks increases in consecutive examples. Notice that the table above shows that n can be reduced from 630 to 175 (i.e. 3.6 to 1) by changing k from 2 to 4. However, here, the sample size was only halved (i.e. 360 to 180) on changing k from 2 to 4.

Example 3

The same products were tested, but this time 240 people were invited to a test centre and asked to taste and rank three cooked sausages. Thus, 60 people ranked each set of three products, as follows:

Set 1   S1, R2, Q3
Set 2   R2, Q3, P4
Set 3   Q3, P4, S1
Set 4   P4, S1, R2

Note that, if the products in each set are presented in the order they are written, each product is tested 1st, 2nd and 3rd by the same number of people. There is thus no need to rotate orders of testing to eliminate bias.

Table 7.5 shows the numbers of people ranking each product 1st, 2nd and 3rd. Since each person ranks three products, the scores for 1st, 2nd and 3rd are 2, 0, -2. Hence, the total net score for S1 is:

$$(2 \times 40) + (0 \times 65) + (-2 \times 75) = 2(40 - 75) = -70$$

The total net score for R2 is 2 $(66 - 62) = 8$, and the other total net scores in Table 7.5 are found similarly.

TABLE 7.5

	1st	2nd	3rd	Total net score	Mean net preferences
S1	40	65	75	-70	-14.58
R2	66	52	62	8	1.67
Q3	55	61	64	-18	-3.75
P4	79	62	39	80	16.67
				0	0

The variance of the difference between two mean net preferences is:

$$\frac{2}{3} \times \frac{t-1}{k} \times \frac{k+1}{k-1} \times \frac{100^2}{n}$$

which in this case is:

$$\frac{2}{3} \times \frac{3}{3} \times \frac{4}{2} \times \frac{100^2}{240} = \frac{100^2}{180} = (7.454)^2$$

$$\Sigma q_i^2 = 70^2 + 8^2 + 18^2 + 80^2 = 11{,}688$$

from Table 7.5. An F value is, with three degrees of freedom:

$$\frac{3}{n(k+1)k(k-1)} \Sigma q_i^2 = \frac{11{,}688}{80 \times 4 \times 3 \times 2} = 6.0875$$

This value of F is highly significant. The interpretation is, of course, the same as in Example 2.

Example 4

The same products were tested in a test centre by 180 people all of whom ranked all four. Table 7.6 shows the results.

Since each person ranks four products, the scores for 1st, 2nd, 3rd and 4th are 3, 1, -1, -3, hence, the total net score for S1 is:

$$3(15 - 50) + (58 - 57) = -105 + 1 = -104$$

The other total net scores in Table 7.6 are found similarly.

TABLE 7.6

	1st	2nd	3rd	4th	Total net score	Mean net preferences
S1	15	58	57	50	-104	-14.44
R2	27	66	63	24	12	1.67
Q3	43	41	45	51	-28	-3.89
P4	95	15	15	55	120	16.67
					0	0

The variance of the difference between two net preferences is, as in Example 3:

$$\frac{2}{3} \times \frac{3}{4} \times \frac{5}{3} \times \frac{100^2}{180} = (6.804)^2$$

$$\Sigma q_i^2 = 104^2 + 12^2 + 28^2 + 120^2 = 26{,}144$$

from Table 7.6. An F value is, as in Example 3:

$$\frac{26{,}144}{60 \times 5 \times 4 \times 3} = 7.262$$

ORDER OF TESTING

Usually, if two or more products are being assessed by each person, it will be necessary for them to use them one after the other and then, after completing the use of the last one, to place them into a rank order. This gives rise to the possibility that a product will be favoured for no other reason than, say, the fact that it was the first one tried. Thus, if A was always used before B, A might appear the better, while if B was always used first, B might appear the better. In fact, this sort of thing very often happens, so, to avoid false results from the test, one must always ensure that every product in a test is used in every possible position by the same number of people. If everyone tests two products, this is best arranged by ensuring that half the people testing any particular pair do it in one order, and half in the other. The analysis is unaffected.

When each person tests more than two products, the equivalent procedure would be to test each set in all possible orders, of which there are, if each person tests k products:

$$k(k-1)(k-2) \ldots 1$$

This is rather large: 6 if $k=3$, 24 if $k=4$, 120 if $k=5$, and so on. There are two ways of achieving what is needed in a simpler way. The first is to use only k orders by rotating the k products cyclically. So if, for example, $k=4$, and one set is the products A, C, E, F, then the four orders of testing could be:

(A, C, E, F) (C, E, F, A) (E, F, A, C) and (F, A, C, E)

But another way which is often, but not always available requires no rotation of orders at all and, simultaneously, reduces the numbers of sets of k that needs to be tested. So, for instance, if seven products are to be tested in threes, one need not test all 35 possible combinations: only seven need to be tested, as follows. Each combination is tested in the order given:

A	B	D
B	C	E
C	D	F
D	E	G
E	F	A
F	G	B
G	A	C

This method is just as precise as testing all 35 possible sets of three with the same total sample, but a statistician must be consulted to find out if such a scheme is available for the number of products to be tested. Designs of this kind are listed in Cochran and Cox.[1]

ATTRIBUTES

It has been implied, so far, that only one question will be asked in a product test — either a scaling of excellence if each person only assesses one product, or ranking by excellence if each person assesses two or more products — but often it will be thought necessary to ask questions about attributes of the products, such as perfume, flavour, strength, lather, texture, and so on, as may be appropriate to the type of product in the test. There are two reasons why these sort of questions are asked: firstly, it may be possible to exploit any particular strengths (or off-set any weaknesses) in advertising the selected product; and, secondly, one might hope to be able to correct any weaknesses in a generally good product by changing it slightly. (One difficulty is that it is often impossible to 'improve', say, the texture of a product without influencing several other attributes, perhaps adversely.)

There are the three commonly used types of scale that can be used for attributes if each person tests just one product:

1. A scale of excellence, e.g. 'Has a very good perfume' . . . . 'Has a very bad perfume'.
2. A 'too much, too little, just right' scale, e.g. 'Much too sweet'. 'Too sweet', 'Just the right sweetness'. 'Not sweet enough', 'Not nearly sweet enough'. If this scale is scored 5, 4, 3, 2, 1, an average score of more than 3 means the product is too sweet, and if the average is less than 3, it is not sweet enough.
3. An 'agree/disagree' scale. This kind of scale is introduced by a statement, e.g. 'This washing powder is suitable for heavily soiled clothes'. The alternative responses are 'Strongly agree', 'Agree', 'Neither agree nor disagree', 'Disagree', 'Strongly disagree', which can be scored 5, 4, 3, 2, 1.

In a ranking test, respondents can be asked to rank in order of preference for perfume or sweetness (or they could be asked to rank in order of sweetness, which might give a different result). They could equally well be asked to rank products in order of suitability for washing heavily-soiled clothes.

The exact method used in a particular case must be a matter of judgement depending on the type and purpose of the test, and one must remember that a ranking test only gives relative information about the products ranked: one does not know how a test product stands in relation to another product that has not been tested.

TEST CONDITIONS

Time and place are the main considerations: either assessors can be brought to a convenient test centre, carry out the test over, say, a half hour period, and go, or assessors can use products in their own homes in a normal way. There are pros and cons for each method. In favour of 'in-home' testing is the fact that it is perhaps more realistic—a test soap will be put in the bathroom and used by family members in the usual way; a test packet of frozen peas will be served as a vegetable with an otherwise normal meal; and so on. Also, a product such as a tablet of soap can be used for, say, a week before an assessment is made.

Against 'in-home' testing is the cost, in that the products have to be delivered to people's homes and one then has to get back the completed questionnaires. If they are collected it is costly, and if people are asked to post them many do not, which is also costly. The proportion returning a questionnaire by post varies greatly with its length and whether respondents find it interesting. One should not expect more than 70% to return them, and of course one can never know whether the views of non-responders are the same as those of responders. Also, different people will use the same product in different ways—some people use a dishwashing liquid as a shampoo or for hand washing, while others use it only for washing dishes. This sort of thing will increase the variability of assessments and so make comparisons between products less clear. On the other hand, product testing in a test centre is quick and cheap, and the conditions of use can be standardised. But assessments can only be on the basis of first impressions.

It is sometimes a good idea to use a test centre to find the best two or three from a number of possible products, and then, as a second stage, to test these 'in home'. The logic of this procedure merits examination. If in-home testing is regarded as the 'right' way to do the test, then one must be assuming that the products which appear worst in a test centre and, therefore, do not go forward for in-home testing, would also appear the worst in an in-home test. If this is true, why should we not assume that the best product in a test centre would also be best in-home? Perhaps both methods would, indeed, give the same ordering of the products, but the procedure may be justified by the increased 'believability' of the in-home test coupled with the cheapness of the test centre as a means of reducing the number of products for in-home testing. The combined cost of the two-stage test would generally be less than that of a single-stage in-home test on all the original products.

BLIND OR BRANDED?

A blind test is one in which the products are not identified by anything other than a code, whereas in a branded test all the products have their brand names attached. They may, or may not, be in their normal packaging in a branded test, but the results might be distorted if some are and some are not in their normal packages.

A blind test is useful as a means of investigating different formulations of a product, divorced from any influence that the brand name may exert.

If a 'blind' product is assessed on its own, it invariably gets a very low mean score, presumably because people do not trust it. But if a branded product is tested on its own, the users of the brand will, naturally, give it a very high score, whereas non-users, because they don't like it, don't need it or can't afford it, can be expected to give a lower score. One must always remember, firstly, that people are giving a comparative answer to the question that is put to them, even if they are assessing just one product, and, secondly, that there are subtleties in questions that may affect the answers, even if alternative questions seem, at first sight, to be measuring the same thing. Thus, for many everyday products a person will give similar scores, high or low, both on a scale running from 'I would definitely buy' to 'I would definitely not buy' and on another running from 'Excellent' to 'Poor'. But a Rolls Royce owner might respond quite differently to these two scales if he was asked to assess a Mini: he might say a Mini is 'Excellent' (for what it is, being implied), but also say: 'I definitely would not buy it'.

In a ranking test, the differences between the results when all the products are presented blind and the results when all products are presented as variants of the *same* brand are often small. The brand name may cause respondents to look for particular characteristics in the test products, however, because they are associated with the brand, which they would ignore if the products were blind; it depends, partly, on whether the respondents are users or non-users of the brand whether these considerations affect the results. When one is testing variants of a brand, it is usually wise to let respondents know this. But one should never mix blind and branded products in the same test.

SAMPLE SIZE

Broadly speaking, the cost of a product test will increase as the number of assessors increases, but so also will the benefit to the user of the results: all that this implies is that a market research client could hardly get anything useful for his money if he commissioned a product test with, say, ten assessors, because the average scores for the products would be far too imprecise for him to know the correct hierarchy of the products. But, if he paid to have 10 000 assessors, the hierarchy would be well enough established for him to feel confident about any decisions he made as a result.

In more detail, the cost of market research can be roughly stated as:

$$T = A \times kS$$

where T is he total cost, made up of a cost, A, for writing a proposal and a report and any other administration costs which are independent of the sample size, and a further cost, kS, which varies directly with the sample size, S.

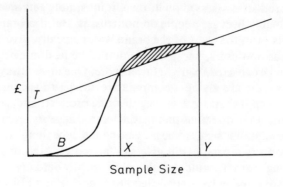

Figure 7.1

Also, for the reasons given above, we may assume that the client gets a benefit, *B*, which, in principle, can be measured in £, which increases with sample size. Moreover, a sample of 20 will hardly yield more benefit than one of ten, and, at the other end of the scale, a sample of 2 million could not give much more benefit than a sample of 1 million.

Hence we could draw two graphs, as shown in Figure 7.1. Unless the sample size lies between X and Y, the market research will cost more than its benefit is worth.

The point of all this is to demonstrate that spending too little can be just as wasteful as spending too much, but, unhappily, there is no way of determining the correct shape of the benefit curve, and we have to use more pragmatic ways of settling the same size.

A reasonable approach is to say that if we saw a net preference of 10% between two products, A and B, after we had analysed a ranking test, we would want to feel reasonably confident (at the 5% level of statistical significance, say) that these two products were at least in the right order.

This criterion is met if the sample size is chosen so that:

$$n = 256\frac{(t-1)(k+1)}{k(k-1)}$$

provided that:

(i) Every assessor ranks *k* products.
(ii) Every product is assessed by the same number of people.

Note:

1. To meet these conditions, the total sample size must be divisible by the number of sets of *k*. *n* as given by the formula may have to be increased a little to ensure this.

2. Small departures from condition (ii) above are unimportant.
3. The formula for n assumes that no tied rankings are given. In practice, they are fairly uncommon if k is 3 or more, and can usually be ignored. If $k = 2$, however, it is common for about 20% of rankings to be tied. If this sort of proportion is expected in the case for which a sample size is being estimated, the value of n as provided by the formula can (and should) be multiplied by 0.8, the proportion expected to state a preference.
4. Although the method outlined for estimating sample sizes is based on the assumption that assessors will rank two or more products, as estimate for a case where each respondent is assessing just one product can be arrived at by calculating n for $k = 2$, and then multiplying the result by 1.75. This is no more than a rule of thumb based on the fact that each respondent is giving less information than if he assesses two or more.
5. Sometimes the sample size is effectively settled by what a client believes he ought to pay. Suppose this gives a total sample of n_1 while the formula above gives n. The net preference between two products that is required for significance at the 5% level changes from 10% to $10 \times \sqrt{n/n_1}$ %.

CONCLUSION

The importance of product testing is very great, and any manufacturer who introduces new or altered products into the market without any testing is running a serious risk of wasting quite a lot of money.

Product testing is also rather difficult. It not only involves the usual administrative and organisational skills required for any successful market research, but it also requires specialised skills in statistics and the design of experiments, together with some understanding of the technology of the products being tested and an appreciation of the marketing problems involved.

For all these reasons, it is a most rewarding field of study to which this chapter can only be regarded as an introduction.

REFERENCE

1. COCHRAN, W. G. and COX, G. M. *Experimental Designs*, John Wiley and Sons 1957 (A specialist's book. Lists many designs that are suitable for product testing)

FURTHER READING

FERBER, R., *Statistical Techniques in Market Research*, McGraw-Hill. (1949) (More detailed and rather more difficult than the two following references)

MORONEY, M. J., *Facts from Figures*, Penguin Books 1984. (This is a simple and readable introduction to statistics. Chapters 10, 13, 18 and 19 are particularly relevent)

WORCESTER, R. M. and DOWNHAM, J. (Eds), *Consumer Market Research Handbook*, 3rd ed., Elsevier North-Holland (1986) (More specialised than *Facts and Figures*, but still quite simple)

APPENDIX 7.1   FACTORIAL TESTS

Suppose the four sausages used in the tests in the examples varied in the amount of meat and water they contained:

	Meat %	Water %	Mean scores
S1	60	10	s
R2	70	10	r
Q3	60	15	q
P4	70	15	p

The n:

$$\frac{(r+p)-(s+q)}{4}$$

is half the difference between the average score for 70% meat and that for 60% meat: it is a measure of the effect of increasing the meat content by 10%. Similarly:

$$\frac{(p+q)-(r+s)}{4}$$

is half the difference between the average score for 15% water and that for 10% water: it is a measure of the effect of increasing the water content by 5%.

Also, $(p-q)$ measures the effect of increasing meat by 10% *when the water content is 15%*, and $(r-s)$ does the same thing *when the water content is 10%*. There is no particular reason to believe that these will be the same, and it would be helpful to know it if they were different. We therefore also measure the 'interaction' between the two variables as:

$$\frac{(p-q)-(r-s)}{4}$$

This argument can easily be extended to deal with any number of different 'factors', such as meat and water, provided they all have just two levels, as in the example. (One can deal with factors at many levels, in fact, but that is too complicated to go into here.)

If n factors are involved, each at two levels, then 2^n products can be made. They will have $(2^n - 1)$ degrees of freedom between them, and if we perform the factorial analysis we can find $(2^n - 1)$ main effects and interactions; each one accounts for a degree of freedom.

Hence, if we measure effects in the way described above, square them and divide by the variance of these effects, we have F-ratios with one degree of freedom with which we can assess the significance of each effect.

If each respondent ranks k products, the variance of an effect is:

$$\frac{1}{3} \times \frac{t-1}{t} \times \frac{k+1}{k(k-1)} \times \frac{100^2}{n}$$

(If $k = 2$ and $p\%$ express a preference, 100^2 in the above formula should be replaced by $100p$.)

APPENDIX 7.2 SEQUENTIAL MONADIC TESTING

In a comparative test it is usual to ask respondents for no more than a ranking of products: 'Which do you like best?', 'Second best?', 'Third?', and so on. The aim is to have a hierarchical ordering from each respondent of the products he or she tested, and a simple ranking, though often the most convenient, is not the only way to do this.

There is no reason, for instance, why each respondent should not be asked to rate a product on a scale, and then be asked to do the same thing for a second product. All possible pairs of products could be dealt with in this way by $t(t-1)/2$ groups of people if t products, in all, were to be tested and, of course, half of each group should test the products in one order, and half in the other to avoid any bias.

To see how data of this kind should be analysed, consider just two products, A and B, and three respondents giving scores on a five-point scale:

Score	A	B
5	1	
4	3	3
3	2	1
2		
1		2

Thus, respondent 1 gives scores to A and B of 5, and 3, respectively; respondent 2 gives score of 3, and 1; and respondent 3 gives both products a score of 4.

The mean score for A is $(5+4+3)/3 = 4$, and, the mean score for B is $(4+3+1)/3 = 2\ 2/3$. The variances of these means are 1/3, and 7/9.

Because the scores for A and B are given by the same people, they are not independent, and so it would be wrong to say that the variance of the difference between the means is the sum of their variances, i.e. that $(4-2\ 2/3) = 1\ 1/3$ has a variance of $(1/3+7/9) = 1\ 1/9$. The correct way to handle the data is to make up a table as follows:

Resp.	A	B	A — B
1	5	3	2
2	3	1	2
3	4	4	0
Means	4	2 2/3	1 1/3

Note that mean (A) (= 4) – mean (B) (= 2 2/3) = mean (A—B) (= 1 1/3).

This will always be true, but also note that the variance of the three values for (A—B) is 4/3, so that the variance of their mean is 4/9. This is the correct variance and it allows for any correlation between scores given to different products by the same person.

This procedure, which can in principle be extended to allow each respondent to give ratings to more than two products, though the analysis is then rather more complicated, usefully combines the advantage of a monadic test (when each respondent rates just one product) in providing a mean score which can be compared with a norm, and the advantage of a paired test in reducing the number of respondents needed.

If the orders of testing are properly organised to remove bias, then every product in the test will be tested an equal number of times first and second. Therefore, if respondents are not told that they will be asked to test more than one product, the data obtained for the first product each person tests will be monadic data and can be analysed as such.

The rest of the analysis is best dealt with by example. Suppose three products, A, B, and C, are rated in pairs by a total of 12 people, i.e. 4/pair.

The scores are:

Resp.	A	B	Resp.	A	C	Resp	B	C
1	5	3	5	5	2	9	5	4
2	4	2	6	5	1	10	4	2
3	4	3	7	4	2	11	3	4
4	2	3	8	3	1	12	5	4
Totals	15	11		17	6		17	14 (80)

Average Score $= 80/24 = 3$ 1/3.

Now subtract each respondent's mean score from the two scores given:

Resp.	A	B	Resp.	A	C	Resp.	B	C
1	1	-1	5	3/2	$-3/2$	9	1/2	$-1/2$
2	1	-1	6	2	-2	10	1	-1
3	1/2	$-1/2$	7	1	-1	11	$-1/2$	1/2
4	$-1/2$	1/2	8	1	-1	12	1/2	$-1/2$
Totals	2	-2		5 1/2	-5 1/2		1 1/2	-1 1/2 0
Sums of squares	2 1/2	2 1/2		8 1/4	8 1/4		1 3/4	1 3/4 25

$$\left.\begin{array}{l} \text{Total for A} = 7\ 1/2 \\ \text{Total for B} = -1/2 \\ \text{Total for C} = -7 \end{array}\right\} \times \frac{t-1}{n(k-1)}\left(= \frac{2}{12 \times 1}\right) = \left\{\begin{array}{l} \text{Mean for A} = 1\ 1/4 \\ \text{Mean for B} = -1/12 \\ \text{Mean for C} = -7/6 \end{array}\right.$$

These means sum to zero. To get them into the range of the scale used, add the average of all the given scores, 3 1/3, to each:

Mean for A $= 4$ 7/12
Mean for B $= 3$ 1/4
Mean for C $= 2$ 1/6

The total sum of squares, as shown above, is 25. This has 12 degrees of freedom because each pair of numbers sums to zero. Therefore, if one number in a pair is known, so is the other. The sum of squares for products can be calculated as:

$$\frac{t-1}{n(k-1)} \times \text{sum of squared product totals, i.e.:}$$

$$\frac{2}{12 \times 1}(7.5^2 + 0.5^2 + 7^2) = \frac{1}{6} \times \frac{211}{2} = 17.583$$

This has two degrees of freedom.
The error sum of squares is then:

$$25 \quad - \frac{211}{12} = \frac{89}{12}, \text{ with } (12-2) = 10 \text{ degrees of freedom.}$$

Finally, the variance of the difference between two product means is:

$$\frac{2(t-1)}{n(k-1)} \times \frac{\text{Error SS}}{\text{Error DF}}$$

$$= \quad \frac{2 \times 2}{12 \times 1} \times \frac{89}{120} = \frac{89}{360} = \quad 0.2472 = (0.4972)^2$$

Note that the crude means, i.e. the averages of the original data, are:

Crude mean for A = 4.00
Crude mean for B = 3.50
Crude mean for C = 2.50

The following table compares the 'crude' and the 'correct' means against the data.

	Mean observed difference	Difference of 'correct' means	Difference of 'crude means
A – B	1	1 1/3	1/2
A – C	2 3/4	2 5/12	1 1/2
B – C	3/4	1 1/12	1

The 'correct' means are chosen to make the discrepancies between the first two columns as small as possible (they are all 1/3, so the sum of their squares is 1/3). The sum of the squares of discrepancies between the first and last column is 1 7/8, indicating that the 'crude' means do not represent the data nearly as well as the 'correct' means.

If a respondent is asked which of two products he prefers, there are only three different values for the difference between them, namely, $+2$, 0, or -2, using the standard scoring system. If, however, each product is rated on a five-point scale, there are nine possible values for the difference between them; 4, 3, 2, 1, 0, -1, -2, -3, -4. This finer scale provides extra information. Thus, the statements 'A is better than B', and 'A is better than C', say nothing about the difference between B and C. However, 'A is 4 points better than B', and 'A is 2 points better than C', implies 'C is 2 points better than B'. Because of this extra information, the sample size when each product in a paired test is rated can be about 70% of that needed if only preferences are asked for.

A disadvantage of the method is that interviewers must approach each respondent three times: once to deliver the first product; once to collect the questionnaire for the first product, and to deliver the second; and, once to collect the second questionnaire. If only preferences are needed, it is usually all right to deliver both products together marked, 'Use first', and 'Use second'. The respondent must then be contacted a second time to collect the questionnaire.

APPENDIX 7.3   A PRODUCT DEVELOPMENT RESEARCH PROGRAMME

Although the methods outlined in this chapter are, perhaps, most often applied to marketed, or at least marketable, products, they can be applied at many stages in the course of developing a new product.

Rather than go to the expense of producing several alternative products and then seeing which of them is the most saleable, it is better to develop and test a number of 'concepts'. These are fairly detailed descriptions of products that could be made in terms the consumer can understand. A personal washing product might be described as, 'A liquid which gently cleans your skin to leave it fresh and soft however hard your water may be'. This concept might be tested along with others, and the most promising one or two turned into real products for testing.

Often, a factorial experiment covering various formulation and processing factors will be helpful at an early stage of development in order to find out how the factors affect acceptability. Armed with this knowledge, the product designer is in a good position to pick the factor levels to achieve a good balance of cost and acceptability. A valuable, but often overlooked, benefit from this procedure is that it can help quality control when the product is in production: if acceptability is more sensitive to variations in some factors than others, these are the ones which should receive most attention.

Once the main details of formulation and processing have been broadly settled, it would be wise to test two or three variants against any competition there might be. This would usually be a blind test so as to avoid any effects of packaging and image. This stage of testing might well suggest changes to improve competitiveness, probably cosmetic ones, such as colour or perfume.

Packaging might be the next matter requiring tests. Packaging is usually required to do much more than protect what is inside from accidental damage. It should be distinctive so that the product is easily recognised and easily identified amongst its competitors, but, at the same time it should suggest desirable qualities in the product: it is usual to assess alternative packages in terms of the qualities they convey, rather than in order of prettiness. There may also be functional properties of packaging such as ease of opening, and, of course, if the product stays in the packing when in use, ease and security of closure. The methods in this chapter can readily be adapted to deal with all these matters, as they can be to allow comparisons of different advertisements. Again, one is usually more concerned with the messages conveyed rather than the memorability or artistic merit of alternative advertising, though these are important as well.

When all these stages have been gone through, one might still wish to run a full test of the final complete marketing mix or even a test market of the product in one town before finally committing the funds necessary for a nationwide launch. It is only then that one really knows if the product will be successful: not all are, but the chances of success are much better if good market research has suggested that the public likes the product than they would be if the whole operation was based on hunch.

Applied Marketing and Social Research 2nd Edition
Edited by Ute Bradley

8. A Cost-Effective Use of Research to Evaluate Sales Promotions

Marc Drake   *Taylor Nelson and Associates*

The writer of this case suggests that 'brands need to have an *overall* communication strategy', covering the product itself, the packaging and label design, PR activity, advertising and promotions. The case is therefore concerned with developing ground rules for assessing future promotional strategic developments, as well as with finding cost-effective ways of pre-testing specific alternative promotions.

The issues involved are fully discussed, sampling implications are stated and data collection methods detailed. For instance, a simple postal questionnaire was devised and by making it a foil printed pre-paid questionnaire, response rates were increased. It had the benefit 'of being completed quickly by simply 'scratching-off' answers. It was felt that such an approach might be useful here partly because of the obvious synergy between this means of data collection and the likely target audience.' Further data interpretation and presentation issues are discussed and the overall approach evaluated.

SUMMARY

This chapter describes how a programme of research based around a novel means of collecting data has enabled Heinz to optimise its performance in the promotions area and develop a framework within which specific promotions can be evaluated.

Though Heinz used traditional research to evaluate the success of consumer promotions, the costs of these relative to the promotion cost meant that no consistent framework for evaluation was used to track the effectiveness of individual promotions.

This chapter describes the development of a more cost-effective way of providing tactical data for marketing, using sales promotion techniques (in the form of foil-printed self-completion questionnaires) to gather profile data from those responding to particular offers.

AN OUTLINE OF THE PROBLEM

H. J. Heinz is one of the UK's largest food manufacturers with a turnover approaching £400 million. The majority of the Company's lines are high penetration items and Figure 8.1 below gives an indication of the size of the main markets within which it operates.

In virtually all of these markets Heinz is brand leader with dominant market shares. However, the environment is fiercely competitive and there is pressure both from other brands and the retailers' own private label goods.

By way of background we offer a few facts about Heinz promotional activities and the Company's current viewpoint on promotions' research.

Most companies with media advertising budgets put a fair amount of effort into the development, pre-testing and subsequent monitoring of their brand advertising. At Heinz there are usually several stages of qualitative and quantitative research undertaken before a commercial is aired. Tracking is then used and attempts are made to assess the impact of that advertising.

However, promotions and specifically consumer promotions had not been the subject of such attention until relatively recently. It is now recognised that brands need to have an *overall* communication strategy. By this we mean any channel used for talking to the consumer of the retail trade should be subject to scrutiny under that strategy. This is to ensure consistency. The areas that fall within this definition are:

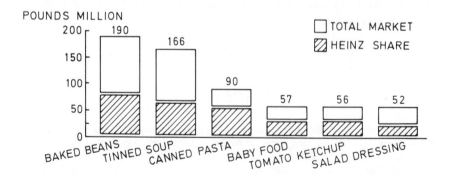

Figure 8.1 *H. J. Heinz— major markets and shares*

—the product itself;
—the packaging and label design;
—public relations activity;
—advertising;
—promotions.

Research can play a key role in ensuring that all of these elements are in harmony and that the brand is deriving the maximum synergy from the efforts being put behind it.

To this end, Heinz have used research to answer a number of strategic promotional issues. For instance:

(i) Who is the primary target audience and are we reaching them?
(ii) What message/impression do we wish to leave with the audience and to what extent have we succeeded?
(iii) Is the activity going to generate incremental sales, and is there a pay-back?
(iv) From a selection of approaches, how do we select the best?

These questions and many like them were addressed for above-the-line advertising almost as a matter of course: they are equally applicable to promotions. As a consequence, it was felt we should consider the degree to which research could help answer these points in a cost-effective way. Heinz were particularly keen to determine the extent to which we could use research to evaluate specific promotions against clearly defined, achievable objectives.

Against this objective Taylor Nelson was commissioned to conduct a programme of research aimed at:

—providing some guidance on how Heinz should evaluate promotional options before committing to final expenditure;
—developing a system which could cost-effectively provide information on who responded to promotions, and some guidance as to how it had affected their apparent purchasing behaviour.

This chapter relates to the findings from the first two stages of research that were carried out against this background.

PROMOTIONS SHOULD BE PRE-TESTED BEFORE COMMITTING TO THE FINAL PACKAGE

Phase I consisted of in-home interviews with 289 buyers of a relevant product field (93% penetration). They were questioned on their awareness of and

Figure 8.2 Levels of participation in various offers. Source: Taylor Nelson and Associates

attitudes to different forms of promotion. In total, the vast majority (86%) claimed to have participated in some form of promotion in the past and over half claimed currently to be participating in at least one promotional offer. We concluded that amongst this target group promotions were very much part of everyday life and as such one would expect them to have some effect on overall purchasing habits at the brand and variety level.

Further investigation showed that both awareness and participation varied considerably by different types of promotion, with those promotions offering money-off future purchase reaching the widest audience; at the other extreme, self-liquidators (i.e. goods purchased ahead by supplier and passed on at cost) and labels collected for vouchers to spend on future groceries were considerably more limited in appeal.

Such variability in levels of participation was either a consequence of the limited appeal of certain sorts of promotion, or because manufacturers were less likely to *offer* these types of promotions. Since one of the objectives to the research was to provide ground rules for future strategic development as well as pre-test some specific alternatives, a number of such promotional concepts were shown to respondents and their degree of interest in each established. Responses to both the question of which type of offer participants personally found most appealing, and which respondents claimed they would actually participate in, all suggest a clear difference in the level of appeal.

Of particular importance was the fact that the relative appeal of promotional concepts *differed* by target group. The possibility of using different promotions as a tactical vehicle to reach specific sectors of the target audience seemed feasible and this objective was adopted by Heinz and incorporated in the research plan.

TABLE 8.1 Differential Appeal of Various Types of Offer

	Most appealing	*Least appealing*	*Would participate in*
Base:	289	289	289
	%	%	%
Offer A	46	16	35
Offer B	27	18	20
Offer C	15	56	11
None	15	15	41

Source: Taylor Nelson and Associates

Pre-testing solely on the basis of respondents' claimed inclination to participate in promotions was, however, deemed a relatively unsatisfactory means of evaluating appeal. We required a pre-testing approach which added a degree of reality, rather than just relying on a mere statement of intent. As a consequence 'interested' respondents were told that if they collected the required number of vouchers, then they would be allowed to participate in the 'pre-test' offers. Monitoring progress with label collection via telephone interviews over a two month period:

—confirmed the *variable* appeal of different types of offers;
—gave some measure of the rates at which respondents were able to collect enough labels to participate in the promotion;
—provided a semi-quantified measure of slippage (people purchasing to participate in the promotion, but not doing so);
—gave a firm base on which further diagnostic questions could be asked, regarding *actual* as opposed to claimed behaviour.

The information provided from this enabled Heinz to quantify a number of issues concerning ways in which they could optimise promotional appeal, as well as providing a pre-test framework which could be used to modify these and future promotions. Additionally, information from these exercises could be used as an input to setting promotional objectives, against which performance of individual promotions could then be evaluated. This led to the second phase of the programme.

PROMOTIONS MUST BE EVALUATED AGAINST SPECIFIC OBJECTIVES

The second stage in the research programme was to provide a tool which could measure the degree to which specific promotions were:

—reaching the correct target market;
—having the desired effect on purchasing;

and which could identify any differences in the profile of responders to each promotion.

To be effective, such an approach had to be potentially applicable to a large number of different promotions over a fairly long time period (approximately 30 potential promotions over 12 months) and to be usable both on promotions where the response was in the order of hundreds of thousands, and also where a far lower level of response was achieved. All of this, we stress, was within a finite research budget, and in an area where research spending has tended to be low.

Taylor Nelson had been conducting experimental work using postal questionnaires as a means of gather 'simple' demographic data on target audiences. As a means of increasing response rate, one alternative evaluated was that of using a foil printed pre-paid questionnaire. It had the benefit of being completed quickly by simple 'scratching-off' answers in the relevant box and so removed the need for writing implements. It was felt that such an approach might be useful here partly because of the obvious synergy between this means of data collection and the likely target audience—and also because the method was highly cost-effective if satisfactory levels of response could be achieved.

An example of the questionnaire is included in Appendix 8.1.

The basis for the research was to select three current Heinz promotions. Promotions differed considerably in terms of the type selected (tailor-made, i.e. promotions specific to a retail chain; versus on-pack), the number of labels required for participation, and also in terms of their likely target audience. For each of the three promotions, 10 000 names and addresses were randomly selected from the total response and a foil printed scratch-off questionnaire returned with their promotional 'prize'. Each questionnaire had been allocated a unique serial number, thereby enabling responses to be matched to respondents' names and address at a later date, should this be required. Questionnaires consisted of eight questions and were consciously kept brief. A test within the agency suggested that eight questions could be completed in one minute.

Specific consideration was given to sampling in light of two requirements:

—that any sample selected had to adequately represent the total sample of redeemers:
—that the administration of any sampling regime had to be practical, given the fact that despatch of questionnaires was to be administered by a third party using outworkers.

Initial consideration was given to a sampling strategy which selected respondents from the total sample using a specified sampling interval and randomly selecting from postal returns by day of week. In the event this was rejected because:

(i) It was extremely difficult to administer 'on the ground' using staff who were unused to such rigorous sampling procedures.

(ii) The alternative of asking a specific worker to mail to all their addresses over a given time period provided a similar random selection procedure. It had the disadvantage, however, of operating over a shorter duration.

In the event, an overall response rate of 67% was finally achieved. Both we and Heinz felt this was particularly satisfactory and justified the use of the 'novelty' approach to the data collection. The resulting data enabled comprehensive analysis to be conducted and has allowed future waves of research to be scaled down, thereby adding to the efficiency of the research programme. Response by promotions was as shown in Table 8.2.

TABLE 8.2   Response by Promotions

		Promotions		
Base size	*Total* 30 000 %	*X* 10 000 %	*Y* 10 000 %	*Z* 10 000 %
Postal response	67	73	66	62
Non-response	33	27	34	38

Source: Taylor Nelson and Associates

Subsequent work has sought to evaluate non-response in terms of type of promotion. From the outset, the objective was to evaluate the *postal* technique as the main means of collecting demographic information on participators. However, because of the uncertainty regarding final response levels and because of the desire to understand differences (if any) between postal responders and non-responders, an additional 1531 telephone interviews amongst non-responders, (split 506—Promotion X; 526—Promotion Y; 499—Promotion Z) were conducted. Comparisons between the demographic data within two means of data collection could then be made.

Information collected from the postal questionnaire was both descriptive (household composition and demographics, main store used for grocery shopping, etc.) and evaluative (what changes in purchasing behaviour did you adopt to take advantage of the Heinz offer?). In the descriptive area,

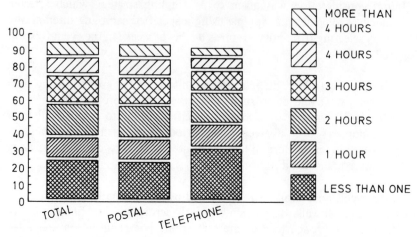

Figure 8.3   Number of hours of ITV watched yesterday. Source: Taylor Nelson and Associates

results from the telephone and postal methods were largely comparable. Responses to the question; 'How many hours of ITV did you personally watch yesterday?' demonstrate this.

Although the telephone sample were significantly lighter viewers (at the 95% confidence level) than the postal sample, in terms of the likely actions taken as a consequence of both sets of data, the two patterns of response were deemed similar.

Similarly, data on the number of people in the household from the postal and telephone response was comparable (3.24 people per household postal study: 3.24 people per household telephone study) and, very interestingly,

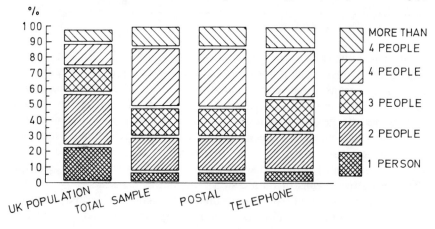

Figure 8.4   Number of people in household. Source: Taylor Nelson and Associates

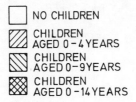

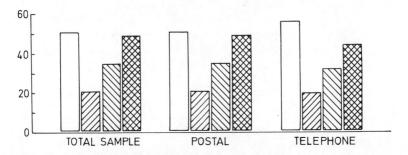

Figure 8.5 Number of children in participating households. Source: Taylor Nelson and Associates

in both instances was shown to be quite different from the UK household population. However, the fact that Heinz brands featured particularly strongly amongst households with children meant the Company was successful in reaching a key target group.

The further area of comparability between methods was in respect to data on the number of children in the household, where the general shape of the postal and telephone response was again similar. Again however, there were differences between the responding sample and the overall UK population.

While there were differences between promotional responders and the UK population in most of these areas, our investigations showed only minor differences between responses from the postal and the telephone responders. Our conclusion on the basis of these data, therefore, was that in respect to factual data regarding household composition and structure, a postal approach of this nature could cost-effectively produce data on the demographic profile of promotion responders.

In all the preceding cases, differences between the postal and the telephone approach were small enough not to affect the action taken by marketing if only postal data had been available. Responses to questions regarding promotional participation, however, suggests that non-responders to the postal questionnaire contacted through the telephone interview were in fact both lighter participators in promotions in general in the last year, and also less likely to have participated in Heinz promotions in the last year.

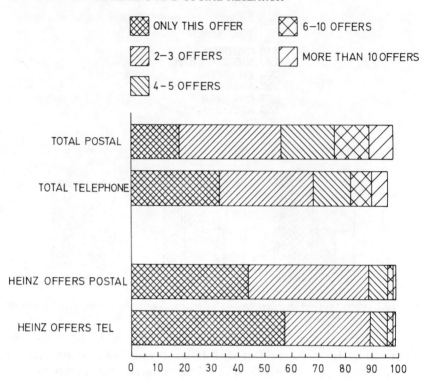

TOTAL NO OF OFFERS MEAN POST 4.1: TEL 3.3
HEINZ OFFERS TOTAL MEAN POST 2.2: TEL 1.9

Figure 8.6 Number of offers involved in over last 12 months. Source: Taylor Nelson and Associates

Responses to questions regarding changes in purchasing to take advantage of the offers showed similar differences between the telephone and the postal sample. In overall terms the result supported the early findings from the in-home study with the majority of offer participators continuing to purchase

TABLE 8.3   Claimed Changes in Behaviour Adopted to Take Advantage of Offer

Base size	*Telephone and Postal response* 21568 %
No change in purchasing/purchased as normal	37
Stocked up on usual purchase	43
Changed brands to Heinz	13
Bought more of a new variety	9

their usual brand or variety rather than switch brands in order to take advantage of the promotion.

While there were differences in response to this question by promotion, the overall implications of this were that Heinz was spending money to:

(i) Change the timing of purchasing, but not to obviously widen the repertoire (most stocked up on usual purchase).

(ii) Gain additional sales *only* from expanding Heinz's *share* of a purchase repertoire; stocking up on 'usual purchases' means that the consumers have a number of 'usual purchases' and Heinz increases its share of these only as a consequence of the promotion).

(iii) By stocking up on 'usual purchase' Heinz have an increased rate of use amongst the existing buyer base and generated additional volumes by stock pressure on consumers.

However, there was little to suggest that those promotions at least were particularly successful in gaining first-time brand or variety trial. The implications were that such promotions were therefore less successful in increasing cumulative penetration, and this point was noted by marketing and fed into calculations for setting future action standards.

Differences between the postal and telephone responders shed a slightly different light on this conclusion, however:

Telephone responders (who were also lighter offer participators) were considerably less likely to modify behaviour. Whilst brand/variety switching still only occurred at a lower level it was considerably higher amongst the more frequent promotions respondents (in the postal sample) and again this was noted for future action standards and allowances made for future comparisons across promotions where only a postal approach was adopted.

TABLE 8.4   Claimed Changes in Behaviour Adopted to Take Advantage of Offers

	Postal responders	Telephone responders
Base size	20 037	1531
	%	%
No change in purchasing/purchased as normal	36	52
Stocked up on usual purchase	44	37
Changed brands to Heinz	14	7
Bought more of a new variety	9	6

SUMMARY AND CONCLUSIONS

The overall objective for the research programme was to provide both strategic information which could enable Heinz to optimise its performance in the promotions area, and a framework within which Heinz could look to evaluate the specific success of a promotion. While it is still somewhat early to say conclusively that we have been successful in this latter area, we can say with confidence that Heinz are now in a better position to evaluate individual promotions than they were prior to the research, and that we have been successful in providing a *cost-effective* vehicle for achieving this. Clearly, evaluating promotions in this way and building up a bank of information which can then be used to evaluate the relative success over a number of alternative promotional concepts provides a valuable framework against which a promotion's ability to meet its objectives can be judged.

Our main conclusions from the chapter are, however, somewhat different. We set out to demonstrate that research does have an important part to play in guiding promotional development and in evaluating the success of promotions at achieving particular objectives. When we started this project we were uncertain that research could effectively meet the objectives with the budgeting constraints set. Thinking carefully about the requirements and creatively about the solutions open to us has produced a vehicle which Heinz can use to aid in the formulation of achievable marketing objectives. It is also one which can be used regularly to determine whether the promotion has achieved these objectives.

This chapter was originally presented at the ESOMAR Conference 'Below the Line Sponsoring', Milan, November 1985.

APPENDIX 8.1

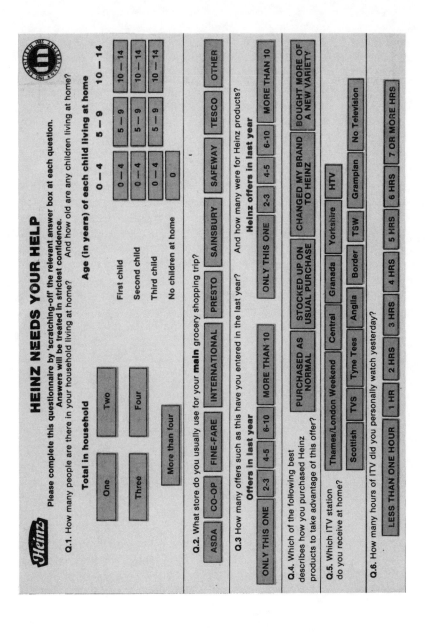

HEINZ NEEDS YOUR HELP

Please complete this questionnaire by 'scratching-off' the relevant answer box at each question. Answers will be treated in strictest confidence.

Q.1. How many people are there in your household living at home? And how old are any children living at home?

Total in household

| One | Two |
| Three | Four |
| More than four |

Age (in years) of each child living at home

	0 — 4	5 — 9	10 — 14
First child	0 — 4	5 — 9	10 — 14
Second child	0 — 4	5 — 9	10 — 14
Third child	0 — 4	5 — 9	10 — 14
No children at home	0

Q.2. What store do you usually use for your **main** grocery shopping trip?

| ASDA | CO-OP | FINE-FARE | INTERNATIONAL | PRESTO | SAINSBURY | SAFEWAY | TESCO | OTHER |

Q.3 How many offers such as this have you entered in the last year? And how many were for Heinz products?

Offers in last year

| ONLY THIS ONE | 2-3 | 4-5 | 6-10 | MORE THAN 10 |

Heinz offers in last year

| ONLY THIS ONE | 2-3 | 4-5 | 6-10 | MORE THAN 10 |

Q.4. Which of the following best describes how you purchased Heinz products to take advantage of this offer?

| PURCHASED AS NORMAL | STOCKED UP ON USUAL PURCHASE | CHANGED MY BRAND TO HEINZ | BOUGHT MORE OF A NEW VARIETY |

Q.5. Which ITV station do you receive at home?

| Thames/London Weekend | Central | Granada | Yorkshire | HTV |
| Scottish | TVS | Tyne Tees | Anglia | Border | TSW | Grampian | No Television |

Q.6. How many hours of ITV did you personally watch yesterday?

| LESS THAN ONE HOUR | 1 HR | 2 HRS | 3 HRS | 4 HRS | 5 HRS | 6 HRS | 7 OR MORE HRS |

Applied Marketing and Social Research 2nd Edition
Edited by Ute Bradley
©Copyright John Wiley 1987

9. The Tracking Study in Market Research

Peter Sampson *Burke Marketing Research Ltd.*

Tracking studies have become firmly established in the market research literature and many refinements have been added to them over the years (see Colman and Brown[6]). In the last decade Pre-test Market Models (e.g. BASES, Sensor, Assessor) have also established themselves, as they provide information that previously only test markets provided and they do so without exposing the new product to the competition (see Factor and Sampson[3] and Sampson and Factor[4]).

In this paper we are fortunate to see the two developments coming together, as it concentrates on the development of the BASES Pre-test Market Model, applied in the area of advertising tracking. Of necessity, a lot of ground needs to be covered by this paper and it assumes the student knows about:

Usership and Attitude studies;

tracking studies;

pre-test market models.

Up-to-date references are provided on all three areas, but in addition the student may wish to consult a basic text, such as Worcester and Downham's *Consumer Market Research Handbook*, 3rd ed. (see Introduction). Once the student has this knowledge, this paper with its many examples, will repay careful study.

INTRODUCTION

During the last decade or so, the tracking study has become a major strategic and planning tool for marketing management. It now ranks along with the market study, or what is often referred to as the 'U and A' (Usage and Attitudes) study, in terms of importance in providing information from market research. From its simple origins (see Sampson and Marshall[1]) the tracking study has developed into a very sophisticated research approach.

Tracking studies are methods of continuous measurement in which market research data are collected in a systematic way at intervals, accumulated and summarised periodically. Depending on the market, the system and what the tracking study is seeking to achieve, the data collection intervals and time frame, in general, can vary.

Unlike the continuous panel— a time series approach, where data are obtained from the same sample of people over a number of points in time— the tracking study is a trend design approach, collecting data from matched samples of the same population over time. Whereas the panel allows data to be analysed for individuals, longitudinal analysis being applied at a micro-behavioural level or on an aggregate basis, with the continuous tracking study, data may only be analysed in aggregate form.

Early tracking took the form of a baseline study that would be followed by periodic checks, usually in response to a particular advertising campaign. A control group, unexposed to the advertising, was often the subject of parallel measurement. The effects of the campaign were evaluated by differences over time in the test area, less any effects that may have occurred in the control area. The use made of tracking studies was mostly in an *ad hoc* context. Nowadays, tracking studies are synonymous with continuous measurement and planning.

Old-style tracking studies were relatively simplistic. The researcher had to consider a number of research design issues such as:

—sampling and matching approach;
—sample size;
—time interval between measurements;
—what key variables to measure for comparisons;
—the actual measurements to take.

The tracking study was regarded as the evaluation of a control strategy both before and after its implementation[2]. Essentially, the research set out to answer the question: 'How successful was the control strategy (e.g. a particular advertising campaign) in achieving its objectives?'

A clear statement of the objectives in advance of design and measurement was necessary. Such a statement required the detailing of such points as:

(i) What is the nature of the objective? For example, is the objective to establish awareness, change attitudes, affect behaviour, etc.?

(ii) Who is the target of the exercise? Is it the total population or segments and, if so, what segments?

   (iii) Is there a single change or are multiple changes sought?
   (iv) When is the desired change supposed to take place? Is it immediately, or medium term or long term?
   (v) How long is the effect intended to last? How permanent is the change intended to be?
   (vi) What magnitude of change determines 'effectiveness'?

Moreover, it was important to distinguish between impact, effectiveness and efficiency. They are not necessarily the same. A campaign may achieve substantial impact (by, say, obtaining a very high degree of awareness and recall) but be ineffective in failing to shift attitudes or change behaviour (like increased sales). It may be effective without being efficient. That is, it may achieve behaviourial change or sales but at an uneconomic cost. Thus efficiency may be regarded as the same thing as cost-effectiveness, not necessarily the same thing as effectiveness *per se*.

While modern-day tracking studies can, of course, still be simply designed to satisfy limited objectives their scope and complexity have been greatly developed. Tracking studies are now totally integrated market studies. They can examine the relative position of key components of the total marketing mix and marketing strategy over time. Tracking studies can be adapted to the analytical approaches used by Simulated Test Market Models also called Pre-test Market Models (see Factor and Sampson[3] and Sampson and Factor[4].) Using these systems (BASES, ASSESSOR, SENSOR, LTM, etc.) it is possible to estimate penetration and volume sales or brand share of a new product via a concept/use test, rather than a test market: hence the term 'Simulated Test Market'. The format of the individual systems vary slightly but, in essence, they require the new product to be communicated via some form of advertising and then intentions to purchase recorded or dummy purchases made. Respondents are given the product to try and reinterviewed. (Again, who is actually asked to try the product varies for the different systems.) From the original interview data and the reinterview, the consumer responses are combined with market-plan and market-place variables to produce the forecast. They deal with consumer responses like awareness, attitudes and buying behaviour; with market plan variables like distribution, advertising and promotional expenditure; and via simulation, allow different aspects of the plan to be altered and the effects on the sales components estimated.

Because the marketing process is continuous and because tracking studies provide continuous information, they are popular with marketing management. The true value of tracking studies is when they become fully integrated into the market planning function and are used to set future performance objectives. This is easily done by combining tracking and Simulated Test Market Model approaches.

Donius[5] in his review of market tracking as a strategic and planning tool describes how tracking studies fit into both the decision making and research processes. Beginning with the planning of strategy, the decision process moves through executional development and testing to an in-market assessment. Intelligently used, market tracking can be a major part of the process of evaluating the marketing plan in an on-going sense, modifying it, remodifying it, and so on, in order to achieve the maximum benefit from the resources employed.

CONTINUOUS ADVERTISING TRACKING

Colman and Brown[6] have discussed how advertising tracking studies may be related to sales effects. Although primarily used to assess the probable effectiveness of advertising campaigns in fast-moving packaged goods markets, they demonstrate how advertising tracking has been used to show why some commercials appear to be more effective than others.

A better measurement approach than conducting all the interviews in a short space of time is to interview continuously. This enables responses to be made over different day of week shopping behaviour and across a campaign. The contemporary viewpoint in tracking favours, say, 100 interviews per week throughout the year, or 20 per working day, in any product field being tracked. Forms of analysis can vary in terms of aggregation, but commonly used is the 'rolling four-weekly window'[7]. Here, weeks one to four are added together and compared with the aggregation of weeks two to five, three to six, and so on, using samples of $N = 400$ per period. The data are plotted against media inputs or weekly TVR (Television Rating Points) delivery.

Regression models are usually used to relate key measures to advertising expenditure and TVR delivery, providing an indication of advertising effectiveness.

Different systems, as they reflect the different objectives, experiences and preferences of different researchers, *can* measure the following kinds of things:

—product category use;
—spontaneous awareness of brands:
    —first mention,
    —other mentions;
—prompted awareness;
—trial;
—past purchase;
—future purchase intent;

—brand images;
—advertising recall;
—advertising content recall.

TRACKING AND SALES FORECASTING FOR ONE BRAND

Increasingly, tracking is being used in conjunction with sales forecasting. Sampson and Standen[8] discuss sales estimation from tracking studies using forecasting models designed for this purpose — BASES IV for a new product or TEL-TRAC for an existing product. The two models are very slightly different because a new product with no previous awareness/experience must be treated differently to an established brand.

Here, a fairly standard Usage and Attitude study is carried out to a market tracking format. Data on awareness, penetration, repeat purchase, purchase frequency, amount purchased etc., are collected and a modeling system based on a regression or econometric forecasting approach is employed. In general, regression is used to model a short-term sales forecast for a new product being tracked, because there are only a few data points available. In the case of a well-established product with, say, three years back data available, an econometric model like Box-Jenkins is preferable.

Whereas market plan measures like Distribution and Awareness have to be estimated in a Simulated Test Market exercise conducted before a product is launched, once it is in the market and being tracked, these inputs can be actual measures rather than estimated ones.

Typical objectives may be to:

—assist users in monitoring the performance of a test brand over time in test market or national introduction;
—monitor sales volume trend (retail or consumer panel, or shipment) versus planned;
—monitor trial build, repeat buying curve of test brand versus expectation;
—monitor brand awareness trend (U and A tracking) versus expectation;
—provide early forecast of test brand performance;
—evaluate the impact of competitive reactions;
—provide direction for better marketing strategy;
—provide simulation for alternative marketing plans.

The BASES IV/TEL-TRAC systems consist of three parts:

(i) Data collection via a multi-wave U and A tracking study.
(ii) Model calibration.
(iii) A sales volume calculation model.

Data Collection

Data are collected by means of a standardised U and A study design with at least four waves (one pre-launch and three post-launch) for a new product, and quarterly or continuous telephone or personal interview tracking for established brands. The pre-launch or 'baseline' check is a feature of most tracking studies. It provides a 'clean' picture of the market, providing measures of claimed awareness, purchasing etc., before the launch of the new product impacts on the market. This does not apply, of course, for an existing product where the first wave is treated as a normal check. The questionnaire design includes all the regular U and A study questions on awareness, usage, diagnostic questions, recalled past purchases, and expected future behaviour. It is important that a standard, fixed-order questionnaire be used with all questions arranged in a particular manner.

1. A pre-wave before launch is often necessary to evaluate the 'ghost' awareness and trial rate for the new product; that is, small percentages of respondents always claim to be aware of a new brand or to have bought it, even though this is impossible. The figure could well be high in the case of a line extension from a familiar brand where there is genuine confusion and respondents are really thinking of the parent brand or some other line extension with the same umbrella brand name.
2. A minimum of two (preferably three or more) post-waves are carried out after product launch.
3. Data collected in each post-wave, in addition to the normal U and A questionnaire, are:
   (a) Past purchases:
      —ever purchased the new test product during the past 12 months;
      —how many times purchased the new product;
      —size or variety purchased;
      —likes/dislikes of the new product;
      —perceived value for money;
      —number of units purchased each time;
      —competitive frame.
   (b) Intended future purchases:
      —purchase intention (buyers and aware non-buyers);
      —intended future purchase frequency;
      —units per future purchase occasion;
      —size and/or variety choice.

The BASES Calibration Model

The BASES consumer response calibration model is an empirically developed model that calibrates consumers' claimed responses for overstatement and confusion. To develop such a model, it is necessary, at the developmental stage, to have both the consumer claimed survey data from standardised U and A tracking and actual panel data from the same market. An example of this type of data for trial and first repeat (i.e. those trialists who buy at least one more time) is given below:

Brand X (new product)

Weeks on Market	Cumulative penetration (first, trial purchase) (Panel data) (%)	U and A tracking claimed ever purchased (%)
4	1.9	6.6
8	4.5	
12	6.4	
16	8.2	
20	8.8	10.4
24	9.3	
28	9.9	
32	10.3	11.8
36	10.8	
40	11.1	
44	11.5	12.4
48	12.1	
52	12.5	

Cumulative first repeat (i.e. subsequent purchasing rate)

Weeks on market	Consumer diary panel data (actual) (%)	U and A tracking (claimed) (%)
4	17	
8	28	38
12	30	
16	33	
20	35	42
24	38	
28	39	
32	39	45
36	41	
40	41	
44	42	47
48	42	
52	43	—

Both tables show a good match between the forecast and the actual results achieved, as measured by the diary panel.

Two key factors were discovered to affect the projected consumer behaviour based on U and A studies. The BASES calibration model takes them into account.

Consumers' Claimed Responses

Consumers' claimed responses of trial purchase, repeat and frequency etc., contain overstatement that tends to be stronger in the earlier months of the brand's life. The longer a brand is on the market, the lower the calibration factor becomes.

Name Used and Product Category

There is a certain amount of confusion among consumers concerning a product name that is used in more than one product category or different product types within a product category. In the USA, for example, Tylenol is the number one brand in the analgesic category, with an awareness of over 90% among all households. However, the Tylenol name is used in many forms: tablets, liquid and capsules. It is expected that if a new Tylenol product is launched, it would generate some consumer confusion, at least initially. Based on degree of confusion, three general groups of calibration models can be identified:

(i) *High level*: line extension situation when the same name is used within the existing product category.

(ii) *Medium level*: different product category but using an old, established name.

(iii) *Low level*: new name in a product category new to that manufacturer.

The degree of confusion also depends on the length of time the product has been on the market. It is expected that the longer the product has been available in the market-place, the less confusion there will be surrounding it.

Separate models have been developed for each type of name/category confusion and for penetration, repeat purchase frequency. The calibration model is aimed at providing estimates of penetration, repeat and purchase cycle each time and projecting these forward to the end of one year with input on future purchase intention from the U and A study.

In the developmental phase, several functional forms of model were attempted, and the multiplicative (or log-linear) form settled upon. For a given confusion level, a penetration calibration model based on claimed ever purchase at time T is taken to be:

$$Y_T = a\ X^b\ T^c, \quad O < b,\ c < 1$$

where T = number of weeks since product availability, X = claimed penetration from U and A study at time T, and a, b and c are 'weights' to be estimated from empirical validation.

The Volume Calculation Model

The projected sales components from the calibration models become the input to the BASES dynamic depth of repeat model for volume forecasting. At this point, other data sources (such as retail audit, panel data etc.) can also be applied, if available, to refine the volume projection. The mathematical expression of the BASES volume calculating model is given below.

By definition, we can express the model as the following:

$$S_t = T_t + R_t \qquad (t = 1, 2, \ldots) \tag{1}$$

where S, T and R are, respectively, Total Sales Volume, Trial Volume and Repeat Volume up to Time Period (week) t.

In addition, Trial Volume (T_t) and Repeat Volume (R_t) can be further defined as:

$$T_t = TM \times P_t \times Uo \tag{2}$$

where TM = Target Market Size (e.g. number of households in the target market area), P_t = Cumulative Trial (or Penetration) Rate up to week t and Uo = average units purchased at trial (or penetration).

$$R_t = \sum_{i=1}^{\infty} N_{i-1,t} Y_{i,t} U_i \ (i = 1, 2, 3 \ldots) \tag{3}$$

where i = repeat level 1, 2, 3 . . . $N_{i-1,t}$ = cumulative number of consumers repeating at least $(i-1)$ times by week t (defining $N_{o,t} = TM \times P_t$), $Y_{i,t}$ = conditional cumulative ith Repeat Rate at week t given that $(i-1)$ Repeat Purchase was made up to week t, and U_i = average units at repeat level i.

Data Input

Data input that can be used for BASES IV tracking include:

(i) Sales data (Nielsen, or factory shipments).
   —awareness, trial and usage (U and A tracking—at least three waves).

    (ii) Plan or expectation of sales volume trend obtained internally or from previous test.

   (iii) Expected trial and repeat curve based on pre-test market estimates. The data set, here, look like consumer diary panel data. These measures include trial/penetration, first repeat, subsequent repeats etc. (i.e. what is called the 'depth of repeat' or 'long-run repeat').

Analysis and Modelling

In addition to tracking data, retail store data and consumer panel data can be used. There is value in taking advantage of what data is available. Clearly data like Nielsen and AGB Panel Data, if available, should be used as actual model parameter inputs. The analysis and modelling approaches will differ depending on the precise data used.

Survey Tracking Data

    (i) The BASES empirically developed calibration model is used to estimate 'true' sales components (trial curve, repeat curve, purchase cycle, purchased units etc.).

   (ii) The BASES dynamic depth of repeat model is used to calculate sales volume, for each set of calibrated sales components.

   (iii) The BASES awareness model and promotion response models are used to simulate likely sales components under alternative marketing plans.

Retail Stores Sales Data

    (i) An econometric modelling approach is used (multiple regression or Box-Jenkins time series analysis depending on how many data points are available) to evaluate the sales responses due to:
        —a test brand's advertising and promotional activities;
        —the sales impact of competitive reaction;
        —estimates of price and advertising elasticities when possible.

   (ii) National sales volume from store sales data is forecast, adjusting for distribution and spending variations.

Consumer Panel Data (e.g. back data available)

    (i) Econometric modelling is used to evaluate sales responses for each sales component due to test brand's marketing activities and competitive activities.
        —The BASES dynamic depth of repeat model is used to estimate sales volume, adjusting for distribution and advertising spend variations.

Case Histories

In 1983, Sampson and Standen[8] published the following BASES IV and TEL-TRAC case histories. By that time, over 35 actual applications and 85 experimental cases had been validated using the system. The overall accuracy of the forecasts were 69% of validations within 10% of actual sales and 31% between 11–20% of actual.

Case 1: A New Product—Brand X (BASES IV)

(a) First, penetration estimates were calibrated from Brand X as stated in the section on calibration models:

Weeks available	8	20	32	44	52
Cumulative penetration (trial) estimate % (model calibration)	3.9	8.0	10.5	11.8	12.9*
Cumulative actual penetration % (from consumer panel data)	4.5	8.8	10.3	11.5	12.5

(b) Cumulative first repeat rate (i.e. subsequent purchase after trial):

Weeks on the market	Claimed (%)	Model estimates (%)	Panel data (actual) (%)
4			17
8	33	25	28
12			30
16			33
20	42	36	35
24			38
28			39
32	45	41	39
36			41
40			41
44	47	43	42
48			42
52		45 (projected)	43

*Projected to end of Year 1 based on model calibrated cumulative penetration trend and future purchase intent at week 44 (wave 4) among aware non-buyers.

(c) Average purchase cycle and average purchase units per purchase occasion were similarly estimated to be five weeks and 1.2 packs, respectively.

(d) Projected Year 1 consumer sales volume, not including pipeline inventory, for the total US (85 million households) was 2 331 000 cases of 12 packs (80% confidence range = 2.05 – 2.61 million cases).

Actual Year 1 factory sales were 2 950 000 cases of 12 packs. Assuming 25% pipeline inventory, the estimated actual Year 1 consumer sales were 2 213 000 cases of 12 packs.

Case 2: A Mature Product — Brand Y (TEL-TRAC)

(a) *Penetration*: forward penetration was projected quarterly based on claimed purchase during past year, adjusted for the future purchase intent and total brand awareness level. Brand Y was continuously tracked and a calibrated model estimate of penetration obtained for each quarter. Other forecasts were made for the period of one year.

Quarter	1 (%)	2 (%)	3 (%)	4 (%)	Annual average (%)
Annual penetration					
Model estimate	13.1	13.5	14.2	13.6	13.6
Actual	NA*	NA	NA	NA	13.9
Repeat rate					
Model estimate	47	49	48	47	48
Actual	NA	NA	NA	NA	50
Purchase cycle (in weeks)					
Model estimate	8.6	7.7	8.8	7.6	8.2
Actual	NA	NA	NA	NA	
Average units per purchase occasion					
Model estimate	2.1	2.2	2.2	2.0	2.1
Actual	NA	NA	NA	NA	2.2
Annual sales volume (in 1000 cases of 24 units)					
Model estimate	1704	1819	1783	1790	1774
Actual	NA	NA	NA	NA	1878

*NA: not applicable

Applications

If the regular U and A study is modified to include the necessary past and future purchase questions with a standard questionnaire, and a calibration model is validated for interpreting consumers' claims, the usefulness of the U and A study will increase greatly. It then can be used to:

— monitor the state of business;
— provide explanation of change (changes in awareness, penetration, repeat, repeat decay, competitive activities etc.);
— evaluate the effects of marketing actions (advertising, promotions, sampling etc.);
— simulate the consumer sales impact due to changes in advertising spending, promotional activities, price action and competitive reactions.

This type of study is especially valuable for those brands that have relatively small penetration levels. Since the cost of obtaining panel data with a large enough buyer base for repeat analysis is sometimes cost-prohibitive, continuous U and A studies are indeed a very viable alternative.

BASES Experience

BASES IV and TEL-TRAC has been used in more than 600 projects since 1979 across the world.

Validation

Out of the 150 brands that used BASES tracking between 1979 and 1983, the accuracy of the Year 1 Sales Volume forecast was:

71% within ± 10% of actual
19% between ± 10% to 15%
10% between ± 15% to 22%

The accuracy of volume estimates depends on:

— the accuracy of marketing plan inputs;
— the amount of data available—number of post waves;
— the quality of cumulation—i.e. the fit of econometric models.

TRACKING AND SALES FORECASTING — SEVERAL BRANDS

The BASES IV and TEL-TRAC systems have been further developed to be able to track up to four brands in a single product category and provide 12 month forward sales forecasts. Whereas the BASES IV and TEL-TRAC questionnaires cover one brand only, collecting the data as previously described and then, in addition, such diagnostic data as may be required, BASES MBT (Multi-Brand Tracking) collects only basic data required for tracking and inputs to the sales forecasting model, for up to four brands, (Pioche[9]).

Using simulation, by changing the values of the different parameters, tactical exercises can be applied to the test and competitors' brands, to estimate the outcomes of different marketing plans and competitive responses.

THE FUTURE OF TRACKING

BASES SUPER-TRAC is currently being developed[10], an advanced, comprehensive tracking system that will use:

— data about the marketing plan from marketing companies and about shipments, promotions and advertising expenditure;
— data about competitive brands;
— data from other research like audits and panels;
— data from continuous tracking.

Information will be provided on:

— sales forecasting (penetration, depth of sales and sales volume for test and competitive brands);
— advertising and promotional elasticities;
— brand switching and market structure dynamics;
— simulation outcomes of changing market plan components.

With the advent of BASES SUPER-TRAC, the tracking study will have achieved a level of sophistication undreamed of by its early developers.

REFERENCES

1. SAMPSON, P. and MARSHALL, K., 'Improving the Efficiency of Research Methods used in Advertising Tracking Studies', *ESOMAR Congress Proceedings*, Oslo (1977)
2. GREEN, O. E. and TULL, D. S., *Research for Marketing Decisions*, Prentice-Hall (1975)
3. FACTOR, S. and SAMPSON, P., 'Making Decisions about Launching New Products', *Market Research Society Annual Conference Proceedings*, Brighton (1983)

4. SAMPSON, P. and FACTOR, S., 'Pre-test Market Models — Take 'em or leave 'em?', *Market Research Society Annual Conference Proceedings*, Brighton (1985)
5. DONIUS, J. F., 'Market Tracking: A Strategic Reassessment and Planning Tool', *Journal of Advertising Research* **25** (1985) 1
6. COLMAN, S. and BROWN, G., 'Advertising Tracking Studies and Sales Effects', *Market Research Society Annual Conference Proceedings*, Brighton (1983)
7. BROWN, G., 'Tracking Studies and Sales Effects: A UK Perspective', *Journal of Advertising Research* **25** (1985) 1
8. SAMPSON, P. and STANDEN, P., 'Predicting Sales Volume and Market Share', *ESOMAR Seminar on New Product Development Proceedings*, Athens (1983)
9. PIOCHE, A. '*BASES MBT — Multi-brand Tracking: A New Tracking System*', Internal Burke Publication, Paris (1986)
10. PIOCHE, A., SAMPSON, P. and STANDEN, P., '*BASES SUPER-TRAC*: Optimising Marketing Plans for New and Established Products', ERC (European Research Centre) Working Document, Munich (1986)

10. On-Line Data Bases: Their Role in Information Retrieval

David Holmes *Consultant*

The role and contribution of Information Technology runs as a theme through many of these cases. This study concentrates on it. The building of an on-line data base is described, using limited in-house computing equipment. The value of being able to access the data produced interactively is fully demonstrated.

The study also stresses the growth of on-line data bases and the developments in linking such data bases, giving some companies the ability to develop systems to support the decision making of their marketing management (Decision Support Systems).

INTRODUCTION

It has been estimated that, in the first half of the 1980s, the total number of 'on-line' bibliographic data bases in the world increased from some 400 to nearly 3000. This is considered by many to be a peak, and there are signs of a down-turn in the trend. Statistical data bases, though fewer in number, are still growing as more and more data that used to be accessed from hard copy is now being made available for direct access by computer.

The implications of this trend to marketing and social researchers are quite considerable, and the writer believes that the speed and flexibility of analysis offered by on-line data bases can significantly increase the *value* of survey data to the end-user.

Over the next few pages, some of these implications will be discussed, and the development of one such data base that has been created for the Pharmaceutical Industry, will be described.

THE DEVELOPMENT OF ON-LINE DATA BASES

First, let us consider what we mean by an 'on-line' data base. Any large volume of information that is held on a computer can be considered to form a data base, and this can include bibliographic and textual data such as news services, or survey results from your last market research survey.

The bibliographic industry was the first to develop computerised data bases when, in the late 1960s, some publishers in the USA who had switched to automatic type setting equipment, realised that the magnetic tapes they were using could be read into a computer. Once the information was stored into memory, it was relatively simple to develop programs that would search through the data for specific bits of information. This was usually on the basis of searching for text or key words.

The fact that the data are held on a computer does not, however, mean that they are readily accessible. Until fairly recently, the user of the information would have to contact the data-processing department responsible for running the computer, specify the requirements and wait for the results. Immediate access was technically possible for computer experts, but not for the layman. As a result, it was often easier to look it up in a book!

The bibliographic data bases were, again, the first to make use of the developing technology enabling non-computer experts to access the data bases through normal telephone lines with a terminal and a modem. No doubt the relative simplicity of the programs required to enable a lay person to search for specific text or key words has helped to accelerate this trend. As the same basic programs can be used for virtually any type of bibliographic data, it is a fairly easy task for a supplier to make new data available for on-line access. Now there are well in excess of 2000 such data bases.

Market research and other providers of survey data have been much slower to develop 'on-line' access for the end-user. This is partially because many surveys are considered to be *ad hoc* in nature, and to have a relatively short life-span, and the suppliers are frequently relatively small research agencies without the resources or expertise to develop such systems for their clients. Add to this the considerably greater degree of complexity needed to analyse data and form tabulations when compared with simple text searching, and it is not surprising that most research data still goes through the age-old stages of analysis. The researcher specifies tabulations, and then waits for them to arrive on his or her desk before commencing the analysis. All too often the researcher wishes that the specification had included something additional, or different, but, time pressures being what they are, has to live with the tabulations that were produced.

In the view of the writer, the use of on-line systems enabling the end-user to access the data from surveys, analyse them immediately, and continue to be able to access them and interrogate them as required, will become the norm rather than the exception. We are just starting to see such systems being used for certain of the larger survey data bases, and some researchers are even using them for small *ad hoc* studies.

Next, let us consider some of the benefits and the problems of such systems.

BENEFITS AND PROBLEMS WITH 'ON-LINE' SURVEY DATA BASES

Benefits

When.discussing on-line data bases in this context, the writer is referring to interactive systems that enable the researcher to interrogate and analyse the data. He is not referring to simple 'page images' that can be accessed by Prestel or other viewdata systems.

The first, and in the writer's opinion, the most important benefit of these interactive systems, is that they allow the researcher to have 'hands-on' access to the data at all times. There is no one else between the researcher and the data; he or she can check hypotheses and follow leads without having to keep going back to the DP department every time they need more tabulations. In the writer's experience, most researchers tend to put too little thought into their specifications for tabulations, and ask for 'everything by everything'. The result is huge mounds of paper, much of it full of zeros, and much of little value.

Even though some of the more searching, and potentially more valuable, analyses may have been omitted, it is rare that a second set of analysis is requested. This is usually because of tight deadlines, and the fact that there is a delay inherent in specifying and receiving tabulations from a remote computer department.

With direct access to the data, the researcher is able to delve into the information on a trial and error basis, follow through hypotheses and work with the information in a much more flexible and sensitive way.

The next benefit relates to the end value of the information. A lot of questions do not get asked of researchers by their marketing management, purely because it takes time to reanalyse data or to conduct a new survey in order to provide an answer. Once management becomes aware that they can expect almost instantaneous answers to their questions, then they are more likely to ask them, and hence make greater use of the research function. This assumes, of course, that the relevent raw data is included in the data base from previous surveys, and that brings us on to the next point.

Being able to access data easily, and on demand, has the effect of extending its life-span. All too often, a survey is forgotten once the report has been produced and the original objectives have been met. When new questions are posed, a new survey is conducted, with all the implications of time and money, rather than reviewing the information that has been collected from previous studies. Frequently this results in duplication of data.

Far too many surveys sit on shelves collecting dust, when forming them into a data base will enable them to be accessed easily in the future, reanalysed if necessary, and used to help answer additional questions. It may still be necessary to conduct another survey, but the data already in-house can often help in its design, pointing to areas for further questions, and avoiding areas that are of no use.

One effect of all this is that the surveys themselves will change in nature. Instead of being designed purely to answer set objectives — a reactive role — they are more likely to be designed to incorporate data to help answer future questions — a much more proactive role. The researcher will need to be much more in tune with management thinking, and predicting the type of questions that may be asked, in order to maintain a data base of relevent information. The researcher will also be more involved in keeping the information regularly updated, especially as management becomes more used to viewing the data in a certain form. This can have the benefit of enabling a much more meaningful study of trends than is possible from a series of often disconnected *ad hoc* studies.

Problems

There are, of course, problems associated with on-line data bases. Leaving aside for a moment the problems of creating the data base in the first place, the most fundamental is whether or not it will be used!

Those who are not used to using computers are very often reluctant to sit in front of a terminal, preferring instead to refer to hard copy (paper). Even if there is sufficient enthusiasm in the early stages to overcome this 'key-board shyness', one often finds that the system starts to fall into disuse once the novelty has worn off.

In this respect, there is still a considerable gap between the available technology and the psychology of the end-user. This has not been helped by many systems that have been developed which, whilst claiming to be easy to use, are incomprehensible to most lay people without a considerable time and effort investment on their part to learn how to use them.

There is a tendency for a lot of system designers to fall short on making the 'front end' of the system friendly. Ideally, the user should not need to worry about the complexities of how the system works. The 'front end' part should consist of a series of menus and help messages that take him or her through the various commands required for the enquiry.

The rapid increase in the number of desk-top microcomputers in offices and the widespread use of word processing has helped enormously to overcome some of the fear of computers. It has also moved the control from the DP department much more into the hands of the end-user of the data.

This brings us to the next problem. In creating an on-line data base, you have to decide who should have access, and whether all enquiries should go through the researcher. In many respects this is recreating a similar situation to the one that we are moving away from, which is all tabulations going through the data processing department. A policy decision needs to be made about this as the implications in terms of departmental functions are quite far reaching. As an example, many organisations insist that the researcher interprets data and provides the conclusions to the marketing personnel. The marketing personnel are not encouraged to access the raw data. With an on-line data base, the marketing personnel may well have access to the raw data, and start drawing their own conclusions without reference to the researcher.

There are also structural decisions to be taken within the research department. One often finds that one person has a particular interest in computers, and that person is frequently given the responsibility of dealing with all data base matters. Unfortunately, this tends to delay the learning and familiarisation process of others in the department, and can even lead to a mini DP department within the department.

Many of these problems are short term, and are a function of the infancy of the subject. Nevertheless, they must all be considered when embarking on such a project.

Most of the other problems are related to the mechanics of setting up an on-line data base, and the writer will address these in the following sections. Before doing that, let us consider the cost aspects. Developing a data base that can be interrogated on-line is an expensive undertaking, both in terms of time and outgoing costs. The potential benefits are considerable, and the writer believes that most organisations will benefit from them. However, the benefits are not easily measured, and many of them result from the development of a different perspective on the business. It is impossible to create an accurate balance sheet showing the costs and benefits, suffice it to say that the costs are likely to be much greater than anticipated, so there must be a real commitment from all concerned.

CREATING AN ON-LINE DATA BASE—A CASE STUDY

Background

The following case study relates to a data base developed for the pharmaceutical industry. This industry is rich in data, and also has a tradition of syndicating information. As a result, there have for many years been regular audits showing monthly or quarterly sales data for all the products, and in considerable detail.

Most pharmaceutical companies purchase these audits, and, in addition, conduct a considerable number of *ad hoc* surveys. The reasons for these additional surveys stem from the rather unusual nature of the industry.

The 'ethical', or prescription market, in the UK is worth some £2000 million in the mid 1980s, and 75% of this is generated from the prescribing of about 30 000 general practitioners. There are over 100 pharmaceutical companies in the UK, of varying sizes, and each tends to specialise in a few therapy areas (e.g. analgesics, cardiovascular drugs and so on).

Unlike consumer markets, a high proportion of promotional spend is allocated to personal calls by representatives. The larger companies can have anything from 50 to 80 or more representatives, at a cost approaching £2 million per year. The unusual thing about this market is that they have no direct information on how successful a call has been, as a representative doesn't take an order and doesn't know how frequently a doctor prescribes the drug, if at all. The doctor is not the final consumer, but he is the decision maker, writing an average of nearly 50 prescriptions every working day.

Against this background, the writer and the research agency that he was working with, ISIS Research Ltd., decided to develop a system that would enable companies to measure the effect of their selling activities, and monitor their progress in relation to that of their competitors. This system was subsequently named *JIGSAW*.

The Basic Concept

The thinking behind JIGSAW was that, if a data base could be created that incorporates the prescribing decisions made by doctors, with information on the sales contacts made on the same doctors, it would be possible to measure cause and effect. It would also need to monitor the selling activity of competitors, so that some comparisons could be made between the performances of different companies.

In order to effectively monitor these elements, it is important that the measures continue over time. This is for two reasons. First, each company only visits about half the GPs in the country, and those they do call on are only visited, on average, about four times a year. To miss one of these calls would weaken the data. Secondly, it is important to measure *trends* in the prescribing of products amongst those doctors being promoted to, and to compare these trends with the prescribing amongst other doctors.

As a result, it was decided to use a panel of doctors, and to get them to record both their prescribing and their sales contacts on a continuous basis. A panel size of 400 was decided on, as this provided sufficient numbers for analysis of subgroups, and over the course of a year, would provide about 20 000 'doctor weeks' of information.

Some Important Considerations

In planning the system, there were a number of major considerations that had to be dealt with. These can be divided under the following headings:

— sampling and data collection:
— data input, quality control and editing;
— data retrieval and analysis;

Sampling and Data Collection

Anyone who has been involved in panel work will understand the problems of sampling and potential fatigue. The sample must be as perfect as possible, because, once recruited, it is difficult to adjust an unrepresentative sample. It is also important that the panel must be retained intact, with planned turnover, and not allowed to deteriorate and become unrepresentative over time. As sampling is not the subject of this chapter, it will simply be said that great pains were taken to ensure that the final panel was representative.

Regarding data collection, it had to be ensured that the recording task was not too great for the respondents. Bearing in mind that continuity of reporting is a prime consideration, the writer decided to concentrate on collecting only that data which is most important for analysis purposes.

Too many research surveys try to collect just about everything that can be crammed into a questionnaire, often to the detriment of the quality of response. In practice, one finds that a relatively small proportion of questions yield a large proportion of the valuable information — an 80/20 rule with 20% of the questionnaire yielding 80% of the information?

In the case of an on-going panel, it is even more important to prune down the data to the most important elements, and not to jeopardise the loyalty of the panel members by demanding too much. There is also another factor to consider. With an on-line data base used by a number of of different companies, the more complex the range of data, the greater the problem in getting people to use it–truly a case of 'small is beautiful'.

In the end, the writer decided to collect prescribing information on only a selection of diagnoses, selecting the most important from the clients' point of view. For each diagnosis, the writer concentrated only on new prescribing decisions. (This meant new patients and cases where the doctor changed a patients therapy, which excluded a large proportion of prescriptions that were simply repeating a course of therapy over a long time-span.) This meant that the data only reflected the *'current behaviour'* of the doctor. The effect of this was to reduce the average number of prescriptions recorded by each doctor from a potential of 50 per day to a much more realistic ten per week, and with no significant loss in value of information.

In addition to the prescribing, they also recorded every sales contact, and provided background information on their demographics etc. The data collection forms are shown in Appendix 10.1. They were self-completed and returned weekly.

Quality Control, Editing and Data Input

Even though the number of pieces of information being collected were reduced, the writer was still faced with some 4000 prescriptions being recorded every week, and 2000 or so sales contacts. The drug names were being written in the doctor's own hand, not the easiest task to decipher, and we had to get all of this information into a usable form on a regular basis, and quickly.

The writer considered precoding the drug names, but with 3000 or so different drugs in the market, this would have been an impossible task, both for the researchers and for the doctors. The rest of the form was, however, reduced to simple ticks.

So, should the forms be edited manually, or using the computer?

Should traditional punch cards be used, or optical reading or some other data input method?

When JIGSAW was started, the agency was primarily involved in qualitative research. Other than a micro computer, there were neither computing facilities nor data entry and coding departments to take responsibility for these functions.

The writer did, however, have a communications package that would enable our micro to talk to a larger computer, and to transfer data down the telephone line. He therefore decided to make use of what he had, and using a simple word-processing package, 'typed' the data in, line by line. The forms in Appendix 10.1 show that letters were ghosted in the background where the respondent was supposed to tick a box. Hence, all that was required was for a line of letters and brand names to be typed for each prescription record etc., preceded by the doctor's reference number and the date.

It was soon realised that there was an additional benefit in this. Copy typists could be used to input the data rather than expensive data input clerks.

A typical entry would look something like this:

3239 35 2 03 35 A   TENORETIC   SU   DYAZIDE

3239 is the respondent number, with a check digit, 35 is the week number, and 2 the day of the week, it is the 3rd patient that week, with hypertension (A), the prescription is for 'Tenoretic', which is a change in drug (S) because the previous drug (Dyazide) was not effective (U).

Typing 6000 lines of information each week is not a mammoth task, but at this stage there has been no editing. The writer did consider building an editing function into the micro computer, with a dictionary of acceptable drug names and spellings. The disadvantage of this, apart from lack of capacity on the micro, is that it slows down the typing speed as everything gets checked and the typist gets out of rhythm and frustrated as errors keep appearing. With something like 300 000 lines of data each year, the system would have to be put up on a large computer, so it was decided to leave the editing to that stage.

Once the data was typed into the micro, and stored onto disk, it was simply transferred to the main computer by transmitting it down the telephone line.

The computer bureau selected for the project, Quantime Ltd., had written some editing programs that enabled a comparison between every typed entry and a dictionary of known drug names. The program then tested for logical errors, such as the wrong drug for a particular diagnosis, or the same doctor being recorded twice. Using a micro as a terminal to the main computer, this effectively increased the in-house computing power and retained 'hands-on' control of the data. We initiated the running of the suite of editing programs, printed off the error listings and corrected the entries before adding the new, clean data to the data base.

Data Retrieval and Analysis

With each week's new data being added, a large data base rapidly developed, covering well over 300 000 pieces of data each year. As this included information on each doctor's prescribing, sales contacts, and basic profile information, the potential for analysis is enormous. Add to this the extra dimension of time, and it soon becomes apparent that the only way to use the information is for it to be made accessible interactively. Providing clients with printed reports could not possibly cover all the various requirements, and such reports would of necessity be summaries.

As companies need to study details of their own activities as well as selected competitors', and their requirements may change over time, we decided to provide the facility for them to access the data base directly themselves.

Quantime already had all the facilities for on-line access, as well as a very flexible interactive data analysis package. This was a prime reason for selecting them, as the task of developing a new interactive survey analysis package is a major undertaking. What the writer had to do was to work with the Bureau in making the data and their system compatible, and to develop a series of front-end menus to help clients make best use of the system.

It must be remembered that there is an enormous difference between text retrieval using key word searching, or the retrieval of preformatted tables, and a system that enables the user to define and conduct a wide range of different analyses, and to obtain the results on-line, virtually immediately.

There must always be a compromise between the flexibility and power of a system, and its simplicity. For a system to have a wide usage, it must be simple to use, and to a certain extent one has to sacrifice some of the more complex facilities. However, the vast majority of analysis requirements *are* relatively simple, and we did not find that there was any real loss in utility, in fact, quite the reverse. The writer strongly believes that there is frequently more to be gained from a series of simple cross tabulations and sensible filtering, conducted in a logical, enquiring manner, than in much of the complex, multivariate analysis that is conducted. It is certainly much easier to communicate.

THE INTERACTIVE SYSTEM

The Basic Concept

The basis of the selected system of analysis is to create an 'axis' for each variable, and to give it a name. Hence, the range of different drugs being prescribed could be called 'drugs', and the different months called 'months'. A simple trend analysis can then be achieved by analysing 'drugs' by 'months', which would print out the drugs down the side of the table and months across the top, showing trends in brand share, month by month.

Every piece of information from the data-recording forms was given an axis name, so the user could specify any combination of variables, and create a table. Add to this the ability to filter the table using any combination of elements from the data base, and the result is a very powerful system. For example, it is possible for a client to specify a table showing trends in brand shares month by month, and to filter this table so that it only includes those doctors they have contacted, and then to compare this with a similar table showing those they have not contacted. This shows the effect of those sales contacts on the doctors' prescribing behaviour, and a similar analysis can be conducted for each competitor.

A further refinement was introduced, giving the user the option of showing data based on market shares (number of prescriptions), or on penetration levels (number of users).

Each enquiry takes an average of two to three minutes to complete, which means that a whole series of 20 or more tables can be completed within an hour, and viewed immediately.

An Example of an Enquiry

This particular system is very easy to use, and the writer believes that this is a major consideration. The user needs to have some form of terminal, or microcomputer with a communication package, and a modem to translate the signals that are transmitted through the telephone lines.

The user simply telephones the computer and types in the relevent log-in name and password. From then on a series of menus takes him to the point when he specifies the tabulation. Even at this point, all of the instructions are in simple English (or whatever the national language is).

A printout of the enquiry described above is shown in Appendix 10.2, and it is hoped that it is clear from this that interrogation of a data base can be a very simple matter. The only real constraint is the users' imagination.

Examples of the System in Use

As an example of the ways in which a system of this nature can be used, Appendix 10.3 shows a series of charts illustrating the results from a typical enquiry. An enquiry of this nature need only take about an hour to conduct, although the production of graphics from the basic figures may take somewhat longer.

This example shows how one set of data can lead on to subsequent questions, which can be posed and answered interactively in the same session.

SUMMARISING THE PROS AND CONS OF AN INTERACTIVE DATA BASE

It is hoped that the benefits of the data base that has been described are evident enough. Without this approach, and the availability of the technology, the writer doubts if the type of analysis that JIGSAW provides could have been achieved. Certainly there is no way he knows whereby a user can have complete flexibility in how they interrogate data, and get immediate results without using an interactive data base of this type. In order to respond to changing market situations, management needs to react quickly, which means that it needs fast information. There is a danger that traditional market research methods are too slow for tactical decision making, and in such circumstances may be ignored. The development of interactive data bases will, the writer believes, greatly enhance the role of the researcher, and will bring the two functions closer together.

This will only occur if both the researcher and the marketing management are prepared to invest their time in understanding the new concepts that are involved. The major benefit is that all concerned will be much closer to the data, and will be more in control of its manipulation. The result will be a considerable increase in its potential value as a decision-making aid.

THE APPLICATIONS OF AN INTERACTIVE DATA BASE

Although this example described a specific application, the writer does believe that many surveys could benefit from being established into a data base of this nature. Certainly if surveys are repeated at regular intervals, there is much to commend keeping them alive and on-line, even though a changing sample may be involved each time.

It is not just survey research that lends itself to such interactive analysis. A lot of in-house data would gain greatly in terms of usage and value if it was more accessible, such as sales and production information, customer enquiries, R and D information etc.

The same basic approach can be used to create a data base for most types of information. The creation of a system that enables the user to access a variety of different types of data, such as sales and promotional expenditure etc., can lead to a decision support system which interconnects all available data. This allows the user to view the relevant information before making a decision, and can even allow him to enter into some 'what if' experiments on the data base.

The trend in all forms of data retrieval is towards speed and accessibility, and the writer predicts that in the next ten years we will see interactive data bases becoming the norm rather than the exception — not just for quantitative data, but also, dare I say, for qualitative information as well.

Indeed, there are trends towards the development of methods that will enable qualitative information to be incorporated into data bases alongside statistical data. The development of fifth generation computer languages and of Artificial Intelligence systems will speed these developments, and will also change the ways in which data is analysed.

NOTES

'JIGSAW' is the copyright of ISIS Research Ltd.
'QUANVERT' (see Appendix 10.2) is the copyright of Quantime Ltd.

ACKNOWLEDGMENT

This chapter is reproduced by permission of ISIS Research.

APPENDIX 10.1(1)

CONFIDENTIAL – COMPANY CONTACT RECORD

WEEK COMMENCING MONDAY

DATE: ....

NAME: ....

ADDRESS: ....

ISIS Research Ltd.
The Boathouse,
The Embankment,
Putney, London,
SW15 1HL.
Tel: 01-788 8819.

ISIS RESEARCH

DAY	COMPANY	PRODUCT	TYPE OF PRODUCT (√)									TYPE OF CONTACT (√)									HOW USEFUL (√)			
	(Please write name)	(Please write name of each product)	ANALGESIC	ANTI-ARTHRITIC	ANTIBIOTIC	ANTI-DEPRESSANT	OTHER PSYCHO	CARDIO PRODUCT	GASTRO INT.	OTHER (Please Specify)	REP VISIT	GROUP MEETING @ SURGERY	GROUP MEETING ELSEWHERE	SYMPOSIUM	FILM/VIDEO	SAMPLE LEFT	OTHER CONTACT (Please Specify)	VERY USEFUL	FAIRLY USEFUL	NOT VERY USEFUL	NOT AT ALL
			A	B	C	E	F	G	I	K	N	O	P	Q	R	S	T	W	X	Y	Z
			A	B	C	E	F	G	I	K	N	O	P	Q	R	S	T	W	X	Y	Z
			A	B	C	E	F	G	I	K	N	O	P	Q	R	S	T	W	X	Y	Z
			A	B	C	E	F	G	I	K	N	O	P	Q	R	S	T	W	X	Y	Z
			A	B	C	E	F	G	I	K	N	O	P	Q	R	S	T	W	X	Y	Z
			A	B	C	E	F	G	I	K	N	O	P	Q	R	S	T	W	X	Y	Z
			A	B	C	E	F	G	I	K	N	O	P	Q	R	S	T	W	X	Y	Z
			A	B	C	E	F	G	I	K	N	O	P	Q	R	S	T	W	X	Y	Z
			A	B	C	E	F	G	I	K	N	O	P	Q	R	S	T	W	X	Y	Z
			A	B	C	E	F	G	I	K	N	O	P	Q	R	S	T	W	X	Y	Z
			A	B	C	E	F	G	I	K	N	O	P	Q	R	S	T	W	X	Y	Z
			A	B	C	E	F	G	I	K	N	O	P	Q	R	S	T	W	X	Y	Z
			A	B	C	E	F	G	I	K	N	O	P	Q	R	S	T	W	X	Y	Z
			A	B	C	E	F	G	I	K	N	O	P	Q	R	S	T	W	X	Y	Z
			A	B	C	E	F	G	I	K	N	O	P	Q	R	S	T	W	X	Y	Z

THANK YOU VERY MUCH – PLEASE RETURN IN ENVELOPE SUPPLIED

APPENDIX 10.1(2)

ISIS RESEARCH

ISIS Research Ltd.
The Boathouse,
The Embankment,
Putney, London,
SW15 1HL
Tel: 01-788 8819.

CONFIDENTIAL PRESCRIPTION RECORD

WEEK COMMENCING MONDAY
DATE: ....

NAME: ....
ADDRESS: ....

THANK YOU VERY MUCH – PLEASE RETURN IN ENVELOPE SUPPLIED

APPENDIX 10.2   EXAMPLE OF AN ENQUIRY

The following shows an example of the way a simple enquiry is conducted.

The prompts are printed in normal type, and the responses typed in by the user are shown in **bold** type.

Good Morning.

Welcome to QUANVERT V6.8e.

This database was last updated on Mon Aug 18 1986

There are 539 cases at level doctor
There are 35791 cases at level script.

> For help, type help or ?
> For available answers, type what or /

Command: **tab**

Axes names for table 1: **drugs month**
Axes names for table 2:
Enter filters if any -
Filter: **contact**
Which elements of contact: **myproduct**
    MYPRODUCT
> Or:
And:
Level: **scripts**
Title: **Trends in Prescribing by Month**
Title: **amongst doctors contacted by Myproduct**
Title:
Enter options -
Option:
Tables file name: **mytable**
Tables printed at terminal?
Starting to process data.

APPENDIX 10.3   EXAMPLE RESULTS FROM AN ENQUIRY

The following figures show a very simple enquiry that would take no more than a few minutes to produce.

The first figure (10.1) shows the market share of a product, 'MYDRUG', for each of four quarterly periods. This shows a gradual upward trend.

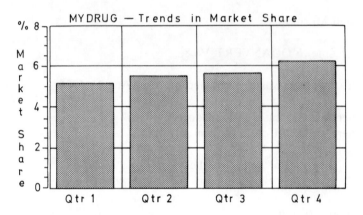

Figure 10.1 Trends in market share

However, most of the promotional cost is spent on visits by representatives, and only about half of the doctors are called on by the Company (Figure 10.2), and then with varying frequencies. Some doctors only receive one call in a year, others two, three, four or more.

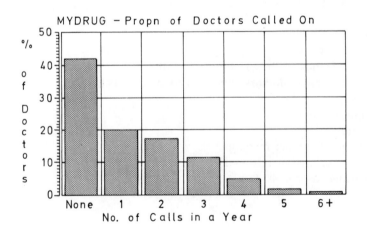

Figure 10.2 Proportion of doctors called on

The next question that a user may ask is, what is the difference in market share between those doctors called on and those not called on? Again, this can be asked of the system, and an almost instantaneous result obtained, illustrated in Figure 10.3.

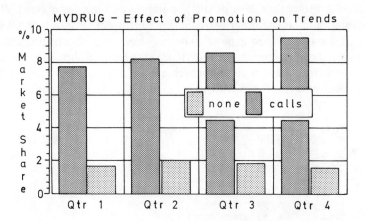

Figure 10.3 Effect of promotion on trends

The doctors who are called on very frequently account for a disproportionately high share of the total promotional cost. It is therefore important to see whether there is an optimal number of calls that should be aimed at, before one starts to see a reduction in marginal benefit. This is illustrated in Figure 10.4, where it can be seen that, after four calls, there is relatively little additional business obtained.

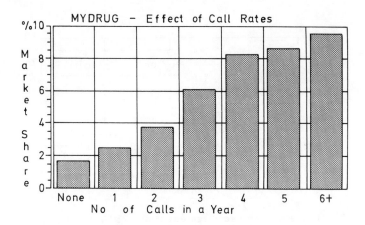

Figure 10.4 Effect of call rates

In this situation, the Company may well decide to redirect these additional calls to some of the doctors who are not being visited.

Finally, the user of the system can study the differing levels of sales potential between prospective customers, and then go on to see whether they are, in fact, calling on those offering the highest potential.

Figure 10.5 shows that 25% of the population account for about half of the potential, and, at the other extreme, the bottom 25% only 10%. When the user of the system then explores whether they are concentrating efforts on this top 25% of potential, the last figure, Figure 10.6 shows that in fact there is considerable room for improvement, with their sales effort being evenly spread between those with high, medium and low potential.

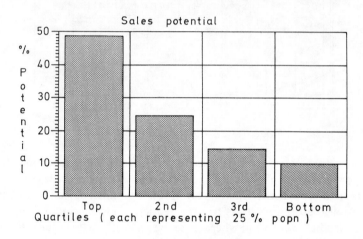

Figure 10.5 Sales potential

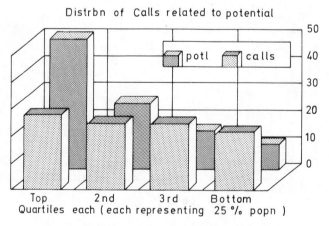

Figure 10.6 Distribution of calls related to potential

A simple series of enquiries of this nature will very quickly provide the user with a picture of their operation, and, possibly of greater significance, will enable a study of the competitor in the same detail. Furthermore, it is possible to monitor subsequent progress, and the effect of marketing decisions, in the following months.

Applied Marketing and Social Research 2nd Edition
Edited by Ute Bradley
©Copyright John Wiley 1987

11.   The Research Benefits of Scanning

Linda R. Morris   *A. C. Nielsen Company Ltd.*

The services provided by Nielsen Marketing Research in the UK are well known. Information technology is making its impact felt in retail businesses and Nielsen have been appointed by the Article Number Association to collect basic sales data from scanning stores. Nielsen have also provided an Added Value Service, Scantrack, and this chapter explores the benefits in data collection to be obtained from these technological advances. The chapter makes it clear that researchers at Nielsen are well aware that these new methods need to be matched by appropriate skills in interpretation. These skills will be appreciated by the student by examining the case studies included in the chapter.

WHAT IS SCANNING?

Bar codes on every product are becoming universal, and they will be the basis of much of future market research.

Two things are required for efficient scanning: firstly, unique codes on all products which are internationally recognisable and readable. Secondly, precise representation of those codes so that they can be read with around 100% accuracy by affordable machines in environments which include busy supermarkets.

Scanning is the technique of using electronics and lasers to recognise numbers. It is shorthand for the employment of Electronic Point Of Sale (EPOS) systems at the checkout but it could also be applied to any technique for capturing data or recognising a number with a device such as a hand-held terminal. This causes interrogation to a price file, allowing that day's price to be brought to the checkout and information to be updated as to the number of sales of each particular item.

Scanning can be achieved via a fixed bed scanner, usually seen as a square of glass set in the checkout counter just beyond the moving belt area; or it can be some form of light pen/scanning wand as more usually seen in DIY stores: after all, it would be rather difficult to scan a bath by placing it over a flat bed scanner. Technology will no doubt come up with other ways of automatically recognising goods, and the TOUCH system currently being trialled by Bloomingdales in the USA[1] is an example of this. However, the method by which the item is recognised is not of importance to the researcher; the benefits of the data collected remain the same.

Scanning in its strictest sense refers to reading an item code by laser scanners, and the most common form of this is to read the bar code. Alternative systems in the retail trade employ the scanning of code numbers held in magnetic form or OCR (Optical Character Recognition) form.

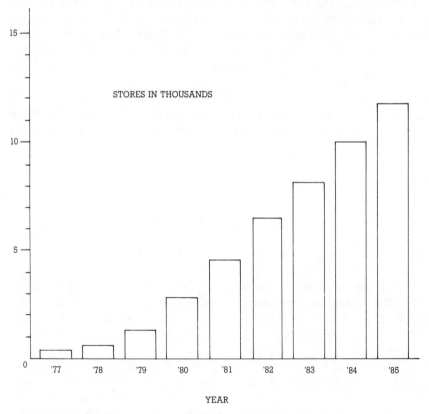

Figure 11.1 Development of scanning installations in Grocers — number of stores in the USA
Source: A. C. Nielsen

The take-off of scanning in the UK was being predicted in the late 1970s, following the introduction of scanning in grocery stores in the USA. Figure 11.1 indicates that in the USA there were 209 such stores by 1977, 4568 by 1981 and 11 600 by 1985.

However, scanning in the UK did not start to take off until the mid 1980s although the first scanning grocery store in the UK was the Keymarket store at Spalding (now Gateway, part of the Dee Corporation) which opened in October 1979.

Figure 11.2 shows the growth of these stores in the UK. During 1980 Argyll, Asda and Sainsbury all started scanning in one store and Keymarkets, as it then was, started scanning in a second store. It was during 1984 that the mark of 100 grocery scanning stores was crossed and by April 1986 there were 374 such stores.

More relevant to the researcher is the percentage of total grocery sales which pass across scanners—all commodity volume or ACV. The general pattern in both the USA and UK is for the large and medium size multiples to install scanning in volume. In the UK, where grocery trade concentration is high, a relatively low number of scanning stores in large outlets covers a high proportion of all grocery sales.

Figure 11.3 shows that 2% of ACV across scanners was reached in the UK in 1984, six years later than in the USA. By mid-1986, the ACV in the States was beyond 50% and in the UK was just over 7%.

So far reference is to the grocery trade because this is where the majority of scanners are installed. However, by the mid-1980s scanning was becoming evident in liquor, DIY, electrical, jewellery and department stores.

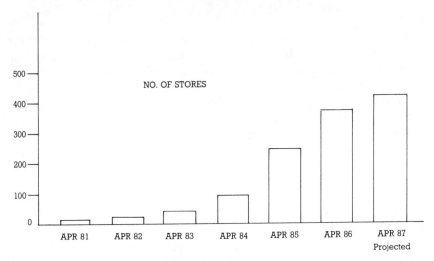

Figure 11.2 Development of scanning installations in Grocers—number of stores in the UK
Source: A. C. Nielsen

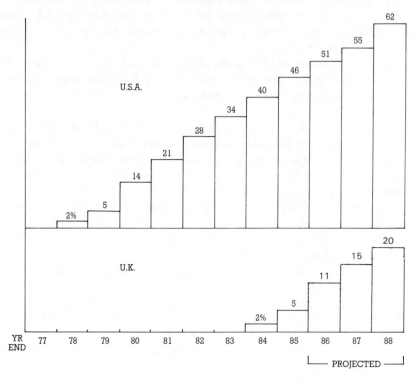

Figure 11.3 Percentage of total grocery sales across scanners
Source: A. C. Nielsen

Table 11.1 estimates the penetration of EPOS terminals by type of retail trade. The estimate source is ICL and refers to electronic point of sale terminals rather than scanning as such. However, some of these sectors of retail trade are scanning, including the store types mentioned above.

To return to the grocery trade, what were the reasons for the slow take off of scanning six years behind the USA?

Firstly, the level of bar coding at source was not high enough to make scanning efficient. Internationally organised code allocation is a prerequisite of cost effective scanning and the EAN, the body who adopted this responsibility, was not formed until 1977.

It takes time for a high percentage of products to be coded — involving the resolution of printing and design as well as code number control issues for thousands of products.

The second reason was the cost of scanning equipment. As with new technology of any kind, the relative cost of scanning equipment has dropped over the past decade.

TABLE 11.1   Penetration of EPOS Terminals by Retail Line of Trade

	1984 %	1985 %	1986 %	1987 %	1988 %	1989 %	1990 %
Beer/Wine/Spirits	15.0	18.0	23.0	30.0	39.0	49.0	57.0
Chemists	1.0	2.0	3.0	6.0	13.0	22.0	33.0
Clothing	5.0	9.0	16.0	25.0	36.0	50.0	65.0
Department Stores	47.0	50.0	57.0	65.0	75.0	83.0	88.0
DIY/Home Improvement	2.5	12.0	24.0	37.0	51.0	65.0	80.0
Electrical	25.0	30.0	36.0	42.0	51.0	58.0	64.0
Speciality Food	3.0	6.0	9.0	13.0	17.0	21.0	27.0
Footwear	2.0	5.0	13.0	22.0	31.0	40.0	50.0
Furniture	4.0	6.0	9.0	13.0	18.0	23.0	30.0
Supermarkets	1.7	4.5	13.0	25.0	39.0	55.0	70.0
Housewares	2.0	10.0	20.0	30.0	37.0	45.0	52.0
Jewellers	15.0	40.0	50.0	60.0	70.0	78.0	85.0
Leisure	20.0	22.0	25.0	29.0	34.0	40.0	47.0
Newsagents	1.0	2.0	5.0	11.0	19.0	27.0	36.0
Variety	10.0	13.0	16.0	20.0	26.0	34.0	46.0
Pubs & Restaurants	1.0	2.5	8.0	17.0	28.0	39.0	50.0
Fast Food	15.0	21.0	29.0	39.0	51.0	63.0	71.0
Petrol	2.0	6.0	12.0	19.0	29.0	40.0	50.0

Source: ICL estimates. The retail categorisations in the above statistics are based on the line of trade of major UK retail organisations and not on their respective operating philosophies.

Thirdly, the economic climate in the late 70s and early 80s did not encourage capital expenditure. But by the mid 1980s the climate and the retailers were ready for scanning.

CUSTOMER VIEWPOINT

What does the customer think of all this new technology?

Most retailers have had a customer education programme, which has proved to be very successful, before introducing scanning. They have described what scanning is and what it means to the customer. They have explained that scanning means fast, accurate checkout procedures, a useful and understandable cash register slip, elimination of wasteful (and costly) pricing of individual goods to keep prices down, giving the opportunities to reduce out-of-stock and improve the range of goods available.

In the UK there has been virtually no customer reaction to item price removal. This is very different to the United States where Ralph Nader led a campaign for retention of item prices. This resulted in individual States legislating for retention and there are numerous areas in the USA today where item pricing is obligatory.

Customers tend to like the checkout slip which details the items they have bought and the price of each. Some customers use it as a basis for their next week's shopping list and others use it to compare prices. An interesting fact reported by most scanning stores is the very low level of checkout slips left at the checkout or found on the floor, at least initially after the introduction of scanning in a store. The customer also likes the shorter checkout queues where this applies but is concerned about the extra time that is needed when an item is not bar coded or its price is not recorded on the computer. However, the efficiency of the retailer in picking up these items and marking them in store before they reach the checkout can reduce checkout delays considerably.

MANUFACTURER VIEWPOINT

With tongue in cheek it can be said that many manufacturers were less delighted than other parties when scanning and bar coding were first mooted. They saw this in terms of incurring extra costs for design, packaging, printing and administration.

However, as it transpires, food item packing is reprinted moderately often and certain government regulations on contents, together with the move to metrication, have meant that bar coding has increased at a time when packaging has been more frequently redesigned. Thus the cost of applying the bar code has been relatively small for many products.

The benefits to manufacturers are in the sales information that can be provided. Manufacturers have always known what they are delivering to each retail group (and possibly even store). What they have not been able to obtain before is actual sales per week of both their own and competitors items. Manufacturers are now more positive about benefits to them which arise from standard product numbering—not only in providing market research data but also through its use in the administration chain or for ordering, delivery, invoicing and payment.

RETAILERS VIEWPOINT

How does the retailer, who wants to see his profits increased by any capital expenditure, justify scanning? The benefits are split between hard and soft benefits.

The hard benefits, those that are quantifiable, include savings on labour costs and those relating to more efficient stock level holding. All scanning food stores in the UK today have chosen not to mark individual item prices, but instead show a shelf price, thus saving related labour costs. The general belief is that scanning improves checkout throughput which means the retailer may choose to decrease his number of checkouts and checkout labour costs and retain his queue length. Or, he can choose to retain the same number of checkouts and reduce queues. The mid-course has been chosen by more retailers.

Scanning tells the retailer actual sales of items by discrete time period: this can be per week, per day, per hour or as chosen by the retailer. To obtain the benefits of lower stock levels the retailer also need to have actionable details, usually held on computer, of stock levels and delivery intervals and such sophisticated computer systems are becoming increasingly common. Analysis of the information relating to sales, stock levels and delivery times has made it possible for the stock held on many items to be reduced.

Most of the soft benefits evolve from better management information. Until this information is analysed and actioned one cannot quantify the level of benefits achieved and, of course, this will vary by retail group, who operate differently and have had different levels of management information prior to scanning. Reducing 'product loss' (shrinkage) is a point which is often cited under this heading. Shrinkage caused by staff will be minimised by the very fact that each item has to be scanned. The checkout design makes it obvious if an item is not charged for, and thus the incidence of uncharged goods passing directly from the customer/relatives trolley to the collection area is minimised. There is a belief that this 'sweethearting' (favouring friends of checkout operator) is relatively common. Another form of it refers to the checkout operator ringing up a lower price than that marked on the item ('under-rings') when family or friends pass through the checkout, which is no longer possible once items are scanned because the standard price is brought back to the checkout. As the extent of sweethearting is unquantifiable, it must remain a soft benefit, as does improving shrinkage caused by the customer.

A further soft benefit is the reduction of another form of 'under-rings'. More recently it might be truer to call this a 'semi-hard' benefit because it is believed that when a price is not on an item, the checkout operator, who is perfectly honest, tends to remember last week's price rather than today's and in a time of inflation this is normally to the customers benefit.

Customer shrinkage is normally perceived to be via one of two general methods. The first is that the customer secretes items and does not present them at the checkout. The other is that the price is removed from an items and that from a cheaper item put in its place.

The changing of the price on an item is not relevant in most food store operations but is more applicable to such areas as department stores. However, where a price is substituted, by scanning the item the true price is brought back to the checkout and charged to the customer. Scanning cannot help the non-presentation of goods by the customer, but what it can highlight, when considered together with stock information, is items which have the highest shrinkage rate. One retailer pinpointed that photographic films had a very high level of shrinkage. On investigation it was found that they were sited in a quiet area at the back of the store and that by moving films to just in front of the checkout area their shrinkage was considerably reduced.

Scanning management information is also helping the retailer to improve the mix of goods in a store. He may choose to de-list slow moving items, which scanning will more quickly define, thus freeing shelf space for other items. It is possible to test more quickly, and economically whether resiting of items increases sales. For instance, do sales of pickled onions increase when sited by, say, the cheeses as opposed to having them sited in the pickles area? By testing within the store, the retailer can answer such questions and thus increase profitability.

Retailers may have sales information from their own scanning system by store, on every item and variant stocked. When the manufacturer's salesman meets the retail buyer, he will have to take into account that the buyer may have the most recent and trended actual sales to hand of not only the salesman's items, but also those of all his competitors.

PROMOTING THE BENEFITS OF SCANNING DATA

The Article Number Association (ANA) was founded in 1976 to help promote the adoption of standard product numbering, bar code symbolisation and the many benefits which can stem from these.

The ANA sets standards and is the UK authority within the International Article Number Association (EAN) for controlling the allocation of numbers to manufacturers of goods. Subsequently the ANA has helped improve business efficiency by promoting standards for electronic data exchange.

The ANA recognized the benefit to its members of scanning sales data and in 1978 set up the Access to Sales Data Subcommittee to recommend the methodology by which scanning data should be made available.

The subcommittee concluded that basic sales data should be made available from the ANA via a specialist agent and the agent chosen was A. C. Nielsen.

The main obligation of the agent is to discharge retailer obligations under the EAN guidelines to provide in an economic way 'basic data at cost'. This is achieved — following the definition of a basic service as detailing a manufacturer's own coded items in a market plus a total for the market — by collecting scanning data from whatever source or type of equipment and aggregating the results into four-weekly reports showing weekly data.

There is no doubt that there is a role for the ANA service and some clients illustrate this. As anticipated, it is a most cost-effective way of monitoring markets where a client is either extremely dominant or very weak. There are some clients who see the need for the ANA service in some markets but require an added value service for others. The ANA service offers excellent value and a specimen report is shown at Appendix 11.1

A further obligation of the agent is to provide an added value service, and thus A. C. Nielsen Company Ltd. has developed the service called 'Scantrack'. This not only details the manufacturer's own coded items, but also those of all his competitors in the market. Additionally, further data types (distribution and volume market share) and trended data are provided.

SCANTRACK

Scantrack 86 started in August 1985 and ran for one year based on data from 35 contributing scanning stores. Scantrack 87 commenced in August 86 based on double the number of contributing stores. Each year for the next few years at least, the Scantrack store base will grow.

Scantrack gives unique new insights into markets by providing the following features:

— actual sales recorded at scanning checkouts;
— weekly sales data;
— trended sales data;
— four-weekly reporting (giving weekly data and four-weekly total);
— provision of competitive data;
— all items identified with an ANA code and electronically captured at the point of sale are described separately (this includes brands, sizes, colours, special offers etc.);
— immediate item availability: as soon as a new item or variant is sold by the contributing stores, data is captured;
— provision of a named list of contributing stores which provide the aggregated Scantrack data;
— prompt production of results, eight working days after the period close.

SCANTRACK APPLICATIONS

Scantrack answers many questions because of its sharp focus on weekly sales for all items. Resultant action can be fast and thus efficient due to the speed of reporting. Examples of applications are:

—seasonality;
—new product launches;
—effect of promotions:
—lag between advertising and sales;
—distribution changes;
—competitive results.

WHAT DATA DOES SCANTRACK SHOW?

Each four-weekly report consists of two sections; the weekly data report and the four-week trend reports. The weekly data report shows the total market, brand sub-totals and individual item sales in units and value. It gives an individual item average retail selling price each week and the share of the market value and volume. Weekly distribution by selling area is shown. This is shown as a percentage:

$$\% = \frac{\text{SALES AREA OF STORES SELLING ITEM}}{\text{TOTAL SALES AREA COVERED BY SCANTRACK BASE}}$$

The trend reports show four-weekly totals both in summary and by item detail, built up over a year and can be produced to value or volume.

A specimen of the weekly data report is shown in Appendix 11.2 and that for the detail trend report in Appendix 11.3

SCANTRACK USES

At the time this paper was written, Scantrack had been in existence for only nine months, yet in that short time the following cases of the uses of Scantrack have been reported to us by our clients.

Case 1—Allied Lyons—Port

Traditionally, most research data has reported sales by four or eight-week periods. Scantrack, showing actual weekly sales, gives finer measurement of market seasonality. Before using Scantrack, Jeff Palmer of the Wine and Spirit Division of Allied Lyons was of course aware of the extreme pattern of seasonality which exists in so many of the wines and spirits markets. As he said at the ANA conference in 1986:

> In some cases more than 50% of the annual volume of our business can occur in the until now 'cloudy' period leading up to Christmas. Just one day's sales in the second week of December can be more than for a whole month in the summer.
> So when your annual sales strategy can be determined by your sales level in, say, 14 days of the year you need the closest measurement you can get.

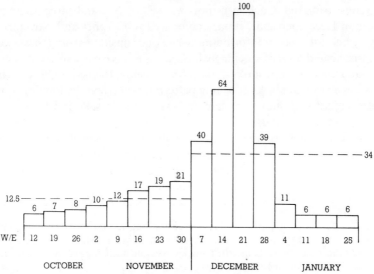

*Figure 11.4 Seasonality of Cockburns Sales port — Scantrack weekly sales index
Reproduced by permission of ICL*

Jeff Palmer wanted to put a microscope on the Christmas period and used Scantrack data to compile the bar chart shown as Figure 11.4.

This shows the actual weekly sales of the pre-Christmas build of Cockburns Port in index form. It highlighted the Christmas sales build-up of Cockburns port and pinpointed sales in the pre-Christmas week were 16 times that of a week in early October. Before using Scantrack, Jeff Palmer had been seeing average sales over a period of weeks, which is indeed very useful for strategic planning in many markets. However, Jeff felt that in his extremely seasonal markets averages could be dangerous.

The dotted line on Figure 11.4 shows the average weekly sales taken over an eight-week period. In looking at eight-weekly data one would come to

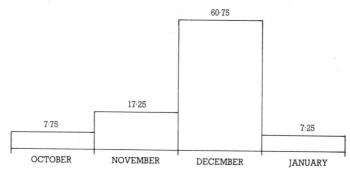

*Figure 11.5 Example of seasonality in the Cockburn port market — four-weekly sales index
Source: A. C. Nielsen*

the conclusion that Cockburns port was selling two-and-three-quarter times more in December and January compared to October and November; not a very helpful piece of information when one considers from the weekly data the timing and level of stocking which needs to take place to satisfy customer demands. Even if one looks at data four-weekly, the actionable conclusions one can draw still mask the selling pattern which is seen by looking at weekly data. Figure 11.5 shows the same market with the sales index consolidated to four-weekly periods.

However, the December average is still only showing 60% of the true pre-Christmas week sales index. On a highly seasonal market like this it is imperative to be aware of the true sales pattern in these four weeks so that distribution can reflect customer demand.

As Jeff Palmer summed up this case study at the ANA Conference 1986:

> We have long hypothosised this situation but had no way of confirming it, let alone quantifying it. The availability of data like this will help manufacturers and retailers better organise their stock cover and shelf facings to optimise these (extremely seasonal) market situations.

A further use which Allied Lyons plan for Scantrack is to measure the

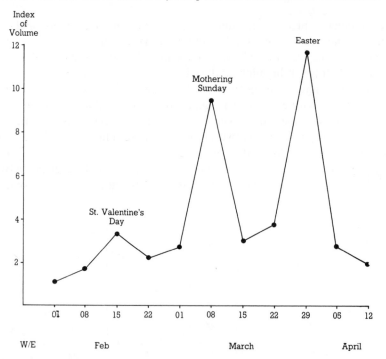

Figure 11.6 Example of special days sales in the confectionery market (weekly data)
Source: A. C. Nielsen

effect of advertising on sales as the incidence of scanning and the Scantrack base of stores increases.

Case 2 — Confectionery Market

Sales patterns related to special days are highlighted by Scantrack. The example shown in Figure 11.6 pinpoints the weekly sales peaks that occurred in a confectionery market.

These can be directly attributed to St Valentine's Day, Mothering Sunday and Easter and have strategic implications for advertising and distribution.

Other factors which affect all markets, including weather, Bank Holidays and stock shortages are all monitored to this level.

Case 3 — New Product

Scantrack gives immediate information on the success of a new product. This example is from the canned drinks market and shows the index of sales value over a number of weeks (see Figure 11.7).

During Week 2 a heavily price-promoted introduction (of Brand B) was made in this market. The introductory price was under 60% of the standard price. Sales while the promotion was in force looked exceedingly good. By Week 5 the heavily-price promoted Brand B was fading out of distribution and in that week the standard-price Brand B drink was introduced.

By Week 12 the price promotion on Brand B was no longer available in the stores and the standard Brand B was showing under 1% (on an index

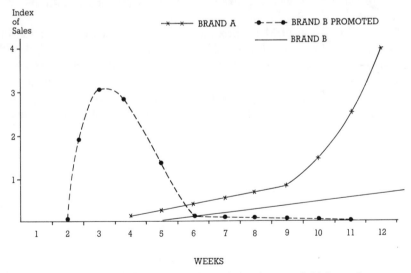

Figure 11.7 Example of new product sales in the canned drinks market
Source: A. C. Nielsen

of sales value) compared to marginally over 3% when the item was price promoted. (Note: indices of sales value are computed for comparative purposes and to avoid revealing actual sales figures). During Week 4 the heavily advertised Brand A, a direct competitor to Brand B, was introduced to the market. During Brand B's price promotional period, Brand A was showing a significantly lower index of sales value. However, as the Brand B price promotion ceased, Brand A took market share and by Week 12 Brand A was registering an index of sales value of over 4%.

Thus Scantrack enables manufacturers to have new evidence about the pattern of their promotional activities, how their levels of advertising have benefitted the product, and how effective their price promotions are both initially and in the longer term. This is especially important when launching new products and new variants. In both cases one can see the effect on the individual item and the effect on the total market; is the new item taking brand share from you or your competitor? Has it expanded the market? What is the effect when a competitor introduces a similar product? Scantrack weekly data will detail when products and promotions start selling to the customers, how long the promotions last and the overall effect on all items in the market.

The varying effects of advertising vs. promotions are highlighted. It has brought into sharper focus how purchasing patterns vary during alternative promotional/advertising activities. In another market, Scantrack has also pinpointed that the same promotion/advertising has quite markedly different effects at different times of year.

It is not only the manufacturer of a new product and his competitors who are interested in the new item: packaging companies also have a vested interest in the success of new products.

The Food Division of Metal Box plc is using Scantrack data to monitor the acceptance of non-traditional packaging from the launch. Scantrack will help them in the decision on whether it would be cost-effective to extend a pilot exercise of manufacturing the new packaging to full production capacity. Scantrack data can also be used to time the entry of new packaging forms, as soon as there are indications that it would be a profitable area.

Case 4—Promotions

This example on the confectionery market (see Figure 11.8) shows how Scantrack can accurately illustrate the life cycle of promotions by monitoring the weekly sales of all bar-coded items.

The market we are looking at is again confectionery and the index is of sales value. The seasonal item in question was available in both its promoted and non-promoted form at the same time. The black sections of the bars show the sales index of the promoted item and the white sections of the bars the sales index of the standard item.

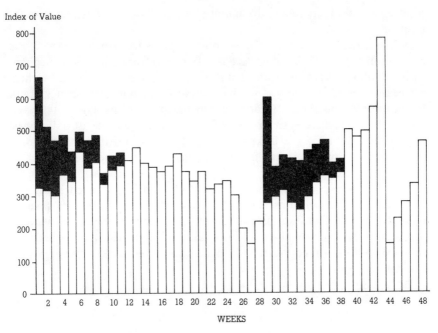

Figure 11.8 Example of promotions in the confectionary market
Source: A. C. Nielsen

Two different promotions were run during the year, the first starting in Week 1 and the second in Week 29. On both occasions Week 1 of the promotion proved to be really effective. An interesting point to note is that the effects of the two promotions were rather different. During the first promotion a marked effect could be seen in Weeks 2–5, although far lower than that in Week 1. In subsequent weeks the effect was minimal and the manufacturer was able to calculate that he was not gaining any revenue from this promotion in Weeks 6–11. Thus, in future, he would choose to promote for a shorter period at this time of year.

During the second promotional period, the activity was seen to be profitable to the manufacturer for the first eight weeks and this information will be used to position further promotional activity.

As Scantrack details the time-spans involved from delivery to sales, the strength of the impact and then the tail-off period, it provides useful and actionable time-scales for planning and maintaining promotions.

FURTHER SCANTRACK USES

One client has used Scantrack to monitor the sell-through of a brand name change. Another client is telling us that he had Scantrack data on his desk showing his pre-Christmas sales pattern earlier than his own internal sales figures.

If it is coded, it shows on the report; every special offer, every price promotion, all promotional packs (20% free, one free in four, free elephant with a jumbo pack). This means that through a leading group of stores which are being monitored, the first week of sales to the public can be picked up. It can be seen how the distribution of the product widens, how it builds to a peak and in some cases, how long it stays in the pipeline. It will not be a surprise to some of you to know that some 1984 Christmas promotional products still have a sale in Christmas 1985, but when they do, they show up in the reports.

The details permits a quicker view to be taken of such things as price/volume relationships. One client has found that there is a good price/volume relationship showing in the 1 Litre size of the brand which is not apparent in the 500 ml size. The detail can also provide a more accurate fix on the precise timing of the take-off of promoted packs compared with standard packs.

FUTURE PLANS FOR SCANNING SERVICES

A whole range of other services are now well established in the USA, based on using the facility of tracking individual customers purchases (which is possible with scanning installations). These data can be linked with television viewing habits, magazine reading habits or other market stimuli and, of course, the whole demographic profile of the people being monitored. This has a terrific potential and the aim is to apply such services in the UK.

We will be following our plan for an annual increase in the number of stores reporting to the ANA & Scantrack Services. By the early 1990's we are likely to be using data from at least 1000 scanning stores and many types of retailer outlets, giving a wide and comprehensive coverage of most goods in the market place.

REFERENCES

1. *Post News* **12** (1986) 2. (Published at Stoke-Sub-Hamdon, Somerset)
2. WOOLFE, A., *The Electronic Revolution in Store*, Ogilvy and Mather (1986).

APPENDIX 11.1 SPECIMEN OF ANA FOUR WEEK DATA

MARKET : HAND CARE ANA SALES DATA SERVICE BREAKDOWN : TOTAL GB

NIELSEN Marketing Research 4-WEEK REPORT BASIS : UNITS (ACTUALS)

ITEM DETAIL

SALES
RSP VALUE
%SHARE

FOR WEEK ENDING	WEEK 1 SALES / RSP	WEEK 1 VALUE / %SHARE	WEEK 2 SALES / RSP	WEEK 2 VALUE / %SHARE	WEEK 3 SALES / RSP	WEEK 3 VALUE / %SHARE	WEEK 4 SALES / RSP	WEEK 4 VALUE / %SHARE	TOTAL SALES / RSP	TOTAL VALUE / %SHARE
TOTAL HAND CARE	152 / 211.2	321 / 100.0	175 / 215.9	378 / 100.0	174 / 218.4	380 / 100.0	169 / 217.9	368 / 100.0	670 / 218.0	1447 / 100.0
MANUFACTURER	151 / 210.7	318 / 99.1	172 / 215.4	370 / 98.0	172 / 218.3	375 / 98.8	168 / 217.4	365 / 99.2	663 / 215.8	1429 / 98.8
BRAND A	104 / 222.8	232 / 72.2	133 / 224.4	298 / 79.0	132 / 229.0	302 / 79.6	128 / 228.8	293 / 79.5	497 / 226.4	1125 / 77.8
150 MLS	91 / 223.4	203 / 63.3	133 / 224.4	298 / 79.0	132 / 229.0	302 / 79.6	128 / 228.8	293 / 79.5	484 / 226.6	1097 / 75.5
150 MLS*+33% EXTRA*	13 / 219.0	28 / 8.9	— / —	— / —	— / —	— / —	— / —	— / —	13 / 219.9	28 / 2.0
BRAND B	16 / 179.0	29 / 8.9	18 / 179.0	32 / 8.5	17 / 179.0	30 / 8.0	16 / 179.0	29 / 7.8	67 / 179.0	120 / 8.3
100 MLS	16 / 179.0	29 / 8.9	18 / 179.0	32 / 8.5	17 / 179.0	30 / 8.0	16 / 179.0	29 / 7.8	67 / 179.0	120 / 8.3
BRAND C	23 / 199.0	46 / 14.3	17 / 199.0	34 / 9.0	17 / 199.0	34 / 8.9	16 / 199.0	32 / 8.6	73 / 199.0	145 / 10.0
25 GM	23 / 199.0	46 / 14.3	17 / 199.0	34 / 9.0	17 / 199.0	34 / 8.9	16 / 199.0	32 / 8.6	73 / 199.0	145 / 10.0
BRAND D	8 / 149.0	12 / 3.7	6 / 149.0	6 / 1.6	6 / 149.0	9 / 2.4	8 / 149.0	12 / 3.2	26 / 149.0	39 / 2.7
100 MLS*+FR COTTON WOOL*	8 / 149.0	12 / 3.7	6 / 149.0	6 / 1.6	6 / 149.0	9 / 2.4	8 / 149.0	12 / 3.2	26 / 149.0	39 / 2.7
ALL OTHERS	1 / 299.0	3 / 0.9	2 / 224.0	7 / 2.0	2 / 224.0	4 / 1.2	3 / 299.0	3 / 0.8	7 / 256.1	18 / 1.2

APPENDIX 11.2
SPECIMEN SCANTRACK 4-WEEK REPORT

MARKET: SOAPS
PERIOD ENDING: 6TH SEPTEMBER 1986   4 WEEK REPORT—ITEM DETAIL

Legend (per cell pair):
- Sales Units / % Share of Units / % Dist of Total Store Selling Space
- Value(£) / % Share of £ / Average RSP

	WEEK ENDING 16TH AUGUST		WEEK ENDING 23RD AUGUST		WEEK ENDING 30TH AUGUST		WEEK ENDING 6TH SEPTEMBER		TOTAL	
	Units	Value(£)	Units	Value(£)	Units	Value(£)	Units	Value(£)	Units	Value(£)
TOTAL SOAPS	5330	2416	5717	2441	5614	2331	5785	2350	22 446	9538
	100	100	100	100	100	100	100	100	100	100
	100	45.3	100	42.7	100	41.5	100	40.6	100	42.5
MANUFACTURER A	1361	809	1514	804	1281	616	1241	546	5397	2775
	25.5	33.5	26.5	33.0	22.8	26.5	21.4	23.2	24.0	29.1
	100	59.4	100	53.1	100	48.1	100	44.0	100	51.4
150 gm	567	175	754	231	689	209	721	224	2731	839
	10.7	7.3	13.2	9.5	12.2	9.0	12.5	9.5	12.2	8.8
	94	30.9	94	30.7	94	30.4	94	31.1	94	30.7
250 gm	420	244	479	281	470	279	489	289	1858	1093
	7.8	10.1	8.4	11.5	8.4	12.0	8.4	12.3	8.3	11.4
	92	58.2	94	58.7	94	59.4	94	59.1	94	58.8
250 gm × 2	374	389	281	292	122	128	31	32	808	842
	7.0	16.1	4.9	12.0	2.2	5.5	0.5	1.4	3.5	8.9
	48	104.1	44	103.8	21	104.7	10	104.6	98	104.1

MANUFACTURER B	1319	500	1334	502	1540	591	1590	599	2193	5783
	24.7	20.8	23.3	20.6	27.4	25.3	27.6	25.5	23.0	25.8
	100	37.9	100	37.6	100	38.4	94	37.7	37.9	100
150 gm	900	264	951	283	864	252	594	175	974	3309
	16.8	10.9	16.6	11.6	15.4	10.8	10.3	7.4	10.2	14.7
	96	29.3	90	29.8	29.1	92	95	29.5	29.4	93
150 gm + 10% Free	*	*	*	*	147	42	495	143	185	642
	*	*	*	*	2.6	1.8	8.6	6.1	1.9	2.9
					13	28.7	28	28.9	28.8	28
250 gm	419	236	383	219	479	269	109	61	785	1390
	7.9	9.8	6.7	9.0	8.5	11.5	1.9	2.6	8.2	6.2
	97	56.3	97	57.1	97	56.2	41	56.4	56.5	97
250 gm + 20% Free	*	*	*	*	50	28	392	220	248	442
	*	*	*	*	0.9	1.2	6.8	9.4	2.7	2.0
					11	56.0	55	56.0	56.0	55
OWN LABEL 150 gm	1079	294	1398	369	1288	334	1316	343	1330	5081
	20.2	11.7	24.5	15.0	22.9	14.3	22.6	14.6	13.9	22.6
	68	26.3	74	26.4	74	25.9	74	26.1	26.2	74

APPENDIX 11.3   SPECIMEN SCANTRACK TREND REPORT

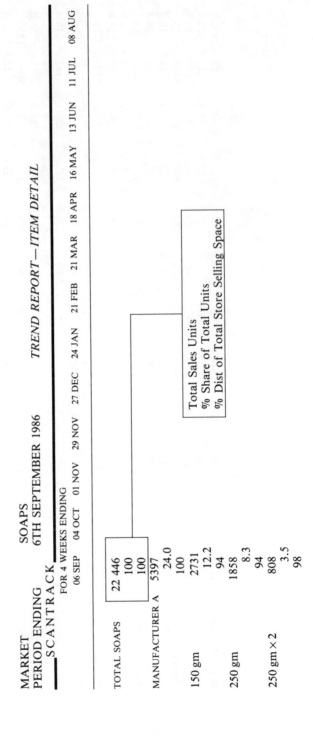

MARKET   SOAPS
PERIOD ENDING   6TH SEPTEMBER 1986   TREND REPORT—ITEM DETAIL
SCANTRACK

FOR 4 WEEKS ENDING

06 SEP   04 OCT   01 NOV   29 NOV   27 DEC   24 JAN   21 FEB   21 MAR   18 APR   16 MAY   13 JUN   11 JUL   08 AUG

TOTAL SOAPS   22 446
                   100
                   100

MANUFACTURER A   5397
                   24.0
                   100

150 gm   2731
                   12.2
                   94

250 gm   1858
                   8.3
                   94

250 gm × 2   808
                   3.5
                   98

Total Sales Units
% Share of Total Units
% Dist of Total Store Selling Space

MANUFACTURER B	5783
	25.8
	100
	3309
	14.7
	93
150 gm	
150 gm + 10% Free	642
	2.9
	28
250 gm	1390
	6.2
	97
250 gm + 20% Free	442
	2.0
	55
OWN LABEL	
150 gm	5081
	22.6
	74

An alternative trend table showing value, share of value and average RSP is available.

Applied Marketing and Social Research 2nd Edition
Edited by Ute Bradley
©Copyright John Wiley 1987

12. Assessing the Effectiveness of Computer-Based Training

Robert J. Mortimer *Barclays Bank plc*
Roger J. Stubbs *MORI*

Information Technology emerges as a dominant theme in a number of these case histories, creating opportunities for both the marketeer and marketing researcher. This particular case should also be of special interest to managers, teachers and students as it explores the advantages and problems of introducing distance learning into an organisation.

MORI were asked to assess the effectiveness of viewdata as a training medium in Barclays Bank, as well as checking on its acceptability to staff. The case raises many interesting issues that need to be considered in personnel research in general and stresses particularly the effect of these issues on research design. These and other problems (e.g. data collection-data interpretation-use made of results) could be usefully explored in classroom discussions.

The three questionnaires used in this study are appended.

SUMMARY

Modern technology has made possible the use of distance learning on a large scale, by means of remote terminals linked by telecommunication land lines to a central computer system. Barclays Bank in the UK has been developing such a system for the last six years for several of its internal training courses. The benefits to the bank, over the traditional 'training course', are readily apparent: each student receives the same message, less time is spent away from the place of work, fewer training personnel, reduced cost of travel and accommodation.

But substantial capital expenditure is involved and no objective information was available either on the effectiveness of computer-based learning or on its acceptability to the staff. The bank asked Market & Opinion Research International (MORI) whether market research techniques could be applied in this new situation to obtain such information. The paper describes the research conducted and some of the findings which emerged.

The research took place in three stages. In the first, bank staff were asked to complete a questionnaire immediately they had finished a training programme. This looked at the physical environment, picture quality, attention span etc, as well as the relevance, comprehensiveness, interest and usefulness of the material. At the second stage the *same individuals* were surveyed three months later and asked how helpful the training had been to them in practice, and how effectively they felt they were doing their job. This latter item is of course extremely subjective, so, as the third component, we asked the *supervisors* of the original staff respondents how effectively *they* felt staff had been doing their job since the training programme. A 'control' of traditional course attenders and their supervisors was also incorporated.

The research showed that computer-based systems can train effectively, but that acceptability varies according to type and length of the programme, age of the participant and the perceived attitude to computer-based learning of senior staff within the work location. The paper concludes with a discussion of how the research has influenced the development of training within the bank and the direction in which the bank is now heading in its use of distance learning.

INTRODUCTION

Barclays staff numbers approximately 47 000 people working in approximately 2100 domestic banking branches spread throughout the whole of Great Britain. This number of staff, combined with the rapidly-changing nature of banking, presents a real challenge as far as training is concerned and the bank is constantly looking at ways in which it can improve the service given to the public through a better trained and informed staff. In 1983 approximately 11 000 Barclays staff were involved in some form of basic procedural training. This ranged from the elementary functions of a new entrant in listing cheques to the more complicated procedures of taking the appropriate legal steps to secure the bank's position when a loan has been made to a customer. Before describing the ways in which, for the last six years, the Bank has been looking at computer-based training using Viewdata as a training medium, it might be helpful to place this medium in the context of the bank's traditional training methods.

BARCLAY'S TRADITIONAL TRAINING METHODS

There are three principal ways in which Barclays Bank undertakes the training of staff: firstly, through centralised courses, secondly, through local courses and seminars, and thirdly through in-branch training.

Centralised Courses

The bank has a residential management training college in Sussex. The two non-residential training centres are in the London suburbs where courses are held covering a diverse range of requirements but all dealing with the day-to-day functions and operation of the bank's branch offices. Centralised courses are not only very disruptive to branches, particularly where there may be less than 20 on the staff, but also very costly. If the student has to travel to London from other parts of the country, 20% of the working week may be lost to allow for the time spent on Monday morning travelling to London and the return home on Friday afternoon. Although the bank has its own residence in which some of the students are accommodated, it is also necessary to use hotels for staff on courses in London. Perhaps the most significant factor of all is that in any form of centralised training it is almost impossible to run courses at the right time for all the students. In 1981 approximately 4000 staff attended a one week Cashier Course of whom 1000 had been working on the counter for six months or more before attending the course. The ideal would be for the formal training course to be undertaken within three months of the member of staff becoming a trainee cashier.

Local Courses and Seminars

Training courses are run in the 30 district offices of the bank within the UK. The instructors are trained and up-dated centrally but much of the student travelling time is eliminated when courses are held locally. It is also possible to meet the specific needs of the locality, for example, to cater for branches in rural areas where specialist training is necessary in agriculture for farming customers.

In-Branch Training

As with many organisations, there is a considerable amount of on-the-job training, but this has been augmented in two ways:

Programmed Learning Manuals

For more than ten years the bank has used programmed learning manuals, particularly for new entrants and cashiers. They are costly to maintain and very dependent upon supervisory skills and the management of the branch for their effectiveness as a training aid.

In-Branch Operator Training Program (IBOT)

Nine years ago the bank introduced a training course to the branch offices for the training of computer terminal operators. The terminal is taken off line and a training program stored on cassette or disc is inserted into the terminal. By reference to a programmed learning text the operator works through a course which not only explains the operation of the terminal itself but, by use of specimen vouchers, the trainee learns the identification and procedure for the different types of entries, cheques, credits and debits which are applied to customers' accounts. The total program lasts approximately 16 hours and this is broken down into three quarters of an hour sessions. The trainees are able to undertake their programs entirely at their own pace and can repeat sessions for clarification as necessary.

The introduction of a simulation program in 1985 allows the student to work in a real live situation, i.e. he/she actually inputs dummy waste through the terminal.

With this background it will be appreciated that the bank has a clear interest in the concept of distance learning.

THE VIEWDATA PROJECT

Viewdata is the generic term for the display on a specially adapted television screen of information, text and simple graphics; it does not provide real pictures, still or moving. The best known example of viewdata is the British Telecom 'Prestel' information system.

Early in 1980 the bank saw this as an opportunity, relatively cheaply, to put a simple terminal into a branch at one end and to provide a computer at the other. By using the ordinary telecom lines to transmit data, branches would be able to access a central computer data base for communication, reference facilities or training. This would not conflict with the mainframe system used for the bank's book-keeping requirements and as viewdata uses a simple authoring language this could be used by the trainers without specialist computer programming knowledge. Rather than use Prestel for access, the bank set up a private viewdata system for the pilot project. Initially in just 33 branches, but more recently in 136 branches spread throughout the London area, the bank has been experimenting with a range of basic procedural training to assess the acceptability and effectiveness of viewdata from the point of view of the students, managers and trainers. Unlike the passive role of the student when using either audio or video, viewdata is a highly interactive computer-based training system. Although simple to operate, usually by just one key depression, the student is required to answer questions and make responses.

Student Interactivity

To maintain the student's interest it is vital that there should be as much variety of interactivity as possible between the student and the program. This may be:

— a simple statement — true or false;
— selection of two alternatives — either one or the other;
— multiple choice question — giving up to nine options;
— free format answers — requiring the student to type in the answer;
— completion of a form — by filling in gaps using an alpha numeric keyboard.

The student is never locked out of the system. During the learning sequence they can always go to a help page to seek guidance. When they return to the teaching page any answers to questions already given on that page will be redisplayed. The use of the seven available colours is also important not just for cosmetic purposes but to give interest and variety to the layout of the information on the screen and to highlight points when necessary. The same standard of presentation is not required when viewdata is used as an information service as it is if a student is expected to absorb knowledge over a period of up to an hour at a time. Simple graphics also enhance presentation.

The student has a personal identification number for each program which is used to gather statistical information. If the student takes a break the program title, date and page last accessed are displayed on the welcome page when the student starts again. The students are locked into that course and are then directed to the point in the program where they finished last time.

One advantage of viewdata is that the information can always be kept up to date and vast quantities of notes or amendments do not have to be printed and circulated.

Reference Facility

If viewdata is to be an effective source of information a referencing index must be carefully structured. The use of the terminal for reference may also have a bearing on the siting as will be mentioned later.

Test Reports

At the end of most viewdata training programs the student is required to complete a short mastery test and the branch where the student works receives a report giving the test results. In addition to a weighted point score for the most important questions, reference is also given to the learning pages to which to refer in the event of incorrect answers. Branch management are thus aided in fulfilling their responsibility in helping students through areas of apparent difficulty. The tests must not be regarded as examinations because there may be individual circumstances known to the branch why a student may not have done well. Neither is the test any measure of the student's practical ability to do the job. It is a guide for the branch management to provide additional supportive training and must be treated as such. The test report is destroyed after examination and is not part of the bank's records.

Contrary to what might be expected, the students look forward to receiving their test results and an element of friendly competition is aroused between students over their scores.

The Effectiveness of Viewdata as a Training Medium

The early experience with viewdata showed that branch management was enthusiastic about the potential concept of this type of in-branch training. Discussion with and comment by students, supervisors and management both at branch and district level showed that viewdata was widely welcomed as an effective training medium.

This enthusiasm has a number of strands:

(a) More flexible manning of branches, because staff are not away on a course.
(b) Timely availability of task-related, as opposed to job-related, training to meet planned needs as and when they arise.
(c) Significantly less supervision of on-the-job training is necessary.
(d) The reports on student comprehension allow in-branch training to be focused on areas of weakness.
(e) The training material is always up-to-date and accurate.

However, the bank had no formal means of objective evaluation. To obtain the best possible information on the effectiveness and acceptability of viewdata training, Market & Opinion Research International (MORI) was asked to design and conduct a survey which would assess:

(i) The physical acceptability of the system: ease of operation, environment in which the training takes place, the adequacy of supporting material.
(ii) The structure of the training programme: level of difficulty, tone, etc.
(iii) The effectiveness of the computer-based training medium: how well it meets its aims and how it compares with course-based training methods.

The Research Design

The first two objectives could have been met by surveying viewdata students immediately on completion of a program of training such as MORI had done for the bank a decade earlier. But the third implied both an extended time-scale (it is really only possible to assess how useful a course has been some time after putting it into practice) and a broader coverage, to compare the new-style training with 'traditional' methods. This would have led to the following three-part research design:

— viewdata students immediately on completion of a training programme;
— the same viewdata students three months later;
— 'traditional' course students (preferably covering the same material as the viewdata students) three months after completing their course.

But the key element — effectiveness of the training — is such a subjective concept, and one which it is arguable whether the member of staff is the best qualified to assess, that two further components were built in:

— supervisors of the viewdata students, three months after students completed a training programme;
— supervisors of 'traditional' course students, also three months on.

These studies served a further purpose, too, in evaluating attitudes of senior staff to the new training system: without their support it could have little future in the bank.

Preliminary qualitative work was undertaken and the questionnaires were designed for self-completion and postal return direct to MORI. This was felt to be the most appropriate technique, since a high response rate would be obtained, confidentiality was ensured and cost-effectiveness maximised. Great stress was laid by MORI and the bank on the fact that the exercise was *not* a performance appraisal of individuals. Responses to all questions — including effectiveness ratings — were strictly confidential, and no completed questionnaire was seen by anybody in the bank. We were encouraged that the response rate exceeded 90%, generating approximately 100 completed questionnaires for each of the five categories.

THE FINDINGS

In this section we have tried to concentrate on those issues of the greatest significance to the use and development of computer-based training in the bank. We will look at each objective in turn:

Physical acceptability

The act of undertaking a session in front of a monitor screen was generally acceptable. Over half felt that the topic coverage and instructions on how to proceed through the session were 'good', with virtually nobody rating them as 'poor' (see Figure 12.1). However, there was substantial criticism of picture quality (a function of the quality of the telephone link), of ease of referring back to earlier material and of the impersonality of the system — a major drawback, particularly when compared with the camaraderie of courses. There was evidence, too, that such irritations became more pronounced the longer the programme being taken.

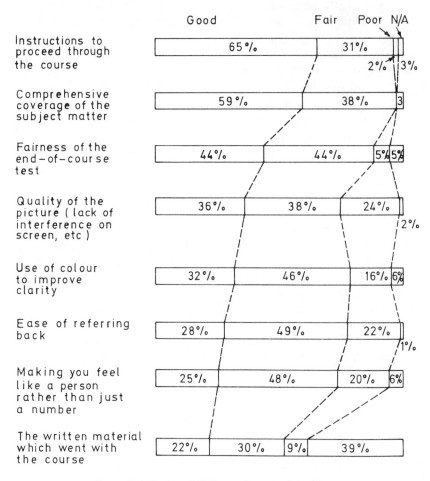

Figure 12.1 Rating of Different Aspects of the Course

The working environment, too, caused some problems. Very few of the branches had the space to allocate a special room to the viewdata system, so the hardware tended to be located in rest rooms, interview rooms or machine rooms, where there were frequent disturbances. Half the respondents were critical on this score, and a third on the level of extraneous noise they had to contend with. It also became clear that factors such as temperature, comfort and illumination in the room were important. More than two students in five complained of eye strain through staring at the screen.

One unexpected finding related to the age of the respondents. The students were generally young (under 30), split roughly evenly above and below age 21. It was the over-21s who tended to be more positive in their views than the youngsters.

Structure of Viewdata Training

There is a delicate balance between making training material too complex and advanced, and appearing to 'talk down to' the students. If anything, the bank's early viewdata courses veered towards the latter: 12% rated them 'too elementary' compared with 2% 'too technical', but an 'about right' figure of 86% was regarded as satisfactory. However, only one student in four found the course 'stimulating', although most of the remainder were neutral rather than critical: one in four found it 'boring'. The over 21s were much more positive in this respect (41% stimulating, 19% boring) than the under-21s (12% and 38%, respectively). Also, the longer the course, the less stimulating it was rated.

Part of each viewdata training programme consisted of an end-of-course test. Figure 12.1 shows that there was little criticism of its fairness, but a fairly common complaint was that trivial errors in some of the responses could lead to them being marked as incorrect (for example 'Taunton High Street' rather than 'High Street, Taunton'). Three-quarters of the students said that this had happened to them on at least one occasion. Half of the supervisors believed that such tests provided a good indication of the person's ability to do the job (but a quarter disagreed).

Effectiveness of Computer-Based Training

Students (from both methods) were asked how effectively they felt they were doing the work since taking the course. The same question was also put to supervisors. The main results, set out in Table 12.1, show that viewdata students — and their supervisors — are more likely to rate performance as 'very effective' than are traditional course students and their supervisors. However, this generalisation hides some major discrepancies: on long courses, traditional effectiveness scores are markedly better than viewdata ones, and the same is true for staff aged under 21.

TABLE 12.1   Perceived Effectiveness of Doing the Work

	'Very effective'	
	Students (%)	Supervisors (%)
Viewdata training	43	46
Traditional training	31	35

In trying to relate on-the-job effectiveness back to training, several different factors can be isolated — interest, comprehensiveness, relevance and ease of remembering the material. Table 12.2 summarises these aspects. On relevance, interest and comprehensiveness of the material, the traditional courses seem to have the edge, though once again the figures vary among particular courses.

Twice as many viewdata students (30%) rated the course 'not very' or 'not at all' interesting, as traditional students (15%). On the face of it, this would seem to be a major drawback for this form of training. But these evaluations were given three months after taking the course. We also asked the same people to rate the same courses immediately on completion, and the 'not interesting' figures were only half the retrospective levels (i.e. 15%). The 'very interesting' scores also dropped during the intervening three months. This suggests that students' memories of taking a viewdata course become less attractive with time: sitting in a hot room staring at a flickering screen late on in the day, rather than the interest and stimulation experienced at the time from the training material itself. This is clearly undesirable in the long term, as it could — somewhat misleadingly — engender a feeling of 'boring old viewdata courses' within the bank. (Encouragingly, in the highest scoring viewdata course, there was no falling off in interest ratings over the months.)

TABLE 12.2   Aspects of Training

	Students		Supervisors	
	Viewdata (%)	Traditional (%)	Viewdata (%)	Traditional (%)
Course rated:				
'very interesting'	11	29	23	25
(not interesting)	(30)	(15)	(15)	(7)
Remembering course material:				
'very well'	31	31	—	—
(not well)	(6)	(8)	—	—
Relevance of material:				
'very relevant'	53	62	59	57
(not very relevant)	(8)	(6)	(4)	(3)
Comprehensiveness of course:				
good	62	79	—	—
(poor)	(1)	(0)	—	—

In the light of this, we were reassured to see the high 'effectiveness' scores, especially from supervisors, and to note that there was no 'falling off' in scores for relevance of the material in the three months following a viewdata course.

It looks, then, as if computer-based training trains bank staff at least as effectively as traditional methods, but that some of the enjoyment, interaction with colleagues, discussion with tutors etc, associated with 'going away on a course' is missed. Further, this drawback becomes magnified over time. These conclusions are reinforced by the findings from two questions which asked all respondent (students and supervisors) which training technique they would recommend, first from the point of view of learning the material and second from the point of view of enjoying the learning experience. Figure 12.2 shows how well the traditional method scores on the latter item, and the affect on attitudes to the former item that actually experiencing a viewdata course can have (very few of the 'traditional' students had ever experienced viewdata training).

a. From the point of view of learning the material ?

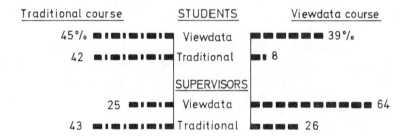

b. From the point of view of enjoying the learning experience ?

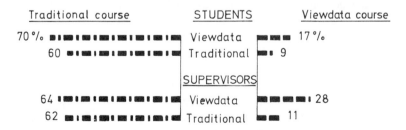

Figure 12.2 Recommendation for Type of Training

TABLE 12.3   Effect of Supervisor's Attitude

	Supervisor judged to be:	
	'Keen supporter' *of viewdata* *(%)*	*Not keen* *supporter* *(%)*
Viewdata material 'very relevant'	60	39

Student
  'very confident' that
  training has enabled him
  to do such work
  unsupervised
	51	32

Student found course 'stimulating'	32	18

The Importance of Supervisors' Views

Supervisors were included in the research partly to act as a check on the effectiveness rating. (Of all those viewdata students who rated their own performance as 'very effective', 71% of supervisors agreed; of those rating their own performance 'fairly effective', 64% of supervisors agreed and a further 30% felt the staff member was being too modest.) But it also became clear in the qualitative work (group discussions) that their attitude towards computer training could have a marked influence on how juniors in the branch felt about it also. The quantitative work bore this out quite sharply (see Table 12.3). Branches in which the supervisor was regarded as a keen advocate of computer-based training tended to generate a much more positive attitude towards it among the staff.

One useful finding from the research was that supervisors claimed a higher level of support for the new system than was perceived by their staff (83% said they were 'keen supporters' compared to 69% of staff, and while 18% of staff believed that their supervisor did not regard viewdata as 'proper' training this view was actually only endorsed by 11% of supervisors themselves). It is thus clearly important for supervisors to convey this support down the line.

We also found strong evidence that 'hands-on' experience of the system by supervisors was likely to instil more favourable attitudes: those who had never used it were much less committed to the system (though not necessarily opposed to it). It is clear that there is a hard core of one supervisor in 20 with the bank who need to be convinced as to the benefits of this type of training.

ACTION AS A RESULT OF MORI SURVEY

The final sentence from the Conclusions of the MORI survey report reads: 'In the long term, this survey suggests that viewdata is a viable medium for a wide range of—preferably short—courses especially at the more junior level'.

However, the survey revealed the following areas of criticism of viewdata training:

1. 'Problem of eye-strain which appears to be a particular problem on the longer courses'.
2. 'More colour and ultimately the use of sound'.
3. 'Location of viewdata terminals'.
4. 'Inability of the system to allow for a sufficiently wide range of correct answers'.
5. The more general need for wider communication in the education of staff as to the objectives and benefits of this training medium.

The response to these criticisms may be listed seriatim as follows:

1. Although taken in one-hourly sessions, the longest individual programme available at the time of the MORI survey was 5½ hours. The group of programmes for Standing Order training took a total of 17 hours, which represented the conversion of a 3½ day course.

   The longest programmes now are 3½ hours with one exception and, although the total length of Standing Order training is still 17 hours, this has been broken down into training for nine job functions, the shortest of which is a three-quarter hour programme and the longest 4½ hours. (This is due to be split in half shortly.)

   The most popular programmes are those lasting an hour to 2¼ hours on new entrant courses.

   The aim now is to produce programmes of no more than about 2½ hours, which means that in just over 2 × 1 hour sessions the training module is completed.

   Within the data base giving details of each programme the student or branch management may now access information which gives the length of each learning sequence and the length of the mastery test at the end of the programme.
2. Each programme is reviewed every six months by making a complete examination of all pages and the student responses. Some standardisation has been introduced not only as to colour but also lay-out. This has been done not to stultify the creativity of the writers but to provide some uniformity of presentation to the student.

3. The location of viewdata terminals has been rearranged due to the closure of one local head office, thus enabling existing districts to have a larger share of terminals. This has alleviated the problem slightly.

4. Enhancements to the computer application programmes have eliminated some of the limitations which restricted the range of acceptable answers. More importantly, the questioning technique has been developed which has restricted some of the possible student responses.

5. With changing management and staff in our branches there is a constant need to enforce the guidance given at the original seminars about viewdata. At first the amount of material available was limited. It is quite clear now that with the development of further courses and information available on screen, communication to users is even more important. This has been achieved in a number of ways:

   (a) A newsletter is sent to all viewdata branches periodically giving details about changes to current courses and the release of new courses.

   (b) A personal visit by one of the senior members of the unit has been made to 74 of the 136 branches with terminals. In addition, Viewdata Unit staff visit branches to validate new courses and every opportunity is taken to develop close user contact.

   (c) The Manager's Assistants (office manager) from 63 branches have visited the Viewdata Unit for a two-hour seminar. They meet Unit staff, see the computer operation, look at new material being prepared and discuss problems.

   (d) A small team has been set up to co-ordinate response to branch problems and provide user support in diagnosing technical difficulties.

PROBLEMS

From the experience gained in the project to date there are three main problem areas, the siting of terminals, time and education.

The Siting of Terminals

Many bank branches or indeed other offices, do not have quiet areas away from the general office noise which would be conducive to the learning environment. Thus, terminals have been installed in a variety of locations from waiting rooms to staff rooms. On the other hand, if viewdata is to be used for reference purposes it is pointless having the terminal sited too far away from the normal working areas because staff are hardly likely to go up two flights of stairs to hunt for a referencing service—it must be immediately accessible. There is therefore a dilemma because the installation of additional terminals adds to the cost.

Ergonomics are important and experience shows that too few students adjust the brightness of the display, adjust the height of their chair for personal comfort or turn the screen so that it does not catch the light.

Time

From the point of view of office organisation it is far easier to send someone on a course for two days than it is to organise one hour training sessions each day until the course is completed. The onus of responsibility is not just on the supervisor or manager but also on the student, as learned when listening to some students' reactions to viewdata. If it is planned to start a one-hour training session at 3.30 pm but the member of staff has some vital work to finish, there is a willingness for staff to finish their work before starting the training programme. If the vital work takes half-an-hour, then at 4.00 pm there is a tendency to say 'I won't start my training programme now — I'll do it tomorrow'. (The MORI research showed that nearly three-quarters of viewdata students had had to postpone at least one session because of work in the branch.) Once the sense of personal discipline has been developed, then the vital work could be handed to a colleague to finish, thus freeing the student to start their training programme today. This needs not only self-discipline but a spirit of understanding and team-work. In fact it needs a new education into the relationship between daily work and on-the-job training.

Education

The concept of computer-based training, although not new in itself, is new to a whole group of staff who, in the past, have had little or no involvement with computers.

Implementation is therefore vital in developing an understanding for staff to appreciate how this type of training can aid them in their work. In this project implementation was carried out in three stages:

   (i) A branch visit by a member of the project team to discuss siting of the terminal.
  (ii) Seminars held in district offices with selected branch staff given a live demonstration of the system and discussion of the concept.
 (iii) In-branch demonstrations when the terminal was installed.

Continuous branch involvement with the users is important. Follow-up visits have been made to branches as well as discussions with district office staff and visits by some staff to see the computers and meet the programme writing teams.

DEVELOPMENT OF COMPUTER-BASED DISTANCE LEARNING IN BARCLAYS BANK

There is no doubt that the Viewdata Project has proved to the bank the acceptability and effectiveness of computer-based distance learning. By the end of April 1985 viewdata training had been used for a total of 45 000 hours and 18 455 student courses had been completed during the six years so far.

The bank has been looking at costs and the feasibility of developing within the UK interactive computer based distance learning. Technology is moving fast and the capital costs, which are high, must reflect the ability of the bank to react quickly to a changing need.

FURTHER READING

MAINWARING, G. and STUBBS, R., 'SPECTRUM: A Marketing Seminar', In BRADLEY, v. (Ed), *Applied Marketing and Social Research*, 1st ed., Van Nostrand Reinhold (1982)

DAWES, R. E., 'Informing the Staff of Product, Services and Supplementary Activities: Training Directed for Optimum Customer Relations', *EFMA/ESOMAR Seminar on How Research can Help Financial Organisations Communicate Internally and Externally Proceedings*, Rome (1982)

WILLOUGHBY, K. and WORCESTER, R., 'Profitability from Research within the Company' *34th Congress of European Society for Opinion and Marketing Research*, Amsterdam, August 1981

STUBBS, R. J., 'Bank Staff—A Neglected Marketing Resource' *EFMA/ESOMAR Seminar Proceedings*, Zurich (1985)

ACKNOWLEDGMENT

The basis for this chapter was a paper read at an EMAC/ESOMAR symposium on 'Methodological Advances in Marketing Research in Theory & Practice' in Copenhagen 1984. Permission has been granted by ESOMAR to reproduce this material.

APPENDIX 12.1 SUPERVISOR'S QUESTIONNAIRE

Market & Opinion Research International

TRAINING SURVEY

SUPERVISOR'S QUESTIONNAIRE

This questionnaire is for completion two-four months after the member of staff has finished the particular training course.

We are trying to assess the effectiveness of the training system, *not* to evaluate an individual's performance in the usual sense. The members of staff will not see your answers, nor will anyone else from the branch or LHO.

How to answer the questions

Most questions have various answers provided, and you circle the number of the answer which comes closest to your own opinion. For example, if you think the member of staff found the course fairly interesting at Q.4, you would answer it like this:

Very interesting 1
Fairly interesting . . . . ②
Not very interesting 3
Not at all interesting 4

Allowance is made for 'don't know' and 'no opinion' replies on some questions, but please try to give a definite answer where possible.

Thank you for your help.

OFFICE USE ONLY

Staff member's name . . . . Branch . . . .

MORI/2054/3   Serial No. . . . . Card 3
     (1–5)   (6–9)   (10)

THIS FORM IS THE PROPERTY OF MARKET & OPINION RESEARCH INTERNATIONAL

Q.1   a) In which of these training areas was the course the member of staff
took recently?

PLEASE CIRCLE ONE NUMBER
(11)

Standing Orders 1
Cashiers 2
Foreign 3
Securities 4   11
Other (PLEASE WRITE IN).......... 5
....

Q.1   b) How did the member of staff take the course?

PLEASE CIRCLE ONE NUMBER
(12)

Attended a course away from the
    branch.......................... 1
Viewdata 2   12

Q.2   Has the member of staff been doing work in the branch relevant to
this course *since* the course?

PLEASE CIRCLE ONE NUMBER
(13)

Yes, as most of their job .... 1] PLEASE ANSWER
Yes, but only as part of their job ...... 2]   Q.3   13

No, not at all 3   — PLEASE GO
                                             STRAIGHT TO Q.4

Q.3   a) How effectively would you say the member of staff has been doing
this work?

PLEASE CIRCLE ONE NUMBER
(14)

Very effectively..................... 1
Fairly effectively.................... 2
Not very effectively 3   14
Not at all effectively 4

Q.3   b) How relevant does the material covered in the course appear to
have been to their work in the branch?

PLEASE CIRCLE ONE NUMBER
(15)

Very relevant 1
Fairly relevant 2
Not very relevant 3
Not at all relevant 4

Q.4   So far as you can judge, how interesting did the member of staff find the course?

PLEASE CIRCLE ONE NUMBER
(16)

Very interesting......................	1
Fairly intereesting....................	2
Not very interesting	3
Not at all interesting	4

16

Q.5   If a member of staff who was about to take this particular course had the choice of doing it in the traditional way — by going away on a course — or by doing it on viewdata, how would you advise them . . .
a.   — from the point of view of learning the material?

PLEASE CIRCLE ONE NUMBER
(17)

Traditional course	1
˙Viewdata	2
No opinion	3

17

b)   — from the point of view of enjoying the learning process?

PLEASE CIRCLE ONE NUMBER
(18)

Traditional course	1
Viewdata	2
No opinion	3

18

Q.6   Below are some statements which have been made concerning the use of viewdata in training. How strongly do you agree or disagree with each one?

PLEASE CIRCLE ONE NUMBER FOR EACH STATEMENT

	Strongly agree	Tend to agree	Neither agree nor disagree	Tend to disagree	Strongly disagree	Not applicable/ no opinion/ don't know	
a. Provision should be made for viewdata training with CWIP	1	2	3	4	5	6	19
b. Viewdata sessions often have to be postponed here because of more pressing work in the branch.........	1	2	3	4	5	6	20
c. I'm a keen supporter of viewdata training	1	2	3	4	5	6	21

d. The viewdata training
centre staff are extremely
helpful to us ....1....2....3....4....5.....6... | 22

e. The end-of-course tests
on viewdata provide a
good indication of the
person's ability to do the
job......................1....2....3....4....5.....6... | 23

f. The viewdata system
has a good index and
reference system ....1....2....3....4....5.....6... | 24

g. I usually go through a
member of staff's wrong
answers with them, after a
viewdata course...........1....2....3....4....5.....6... | 25

h. I don't regard viewdata
as 'proper' training ....1....2....3....4....5.....6... | 26

i. There are some courses
which could never be suc-
cessfully done on viewdata ..1....2....3....4....5.....6... | 27

Which are they? (PLEASE WRITE IN) | (28)
.... | 1 2
.... | 3 4
.... | 5 6
.... | 7 8
.... | 9 0
.... | X Y
.... | (29)
| 1 2
| 3 4
| 5 6
| 7 8
| 9 0
| X Y

Q.7   a) Do you have a viewdata training facility at your branch?

PLEASE CIRCLE ONE NUMBER
(30)

Yes .... 1— PLEASE CONTINUE
                                        WITH Q.7b | 30
No .... 2—   PLEASE GO
                                    STRAIGHT TO Q.8

Q.7 b) On balance, has the viewdata made your life easier or more difficult?

PLEASE CIRCLE ONE NUMBER
(31)

Made it easier	1
Made no real difference	2
Made it more difficult	3
Too early to tell	4
No opinion	5

31

Q.7 c) How well was the viewdata system of training introduced and explained to you?

PLEASE CIRCLE ONE NUMBER
(32)

Very well	1
Fairly well	2
Not very well......................	3
Not at all well.....................	4
No opinion/not applicable	5

32

Q.7 d) Where is the viewdata terminal located in your branch?

PLEASE CIRCLE ONE NUMBER
(33)

Rest room	1
Securities	2
Mech. room.......................	3
Interview room	4
Special room for viewdata	5
Other (PLEASE RING '6' AND WRITE IN)	6

....

33

Q.7 e) Ideally, where *should* the terminal be located?

PLEASE CIRCLE ONE NUMBER
(34)

Rest room	1
Securities	2
Mech. room.......................	3
Interview room	4
Special room for viewdata	5
Other (PLEASE RING '6' AND WRITE IN)	6

....

34

Q.7   f) How long have you *personally* spent operating the viewdata system in your branch?

PLEASE CIRCLE ONE NUMBER

(35)

Operated it personally for 2 hours	1
Operated it personally for 1–2 hours . . .	2
Operated it personally for ½ hour to 1 hour	3
Operated it personally for a short while (less than 30 minutes)	4
Have not personally operated it, but have spent time watching others	5
Have not operated the system at all	6

35

THE FOLLOWING INFORMATION ABOUT YOU WILL HELP US COMPARE THE VIEWS OF DIFFERENT TYPES OF SUPERVISORS. GROUPINGS OF LESS THAN 12 WILL NOT BE USED.

PLEASE CIRCLE ONE NUMBER FOR EACH QUESTION

Q.8   a) *Your age group*:   (36)

Under 25	1
25–34	2
35–44	3
45–54	4
55 or over	5

36

Q.8   b) *Your job title*:   (37)

Securities Officer	1
Manager's Assistant	2
Assistant Manager	3
Deputy Manager	4
Manager	5
Other (WRITE IN)	6

. . . .

37

Q.8   c)*Total (actual) number of staff in your branch*:

(38)

Under 10 staff	1
10–19	2
20–29	3
30–39	4
40–49	5
50–74	6
75–99	7
100 or more	8

38

Q8   d) On average, how many under or over basic has your branch been
over the last six months or so?

PLEASE CIRCLE ONE NUMBER

(39)

3 or more under basic	1
2 under basic	2
1 under basic	3
On basic	4
1 over basic	5
2 over basic	6
3 or more over basic	7

39

Q.8   e) *District*   (40)

Windsor	1
London	2

40

Q.9   Finally, what other comments would you like to make about viewdata
training?
PLEASE WRITE IN

. . . .   (41)

. . . .   1 2 3

. . . .   4 5 6

. . . .   7 8 9

. . . .   0 X Y

. . . .   (42)

1 2 3

4 5 6

7 8 9

0 X Y

Note: in the reproduction of these three questionnaires the original question
layout has been retained as far as possible, but not the page layout.

APPENDIX 12.2   RETROSPECTIVE QUESTIONNAIRE

Market & Opinion Research International

TRAINING SURVEY

RETROSPECTIVE QUESTIONNAIRE

This questionnaire is for completion two-four months after your have finished the particular training course.

THIS IS *NOT* A TEST

It is a survey of your *opinions* of the course — there are no "right answers". We are trying to assess the effectiveness of the training system, *not* your performance. Nobody from your branch or LHO will every know how you — as an individual — answered these questions.

How to answer the questions

Most questions have various answers provided, and you circle the number of the answer which comes closest to your own opinion. For example, if you completed the course 3 or 4 months' ago, you would answer Q.1b like this:

```
Less than 2 months ...................................1
Between 2 and 3 months...............................2
Between 3 and 4 months.............................. (3)
Between 4 and 6 months...............................4
More than 6 months ago ..............................5
```

Allowance is made for 'don't know' and 'no opinion' replies on some questions, but please try to give a definite answer where possible.

Thank you for your help.

OFFICE USE ONLY

Name ....   Branch ....

MORI/2054/2   Serial No.............   Card 2
    (1–5)   (6–9)   (10)

THIS FORM IS THE PROPERTY OF MARKET & OPINION RESEARCH INTERNATIONAL

Q.1 a) In which of these training areas was the course you took recently?

PLEASE CIRCLE ONE NUMBER
(11)

Standing Orders 1
Cashiers 2
Foreign 3
Securities 4
Other (PLEASE WRITE IN).......... 5
....

11

Q.1 b) Please specify exactly which course you attended or viewdata training programme you completed?

PLEASE WRITE IN

(12)
1 2 3
4 5 6
7 8 9
0 X Y

Q.1 c) How did you take the course?

PLEASE CIRCLE ONE NUMBER
(13)

Attended a course away from the
branch.......................... 1
Viewdata 2

13

Q.1 d) How long ago did you complete this course?

PLEASE CIRCLE ONE NUMBER
(14)

Less than two months 1
Between 2 and 3 months............. 2
Between 3 and 4 months............. 3
Between 4 and 6 months............. 4
More than 6 months ago
(PLEASE SPECIFY).............. 5

14

Q.2 a) Had you been doing work in the branch relevant to this course *before* the course?

PLEASE CIRCLE ONE NUMBER
(15)

Yes—for more than 3 months before .. 1
Yes—for more than 1 month but less
than 3 months before 2
Yes—for more than 2 weeks but less   PLEASE
than 1 month before 3   ANSWER Q.2b   15
Yes—for more than 1 week but less
than 2 weeks before............... 4
Yes—for less than a week before...... 5
No—not at all 6   —PLEASE GO
STRAIGHT TO Q.2c ➡
⇒

Q.2 b) Was there any gap between doing this work and taking the course?

PLEASE CIRCLE ONE NUMBER
(16)

No — no gap 1
Yes — gap of less than a month 2
Yes — gap of 1–3 months 3
Yes — gap of 3–6 months 4
Yes — gap of 6–12 months 5
Yes — gap of more than 12 months 6

16

Q.2 c) Have you been doing work in the branch relevant to this course *since* the course?

PLEASE CIRCLE ONE NUMBER
(17)

17

Yes — as most of my job.............. 1 ⎤ PLEASE
Yes, but as only a small   ANSWER
  part of my job .... 2 ⎦ Q.3
No — not at all 3   — PLEASE GO
                              STRAIGHT TO Q.4a

Q.3 a) How relevant was the material covered in the course to your work in the branch?

PLEASE CIRCLE ONE NUMBER
(18)

Very relevant 1
Fairly relevant 2
Not very relevant 3
Not at all relevant 4

18

Q.3 b) How would you rate the course, overall, on how fully it covered the subject matter?

PLEASE CIRCLE ONE NUMBER
(19)

Good............................. 1
Fair 2
Poor 3

19

Q.3 c) What — if anything — should have been covered better, or in more depth?

(20)

PLEASE WRITE IN

....

....

....

....

....

....

1 2 3 4
5 6 7 8
9 0 X Y
(21)
1 2 3 4
5 6 7 8
9 0 X Y

Q.3   d) How effectively would you say you have been doing this work in
the branch, since you took the course?

PLEASE CIRCLE ONE NUMBER
(22)

Very effectively...................... 1
Fairly effectively.................... 2
Not very effectively 3
Not at all effectively 4   22

Q.4   a) How often — if at all — have you referred back to your course notes?

PLEASE CIRCLE ONE NUMBER
(23)

Never 1
Less than 5 times 2
5–10 times 3   23
11–20 times 4
More than 20 times
    (PLEASE SPECIFY).............. 5
....
No course notes 6

VIEWDATA STUDENTS ONLY. OTHERS PLEASE GO ON TO Q.5
Q.4   b) How often — if at all — have you referred back to the material, using
the viewdata equipment?

PLEASE CIRCLE ONE NUMBER
(24)

Never 1   24
Less than 5 times 2
5–10 times 3
11–20 times 4
More than 20 times 5

PLEASE CONTINUE WITH Q.5

Q.5   How well would you say you have been able to remember the material
you learned in the course?

PLEASE CIRCLE ONE NUMBER
(25)

Very well 1
Fairly well 2
Not very well....................... 3   25
Not at all well...................... 4
No opinion 5

Q.6   Overall, how interesting did you find the course?

PLEASE CIRCLE ONE NUMBER
(26)

Very interesting...................... 1
Fairly interesting.................... 2
Not very interesting 3   26
Not at all interesting 4

Q.7 Looking back, what improvements would you like to have seen on the course or in the equipment? (27)

PLEASE WRITE IN

	1 2 3 4
....	5 6 7 8
....	9 0 X Y
....	(28)
....	1 2 3 4
....	5 6 7 8
....	9 0 X Y

Q.8 If somebody who was about to take this course had the choice of doing it in the traditional way — by going away on a course — or by doing it on viewdata, how would you advise them . . .
a) — from the point of view of learning the material?

PLEASE CIRCLE ONE NUMBER
(29)

Traditional course	1
Viewdata	2
Don't know	3

29

b) — from the point of view of enjoying the learning process?

PLEASE CIRCLE ONE NUMBER
(30)

Traditional course	1
Viewdata	2
Don't know	3

30

THE FOLLOWING INFORMATION WILL HELP US TO COMPARE THE VIEWS OF DIFFERENT TYPES OF BANK STAFF. NO GROUPS OF LESS THAN 12 STAFF WILL BE USED.

PLEASE CIRCLE ONE NUMBER FOR EACH QUESTION

Q.9 a) *Are you* . . .

(31)   31

Male	1
Female	2

Q.9 b) *Age group*:

(32)

Under 21	1
21–25	2
26–30	3
31–35	4
36–40	5
Over 40..........................	6

32

Q.9 c) *Length of service with Barclays*:

	(33)	
Less than a year	1	
A year but less than 3 years	2	
3 years but less than 5 years	3	
5 years but less than 10 years	4	
10 years or more....................	5	33

Q.9 d) *Grade at present*:

	(34)	
CG1..............................	1	
CG2..............................	2	
CG3..............................	3	
CG4..............................	4	
SCG1	5	
SCG2	6	34
Other (WRITE IN)	7	
....		

Q.9 e) *Total number of staff in your branch*:

	(35)	
Under 10 staff.....................	1	
10–19	2	
20–29	3	
30–39	4	
40–49	5	
50–74	6	
75–99	7	35
100 or more.......................	8	
Don't know	9	

Q.9 f) *District*

	(36)	36
Windsor	1	
London...........................	2	

VIEWDATA STUDENTS ONLY	TRADITIONAL COURSE STUDENTS ONLY	
g. Have you ever been on a 'traditional' (non-viewdata) Bank training course?	g. Have you ever taken a viewdata programme in the Bank?	
(37)	(37)	37
Yes 1	Yes 3	
No 2	No 4	

APPENDIX 12.3 IMMEDIATE QUESTIONNAIRE

Market & Opinion Research International

SURVEY OF VIEWDATA TRAINING

IMMEDIATE QUESTIONNAIRE

This questionnaire is for completion soon after you finish the viewdata training course.

THIS IS *NOT* A TEST

It is a survey of your *opinions* of the course — there are no "right answers". We are trying to assess the effectiveness of the training system, *not* your performance. Nobody from your branch or LHO will every know how you — as an individual — answered these questions, and your answers will *not* be compared with your end-of-course test results.

How to answer the questions

Most questions have various answers provided, and you circle the number of the answer which comes closest to your own opinion. For example, if you prefer using viewdata in the afternoons, you would answer Q.3b like this:

```
Morning .............................................1
Afternoon ........................................... ②
No preference either way ............................3
```

If you want to change your answer, just put a cross through the one you want to remove. Allowance is made for 'don't know' and 'no opinion' replies on some questions, but please try to give a definite answer where possible.

Thank you for your help.

OFFICE USE ONLY

Name ....   Branch ....

MORI/2054/1   Serial No.............   Card 1
      (1–5)   (6–9)   (10)

THIS FORM IS THE PROPERTY OF MARKET & OPINION RESEARCH INTERNATIONAL

Q.1   Which viewdata course have you just taken?

PLEASE CIRCLE ONE NUMBER
(11)

Cashiers
Operation of a Pooled Till   1
Balancing the Pooled Till   2
Tracing Till Errors   3
Foreign:
Collections and Negotiations   4
Sale of Foreign Notes and Coins   5
Telegraphic Transfers   6   11
Securities:
Branch Bid Deposits   7
Life Policies   8
Release of Safe Custody Items   9
Immediate Money Transfers   0
Standing orders (any section(s))   X

Q.2   In how many distinct sessions did you complete the course?

CIRCLE ONE NUMBER
1   2   3   4   5   6   7   8   9 or more   12

Q.3   a) When were these sessions?

PLEASE CIRCLE ONE NUMBER
(13)
All in the morning   1
Mainly in the morning   2
Half morning, half afternoon   3
Mainly in the afternoon   4
All in the afternoon   5   13

Q.3   b) In general, do you prefer morning or afternoon sessions?

PLEASE CIRCLE ONE NUMBER
(14)
Morning   1
Afternoon   2
No preference either way   3   14

Q.4   Over how long were the sessions spread out?

PLEASE CIRCLE ONE NUMBER
(15)
All in one day   1
Within 1 week   2
More than 1 week but within 2   3
More than 2 weeks but within 1 month .   4
More than a month   5   15

Q.5 Overall, how interesting was this course to do?

PLEASE CIRCLE ONE NUMBER

(16)

Very interesting 1
Fairly interesting 2
Not very interesting 3
Not at all interesting 4   16

Q.6 How relevant do you think the material covered in this course will be to you in your work?

PLEASE CIRCLE ONE NUMBER

(17)

Very relevant 1
Fairly relevant 2
Not very relevant 3   17
Not at all relevant 4

Q.7 a) Had you been doing work in the branch relevant to this course *before* you took it?

PLEASE CIRCLE ONE NUMBER

(18)

Yes—for more than 3 months
  before I took it 1
Yes—for more than 1 month but
  less than 3 months before 2
Yes—for more than 2 weeks but
  less than 1 month before 3
Yes—for more than 1 week but
  less than 2 weeks before 4
Yes—for less than a week before
  I took it 5   18
No—not at all 6

Q.7 b) Now that you have finished the course, when will you be doing work in the branch relevant to this course?

PLEASE CIRCLE ONE NUMBER

(19)

Straight away 1
Within a month 2
Within 3 months 3
Not for at least 3 months 4   19
I have no idea 5

Q.7 c) How confident are you that you can now do this work with little
or no help from others in the branch?

PLEASE CIRCLE ONE NUMBER

	(20)	
Very confident	1	
Fairly confident	2	
Not very confident	3	20
Not at all confident	4	

Q.8 How do you rate each of the following aspects of the viewdata course
you have just completed?

PLEASE CIRCLE ONE NUMBER FOR EACH ASPECT

	Good	Fair	Poor	Not applicable	
a. Instructions on how to proceed through the course.....................	1	2	3	4	21
b. Ease of referring back	1	2	3	4	22
c. Use of colour to improve clarity	1	2	3	4	23
d. Comprehensive coverage of the subject matter.............................	1	2	3	4	24
e. Making you feel like a person rather than just a number	1	2	3	4	25
f. The written material which went with the course	1	2	3	4	26
g. Fairness of the end-of-course test	1	2	3	4	27
h. Quality of the picture (lack of interference on screen etc.	1	2	3	4	28

Q.9 a) Where was the viewdata terminal located when you were doing the
course?

PLEASE CIRCLE ONE NUMBER

	(29)	
Rest room	1	
Securities	2	
Mech. Room	3	
Interview room	4	
Special room for viewdata	5	
Other (PLEASE WRITE IN		
& RING '6')	6	30

....

Q.9   b) How do you rate the conditions in which you took the course?

PLEASE CIRCLE ONE NUMBER FOR EACH ASPECT

	Good	Fair	Poor	Not applicable	
a. Temperature of the room	1	2	3	4	30
b. Comfort of the chair	1	2	3	4	31
c. Enough work-space.	1	2	3	4	32
d. Lack of interruptions/disturbances . . .	1	2	3	4	33
e. Quiet	1	2	3	4	34
f. Lighting.	1	2	3	4	35
g. No eye-strain from looking at the screen	1	2	3	4	36

Q.10   a) How would you describe the tone used in the course?

PLEASE CIRCLE ONE NUMBER
(37)

Too technical, difficult to follow .	1
About right .	2
Too elementary	3

37

Q.10   b) People have told us that answers in the test are sometimes marked wrong unreasonably. For example, if 'Taunton High Street' is answered instead of 'High Street, Taunton'. To what extent did this sort of thing happen to you?

PLEASE CIRCLE ONE NUMBER
(38)

Never	1
Once or twice only	2
More than twice	3
Don't know	4

38

Q.11   Below are some statements which have been made about viewdata training. How strongly do you agree or disagree with each?

PLEASE CIRCLE ONE NUMBER FOR EACH STATEMENT

	Strongly agree	Tend to agree	Neither agree nor disagree	Tend to disagree	Strongly disagree	
a. I found doing the course stimulating.	1	2	3	4	5	39
b. Senior people in the branch don't regard viewdata as 'proper' training	1	2	3	4	5	40

c. Some of my scheduled
viewdata sessions had to
be postponed because of
work in the branch.........1....2....3....4....5.. | 41

d. I found doing the
course boring..............1....2....3....4....5.. | 42

e. My MA is a keen
supporter of viewdata
training...................1....2....3....4....5.. | 43

Q.12 In general how often would you say the viewdata terminal is used in
your branch?

PLEASE CIRCLE ONE NUMBER

	(44)	
Just about every day	1	
Every two days	2	
Once or twice a week	3	
Once or twice a month	4	44
Less often than once a month	5	
Other (PLEASE WRITE IN)..........	6	
Don't know	7	

THE FOLLOWING INFORMATION WILL HELP US TO
COMPARE THE VIEWS OF DIFFERENT TYPES OF BANK
STAFF. NO GROUPS OF LESS THAN 12 STAFF WILL BE USED.

PLEASE CIRCLE ONE NUMBER FOR EACH QUESTION

Q.13 a) *Are you* . . .

	(45)	
Male	1	
Female	2	45

Q.13 b) *Age group*:

	(46)	
Under 21	1	
21–25	2	
26–30	3	
31–35	4	
36–40	5	46
Over 40..........................	6	

Q.13 c) *Length of service with Barclays*:

	(47)	
Less than a year	1	
A year but less than 3 years...........	2	
3 years but less than 5 years	3	
5 years but less than 10 years	4	
10 years or more....................	5	47

Q.13 d) *Grade at present*:

	(48)	
CG1...............................	1	
CG2...............................	2	
CG3...............................	3	
CG4...............................	4	
SCG1	5	
SCG2	6	48
Other (WRITE IN)	7	
....		

Q.13 e) *Total number of staff in your branch*:

	(49)	
Under 10 staff......................	1	
10–19	2	
20–29	3	
30–39	4	
40–49	5	
50–74	6	
75–99	7	49
100 or more.......................	8	
Don't know	9	

Q.13 f) *District*

	(50)	50
Windsor	1	
London............................	2	

Q.14 What other comments would you like to make about the viewdata course you have recently completed? PLEASE WRITE IN

	(51)
....	1 2 3
....	4 5 6
....	7 8 9
....	0 X Y
....	(52)
....	1 2 3
....	4 5 6
....	7 8 9
....	0 X Y

13. Multi-Country Research

D. N. Aldridge   *RBL Overseas Research Ltd. (Research International)*

Undertaking research in one country often presents the researcher with difficulties; the problems tend to increase when research is carried out in more than one country. This paper looks at multi-country research in both sophisticated and developing markets and stresses the need for local knowledge to develop appropriate research designs and appropriate responses at the data collection and data interpretation stages. Such knowledge and understanding is particularly important in research projects where comparability between countries needs to be achieved. The student can discuss many interesting examples, working out the ways and means of achieving comparability.

INTRODUCTION

Much of the research undertaken by agencies has an international dimension. The largest buyers of market research are multinational corporations who, whilst they may commission most of their research locally, are likely to have a centrally developed philosophy, even strict guidelines, regarding how studies are to be conducted. An increasing number of their projects are overtly multi-country, conducted simultaneously or sequentially, but others, apparently one-off, will replicate an earlier study carried out in their home market. Generally, however, the term 'multi-country' is used to distinguish similar research conducted in more than one country at approximately the same time, with the intention of comparing results between countries, and it is this type of research which will be considered here in detail. The first half of the paper will consider some issues affecting multi-country research in general, whilst the second half will examine additional challenges posed by research in the Third World developing countries of the Middle East, Africa, Asia and Latin America.

WHO DOES IT?

Multi-country research may be commissioned by multinational companies, either centrally from their international headquarters, or regionally by a regional head office. Other buyers of such research will be national companies looking to establish or develop export markets. Advertising agencies and consultancies may commission projects directly or provide advice to their clients on how to go about it. Non-commercial organisations, including governments and their agencies, supra-governmental organisations (UN, EEC) and charities are also involved in this type of work.

Buyers may visit each country of interest themselves, conducting their own research or commissioning a local supplier in each market and putting together the results of the various sub-projects into a unified whole. Alternatively they may, for certain types of projects (generally qualitative or trade-oriented), commission an agency in their local country to travel to each market and conduct the work for them directly. The third, and most likely, option is for the buyer to approach an organisation specialising in international research, fieldwork generally being conducted by local associates or affiliates of the specialist agency.

In choosing a supplier, research buyers tend to consider six main criteria when evaluating international research organisations (Barnard[1]):

—resources;
—management/geographical structure;
—systems and procedures;
—technical capability;
—business sector knowledge;
—experience.

Different types of agencies may specialise in multi-country research. Some have no formal links with their suppliers, buying in the services of local agencies as and when required. Others are members of a 'chain' of agencies (e.g. INRA, Gallup), who entrust work to chain members around the world but do not normally have direct management control over them. Finally, there are those who are members of a multinational research company, with units around the world under common ownership and management control, with common philosophy and methodologies (e.g. Research International, MRBI). Because of the particular expertise and experience required for this type of work, such multinational agencies may themselves contain units specialising in international research co-ordination on a worldwide basis, such as my own agency, RBL Overseas, within Research International.

THE BENEFITS OF CO-ORDINATION

Essentially co-ordination involves bridging cultural gaps, providing a framework for identifying similarities and differences between markets, or simply interpreting one culture to members of another. The role of the co-ordinator varies according to the type of study and the marketing philosophy behind it. A study may be tightly co-ordinated, employing the same methodology across several markets with essentially identical questionnaires to ensure maximum comparability of results, or the approach may be looser, possibly sacrificing some comparability for the sake of greater relevance to the individual markets. One philosophy is not necessarily better or worse than the other — it is a question of objectives. However, where possible it makes sense, with regard to cost-effectiveness of project management, but more crucially in usability and value of results, to achieve comparability wherever possible.

The essential reason for co-ordination was succinctly stated by Richard Halpern of Coca-Cola in his 1981 ESOMAR Congress paper[2]: 'Data from different countries is difficult enough, without also having to aim off for variations due simply to use of different research approaches.'

If inter-country comparisons are of prime importance in a survey, it is usually preferable to employ the same data collection method across countries, to achieve comparability. Further, if the marketing problem underlying the study forms the basis of an *international* marketing decision, as distinct from a series of independent *national* decisions, it is incumbent upon the researcher to provide comparable results by means of co-ordinated methodology.

Differences which emerge should reflect genuine differences between markets; conversely similarities should be due to genuinely similar market conditions, and not to strait-jacketing and force-fitting of results. There are potential dangers in an over-rigid approach, which may mask or distort the very aspects we are trying to measure; indeed, co-ordination can involve variations in data collection, sampling, questionnaire and timing if appropriate. There is also a potential danger that the client may feel too divorced from the action, so it is important for the co-ordinator to provide the appropriate level of feedback. Co-ordination can have benefits of speed and of cost (if *all* the elements, including client time, are taken into account); it can provide standardisation, centralisation of communication, design and analysis, quality control, expertise and advice, and a minimisation of problems.

SOME CONSIDERATIONS

Life-Style, Habits, Market Structure

Despite the tendency of modern media influences and growing international travel to reduce inter-country differences, Europe, for instance, is by no means one market (save possibly for certain durables and industrial/ commercial products). Whilst such differences are frequently the *raison d'etre* for multi-country projects, they may in themselves affect the design of the project itself. For example, money in Europe has many different forms, whose relative importance varies widely between countries. Only in the UK do cards of the Access and Visa type have widespread penetration. In the Netherlands, and several other countries, the Post Office Giro dominates regular transactions, and it may be normal to carry large amounts of cash when making a substantial purchase. Similarly, the use of current accounts and cheque facilities varies considerably between markets, and such factors have to be borne in mind when designing and interpreting studies; a survey concentrating upon only certain types of 'money', to the exclusion of those normal in particular markets, would obviously produce misleading results.

It is expected that eating habits will differ between countries, but it is perhaps more surprising to learn that 'basic', 'simple' behaviours such as dishwashing vary dramatically from country to country. By no means everyone fills a bowl or sink with water and a squirt of dishwashing liquid: in some countries it is normal to mix up a concentrated solution of the liquid plus a little water in a small bowl, and to apply this to dishes with a cloth or sponge, afterwards rinsing under a running tap. Such differences can mean that a product use sequence in a television commercial for one market is incomprehensible to consumers from a neighbouring country; under these circumstances, designing one questionnaire to cover both types of behaviour (and indeed others which may exist amongst minorities) can be extremely difficult, if not impossible.

The structure of the retail trade likewise varies dramatically across geographical borders. France has perhaps the most highly developed retailing in Europe, with enormous, highly automated, highly professionalised organisations predominating. Italy, on the other hand, is still preponderantly served by small, traditional stores. Any study involving the views of retailers, or studying their throughput and behaviour, has to allow for such differences.

Religion and Culture

Religion has a significant influence, even within Europe, upon habits and attitudes. Several countries have strong historical divisions between Protestant and Catholic, and these can in extreme cases affect choice of interviewers. Certainly the consumption of particular foods, notably fish on Fridays, will be correlated with religious allegiance. Nor is categorisation of religious belief always a simple matter—in Japan many will acknowledge Buddhism as their creed whilst also practising the rituals of traditional Shintoism. Nevertheless, religion generally assumes lower importance within the industrialised world than in developing countries and it will therefore be examined more fully in a later section.

Cultural differences are naturally of major significance, and affect research projects in a variety of ways. It is imperative that the researcher stays alive to the possibility that apparent similarities can hide important differences. The late Paul Berent, in the first edition of this book[4], cited a study on diamond rings which needed to establish whether ladies were married or engaged, before enquiring about the type of engagement ring received, if any. In applying an apparently simple series of questions to Spain, Italy, Germany and Sweden, it became clear that, whereas the term 'engaged' can be translated into Italian and Spanish it has by no means the same significance in those countries as in the UK. A Spanish or Italian lady will refer to almost any man who has taken her to the cinema more than once as her fiancé, whether or not she intends to marry him. Thus to be engaged simply means to have a boyfriend, a definition which would have produced a serious underestimation of receipt of diamond rings amongst the target group. Elsewhere there were different problems—many German ladies receive a plain gold band on engagement, and transfer it to the other hand on marriage, whilst in Japan and France pearl rings account for a significant proportion of the engagement market.

Culture can impinge upon research in many subtle ways. Researchers often have to use scales for measuring differences. In certain cases these are even used, with the help of market norms, to predict future sales. Yet the use of scales for any cross-cultural comparison, including the relation of scores to norms derived from other countries, has to take account of the fact that a 'good' score in the UK or USA is not necessarily a 'good' score elsewhere. Consumers in most countries, when given their usual brand 'blind' in a test, will generally rate it better than their usual product, yet in Japan we have found the reverse. Latin countries both in Europe and the Americas tend, on available evidence (e.g. Jarret and Crossman[3]) to give more positive scores than average, whereas Scandinavian countries apart from Finland are less positive than most Europeans.

How can we deal with the problem in order to provide comparable data? Firstly, it may be feasible to avoid the problem, or minimise it, by using a standard reference point (e.g. a marker brand, to which others are compared). Alternatively, results can be transformed statistically so that each is expressed in terms of deviation from the country mean, while less formal consideration of inter-brand relationships within the data may also help.

Generally it is sufficient to know relative positions in one market compared to those in another, rather than having to state categorically that the brand in question actually performs better here than there, in some absolute sense. It is normally the comparison of one country's relative brand positions with those in another which is of most interest and relevance. However, if absolute measures are required, there is no substitute for experience and the systematic collection of norms on standard scales for each product field within each country — clearly a situation where long-term agency/client relationships will significantly enhance the value of the data collected.

Language

A number of countries, including Belgium, Switzerland and Canada, have more than one official language. It is generally necessary to translate questionnaires into all major languages, but seldom is it cost-effective to cover small minorities such as Italian-speaking Swiss. Of considerable significance is the difference in the way ostensibly the same language is used in different countries — the joke about the USA and Britain being divided by a common language is all too true, in that US questionnaires cannot be used here without translation, nor vice versa. Similarly, Swiss German is not the German of Germany, whilst Canadian French is more akin to that spoken in 17th century France than to modern Parisian.

Furthermore, many concepts are essentially untranslatable — the German 'gemutlich' or Dutch 'gezellig', which describe a warm, cosy experience such as an evening around the fire with close friends, do not have an English equivalent. Even if meanings are broadly similar, there are likely to be differences in the extent to which a term is applicable in different cultures.

Sampling

Whilst most sampling methods are feasible in most countries, availability and quality of information for random methods varies considerably. Furthermore, what is normal sampling methodology differs widely between countries; quota sampling is very common in France, for example, even for national surveys. In countries where quota sampling is widely used, there may be a high level of control over what the interviewer is permitted to do, thus reducing the dangers of an interviewer-selected sample.

It is important to understand exactly what type of sampling will be employed, but unless there are over-riding considerations, e.g. the inappropriateness of the method for the task, it is generally preferable to allow local agencies to use their standard methods; these will be less prone to misunderstanding and error, and should be more cost-effective than theoretically preferable methods imposed from outside.

In cases where the proportion of eligible individuals differs dramatically between countries, it may prove necessary to adopt different sampling methods for reasons of cost-effectiveness. This may mean either redefining the target group, e.g. by ignoring a particularly low incidence sector or easing the recruitment criteria (including potential as well as actual owners, for example), or using lower-cost methods of recruitment such as pre-recruiting via an omnibus or contacting at work-places. Of course, the potential effects in terms of timing, skewing of the sample or whatever need to be carefully considered in the light of the survey aims, in order to evaluate such a change.

Data Collection

In the USA telephone interviewing predominates, followed by postal surveys and so-called 'mall intercept' interviewing, the latter conducted in the many hundreds of enclosed shopping centres ('malls') that abound. Face-to-face interviewing on the doorstep or in the home is comparatively rare, both because of the availability and cost-effectiveness of alternative methods and because door-to-door interviewing is increasingly difficult and dangerous.

In Europe, on the other hand, the door-step interview is the norm for household survey work, save in those Scandinavian markets where population spread and harsh climate have made telephone work more attractive. Nevertheless, telephone interviewing has certainly grown elsewhere in Europe, although particular cultures, e.g. the German, have shown greater resistance than others.

For international research telephone interviewing is becoming more popular, partly because American multinationals are more telephone-research oriented, partly because interviewing from a centralised location in one country, using nationals from the countries being surveyed, has considerable potential for overcoming at least some of the difficulties inherent in co-ordinating multi-country work. Such an approach may be extremely cost-effective, for example when interviewing businessmen and professionals (membership studies for ESOMAR, the European Study for Opinion and Marketing Research, have been carried out by our organisation, on one occasion by telephone from each of our 15 units around Europe, on another, from one central location in the UK, using nationals of the various countries as interviewers); it also has the benefit of allowing a large number of interviews to be arranged and conducted very quickly, as in cases where awareness of World Cup Sponsorship was being monitored.

HOW IS IT DONE?

Many of the co-ordinator's tasks are those of the UK-only researcher, but there are added dimensions and complications. Firstly, the client will often come to the briefing with much less certainty about market data, about ways of researching abroad, even about the real aims of the study, than is typical in the UK. Given that quotations or proposals are frequently required with great urgency, and local suppliers must be involved, it is extremely important that as full a picture as possible is obtained at the initial meeting.

Even at this stage the experienced researcher will play an important role in helping the client to develop their thinking, by suggesting appropriate methods, warning of pitfalls, querying reliability of market share data or optimistic timings for product delivery in market, and suchlike. It is important to establish from the outset who are the decision-makers, what role the client's in-market organisation will play, who will be paying and in what currency.

Local Agency Selection and Initial Briefing

The co-ordinator who already has long established relationships with local suppliers, whether part of his own organisation or not, is at a considerable advantage. It makes sense to cultivate relations with a small number of agencies in each country, enough to obtain alternative quotations whilst providing a spread of expertise, but few enough to make you a valued client. It is important to obtain as much information about suppliers' organisations and methods as possible, both to aid in selection for a specific project and to avoid asking for totally unfamiliar methods, which will almost certainly add to cost. Price is obviously a consideration, but it is particularly important in international research to ensure that the required quality is there; standards can vary enormously.

In addition to technical competence, local suppliers should have flexibility and tolerance, the confidence to say what they think, the breadth to see the wider issues and the sense to quote for your requested specification as well as their preferred alternative. They should also speak good English, unless you have bilingual staff. Building good relations is extremely important — pay promptly (including reasonable extras) and treat them as colleagues rather than slaves. In short, do as you would be done by — indeed, a reversal of roles can be highly illuminating to all concerned. Nevertheless, the co-ordinator is the client of the local agency, and it must be clear who has the ultimate say.

When giving the initial briefing, for the purposes of quotation or proposals, it is essential to give details in writing and to consider, and if necessary specify, a host of issues. Our own briefing procedures include a checklist of over 50 items, covering executive tasks, data collection and processing, production, timing and commercial aspects. In addition, if you want your local supplier to be more than a dumb robot, it is important to tell him the objective — frequently omitted. (This does *not*, of course apply to those circumstances where you are forced to use suppliers whose security is not above question.)

Communication

Quotes should be in writing, but a process of telephone clarification and discussion may well precede this. Telephoned changes should of course be confirmed in writing, since whilst the telephone is immediate, it is expensive, leaves no record, and requires linguistic fluency. Telex is fast, cheaper, leaves hard copy and is clearer for those less fluent; however, it can be garbled, and lack of pound sterling signs overseas can cause expensive confusion. Cable is a slower, dearer, poor alternative, whilst mail is slower still but cheaper. Its valuable role in transmitting detailed documents such as questionnaires and instructions has to a considerable extent been superseded by courier services, though these can be expensive and are not always reliable, and by fax. This latest 'toy' is marvellous for rapid transmission of documents *provided* it works, but frustrating when difficult-to-pinpoint faults occur.

The Proposal

Here the principles are similar to the UK, but there is often greater need to explain methodology, including cost-sensitive areas, clarify ambiguity and delineate roles and tasks. Particular attention needs to be paid to timing and cost: co-ordination is time-consuming, whoever does it, and schedules can be affected by holidays and festivals, transportation problems (including customs strikes), delays to test materials, co-ordination of code frames etc. Research costs vary considerably by country (see next section), as do inflation rates, taxes, contract law, codes of practice and suchlike. Exchange rates and convertibility (or not!) of currency pose particular traps for the unwary, and can lead to major losses.

Costs

Research prices vary enormously, as demonstrated by the following table (Table 13.1) of European costs, taken from a paper presented by Peter Hayes of Research International to a joint ICC/ESOMAR Symposium on International Market Research in 1984[5]. Not only is the top country more than twice as expensive as the bottom, but the order varies according to the type of research, the Netherlands being average in terms of quantitative research but almost top for qualitative costs, and Germany showing the reverse pattern. The UK is average or a little below, by European standards.

   Of course, such cost comparisons are only reliable for the particular type of study under consideration, and at the time of study. Levels can and do change, as the result of social legislation, inflation and salary increases, and especially fluctuations in exchange rates. Not so long ago US research was relatively 'reasonable' by European standards, but is now at the top of the

TABLE 13.1   Quantitative/Qualitative Job Cost Comparison

	Quantitative			*Qualitative*	
1.	Switzerland	132	1.	France	149
2.	France	130	2.	Netherlands	134
3.	W. Germany	121	3.	Norway	125
4.	Norway	118	4.	Switzerland	114
5.	Italy	112	5.	Denmark	107
6.	Sweden	106	6.	Sweden	99
7.	Denmark	105	7.	Spain	96
8.	Netherlands	103	8.	Italy	96
9.	UK	98	9.	UK	95
10.	Spain	96	10.	W. Germany	89
11.	Finland	75	11.	Finland	80
12.	Belgium	69	12.	Belgium	79
13.	Greece	69	13.	Austria	75
14.	Austria	68	14.	Greece	63

Ranking and indices based on 1982 and 1984 data
From Hayes: The Cost Comparison of Market Research in Western Europe, *in ICC/ESOMAR Symposium, International Market Research, Paris, 26–28 November 1984*
Reproduced by permission of ESOMAR

list, whilst Japan is even higher. A point of value to the UK-based research co-ordinator is that high calibre thinking time (research executive level) is relatively cheap here, by international standards.

The Questionnaire

The master questionnaire should be as simple and uncluttered as possible, with logical, easy flow and routing; complex grids should be avoided. Use straightforward wording, with well-spaced DP codes and easily located classification information. Country-specific questions should go at the end, if possible, and the local agencies should use their usual layout, to avoid confusing interviewers. Pilot if possible.

Translation should be by a *local researcher* fluent in English, with as careful a check as possible by means of independent back translation, again by a researcher, local client vetting, and in-depth discussion. Translator's notes and a glossary are invaluable; particular attention must be paid to attribute statements and usership questions.

Final Briefing

This should include instructions for the executive and for interviewing, editing and coding, with detailed explanation of the sample method, questionnaire, visual aids (and their use). Roles and communication chains should be confirmed, together with the timetable and any progress reports. Where possible, actual interviewing, as well as interviewer briefing, should be attended. This of course requires travel, which adds to the cost of the research but is a major factor in the successful conduct of a project.

Being there gives a far greater opportunity to explain (again, if necessary) and to check whether there is genuine understanding, both in conversation and by seeing what is done. It also permits a check on materials (ads, product, concepts), and on the latest market changes, which can if necessary be incorporated into the study. It keeps the local agency on its toes (one may do independent checking) whilst strengthening relationships, and may permit visiting the client's local office to help them feel involved (if the client so desires). A further benefit to the client comes from the greater depth and confidence of interpretation provided by in-market experience, coupled with the future benefit of increased understanding when new projects arise.

Data Processing

Centralisation of DP has considerable benefits in terms of comparability, both technically (treatment of unanswered questions, table bases etc.) and 'cosmetically'—it is easier and neater to compare countries when they are all on one page. It also permits greater quality control and flexibility for further analysis, whilst use of sophisticated analytical techniques is facilitated. There is the additional bonus of greater security.

Whether one takes questionnaires, cards or tape is debatable. Questionnaires are more expensive to transport and there is the potential risk of loss (we have lost one parcel in 15 years: we re-did the work), but there is greater flexibility and control, and the opportunity to check fieldwork standards. Tapes can get wiped by X-ray machines, and there can be format and labelling problems, whilst cards can get bent or wet. Data protection laws, as in Germany, may affect transfer of information.

On a study where comparability is crucial, coding is best handled by use of a master frame, developed on the basis of prior knowledge or ideally the first questionnaires from each market. This frame may have local codes added to it in order to avoid undue force-fitting; given sufficient time, these extra codes may be supplied to other markets, too.

Presentations and Reports

At the client briefing the number and language of presentation and reports, as well as the location of all overseas client meetings, should be established. Unplanned meetings abroad, or requests for a change of language, can wreak havoc with timings and cost. It is particularly important to allow the necessary time for preparation of presentations in-market; staged presentations, first to the client and then to his local counterparts, are often valuable, but roles need to be carefully considered. Presentations and reports in 'English' by local agencies can be less than ideal (as, of course, can presentations by co-ordinators in local languages!)

Qualitative Research

Qualitative studies raise extra issues, since there is the possibility that the co-ordinator will actually do some or all of the fieldwork. Opinions differ, but our view is that even if you have nationals of the country concerned working in the UK, it can be risky to use them as moderators since they are likely to be out of touch with the latest subtleties of the culture. Non-nationals with less than bilingual fluency are unlikely to cope adequately with moderation, whilst working through translators is fraught in the extreme. We prefer to use local moderators but have experienced qualitative researchers, fluent in the language, to sit in, brief, debrief and develop the study dynamically. Of course, unusual languages may call for sub-optimal solutions, particularly where local qualitative skills are limited. Output from groups or depth interviews may be tapes or transcripts (local language or English). You may choose to take full reports, but unless accompanied by tapes or transcripts they can lead to a lack of real feel for cultural differences, local researchers often not being aware of how their market is similar or different from others.

Even in the qualitative field, techniques and terminology differ across countries — most dangerously, the concept of a 'depth interview' can vary from a three hour psychoanalytical 'therapy session' to a series of open questions. Reporting styles are equally varied. Nevertheless, with patience and in-depth involvement, it is possible to co-ordinate qualitative studies successfully.

RESEARCH IN DEVELOPING COUNTRIES: ADDITIONAL CONSIDERATIONS

Research in the developing world poses all the problems encountered by multi-country researchers in Europe, but at a more extreme level. Furthermore, there are additional issues which are generally inconsequential in the developed world, but which loom large in less developed markets.

Diversity

Different countries pose very different problems for the researcher. Indeed, diversity is one of the most striking features of the developing world. The advanced developing nations of Singapore, South Korea, Taiwan and Brazil have little if anything in common either with the oil exporting countries of the Middle East, struggling with fluctuating revenues to avoid the cultural and political upheavals of Iran, or with countries such as Haiti or Kampuchea, desperately poor and getting poorer. Research techniques may need to take account of widely differing levels of infrastructure — telephone interviewing is feasible for consumer work in Hong Kong, with 90% household penetration, but pointless in most of its neighbours. Postal services are generally poor or non-existent, so there may be little alternative to personal interviewing, although observation techniques have worked well in many countries (we have successfully stationed observers in the homes of Saudi Arabian ladies to watch them performing household tasks and take samples of products and ingredients).

Diversity is not only faced in multi-country research — within the same market one may find incredibly rich people with all imaginable luxuries and others so poor they have to pawn their meagre belongings in order to buy the basic essentials. Apparently simple questions on washing habits may have to embrace the use of gold-plated showers and of the local river or canal, without giving offence to either user group. Concepts of value for money can be meaningless, either if money is inexhaustible or when branded products cost more than the housewife ever has in her pocket — hence very small pack sizes, and the retail practices of 'spooning' from bulk containers or breaking multi-unit packaging down into individual items (cigarettes sold by the 'stick', for example).

Of course, diversity is not simply a function of socio-economic status. Many markets have major ethnic divisions. The majority of the population of Kuwait and the United Arab Emirates are aliens; in the latter case they are not even Arab. In Malaysia, only just over half the population are racially Malay; Chinese form a third of the total and in towns constitute the majority, whilst there is also a sizeable Indian minority. Singapore has the same ethnic groups, but here the Chinese predominate to the extent that research may sometimes confine itself to them, for reasons of cost-effectiveness. In Malaysia, that approach is clearly inappropriate, and major surveys may not only cover the three major ethnic groups but sub-divide each into urban and rural dwellers because of substantial differences in behaviour and attitudes.

It may be necessary to match interviewers to respondents in terms of ethnicity, because of strong racial or tribal antipathy, as was the case in Nigeria. The use of Europeans (or, for the matter, black Americans) to interview Africans has considerable dangers, both because their different cultural and linguistic backgrounds can lead to misunderstanding, and also because a European may be seen as someone to please or even deceive.

The urban/rural divide is of considerable relevance to research, as it is to marketing. In essentially urban societies such as Singapore, Hong Kong or the UAE, the tiny rural population may not warrant separate consideration. In other markets, increasing attention is being paid to rural consumers since, despite rapid urbanisation, countries such as Thailand, Indonesia, India and Nigeria are still predominantly rural, and purchasing power is increasing outside the cities. These markets are not yet mass societies, and rural dwellers may contrast markedly with their urban counterparts.

Because of the enormous disparity between 'the masses' and the very up-market elite from whom local developing country researchers will be drawn, it is dangerous to assume that the native researcher will automatically be *au fait* with the behaviour of the 'average' consumer. I have been assured by a highly professional researcher that everyone in her country drank bottled mineral water rather than tap water; probing elicited the evidence as simply that she and all her friends did so. This atypicality of the researcher makes piloting of questionnaires, amongst normal consumers, particularly essential.

Religion and Culture

Religion poses traps for the unwary. At the logistical level, religious observance can interrupt fieldwork; Muslims go to prayer five times a day. More seriously, eating habits may alter drastically during the fast period of Ramadan — it is not simply that no food is consumed during daylight hours, but that the very nature of the food changes. This can naturally play havoc with research on eating habits, or with food product tests, and it may be necessary to conduct interviews in the middle of the night because of changed working hours and respondent irritability during the day.

Fear about the animal fat content of ammunition is said to have sparked off the Indian Mutiny. Fears of food containing taboo ingredients such as beef (sacred to Hindus, whilst it 'irritates the noses' of Taoist gods), pork (abhorred by Muslims) or indeed any meat (all life is sacred to Buddhists) can have equally drastic effects upon a product test. Even if the species is acceptable, it may have to be slaughtered in a particular manner; the true Muslim will examine packaging for assurance that the contents are 'halal'. Similarly, we have seen test products hung on a ju-ju tree because a local witch-doctor considered them unclean.

Intimately linked to religion in many cases are the cultural norms which researchers ignore at their peril. Purdah imposes restrictions upon freedom of movement for women in strict Muslim countries, and likewise can make it difficult for researchers to interview them. In Saudi Arabia a classic 'Catch 22' situation operates — you need women to interview women, yet they are barred from occupations which could bring them into contact with males. Thus complex procedures may be necessary to conduct fieldwork, and attempts to interview in the street or at random addresses have led to researchers being arrested (not ours, I hasten to add). Under such circumstances it is essential to work from within the culture, with the assistance of a knowledgeable and influential local partner.

Other cultural factors may affect fieldwork: age deference, as found amongst Chinese and Africans, calls for tighter controls on group recruitment. Unwillingness to give offence, or to lose face by showing ignorance of the 'right' answer, may necessitate sensitive and sometimes unorthodox probing techniques. Certain topics may be taboo (e.g. alcohol, or female smoking, amongst strict Muslims), but other subjects such as sexual behaviour may be freely discussed.

Individual interviews in the Middle East or Africa can easily turn into group discussions as friends and relatives are invited to share the novel experience. Whilst there may be initial reluctance to participate (from fear of espionage or the taxman) the problem frequently becomes one of departing without giving offence so as to adhere to fieldwork schedules; respondents on the Indian Subcontinent and in Africa (though not in the Middle East) are often much more willing than their Western counterparts to give up their time. Hall tests may be besieged as word of free product gets around, necessitating frequent changes of venue (hall tests have other potential problems, relating to the representativeness of samples and of test situations).

Certain countries, particularly those with an Islamic culture, require governmental permission for large-scale survey work, often from two different ministries. In addition, topics such as cigarette smoking may be banned entirely, whilst apparently harmless questions, even profile data, can cause problems because of political sensitivities. Caution is advisable, and one needs to know when official permission is a necessity. Photography, a useful adjunct to written reporting, can lead to difficulties, even arrest, in certain markets because of spy mania and fear of the 'evil eye' or foreign ridicule; it is generally safer to ask local colleagues to take the pictures.

Language and Literacy

Linguistic variety can be daunting. In Singapore, with only 2.5 million inhabitants, Mandarin, Hokkien, Cantonese, Malay, Tamil and English are all needed, and other languages or dialects may be required. India has 16 totally different languages, with 1652 known dialects. Nigerians use over 230 different tongues, although thankfully Hausa, Yoruba, Ibo, English and Pidgin are adequate for most purposes. Where English is commonly employed, it is not necessarily *our* English — to one Nigerian 'too sweet' will mean 'over sugary', but to another it can mean 'delicious',

Of course, translation is even more of a headache than in Europe, not only because languages vary in their ability to convey subtle distinctions (e.g. between 'inclined to agree' and 'definitely agree') but also because even the best translation cannot convey precisely the same meaning. Ideally any translation for research purposes is done by a *researcher* who is *locally based* and also *fluent in English* — not all these conditions may be feasible, which places even more importance on translators' notes. Furthermore, independent back-translation or in-depth discussion of the wording is needed to minimise the risk of 'body odour' appearing in a deodorant questionnaire as 'the stench of corpses'.

Further linguistic pitfalls concern the use of brand names. Some, usually the first in a new category, become generic—'Kodak' for film, 'Surf' for washing powder,—leading to statements such as 'that Knorr Maggi'. (Of course, these sound amusing to our ears as we sip our 'Britvic' orange, quite possibly Schweppes, or do the 'Hoovering'.) Brand names can also cause confusion if they are different in the local language—Lux toilet soap is 'Lak Tse' in Cantonese, which sounds similar but means 'strong man', whilst to Saudis it can be known as 'abu bint'—'the one with the girl' (Lux packs carry the face of a young lady). Such names may be adopted because the local population are unable to read the name in English. I have heard a Chinese housewife refer to English writing as 'those squiggly chicken intestines'. Even though companies are increasingly putting local languages on packs, the problem can remain—illiteracy is still high in many countries, particularly amongst older women.

All these factors can lead to low spontaneous brand recall, and argue strongly for the use of photographs or packs as prompts. However, the presence in many markets of 'grey' imports (i.e. products obtained from abroad through other than the 'official' channels) and of look-alikes, or even highly professional fakes, makes the selection of the correct stimuli a crucial issue, whether for visual prompts or when testing against competition.

Illiteracy has other implications besides reducing brand awareness. Complex, wordy scales should be avoided, as of course should self-completion questionnaires. The lack of a large group of literate, mobile housewives willing to act as interviewers may mean greater use of males, and also of student interviewers, but the term 'student' may cover a much wider age-range than it does in the West.

Sampling

Paucity of reliable statistics means that adequate sampling frames are seldom readily available. No-one knows the population of Nigeria even to the nearest ten million, and similar problems abound in the Middle East. Korea and Taiwan have up-to-date registers of inhabitants by locality. Indonesia is divided into small administrative areas, and each local head man is supposed to maintain a list of inhabitants, but the lists are often out of date and available only at the local level.

Random walk techniques must be modified to cope where there are no clearly defined streets, or where multi-family households are the norm, and agencies often construct their own sampling frames by mapping the dwellings in randomly selected areas.

In rural communities the relative availability of the sexes may vary by time of year, since certain agricultural tasks are sex-role specific, or because the men leave the village to work. In the Middle East, the summer may be the time for leaving the home district, even the country, for more congenial climes.

Because of lack of data, quota sampling is best avoided, at least until an adequate information base has been derived from large-scale random samples. Similarly, street sampling can be dangerous since in many markets individuals frequenting major thoroughfares are highly atypical of the general population; in Singapore, we found usership of a particular European drink to be ten times as high amongst those interviewed in main streets as it was amongst adults randomly sampled at home. Of course, local conditions may mean that non-ideal methods must be used, as in the Middle East where men can be very difficult to contact at home, often necessitating interviews at place of work, or coffee shops, for reasons of cost-effectiveness.

Respondent definition requires careful thought. Multi-generation households are common; the Hong Kong 'housewife' and 'head of household' may be the oldest of three generations and perhaps not closely involved in the economic life of the family unit. Muslim men may have a much greater role in purchasing than is normal in the West; of course, what usually matters more is the identity of the decision-maker — we have found that females have a much greater role in brand choice, for many product areas, than might be imagined either from public behaviour or male claims. Servants may be important for certain product fields. Even the very concept of a household may require consideration in the light of local circumstances and the needs of the research; and migrant labour may mean large numbers of house-holds containing only males, with each man taking it in turn to shop and cook.

Scaling

Market research techniques generally transfer well across cultures. However, certain methods such as the Flachenskala ('area scale' — a series of boxes of descending size, each containing the same statement) are extremely effective in some markets, less so in other. Scaling methods generally rely on a certain standard of literacy, and this cannot be taken for granted. Use has been made of visual techniques such as the 'Smiley' scale, a series of faces with expressions running from very happy to very unhappy, but it is essential to ensure that they do not lead to confusion (see van der Reis[6]). Attempts to use 'mountain scales', whereby the respondent indicates how high up on a 'mountain' diagram the product should be placed (higher implying better), amongst respondents who have either never seen a mountain or are valley-dwellers and despise those who live in the mountains, have proved unsuccessful!

Clearly it helps when dealing with illiterates to reduce verbal content to a minimum. One effective solution is to employ associative techniques, in which a brief statement is read out and the respondent asked to indicate which of a number of brands, indicated by photos or pack fronts, the statement applies to. As well as reducing memory load, this technique allows a large number of stimuli to be handled economically and works well in many markets. (It should be noted that illiterates can be extremely clever at hiding their inability to read; where level of literacy is important, as in media surveys, objective tests must be employed.)

The use of scales raises issues of norms and sensitivity. As indicated above, different cultures exhibit different scale norms and if positive bias is particularly marked this can lead to reduced sensitivity. However, before blaming the scale certain factors should be checked — for example, shortages can produce very positive reactions to *any* product, whilst poor competition can make minor variations in a brand leader unimportant. If the problem is definitely positive bias, scales can be modified to cope. Where between-market comparability is important it is possible to select techniques suited to the task, always bearing in mind that it is comparability of results rather than of techniques *per se* which should be the goal.

Costs

The diversity of the developing world extends to the area of research costs. In markets such as Singapore and Hong Kong, with a highly educated, highly efficient business community, costs compare favourably with the UK. At the other extreme, Nigerian and Middle East prices can be two to three times as high for good quality research, reflecting both the cost and potential benefit of doing business in such markets and the shortage of trained research personnel.

CONCLUSION

In this section I have deliberately dwelt upon areas of contrast, and normally of increased difficulty, compared to research in the developed world. This does not, however, imply that research quality need be in any way inferior to that conducted in Europe or the USA, simply that there are a number of extra hurdles to be surmounted. The problems, and their solutions, are essentially practical; in certain respects research in developing countries may be superior to that conducted nearer home. Interviewers frequently work as a team under an experienced, on-the-spot supervisor able to detect and rectify errors as they occur, in a situation which makes cheating pointless. Furthermore, piloting, random sampling methods and executive involvement with fieldwork are probably more common than in the developed world.

Despite the practical difficulties, sophisticated methods such as trade-off, mapping and other multivariate techniques can be used successfully in supposedly unsophisticated markets (for examples see Aldridge[7]). Whilst it is certainly desirable to keep the interview straightforward, this is not only true of developing countries, and besides, sophistication can be used at the design and analysis stages, for example in factorial-design product tests (Aldridge *et al.*[8]). The secret is to combine practical experience with a thorough grounding in research theory, knowing when to adapt to local conditions, when to stand firm, and also to think flexibly, envisaging unfamiliar uses for familiar products and constructing questionnaires which respect the logical sequence of the respondent's thinking.

REFERENCES

1. BARNARD, P., 'Conducting and Co-ordinating Multi-Country Quantitative Studies across Europe', *Journal of the Market Research Society* **24**, (1982) 1
2. HALPERN, R. S., 'The Position and Role of Research within Strategic Market Planning', *ESOMAR Congress Proceedings, Amsterdam* (1981)
3. JARRETT, C. and CROSSMAN, S., 'The Change from National to International Research — a Case History', *ESOMAR Congress Proceedings, Vienna* (1982)
4. BERENT, P. H., 'Multi-Country Research', in *Applied Marketing and Social Research*, 1st ed., Bradley, U. (ed.), Van Nostrand Reinhold (1982)
5. HAYES, P. J., 'The Cost Comparison of Market Research in Western Europe', *ICC/ESOMAR Symposium on International Marketing Research Proceedings* (1984)
6. van der REIS, A. P., 'Problems in the Use of Rating Scales in Cross-Cultural Research', *ICC/ESOMAR Symposium on International Marketing Research Proceedings* (1984)
7. ALDRIDGE, D., 'Highly Developed Research in Less Developed Countries', *ICC/ESOMAR Symposium on International Marketing Research Proceedings* (1984)
8. ALDRIDGE, D., SHORE, A. J. and WILLEY, M., 'Finding the Cube Route', *ESOMAR Congress Proceedings, Barcelona* (1983)

Applied Marketing and Social Research 2nd Edition
Edited by Ute Bradley
©Copyright John Wiley 1987

14. Evaluating the Effectiveness of Anti-Drinking and Driving Advertising: Increasing the Cost Efficiency of Research

Robin Jones   *Central Office of Information*
Simon Godfrey and Tony Twyman
Research Bureau Limited — Research International

The Central Office of Information presents each year a campaign against drinking and driving. This case deals with the problems of pre-post campaign evaluation for anti-drinking and driving advertising. The problems are fully discussed, but this case is of particular interest on two further accounts:

(i) It reports on an experiment, checking on possible conditioning of respondents through repeat interviewing.
(ii) It employed a most interesting questionnaire to obtain information on the sensitive subject of drinking and driving.

Both the experiment and the questionnaire structure could provide a useful basis for classroom exercises or discussions.

References are also provided which indicate the role research played in the creative development and evaluation of these campaigns, widening the scope of this case.

In addition, Tony Twyman produced a paper for *Survey* (June 1984) entitled 'Evaluating Public Service Campaigns'. In this paper he discusses some of the differences between public service campaigns (like the above) and consumer campaigns in terms of the type of behaviour, the role of attitudes and attitude change involved. He concludes:

'Surveys have a major role in evaluating the effects of public service campaigns. They are particularly valuable where no direct measure of response is available or in suitable form (e.g. accident statistics). By relating changes in behaviour to other changes such as attitudes and knowledge it is possible to begin to understand how campaigns are working in addition to whether they are having an effect.'

SUMMARY

Each year the Central Office of Information presents a campaign against drinking and driving at Christmas, and usually evaluates its effectiveness by surveys before and after the campaign.

Increasing budgetary pressures have led to the seeking of more cost-effective methods of carrying out the research.

Repeat interviewing on the same respondents is one way in which the cost-effectiveness of surveys can be increased but this had previously been ruled out because of the obvious dangers of conditioning the second interview by the knowledge gained by respondents of the purpose of the survey from the first. This paper describes an experiment to devise and test a limited first interview confined to the behavioural elements of the questionnaire, which would be capable of repeat administration without conditioning.

The experiment concluded that such an approach was feasible, and the following year a full half of the effective sample size of the survey was contributed by repeat interviewing.

INTRODUCTION

Recession brings both pressure to demonstrate the value of advertising expenditure and the need to find more cost-efficient means of doing this.

Each year the Central Office of Information (COI) in the UK presents a campaign against drinking and driving. This campaign has been traditionally timed for the Christmas period. Its effectiveness has been evaluated by surveys of behaviour and attitudes before and after the campaign. Increasing budgeting pressures have led to a search for more cost-effective methods of carrying out the research.

DISCUSSION OF REPEAT INTERVIEWING

The campaign evaluation design has involved the use of identical matching samples before and after the campaigns. An obvious source of economy would be to interview the same sample twice. This would have the advantages of removing differences due to chance variations arising between two independently selected samples. All other things being equal this would allow real changes over time to be detected at a criterion level of significance with a substantially smaller sample than when using two independent samples. It would also allow investigation of the correlates of change on a within-individual basis.

Such a repeat interviewing method had been ruled out previously because of the obvious dangers of conditioning engendered by conducting a study involving questioning on attitudes to drinking and driving before:

—exposure to the campaign;
—a further survey of behaviour and attitudes.

Conditioning could arise both from sensitisation to the issues and awareness of the purposes of the survey.

Repeat interviewing on the same sample is the basis of panels but can also be carried out at a more limited frequency.

Whilst conditioning is of great concern in relation to panels, evidence is more likely to be worthy of publication when it fails to appear than when it does. Sheth[1], reviewing consumer purchasing panels found some conditioning of attitudes but very little evidence of conditioning of behaviour unless isolated product fields were singled out for recording. Twyman[2] quoted findings that television viewing records kept by panels showed very little evidence of conditioning. Budge *et al.*[3] concluded that interviewing can change attitudes if respondents are made to feel, by questioning, that they have insufficient information or opinions on something perceived as important. This seems likely to apply to a sensitive area like drinking and driving.

This kind of evidence suggested that repeat interviewing might not lead to conditioning of reported behaviour if it were possible to avoid making the respondent aware of any specific purpose of the interview other than to establish an objective record of behaviour.

Some earlier work by the COI is also relevant. Mills and Nelson[4] reported a programme of research concerned with measuring households' intentions about home insulation. They used a reinterviewing approach in order to evaluate the predictiveness of the original questioning and also to attempt to measure changes in attitudes more precisely. The technique was useful for the former purpose but they did find some conditioning of attitudes. They concluded that reinterviews 'are therefore probably most useful when dealing with facts and preferably checked by observation, and not with attitudes'.

The potential benefits of the statistical sensitivity of panels in measuring change have been discussed in a number of papers, e.g. Buck *et al.*[5]. In a programme of research on home security Chardin and McCallum[6] found greater sensitivity to measuring sales change from a retail panel compared with measuring installation intentions and attitudes in a series of consumer surveys. Whilst many other factors were involved it is probable that some of this advantage came from the statistical sensitivity of panels.

From reviewing this kind of evidence we concluded that the only possibility of measuring something about drinking and driving on a repeat interview basis would arise if the initial survey could:

— be confined to the factual reporting of behaviour without any evaluative overtones;
— avoid all attitudinal questions;
— avoid any direct reference to the emotive issue of drinking and driving.

We therefore proposed to carry out repeat interviews on the apparently factual basis of reporting recent leisure behaviour in respect of eating and drinking, its location, who was present, and mode of transport. Whether reporting such behaviour twice could be done objectively and without conditioning from the first interview was the question to which the experimental stage was directed.

DRINKING AND DRIVING

Drinking and driving continues to be one of the UK's most serious road safety problems, with in 1982 over 70 000 persons being found guilty of offences of drinking after consuming alcohol or taking drugs.

Successive governments accorded high priority to measures to help alleviate the problem, including firm legal sanctions on the one hand and drink/driving publicity campaigns, using both advertising and various 'below-the-line' activities on the other.

The Road Safety Act of 1967 made it an offence to drive with a blood alcohol content of 80 milligrams of alcohol in 100 millilitres of blood or over. Legal sanctions included disqualification for a year (or longer at the Court's discretion) for a first offence with provisions also for fines and imprisonment.

There was a marked decrease in road accidents during the full year after the introduction of the legislation, but the effects then appeared to wear off somewhat over the following years. Nonetheless it has been estimated that over a period of seven years at least 5000 deaths and 200 000 casualties were saved as a result (see Beaumont and Newby[7]; Sabey and Codling[8]; Sabey[9]).

Concern about the upward trend led to the setting-up of a Government Committee of Enquiry in 1974 (the Blennerhassett Committee) which published its report in 1976. This recommended, among other measures, a continuing programme of publicity against drink and driving to help enlist public support for the law and the development of informed and responsible attitudes.

More effective enforcement alone is not enough. It is essential that the police should have the full support of public opinion for their work to be practical and effective . . .

There should be continuing programmes of publicity having particular regard to the education of young drivers, to develop informed and responsible attitudes to drinking and enlist public support for the law . . .

We recommend that publicity should be used not only to draw attention to new measures to strengthen the law, but also on a continuing basis, and that it should include educational measures, particularly directed at the young, as well as campaigns in the mass media . . .

The ultimate aim, which can never be fully realised, is not a temporary remission of casualties due to drinking, but the progressive development of responsible habits among all drivers, from the time when they first qualify the licences.

The introduction of the 1967 Act had been supported by a national publicity campaign mounted by the Department of Transport. Due primarily to lack of funds, no further national campaigns were run between 1968 and 1975 but from Christmas 1976 onwards national campaigns have been run on an annual basis around the Christmas period, using television as the primary medium.

The Role of Research in these Campaigns

The role which research has played in the planning, creative-development and evaluation of these campaigns has been reviewed elsewhere (see Ellis and Ford-Hutchinson[10] and Samuels and Lee[11]). One major element in the research programme has been the undertaking of pre- and post-quantitative surveys for each campaign from 1976 onwards. These surveys have provided information about public attitudes towards 'Drink and Drive' especially among the main target groups, and about how these attitudes have changed over the period. For example, we are able to infer that heavy drinking followed by driving is nowadays less socially acceptable, less 'Macho', than it was and that this is especially true among young and new drivers.

The surveys have also provided a means of measuring shorter-term 'campaign effects' for each years' campaign.

These quantitative surveys are costly, reflecting the quite large sample sizes needed to measure change and the fact that those in the main target group ('young heavier drinkers') are relatively difficult to interview.

Another factor is the need for a long questionnaire, this in turn reflecting the complexity of drinking and driving attitudes and beliefs.

At the beginning of the interviewing the survey is positioned as a 'Leisure Study' to avoid initially focussing the attention of respondents upon the drinking and driving issue. They are asked about a series of leisure activities, and then taken back over the past week, day by day, and asked to recall when they had any alcoholic drink inside or outside the home. Having established when all the occasions outside the home took place, respondents are asked about each one in detail, covering time, location, who they were with, what they drank and ate, where they went afterwards, and how they left (walked, drove, taxi etc). The important pieces of information are, of course, the amount drunk, and whether they drove or not afterwards. This is done in such a way as to enable us to build up a picture of the respondent's drinking and driving behaviour without initially revealing that drinking and driving is the subject of interest.

Once this behavioural information is established, the interviewer moves on to other subjects which increasingly make clear the interest in drinking and driving: attitudes to road safety and to drinking and driving in particular, including the respondent's opinions about how much alcohol he personally can take yet still drive safely, and the likelihood of being detected by the police. The questionnaire also measures various items of knowledge such as beliefs about the legal penalties if convicted of driving over the limit. Awareness of publicity about 'Drinking and Driving' and recognition levels of the present and previous commercials are also measured.

During late 1981 the COI began to explore whether the cost-effectiveness of these surveys could be enhanced by the use of repeat interviewing of the same respondents and the outcome of these deliberations was the experiment described in this paper.

Description of the Experiment

Prior to the experiment, repeat interviewing of the same respondents had been ruled out because of the obvious dangers of conditioning.

On the other hand, because of the steps taken early in the interview to disguise the interest in drinking and driving it should be possible, in theory at least, to elicit the behavioural information without the respondent realising that 'drinking and driving' is the subject of interest, so enabling subsequent reinterviewing to take place without conditioning. One objective of the experiment was to test the correctness of this 'no-conditioning' hypothesis.

General Design

The experiment ran the reinterview method in parallel with a 'traditional' pre-post survey using independent samples so results of the latter could provide a baseline for checking whether or not conditioning had taken place.

For the pre-stage interview of the experimental study, questions were confined to behavioural measures alone. When reinterviewed, these behavioural questions were repeated, followed by the remainder of the questions from the 'traditional' survey covering attitudes, knowledge, advertising awareness and so on. This questionnaire was therefore exactly the same as that used on the main survey . . .

	Questions asked	
Survey	Pre	Post
The Experimental Survey (Same respondents interviewed at both stages)	Behaviour	Behaviour, Attitudes Advertising Recall
The Main Survey (Independent samples at each stage)	Behaviour Attitudes Advertising recall	Behaviour Attitudes Advertising recall

Sampling

The samples used for the Main and Experimental surveys were matched.

The same general sampling procedure was adopted as for the previous studies, selecting constituencies with probability proportional to number of households with cars, and then randomly selecting starting points within each constituency.

The required number of 100 constituency starting points was selected using the identical procedure as before. In order to maximise the precision of comparisons between this campaign evaluation and that conducted in previous years, as many as possible of the constituencies used in both of the last two studies were employed again, although the new starting points were constrained to different wards.

Around each starting point, eight interviews were conducted, selected by the same procedure as before.

In each of the 100 constituencies a starting address was randomly selected from electoral registers, using random number tables on the list of electors. This address predefined a group of 200 households specified by the random route procedure at each stage of the survey, within which the interviewer had to contact all six of her main sample quota.

Once an interview had been conducted in a household, no other interviews were sought within four houses of that household. In particular, only one full interview was permitted per household. Where a respondent was eligible for both the main and boost sample the interviewer always allocated him to the main sample until she had obtained all six main interviews.

If the interviewer had not also obtained her quota of two boost sample interviews within the locations used for the main sample respondents, she was permitted to go outside the 200 households but had to stay within one mile of the starting address. The group of households for use at the post-stage was defined by a random route which started on the opposite side of the road from the original pre-stage starting address.

Quotas were set for age breaks and all data were weighted to the class and age profile of men who drink away from home obtained from another source.

In order to minimise the loss between the first and second stages, co-operation at a second interview was invited at the end of the first interview and respondents refusing to be reinterviewed were discarded from the sample at this point. Interviewers reported few refusals at this stage although inevitably some respondents subsequently refused the second interview at the time when their co-operation was sought.

The pre-stage interviews took place in October/November 1981, and the post-stage in January 1982 (see Appendix 14.2). The advertising campaign ran in December 1981.

THE SURVEY RESULTS

Introduction to the Results

Two groups of respondents were recruited in the surveys in 1981/2, a 'main' sample of any male who drove a car or van, and drank alcohol away from home, and a 'primary target group' sample of males who drove, and drank away from home, and who were aged between 20 and 34 years, and were in the C2 social class.

The amount drunk is classified into the number of 'units', one unit being a half pint of beer, lager, or cider, or a single glass of wine, or a single measure of spirits. Occasions are classified into four main groups (which are not mutually exclusive):

(i) *All drinking occasions* outside the home, regardless of the amount drunk, or whether they drove afterwards or not.

(ii) *All six plus unit drinking occasions* outside the home, when six or more units of alcohol were consumed.

(iii) *All drinking and driving occasions* outside the home, when they drove afterwards, but regardless of how much alcohol was consumed.

(iv) *All six plus drinking and driving occasions* outside the home, when they drove after consuming six or more units of alcohol.

The primary aim of the anti-drinking and driving campaign is to reduce the number of heavy drinking and driving occasions. There are a number of possible strategies for doing this which could lead to different kinds of change in the pre-post comparison of the survey data. Briefly, the two main possibilities are:

1. To persuade people not to drink and drive *at all*, leading to a reduction in the total number of drinking occasions, but not necessarily the

proportion of drinking and driving occasions on which six plus units were consumed.

2. To persuade people to drink *less* when they are going to drive, leading to a reduction in the six plus drinking and driving occasions as a proportion of all drinking and driving occasions, but not necessarily reducing the total number of drinking and driving occasions.

In practice, most campaigns have been found to affect behaviour in a mixture of these two ways, and results are always examined with an eye to both possibilities.

In addition to reported behaviour, several attitudinal and other questions were asked in the survey.

The comparison of the independent and repeat interview surveys was made along a number of dimensions, each of which is described in more detail in the following sections. These dimensions are:

(a) The drop-out between the pre- and post-stages of the repeat interview survey, in terms of respondent profile.
(b) The absolute levels of drinking, and drinking and driving at each stage of the survey.
(c) The changes in drinking, and drinking and driving behaviour between the pre- and post-stages.
(d) The sensitivity of measurement of changes in behaviour.
(e) The attitudes of respondents at the post-stage (attitudes at the pre-stage not being measured amongst the repeat interview sample).
(f) The connection between attitudes and changes in behaviour (this can only be examined amongst the repeat interview sample).

Drop-Out between the Two Stages of the Repeat Interview Survey

A total of 788 respondents were interviewed at the pre-campaign stage, and of these, 689 were interviewed after the campaign, leaving 99 who dropped-out. Respondents at the first stage were only counted as effective if, at the end of the interview, they agreed to be interviewed again. Nevertheless, refusal to be interviewed when contacted at the second stage was still the main reason for dropping-out. Failure to make contact, either because the respondent was not found in or because they were otherwise unavailable (moved, away on holiday) was the other main reason.

In all respects, however, the profile of those who dropped-out at the second stage, was similar to that of those who completed both stages.

Thus, those who were non-effective at the second stage did not appear to behave differently in terms of drinking away from home behaviour, to those who completed both stages.

TABLE 14.1   Average Number of Drinking Occasions out of Home Last Week

	Pre			Post		
	Independent samples	*Repeat interview*	*Difference*	*Independent samples*	*Repeat interview*	*Difference*
Main sample						
All drinking occasions	2.36	2.55	(+0.19)	1.96	2.11	(+0.15)
All 6+ drink occasions	0.82	0.94	(+0.12)	0.78	0.74	(−0.04)
All D and D occasions	1.02	1.06	(+0.04)	0.79	0.83	(+0.04)
All 6+ D and D occasions	0.24	0.24	(=)	0.18	0.15	(−0.03)
Primary target group						
All drinking occasions	2.88	2.71	(−0.17)	2.65	2.17	(−0.48)
All 6+ drink occasions	1.25	1.36	(+0.11)	1.34	1.13	(−0.21)
All D and D occasions	1.21	1.00	(−0.21)	0.99	0.78	(−0.21)
All 6+ D and D occasions	0.36	0.37	(+0.01)	0.26	0.26	(=)

Comparison of the Absolute Levels of Results between the Repeat Interview and Independent Sample Methods

Table 14.1 shows the average number of drinking occasions out of home last week.

An examination of the figures at each stage, comparing those of the independent samples and those of the repeat interview samples showed a certain amount of variation between the absolute levels, although these were not substantial. Possible sources of difference are:

(i)   Slightly later timing of the pre-stage for the repeat interview sample; deeper into winter, closer to Christmas.

(ii) Possible differential levels of initial co-operation, given that the interview was shorter, but that agreement had to be obtained for a further interview. (Field-staff reports discount this as a possible source of difference.)

(iii) Sampling error; difficult to assess theoretically, given both the kind of statistic being compared and the type of sampling involved.

TABLE 14.2 Amount Drunk (Number of Units)

	Pre			Post		
	Independent samples	*Repeat interview*	*Difference*	*Independent samples*	*Repeat interview*	*Difference*
Main sample						
Total in week	11.9	12.8	(+0.9)	10.3	10.4	(+0.1)
Average per occasion	5.0	5.0	(=)	5.3	4.9	(−0.4)
Average per driving occasion	4.1	3.9	(−0.2)	4.0	3.8	(−0.2)
Highest number on any driving occasion	4.4	4.3	(−0.1)	4.3	4.2	(−0.1)
Primary target group						
Total in week	16.0	16.5	(+0.5)	16.3	13.5	(−2.8)
Average per occasion	5.6	6.1	(+0.5)	6.2	6.2	(=)
Average per driving occasion	4.6	4.8	(+0.2)	4.2	4.6	(+0.4)
Highest number on any driving occasion	5.0	5.3	(+0.3)	4.9	5.1	(+0.2)

It seems most likely that the differences were attributed to some degree to a seasonal effect, but mostly to sampling variation. The fact that the differences go in various directions and are greater for the primary target group than for the main sample confirm this.

Table 14.2 shows the amount drunk. Once again, the variations between the two methods do not show consistent biases and look like possible sampling variations.

Concerning where drinking took place, the profiles of places of drinking and mode of transport used were very similar between the two surveys.

Comparison of Changes between Stages from the Different Methods

This is shown in Table 14.3

When the two studies are compared, not in terms of their absolute levels but in terms of the changes found between the pre- and post-stages, there is a fair degree of consistency as to the conclusions reached.

TABLE 14.3   Average Number of Drinking Occasions out of Home Last Week

	Independent samples		Repeat interview		Independent samples	Repeat interviews
	Pre	Post	Pre	Post	Change (%)	
Main sample						
All drinking occasions	2.36	1.96	2.55	2.11	− 17	− 17
All 6+ drinking occasions	0.82	0.78	0.94	0.74	− 5	− 21
All D and D occasions	1.02	0.79	1.06	0.83	− 23	− 22
All 6+ D and D occasions	0.24	0.18	0.24	0.15	− 25	− 37
Primary target group						
All drinking occasions	2.88	2.65	2.71	2.17	− 8	− 20
All 6+ drinking occasions	1.25	1.34	1.36	1.13	+ 7	− 17
All D and D occasions	1.21	0.99	1.00	0.78	− 18	− 22
All 6+ D and D occasions	0.36	0.26	0.37	0.26	− 28	− 30

In the Repeat Interview survey the main sample show similar reductions in drinking and driving occasions, but a sharper decline in six plus drinking occasions, particularly when driving.

A similar result is found for the primary target group, except that the fall in the number of drinking occasions is more consistent with the main sample in the Repeat Interview survey than in the Independent Sample study.

Overall, therefore, the conclusions from the two studies on campaign effects would be fairly similar but with a slightly sharper result for the main sample on the Repeat Interview study. The results perhaps also look more internally consistent in this survey.

Attitudes, Knowledge and Advertising Awareness

So as to avoid any conditioning effect through repeat questioning, these data were only obtained at the post-stage of the Repeat Interview survey and were therefore compared with the figures from the corresponding stage of the Independent Sample study.

Although there were inevitably some differences between the results obtained from the two surveys, these were generally small, and similar conclusions would be drawn from either method.

It did not appear that the first interview with the repeat sample had any substantial effect on respondents' attitudes, or on their sensitivity to anti-drinking and driving publicity.

Sensitivity of Measurement of Behavioural Change in the Two Methods

A comparison of the sensitivity of the two alternative interviewing approaches involves consideration of two factors:

— the drop-out between pre- and post-stages in the interviewing method;
— the correlation between the pre- and post-scores for respondents in the repeat interviewing study who are interviewed at both stages.

The drop-out rate, and the profile of those respondents who were not interviewed at the post-stage is important in assessing the validity of the repeat interviewing method as already described. It is also important from the point of view of sensitivity, since respondents who drop out only contribute precision to the pre-campaign measure.

The objective of this section is to show the pre-stage sample size that would lead, in the repeat interviewing method, to an equivalent precision in the measurement of reported behavioural change, as the method using two independent samples. Knowing this sample size enables an assessment of the relative cost-efficiencies of the two methods to be made.

The calculation of the variance of the pre-post change for each of the two interviewing methods is shown below in Appendix 14.1 together with the implications on sample size.

The correlation coefficients (ϱ) between the main measures in the repeat interview study were all found to be positive, indicating that the changes in individual respondents' behaviour between the two stages of the survey were relatively small, compared with the variations in behaviour across respondents. This result was as expected.

The correlations for the main sample were of a slightly higher order than those for the primary target group, possibly indicating a more regular pattern of behaviour for older men. For calculating equivalent sample sizes for the two interviewing methods, it is appropriate to take an average across all the main behavioural measures yielding the following values:

ϱ (primary target group) $= 0.54$
ϱ (main sample) $= 0.67$

The drop out rates for the two groups were:

d (primary target group)   = 9.5%
d (main sample)   = 13.5%

Using the formula shown in Appendix 14.1, the equivalent recruitment sample sizes with the repeat interview method to replace two independent 600 main, and 200 primary target group boost samples are as follows:

Two Independent Samples	Equivalent Repeat Interview Samples
600 main	182 main
200 boost	91 boost

It is seen that very substantial savings in sample size can be achieved, due to the high correlations found between individuals' results at the two stages of the interview. The findings from this section show that the repeat interviewing method is highly cost-effective.

The Connection between Attitudes and Behavioural Change

For the reasons discussed earlier in the paper, attitudes to drinking and driving were only measured amongst the repeat interview sample at the post-campaign stage. A direct examination of the connections between attitudinal and behavioural changes was therefore impossible. However, it was possible to compare the post-campaign attitudes of those respondents who had 'improved' in their reported drinking and driving behaviour with those whose behaviour had not changed, and those whose behaviour had 'worsened'. Improvement or deterioration was defined by whether the reported number of driving occasions after excess alcohol had been fewer or greater in the weeks preceding the post- compared with the pre-stage interviews.

The post-campaign attitudes of improvers were consistently more positive than those who had deteriorated, over a wide range of measures. For example, improvers felt that driving after one or two alcoholic drinks was considerably more dangerous than did those who had deteriorated. Improvers were more likely to agree that the police were catching more drinking drivers, and, that those who drink and drive should be sent to prison. They were also more likely to claim that they themselves tried to stop other people from drinking too much when they were going to drive.

These results show that a strong correlation does exist between reported behaviour and a number of the attitudes that many of the anti-drinking and driving advertising campaigns have tried to encourage. A direct cause and effect relationship is not, of course, possible to establish, but in the sense that a lack of correlation would have tended to disprove such a relationship, these findings may be regarded as encouraging.

CONCLUSIONS

Point One

The results suggested that repeat interviewing offers an opportunity to substantially reduce the sample size needed for future drink and drive evaluation surveys

The limitation of the approach is that no attitudinal or advertising questions can be asked at the pre-stage and this informaton is of interest, (although of less interest than behaviour, which has always been regarded as the primary measure of interest when measuring campaign effectiveness of these campaigns).

Point Two

Furthermore, the results of the experiment suggested that the technique produces valid results:

1. Roughly one-in-eight of the sample dropped out between stages but their profiles and behaviour patterns looked broadly similar to those of the remainder who were interviewed at both stages.
2. The main measures of interest (pre-post shifts in the key behavioural measures) showed considerable consistency between the repeat interviewing and traditional surveys, showing the same direction and similar magnitude. Thus, conclusions about the effectiveness of the campaign would have been similar whichever technique had been used.

Point Three

Based on these experimental results we were able to formulate two options for use in future Drink and Drive campaign evaluations:

Option One

Dispense with the attitudinal/advertising information altogether at the pre-stage. Use repeat interviews for measuring changes in reported behaviour, with much lower sample sizes (and a shorter questionnaire) than used traditionally.

Advantages — Substantially lower sample sizes (and so much lower cost). For every 100 interviews required using the traditional method the use of repeat interviewing would need only 30 interviews (main sample) or 45 interviews (primary target group) respectively for a given level of statistical precision.

Disadvantage — Loss of advertising/attitudinal trend data.

Option Two

Undertake two research exercises in parallel: a repeat interviewing survey (to measure trends in behaviour) and a 'traditional' survey (to measure trends in 'attitudes' and 'advertising recall' as well as behaviour.

Advantages — (i) Substantial savings in cost for the behavioural data (compared with the cost of an equivalent effective sample size using traditional techniques).

(ii) Some basis of assessing trends in the 'attitudinal' and 'advertising recall[1] but this part of the exercise being (properly) given a lower share of resources than measuring trends in the behavioural data.

Disadvantage — Having *two* independent figures for each behavioural measure of interest raises the problem of whether and how to pool them, especially if the absolute figures at the pre-stage for the two surveys ('traditional' and 'repeat') are fairly different. In other words, data processing and interpretation become more complex.

Point Four

More generally, the repeat-interviewing approach offers a possible method of enhancing the cost-effectiveness of similar 'pre- and post-' studies for other campaign subjects, provided that certain conditions are met. Briefly those conditions are:

1. Some means needs to be found of disguising the purpose of the survey at the pre-stage to minimise conditioning. This will doubtless mean having to cut out certain questions of interest as they would make the purpose of the study too apparent.
2. The 'loss' of information when the pre-stage questionnaire is cut down (to avoid conditioning) must be acceptable. In the case of Drink and Drive the existing behaviour questions had been designed initially to cover up the subject of the survey. Fortunately too, these (behavioural) questions were the ones of primary interest, and the loss of the other questions (attitudes and advertising) was regarded as an acceptable trade-off. In other instances it would be more difficult to curtail the pre-stage questionnaire in such a way as to disguise the subject and yet retain enough information to be of use in assessing campaign effectiveness.

3. There needs to be a high level of correlation between individuals' responses at the initial interview and when repeat interviewed for each of the various measures of interest. In the case of Drink and Drive these correlations were indeed high enough (at around 0.55 for the primary target group, and 0.67 for the main sample) enabling substantial reductions in sample size for given levels of precision in measuring trends.
4. Given that there is bound to be some loss in sample at the second stage due to refusals or inability to contact, it is important that this should not happen in such a way as to distort the results. As mentioned earlier, roughly one-in-eight of the experimental sample was lost at the post-stage but the characteristics of the drop-outs were closely in line with the remainder. In other words, in this instance there was no evidence that the samples were distorted by sample loss at the second stage.

AN APPLICATION OF THE RESULTS

The year after the experiment the Department of Transport decided to undertake an area test to evaluate two different campaigns. For this purpose the country was divided into three 'test areas', one of which would act as a control by not having any advertising during the test period.

The cost of replicating the traditional 'before' and 'after' research technique on the scale of earlier years in each of three areas would have been very high and it was decided to use repeat interviewing for a segment of each sample to reduce the costs.

Thus in each of the three areas 300 interviews were carried out at each stage amongst the primary target group only. Of these, 200 used the traditional questionnaire (behaviour, attitudes, advertising) and 100 used the shortened version (behaviour only at the pre-stage) for repeat interviews. In total, 1800 interviews were carried out representing an 'equivalent sample size', for the behaviour data, of around 2400 (see Table 14.4).

TABLE 14.4   **Survey design for Evaluation of 1982/83 Drink and Drive Campaign:**

	Area			Total:
	Campaign 'A'	Campaign 'B'	Control	all 3 areas
Interviewing at *each stage*:				
traditional	200	200	200	600
repeat	100	100	100	300
total	300	300	300	900
Both stages combined:	600	600	600	1800
Effective sample sizes:	800	800	800	2400

On the whole there were few differences between the traditional and repeat interview sample and their data were accordingly pooled at the data analysis stage. The use of repeat interviewing on this survey led to a saving of around 30% in survey costs.

REFERENCES

1. SHETH, J. N., 'A Report on Conditioning Bias in Fixed Panels', University of Illinois (1981).
2. TWYMAN, W. A., 'Television Media Research' in *Consumer Market Research Handbook*, 2nd ed., Worcester, R. M. and Downham, J. (eds) van Nostrand Reinhold (1978)
3. BUDGE, R. G. *et al.*, 'Interviewing Changes Attitudes — Sometimes' *Public Opinion Quarterly* **41** (1977)
4. MILLS, P. and NELSON, E. H., 'Reinterviewing in Attitude Surveys: An Experimental Study' *ESOMAR Seminar, on Socal Proceedings, Research* London · (1977)
5. BUCK S. E. Sherwood, R., and TWYMAN, W. A., 'Panels and the Measurement of Change', *ESMOMAR/WAPOR Congress Proceedings*, Montreux (1974)
6. CHARDIN, C. and McCALLUM, D., 'Enhancing the Contribution of Research to Central Government Advertising — A Practical Approach to Evaluating a Crime Prevention Campaign', *36th ESOMAR Congress Proceedings*, Barcelona (1983)
7. BEAUMONT, D. and NEWBY, R. F., 'Traffic Law and Road Safety Research in the United Kingdom — British Countermeasures', *National Road Safety Symposium*, Canberra, Australia (1972)
8. SABEY, B. E. and CODLING, P. J., 'Alcohol and Road Accidents in Great Britain', *6th International Conference on Alcohol, Drugs and Traffic Safety*, Toronto (1974)
9. SABEY, B. E. 'A Review of Drinking and Drug-Taking in Road Accidents in Great Britain', *7th International Conference of the International Association for Accident and Traffic Medicine*. Ann Arbor, Michigan, (1978). TRRL Report SR 441, Crowthorne, England (1978)
10. ELLIS, S. and FORD-HUTCHINSON, S. 'The Use of Research in Planning the Drinking and Driving Advertising Campaign' *Market Research Society Conference Proceedings* (1982)
11. SAMUELS, J. and LEE, B. 'The Evaluation of the Drink and Drive Advertising Campaign 1976/77', *31st ESOMAR Congress Proceedings*, Bristol (1978).

ACKNOWLEDGMENT

This paper was first presented by Robin Jones, Simon Godfrey and Tony Twyman at the 37th ESOMAR Congress, Rome 1984 where it won the Conference prize for the best case history. Permission for reprinting has been granted by the European Society for Opinion and Marketing Research, ESOMAR, J. J. Viottastraat 29, 1071 JP Amsterdam. The Netherlands, from whom the papers of this Congress may be obtained.

APPENDIX 14.1   PRECISION OF PRE-POST CHANGES IN REPORTED BEHAVIOUR

1. Independent Sample Method

Two independent samples of size $= Ni$ (the same at both stages)

Variance of pre-post change $= \dfrac{2\sigma^2}{Ni}$

Where σ^2 is the variance of the result of the question from individual respondents at each stage.*

2. Repeat Interviewing Method

Where the recruitment sample $= Nr$
The drop out percentage $= d\%$
The correlation coefficient
between stages $= \varrho$

$$\textit{Variance of Pre-Post Change} = \frac{\sigma^2}{Nr} \left(1 + \frac{100\ (1 - 2\varrho)}{(100 - d)}\right)$$

To obtain an equal precision of pre-post change from the two methods:

$$Nr = Ni \frac{\left(1 + \dfrac{100(1 - 2\varrho)}{(100 - d)}\right)}{2}$$

*Assumed the same for both interviewing methods.

APPENDIX 14.2   BEHAVIOUR STUDY QUESTIONNAIRE

The shorter interview referred to in the text terminated after all occasion pages had been completed. Respondents were then asked if they would be prepared to be interviewed at a later date, when the full version of the questionnaire shown here was administered. The questionnaire shown here is simplified for typesetting purposes; it does not represent the original layout.

RESEARCH BUREAU LTD., GREENBANK, LONDON, E1 9PA

M.S.   *RBL 11993*

M.R.S.   W.A. TWYMAN

BEHAVIOUR STUDY	D.P. USE ONLY
January 1982	COLS 1–4 Serial No.
Interviewer Name	
Respondent Name	
Address	Col. 5 Card No. 1
....	INTERVIEWER NO. Cols 6–9
Phone No............... Date...............	

P1   *RBL REGION*
Col. 10

LN	LS	MID	NW	YKS	NE	SCOT	SW	ANG	STHN
1	2	3	4	5	6	7	8	9	0

P2   *AGE*   Col. 11

18–19 years......1
20–24 years......2
25–29 years......3
30–34 years......4
35–39 years......5
40–44 years......6
45–49 years......7
50–54 years......8
55–59 years......9
60–64 years......0
65–69 years......X
70 years of more . V

P3   *TIME CONTACT TOOK PLACE*
Col. 14

Weekday between 5.30
   and 8.30........1
Weekend before
   8.30 p.m. 2

P4   *OCCUPATION OF HEAD OF HOUSEHOLD*

WRITE IN BOX AND RING APPROPRIATE CODE

	Col. 12	OCCUPATION OF HEAD OF HOUSEHOLD
A	Higher Manager..1	
B	Intermediate Man.2	
C1	Jun. Man/clerical.3	
C2	Skilled...........4	
D	Semi-skilled......5	
E	State Pensions....6	

P5   *MARITAL STATUS*   Col. 13

Married....................................1
Single (inc. widowed/divorced) 2

P6   *PRESENCE OF OTHERS AT INTERVIEW*
Col. 15

Interviewed alone 1
Wife present................................2
Other female(s) present (incl. child) 3
Males present (inc. child).....................4

P7   *STAGE OF SURVEY*   Col. 16

First stage .1

Second stage 2

P8   *COMMERCIAL RADIO LISTENING*   Col. 17

Do you listen to commercial radio stations at all nowadays — by that I mean independent radio, not BBC!

Yes 1

No 2

P9   *SAMPLE*   Col. 18

Main 1

Boost 2

P10   *ITV AREA* — Which ITV station can you normally get on your TV set? PROMPT IF NECESSARY.
IF MORE THAN ONE ASK: Which do you normally watch?

Col. 19

London (Thames/London Weekend 1

Southern 2

Westward (South West) 3

HTV (Harlech/Wales & West) . . .4

Anglia 5

Midlands (ATV) 6

Yorkshire .7

Tyne Tees (North East) 8

Granada .9

Border 0

Scottish (Central Scotland X

Grampian (N.E. Scotland) . . . . . .Y

P11 *ITV VIEWING*
On an average day, for about how many hours do you watch ITV — that is Independent TV, not BBC?

Col. 21

None 1

1 hour or less 2

Over 1 up to 2 hours 3

Over 2 up to 3 hours 4

Over 3 up to 4 hours 5

Over 4 up to 5 hours 6

Over 5 up to 6 hours 7

Over 6 up to 7 hours 8

More than 7 hours 9

P.12 *DAY OF WEEK OF INTERVIEW*   Col. 22

Monday 1

Tuesday 2

Wednesday 3

Thursday .4

Friday 5

Saturday .6

Sunday 7

P.13 *TYPE OF SURVEY*   Col. 20

Behaviour Study 1

Leisure Study 2

At the end of last year, you were kind enough to take part in an interview for us. We are now conducting the last stage of the survey on some aspects of peoples' lives and leisure activities, like eating out, sports and their attitudes on several issues.

Q.1   SHOW CARD A

Please would you look at this card and tell me which, if any, of these things you do nowadays. Please start at the top and work down.

Col. 23

	YES	NO
Go to the cinema................................1		☐
Eat out in a restaurant............................2		☐
Eat out at a friend's house 3		☐
Watch television at home..........................4		☐
Take part in sport, as a player......................5		☐
Drink at home (wines, spirits, beer etc.)...............6		☐
Drink away from home in a pub, hotel, bar, club etc. (including when you have a meal out) 7		☐
Drink at a friend's house (including when you go for a meal) 8		☐
Go to a football match 9		☐
Smoke cigarettes 10		☐
Smoke cigars or a pipe...........................11		☐
Drive a car or van...............................12		☐

Col.24

Ride a motor bike.................................1		☐

—PUT A CROSS IN BOX FOR NO

—RING NUMBER FOR YES

Q.2a *SHOW CARD 3*	Q.2c *SHOW CARD B*	Q.2e *SHOW CARD B*
How often do you watch television at home nowadays?	How often do you eat out in a restaurant nowadays?	How often do you drink away from home, in a pub, restaurant, friend's house nowadays?

	Col. 25	Col. 26	Col. 27

Does not apply..1–Q.2c (Check Q.1 — not code 4)

Does not apply..1–Q.2e (Check Q.1 — not code 2)

7 or more 2	7 or more 2	7 or more 2
6 times a week 3	6 times a week 3	6 times a week 3
5 times a week 4	5 times a week 4	5 times a week 4
4 times a week 5	4 times a week 5	4 times a week 5
3 times a week 6	3 times a week 6	3 times a week 6
1–2 times a week . . 7	1–2 times a week . . 7	1–2 times a week . . 7
2–3 times a month . 8	2–3 times a month . 8	2–3 times a month . 8
Once a month 9	Once a month 9	Once a month 9
Less often than once a month 0	Less often than once a month 0	Less often than once a month 0

↓ ↓ ↓

Q.2b *SHOW CARD C*	Q.2d *SHOW CARD C*	Q.2f *SHOW CARD C*
And how does this compare with what you did 3 months ago?	And how does this compare with what you did 3 months ago?	And how does this compare with what you did 3 months ago?

	Col. 28	Col. 29	Col. 30

More often 1	More often 1	More often 1
About the same 2	About the same 2	About the same 2
Less often 3	Less often 3	Less often 3

I should now like to ask you about some of these activities in more detail. Still thinking about eating or drinking *outside your own home*, I'd like to ask you about the last seven days.

Q.3 First of all, did you have any kind of alcoholic drink *outside your home*, including when eating out, yesterday, that is . . . . day?

RECORD YES OR NO IN GRID AT BOTTOM.

Q.4 And on how many different occasions on . . . . day did you have an alcoholic drink *outside your home*? *By occasions, I mean different times, or different places.

RECORD NUMBER IN GRID AT BOTTOM.

Q.5 Did you have an alcoholic drink at home on . . . . day?

RECORD YES OR NO IN GRID AT BOTTOM.

Q.6 And on how many different occasions on . . . . day did you have a drink at home?

> REPEAT QUESTIONS Q.3–6 FOR ALL OTHER DAYS OF THE
> WEEK, WORKING BACKWARDS THROUGH THE WEEK

—NOW TAKE EACH DRINKING AWAY FROM HOME OCCASION
SEPARATELY, STARTING WITH THE NEAREST TO TODAY.

—RECORD ONTO OCCASION PAGE AND ASK Q.7A–13.

—WORK THROUGH EACH OCCASION ONE AT A TIME.

—USE ONE OCCASION (PAGE) FOR EACH AWAY FROM HOME OCCASION.

NB. IF WHEN RESPONDENT STARTS DESCRIBING AN OCCASION, IT
BECOMES CLEAR THAT HE VISITED SEVERAL DIFFERENT PLACES (i.e.
went from one pub, to another, or to a friend's house, or to a restaurant) TREAT
EACH PLACE AS A SEPARATE DRINKING OCCASION, AND USE A
SEPARATE PAGE—ALSO MAKE SURE THAT *NUMBER* OF OCCASIONS IS
CORRECTLY CODED UP FOR THAT DAY.

MARK CROSS ABOVE YESTERDAY, THEN FOLLOW ARROWS			Sun	Sat	Fri	Thu	Wed	Tue	Mon
Q.3	Did you have any drink *outside your* *home* on . . . . . . day?	No — (Go to Q.5 Yes	1(34) 2	1(35) 2	1(36) 2	1(37) 2	1(38) 2	1(39) 2	1(40) 2
Q.4	On how many dif- ferent occasions did you have a drink *out-* *side* your home on	1 occ 2 ocs 3 ocs 4 + ocs	3 4 5 6	3 4 5 6	3 4 5 6	3 4 5 6	3 4 5 6	3 4 5 6	3 4 5 6
Q.5	And did you have any drink at home on . . . . . . day?	No — (Go to next day) Yes	1(41) 2	1(42) 2	1(43) 2	1(44) 2	1(45) 2	1(46) 2	1(47) 2
Q.6	On how many dif- ferent occasions did you have a *drink at* *home* on . . . . . . day?	1 occ 2 ocs 3 ocs 4 + ocs	3 4 5 6	3 4 5 6	3 4 5 6	3 4 5 6	3 4 5 6	3 4 5 6	3 4 5 6

EXAMPLE OF
OCCASION PAGE

CARD 4 repeat cols
1-4   Col. 5/4

Now thinking about when you had a drink *away from home* on . . . (DAY OF WEEK)

	Col. 6
Day of week	Sunday 1
	Monday 2
RECORD FROM LIST AT BOTTOM OF PAGE	Tuesday 3
	Wednesday 4
	Thursday 5
	Friday 6
	Saturday 7

Q.7a Thinking of (the . . . 1st/2nd occasion) . . . day, approximately what time was it?

Show card D   Col. 7
Morning 1
Lunchtime 2
Afternoon 3
Early evening 4
Evening 5

Q.7b and where were you?
Show card E   Col. 8
Pub 1
Hotel bar 2
Club 3
Restaurant/cafe 4
Boat/plane/train 5
Place of work 6
Other' home 7

Q.7c and who was with you?
Show card F   Col. 9
On my own 1
One other person — man 2
One other person — woman 3
Several others — males 4
Several others — females 5
Several others — mixed 6
Others 7

Q.8 and what did you drink? →
Show card G   Col. 14
Beer/Stout/Lager* 1
Cider* 2
Sherry/wine/vermouth 3
Spirits 4
Other (code only if alcoholic) 5
* If respondent says bottle, ask how much in bottle.

Q.10 Did you eat anything on that occasion?
Show card H   Col. 10
Snack (crisps, nuts etc) 1
Bar food (sandwiches, pies etc.) 2
Full meal 3
Other 4
Nothing to eat 5

Q.11 About what time did you leave . . . .(Name location)?
                                 Col. 11
Up to 12 noon 1
12.01-3 pm 2
3.01 — 5 pm 3
5.01 — 9 pm 4
9.01 — 11.15 pm 5
11.16 pm or later 6
Stayed there, go to next occasion 7

Q.12 Where did you go afterwards?
Show card I   Col. 12
Own home 1
Other's home 2
Place of work 3
Somewhere else 4

Q.13 and how did you leave . . .
(Name location at Q.7b)
Show card J   Col. 13
Walked 1
Drove car/van 2
Rode as passenger in car/van 3
Took a taxi/minicab 4
Drove a motorbike/moped 5
Rode as passenger on
    motorbike/moped 6
Went by public transport 7
Other 8

Q.9 . . . and how much? Ask for each type separately. Record in pints. If

Pints ( )	½ Pints	If total includes ½
(15) (16)	(17)	pint put 0.5 in
(18) (19)	(20)	right column
(21) (22)		— Record in single glasses
(23) (24)		— Record in single measures
(25) (26)		— Record in single glasses

Now I should like to ask you some questions about other activities you mentioned earlier. You said that you drive a car or van.

Q.14 *Show card B* How often do you drive on average nowadays?

Col. 48

7 or more times a week..............	1
6 times a week	2
5 times a week	3
4 times a week	4
3 times a week	5
1–2 a week:.........................	6
2–3 a month	7
Once a month	8
Less often than once a month	9

SKIP COL. (49)–(51)

Now I would like to ask you some questions about road safety.

Q.15 I would like you to tell me, for each of the statements I shall read out to you, how dangerous you think this is, from this card here — *Show card M*. As you can see, the less dangerous you think it is, the lower the score you give, and the more dangerous you think it is the higher the score you give. So please give a score between 0 and 5, depending on how dangerous you think it is.

Read out each statement in turn and code answer for each separately.

Read the statements in the order given in the instructions.

	NOT AT ALL DANGEROUS					EXTREMELY DANGEROUS	
Turning right without signalling first	0	1	2	3	4	5	Col. 52
Parking on a double yellow line	0	1	2	3	4	5	Col. 53
Overtaking when you have to cross double white lines..................	0	1	2	3	4	5	Col. 54
Doing a U-turn in a busy street..................	0	1	2	3	4	5	Col. 55
Driving soon after having just one or two alcoholic drinks	0	1	2	3	4	5	Col. 56
Driving at 35 mph in a 30 mph zone	0	1	2	3	4	5	Col. 57
Driving when tired	0	1	2	3	4	5	Col. 58
Driving slowly on a motorway.............	0	1	2	3	4	5	Col. 59

Q.16 I would like now to ask your opinion about drinking and driving. I shall read out some things that people have said and after each, I would like you to tell me how much you agree or disagree from this card. *Show card O and read out each statement in turn.*

	Agree a lot	Agree a little	Dis- agree a little	Dis- agree a lot	Don't know	Col.
Some people drive better after one or two drinks	1	2	3	4	5	(6)
Even if a person has only one drink, he cannot drive so well	1	2	3	4	5	(7)
The police are now catching more drinking drivers	1	2	3	4	5	(8)
I am most concerned about drinking and driving when I have my girlfriend/ wife or a close member of my family in the car	1	2	3	4	5	(9)
I think people who ever drink and drive should be sent to prison	1	2	3	4	5	(10)
Most car accidents that happen to people who have been drinking would probably have happened anyway	1	2	3	4	5	(11)
The legal limit on drinking when driving is not strict enough and should be tightened up	1	2	3	4	5	(12)
It's people like me that the police are most keen to pick on, when stopping people for breath test	1	2	3	4	5	(13)
I myself try to stop other people from drinking too much when they are going to drive	1	2	3	4	5	(17)
If I drive carefully after drinking, I am not likely to get caught by the police	1	2	3	4	5	(18)
I think its bad luck if someone is caught drinking and driving because lots of people do it	1	2	3	4	5	(20)
People are always nagging me about drinking and driving	1	2	3	4	5	(22)

SKIP COL. (14)–(16)

SKIP COL. (19)

SKIP COL. (21)

SKIP COL. (23)

You're less likely to be stopped by the police these days for drinking and driving	1	2	3	4	5 (24)
Drinking a little bit over the legal limit does not really make me more likely to have an accident	1	2	3	4	5 (25)
When you're going to drive, its better to limit your drinking by how you feel, rather than by a set number of drinks	1	2	3	4	5 (27)
If you have had a few drinks and someone else crashes into you, you would still be at fault as far as the law is concerned	1	2	3	4	5 (28)
It is difficult to avoid some drinking and driving, if you are going to have any kind of social life	1	2	3	4	5 (29)
The police are getting more expert at spotting the drinking driver	1	2	3	4	5 (30)

SKIP COL. (26)

Q.17a What is the *most* beer you think that you *personally* can drink, without it affecting your driving?

Q.17b What is the *most* spirits you think that you *personally* can drink, without it affecting your driving — how many glasses of spirits, I mean singles?

Col.31		Col. 32	
Never drink beer at all	1	Never drink spirits at all	1
None at all	2	None at all	2
½ pint	3	1 measure	3
1 pint	4	2 measures	4
1½ pints	5	3 measures	5
2 pints	6	4 measures	6
2½ pints	7	5 measures	7
3–3½ pints	8	6 measures	8
4–4½ pints	9	7 measures	9
5–5½ pints	0	8+ measures	0
6+ pints	X	Don't know	V
Don't know	V		

Ask all
Under the present law, how much do you think a driver can drink, without fear of prosecution?

Ask for both beer and spirits even if not drunk.

Q.18a That is how much beer? (PROBE FOR PINTS)

Q.18b And how much spirits, how many glasses, I mean single measures?

BEER	Col. 33	SPIRITS	Col. 34
None at all	1	None at all	1
½ pint	2	1 measure	2
1 pint	3	2 measures	3
1½ pints	4	3 measures	4
2 pints	5	4 measures	5
2½ pints	6	5 measures	6
3–3½ pints	7	6 measures	7
4–4½ pints	8	7 measures	8

Q.19 If you were to *drive after drinking over the limit,* how likely do you think it is that you would be stopped by the police? Please show me by choosing one of the boxes on this card. The *more likely* you think it is, the nearer the top the box would be and the *less likely* you think it is, the nearer the bottom the box would be. *Show card S*

VERY LIKELY   Col. 37

	a	1
	b	2
	c	3
	d	4
	e	5
	f	6
	g	7
	h	8
	i	9
	j	0

PLEASE RING ONE CODE OPPOSITE THE BOX HE CHOOSES

NO CHANCE AT ALL

Q.20 Can you tell me what you think are the types of legal penalties for a first time conviction for drinking and driving? *Record in grid below*

Q.21 And do you know of any other ways in which a first time conviction for drinking and driving could affect a driver? *Record in grid below*

Q.22 *Show card Q.* Are there any (other) of these which you think might be penalties or consequences for a first time conviction for drinking and driving?

Penalties/other consequences	Spontaneous Q.20/21 Col. 38	Prompted Q.22 Col. 39
Fine	1	1
Imprisonment	2	2
Licence endorsed	3	3
Driving ban/disqualification	4	4
Increased insurance premium	5	5
Unable to hire a car	6	6
Others (specify)	7	7
No others	8	8
Don't know	9	9

Q.23 *Show card Q* Which *one* of these do you think is *most* likely to influence you not to drink and drive?

And which is *least* likely to influence you?

	Most Likely Col. 40	Least Likely Col. 41
Fine	1	1
Possibility of imprisonment	2 .. MARK ONE ...	2
Licence endorsed	3 .. CODE ONLY ..	3
Driving ban/disqualification	4 ... FOR EACH ...	4
Increased insurance premium	5	5
Unable to hire a car	6	6
None of them	7	7

Q.24 One of the possible consequences of a conviction for drinking and driving is a much higher insurance premium. Could you tell me from this card, *Show card R*, how much this would matter to you?

An increased insurance premium —

	Col. 42
Would bother me a great deal	1
Would bother me a little	2
Would bother me much	3
Wouldn't bother me at all	4

Q.25 Where at all, can you remember hearing or seeing things about *drinking and driving* in the *last 12 months?*

Do not prompt. If unclear probe whether advertisement/programme/article intended

Probe: Anything else?

Q.26 In the last 12 months, do you remember . . . (*read out as appropriate*) about *drinking and driving?*

	Col. 43			Yes	No

Col. 44

TELEVISION (programme........ 1
            (advertisement ..... 2 * ....Seeing any TELEVISION
                              advertisement ....1 ☐

RADIO   (programme........ 3
            (advertisement ..... 4 *........Hearing any RADIO
                              advertisement ....2 ☐

NEWSPAPER (article 5
            (advertisement ..... 6 * ....Seeing any NEWSPAPER
                              advertisements ....3 ☐

MAGAZINE (article 7
            (advertisement 8

CINEMA   (film 9
            (advertisement ..... 0 * ....Seeing any CINEMA
                              advertisements ....4 ☐

POSTER/   (in the street .... X *........Seeing any POSTERS
HOARDING (elsewhere V   in the street............5 ☐

Col. 45

Back of buses 1
Leaflets...................... 2
People talking about it 3
Beer mat..................... 4
Others (write in) 5
.... 6
None seen/heard............... 7

If neither TV nor cinema advertising mentioned at Q.25 or Q.26, ask Q.27 otherwise go to Q.28.

(If at Q.1 code 1 (cinema) *and* code 4 not rung, and respondent insists he never goes to the cinema or watches television, go on to Q.32 and check if it is to be asked. If not, go straight to classification)

Q.27 a Can you remember seeing this advertisement on television or in the cinema before?

Col. 46

Yes 1
No 2

Q.27 b *Show photo J*
Can you remember seeing this advertisement on television or in the cinema before?

Col. 47

Yes 1
No 2

Q.27 c *Show photo Q*
Can you remember seeing this advertisement on television or in the cinema before?

                                              Col. 48
    Yes   1
    No...............................   2

Q.27 d *Show photo R*
Can you remember seeing this advertisement on television or in the cinema before?

                                              Col. 49
    Yes   1
    No...............................   2

Q.27 e *Show photo S*
Can you remember seeing this advertisement on television or in the cinema before?

                                              Col. 50
    Yes   1
    No...............................   2

Q.27 f *Show photo T*
Can you remember seeing this advertisement on television or in the cinema before?

                                              Col. 50
    Yes   3
    No...............................   4

Now go to Q.32 and check if it is to be asked. If not, go straight to classification.

Q.28 *Ask if television or cinema advertising mentioned at Q.25 or Q.26*
Please would you describe to me any television/cinema advertisements that you have seen in the last 12 months about drinking and driving. Please would you tell me anything that you remember about what happened in the advertisement? *Probe vague/ambiguous answers.* Ask 'Anything else?' *Twice (Max) and record probed answers in brackets*
Do you remember any other recent TV/cinema advertisement? What happened in that?
Keep different ads separate as far as possible

D.P. USE ONLY

	Col. 51–62

Hand respondent Photos G, J, Q, R, S, T
These are photograph stills from 6 different advertisements.

Q.29 Is any of these the advertisement(s) you were just describing?

	Col. 63 Yes (Ring)	No (Tick)
Photo G.............................1..........		☐
Photo J ....2..........		☐
Photo Q.............................3..........		☐
Photo R.............................4..........		☐
Photo S ....5..........		☐
Photo T.............................6..........		☐

Q.31   Q.30

Q.30 *For each 'No' (was not describing) At Q.29, ask Q.30 but not Q.31 for that photo*

Can you remember seeing this advertisement on television or in the cinema before?

	Col. 64 Yes (Ring)	No (Tick)
Photo G.............................1..........		☐
Photo J ....2..........		☐
Photo Q.............................3..........		☐
Photo R.............................4..........		☐
Photo S ....5..........		☐
Photo T.............................6..........		☐

For each 'Yes' (was describing) at Q.29, ask Q.31

*Point to photo, then remove from sight**

Q.31 What was this particular advertisement trying to tell you?

Probe vague/ambiguous answers. Ask 'Anything else?' Twice Max. and record answers in brackets.

	DP USE ONLY Cols 65–77
PHOTO G:	
PHOTO J:	
PHOTO Q:	
PHOTO R:	
PHOTO S:	

Q.32 *Ask Q.32 if radio advertising mentioned at Q.25 code 4 or Q.26 code 2*

Please would you describe to me any radio advertisements that you have heard in the last 12 months about drinking and driving? Please would you tell me everything that you remember from the advertisement.
Probe vague/ambiguous answers. Ask 'anything else?' Twice (max) and record probed answers in brackets.

	DP USE ONLY Cols. 78–79

Q.33 When we came to see you before, what did you think was the main point of *that* stage of the survey?
Probe vague/ambiguous answers. Ask 'anything else?' Twice (max) and record probed answers in brackets.

Carry on with classification at beginning of questionnaire, then thank respondent for taking part.

OFFICE USE ONLY | Card 2 Repeat Cols — Col. 5/2

RECORD
IN HALF
PINTS

TOTAL BEER CONSUMPTION | (6) | (7) | (8) |

TOTAL CIDER CONSUMPTION | (9) | (10) |

TOTAL SPIRITS CONSUMPTION | (11) | (12) |

TOTAL SHERRY/WINE CONSUMPTION | (13) | (14) |

TOTAL OTHER DRINKS CONSUMPTION | (15) | (16) |

TOTAL DRINKS CONSUMPTION | (17) | (18) | (19) |

HIGHEST DRINK CONSUMPTION ON
ANY ONE OCCASION | (20) | (21) |

HIGHEST DRINK CONSUMPTION ON
OCCASION WHEN DROVE | (22) | (23) |

TOTAL OCCASIONS | (24) | (25) |

TOTAL OCCASIONS WHEN DRANK
FOUR OR MORE UNITS | (26) | (27) |

TOTAL OCCASIONS WHEN DROVE | (28) | (29) |

TOTAL OCCASIONS WHEN DRANK
FOUR OR MORE UNITS *AND* DROVE | (30) | (31) |

| (32) | (33) |

Applied Marketing and Social Research 2nd Edition
Edited by Ute Bradley
©Copyright John Wiley 1987

15. Developing a New Index of Crime: The British Crime Survey

Mike Hough *Home Office Research and Planning Unit*

While students may be aware of the wealth of statistics produced by government, fewer may know about the nature and extent of government survey research activities.

The British Crime Survey, sponsored by the Home Office and discussed here, demonstrates many of the problems which have to be tackled in social research. For example:

— the need to develop clear definitions;
— to compare different data sets (e.g. police statistics and survey data);
— to make empirical contributions to understand the issues involved. In this particular case, contributions were made to a better understanding of the extent and fear of crime, attitudes to the punishment of offenders and the geographical distribution of crime.

The data sets from the British Crime Survey are held by the ESRC Archive and teachers and students alike may wish to undertake secondary analysis of the data, with the sample questionnaires and the follow-up references to guide them. Even on a small scale, re-analysis of data would provide a most useful exercise in the development of research hypotheses.

The British Crime Survey (BCS) is a large sample survey whose main purpose is to provide an index of crime. This paper discusses the rationale of crime surveys, describes the design and organisation of the BCS, presents some of its main findings and discusses its impact and future.

THE RATIONALE FOR CRIME SURVEYS

Recorded crime has increased sevenfold since the war. But this apparently stark fact may not mean all that it seems at first sight. Far from all crimes are reported to the police, and not all of reported crimes are recorded; there is a large proportion of crimes which never find their way into police records — which criminologists refer to as the 'Dark Figure'. Changes in the level of recorded crime may thus reflect either changes in crimes *committed* or changes in the proportion *recorded*. The implication is that statistics of recorded crime can only be used to measure the extent of crime if the proportions reported and recorded, are constant over place and time.

Despite the improbability of a constant 'Dark Figure', recorded crime statistics have for generations been pressed into service not only to measure the workload imposed on the system, but also to show the extent of crime. In the absence of alternatives, it is hardly surprising that police statistics have been used in this way; in the formation of social policy, some information is usually better than none at all. What is needed, of course, is a measure of crime independent of processes designed to control crime. It is only recently — with improved facilities for computer analysis, and better survey methodology — that crime surveys have made such measures possible.

Surveys of victimisation — crime surveys for short — typically question a randomly selected sample of the population about their experiences as victims of selected crimes. Grossed up, the results yield estimates of the extent of these crimes, and surveys repeated over time can help show crime trends. National crime surveys have now been carried out in several countries including the United States (annually since 1972), Canada, Australia, Holland and the Republic of Ireland. In this country, the General Household Survey has intermittently carried questions on residential burglary since 1972. The British Crime Survey (BCS) was first carried out in 1982 in England and Wales (Hough and Mayhew[1]) and in Scotland (Chambers and Tombs[2]); the second sweep was conducted two years later — but not in Scotland — (Hough and Mayhew[3]), and a third is planned for 1988. A number of local surveys have also been carried out in Britain, notably in Nottinghamshire and adjacent counties (Farrington and Dowds[4]), in Merseyside (Kinsey[5]) and in Islington (Young et al.[6])

The great strength of crime surveys is that their image of crime has not been refracted through the workings of the criminal justice system. There are many counterbalancing limitations, however (see, e.g. Skogan[7] and Sparks[8]). They can only uncover crimes which have clearly identifiable people as victims — they cannot easily count crimes against organisations (such as company fraud, shoplifting or fare evasion) and 'victimless crimes' involving, for example, drug abuse or some sexual offences. It is also well established that people fail to report to interviewers all the relevant incidents which they have experienced within the so-called 'recall' period, and that they also report incidents which had in fact occurred earlier — a phenomenon referred to as 'telescoping'. There is some evidence of systematic 'response bias': for example, better-educated respondents seem more adept at recalling relevant events at interview; and middle-class respondents seem more prepared than others to define certain classes of incident as assaults. It must be remembered that crime survey findings are based on only a sample of the population and error may arise because of this; the percentage sampling error is particularly large for relatively rare crimes such as robbery and rape. The extent of the error depends on sample size, so there is an inevitable trade-off between the expense of a survey and its precision. Crime surveys always seem to their sponsors to cost too much (the two sweeps of the BCS costed in the region of £240,000 each), and researchers always feel that the samples they are permitted are too small.

Finally, there are some important conceptual issues to do with the nature of incidents counted by crime surveys — are these crimes as defined by criminal law? Or according to the definitions embedded in police practice? Or as popularly defined — however that might be? Crime surveys employ more inclusive definitions of the offences with which they are concerned than do the police or — quite possibly — the public. To summarise a complex argument, statistics of recorded crime count incidents reported to the police which could be punished by a court and *should* occupy the attention of the criminal justice system. Both public and police inevitably make value judgements in deciding whether an incident requires the attention of the criminal justice system — and the resultant count of recorded crime reflects these judgements. The BCS, on the other hand, counts a category of actions which, according to the letter of the law and regardless of the value in doing so, *could* be punished. Crime surveys count a broader, and more value-free category of incidents than police statistics — of necessity if they are to be able to detect shifts in reporting and recording practice over place or time.

Many crime surveys, including the BCS, do not simply count crimes, but collect extra information about crime and victims. Police statistics to date provide surprisingly little information about the characteristics of victims or about the detail of offences. By collecting detailed information about crimes and victims, crime surveys can offer — at least for the offences they cover — a fuller picture of people at risk, the reasons why they are at risk, and the nature of both reported and unreported offences. The BCS has also collected information on a wide range of other crime-related topics including fear of crime, experience of the police and attitudes to punishment.

SOME FEATURES OF THE BCS DESIGN

The decision to go ahead with a national crime survey in England and Wales was taken by the Home Office in 1981. The potential benefits of crime surveys had been recognised for some time, but the financial cost, and the risk of uncovering a politically damaging 'Dark Figure' had previously acted as disincentives. Once the decision to go ahead had been taken, the Home Office Research and Planning Unit (RPU) placed a contract with Social and Community Planning Research (SCPR). The design of the first BCS was shared between the RPU and SCPR; SCPR were responsible for fieldwork which took place in early 1982, and data preparation, whilst the RPU carried out analysis and preparation of reports. The Scottish Home and Health Department commissioned a parallel survey in Scotland, using the same design and questionnaire. A second sweep of the survey was carried out in early 1984, with NOP Market Research as contractors—though only in England and Wales—and a third sweep is planned for 1988. In the first and second sweeps of the survey, a number of academic researchers were engaged as consultants; they provided valuable help both in designing the survey and in presenting findings. The first two sweeps share very similar designs, of course; the need for comparability between sweeps places a strong disincentive on reconsidering decisions taken for the first sweep. The design discussed below is that of the second sweep.

The Questionnaire

The BCS aimed not only to estimate crime levels, but to provide a range of extra information on matters related to crime. The full 1984 questionnaire covered victimisation, demographic details and questions relating to: fear of crime; perceptions of crime risk; attitudes to the seriousness of crime; attitudes to punishment and the sentencing of offenders; attitudes to Neighbourhood Watch schemes; the impact of crime on victims and their views about Victim Support schemes; and self-reported offending.

The questionnaire was divided into four parts: the Main Questionnaire; the Victim Form—which collected detailed information about victimisation; the Follow-up Questionnaire; and the Demographic Questionnaire. The Main Questionnaire 'screened' people to see if they or other members of their household had been the victim of crime. For *personal crimes*—assaults, robberies, thefts from the person, other personal thefts and sexual offences—respondents were asked only about their own experience. For *household crimes*—burglary, thefts of and from vehicles, vandalism and theft from the home—they were also asked about the experience of others in their household. This distinction reflects the fact that for some crimes, such as burglary, the household is the natural unit of analysis, whilst for others, the individual is a more sensible choice. The 'reference period' which respondents had to scan for victimisations was the previous calendar year, 1983, together with the month or so in 1984 preceding interview. Methodological studies indicate that with a reference period this long, people both forget trivial incidents, and 'telescope' the date of incidents occurring earlier, reporting them as occurring within the reference period. The American National Crime Survey employs a panel design to avoid the problems associated with telescoping, and uses only a six month reference period, but both these options were ruled out on grounds of cost for the BCS. Given the sample size with which the Home Office could afford, a six month reference period would yield too few victims for sub-group analysis; and a panel design would have involved wasted interviews.

Respondents were not asked to report by proxy on personal crimes experienced by other members of the household, because American work suggested that this leads to substantial undercounting; and the additional cost ruled out interviewing the entire household. There were two versions of the Main Questionnaire; half of all Main Questionnaires required Victim Forms to be completed when respondents reported experience of vandalism; the other half did not. This was done — given the frequency of incidents of vandalism — again to reduce costs and interviewer workloads.

Details of each incident revealed by the screen questions were collected on *Victim Forms*. An arbitrary limit of four forms was imposed. All victims and two out of five non-victims completed a *Follow-up* Questionnaire, which covered most of the attitudinal items on fear of crime, attitudes to punishment, crime seriousness etc. Only a sub-sample completed the Follow-up Questionnaire, as the items in it did not require the same precision as those on victimisation; with financial savings in mind, the sample was reduced. Demographic details were collected at the end of the interview from all respondents.

Interviews, conducted in respondents' homes, were often very long. Those victims answering all four parts of the questionnaire were interviewed on average for an hour and ten minutes; non-victims who completed the Follow-up Questionnaire were interviewed for just over 45 minutes; interviews with non-victims who were issued only the Main Questionnaire took on average 25 minutes.

The Sample

The BCS sample was designed to give a representative cross-section of people aged 16 and over living in private households whose addresses appear in the Electoral Register. Although the American National Crime Survey interviews people aged 12 or over — and teenagers emerge as frequent victims — it was not regarded as practicable to interview people under 16 in this country. The

Electoral Register was chosen in 1981 as the most convenient sampling frame at the time, and in the interests of continuity this decision was not reconsidered in the second sweep. This sampling frame does not cover all addresses of private households: about 4% are omitted nationally—more in inner cities. Methods are available to fill the gaps, but as these are of questionable reliability and pose difficulties for interviewers, no use was made of them. People living in institutions were not sampled, again to minimise the complexity of the survey.

A five-stage sample design was chosen, the selection stages being: parliamentary constituencies; wards; polling districts; addresses; and individuals. Of the 561 constituencies in England and Wales, 300 were selected for sampling. Because of high crime levels in inner city areas, these were sampled in higher proportion than their population would justify (restoring representativeness in analysis by weighting). Two wards were selected from each constituency, and one polling district from each ward. The comparatively large number of sampling points—600—was chosen to minimise sampling error. As for the selection of individuals at addresses, where the household composition was as specified on the electoral register, interviewers were required to interview only a prespecified 'named elector'. Where the composition of the household differed from the register, interviewers used a randomised grid (Kish grid) to select someone for interview.

Fieldwork

A total of 309 interviewers worked on the second sweep. Of the issued sample of 14 874 addresses, 4% were empty, demolished, or ineligible for interview for other reasons. The remaining 14 277 addresses yielded 11 030 processed interviews, a response rate of 77.3%. In general, the representativeness of the sample was sound, though—as is common—there was a slight shortfall in the 16–19 age group. At 53% of the addresses where no successful interview took place, the selected respondent refused to be interviewed; no contact accounted for most of the other failures. The response rate was 73% in inner cities, 80% elsewhere. The 1982 BCS also had a sample of 11 000, and achieved a slightly higher response rate of 80%.

Weighting

Data from the survey were weighted in a number of ways at the data processing stage. Weighting served two main purposes: to correct imbalances introduced in sampling; and to correct imbalances created by the design of the interview. Weights were applied to correct for the following.

   (i) The inner city imbalance.
  (ii) The mismatch between electors and persons at addresses when data were used to represent the adult population.
 (iii) Household crimes: for crimes (e.g. burglary) where the victim is the household rather than the individual respondent, each record was weighted by a factor of $1/e$, where e was the number of electors relevant to the household;
 (iv) Omission of Follow-up Questionnaire: weighting was applied to restore the correct balance between victims and non-victims.
  (v) Series offences: for series offences (see below), only a single Victim Form was completed. In the analysis of victim incidents, these forms were weighted by the number of incidents involved, with an arbitrary top limit of five.

Series victimisations

When a person is a victim of a number of very similar offences, it is not always possible for him or her to separate them into discrete events. For example, in cases of domestic assault, the victim might have been attacked once a month or more often. In an already lengthy interview, it is also very demanding—if not impossible—for respondents to report on all the incidents separately. Offences of this kind are usually called *series incidents*. In the BCS, interviewers could treat incidents as series provided that they were all very similar in type, were done under the same circumstances and probably committed by the same person(s).

For crimes classified as a series offences, full details were collected only about the most recent incident. In calculating offence rates for 1983, series incidents were given a score equal to the number of incidents in the series occurring in 1983, with an arbitrary top limit of five.

Classifying and Counting Incidents

Incidents were classified by coders using a coding manual drawn up for the first BCS; this was designed in consultation with the Home Office Statistical Department and with the statistics branches of a number of police forces, so as to enable comparison with statistics of offences recorded by the police. A number of incidents in the survey (7% of those for which Victim Forms were completed) were not included in any of the analyses of offences, either because they fell outside the survey's coverage (e.g. burglary of business premises) or because there was insufficient evidence that an offence had occurred. For some categories of offence, there was evidence of coding inconsistency between the two surveys; for example, the threshold at which an assault becomes a wounding seemed to have altered. Computer coding of incidents will be examined as a possibility in the third sweep.

FINDINGS FROM THE BCS

The two sweeps of the BCS amount to a very substantial data-set, and in analysis and report writing, a number of strategies were considered. One option was to attempt to write a definitive and exhaustive report for each sweep. This was rejected on grounds of timeliness: two years could well elapse between fieldwork and publication, by which time the information about the extent of crime would be three years out of date. For the first sweep, therefore, it was decided to prepare a short overview report, and to follow this up with a number of more detailed studies of separate topics. The overview (Hough and Mayhew[1]) was published some six months after the data were handed over to the RPU, and this was followed over the next two years by a dozen or so reports and papers. For the second sweep, a slightly modified strategy was followed, in which a fuller — but by no means comprehensive — report was published within nine months of receipt of a data-tape, again followed by a number of more detailed and focused reports and papers. Some of the key findings to do with the extent of crime are presented below; no attempt is made to cover the full range of findings on attitudes to crime and the criminal justice system.

Figure 15.1 shows BCS estimates of the number of incidents in 1983, by crime type. These estimates have been derived by applying rates for the 1983 sample to the household and adult populations in England and Wales. It should be said that as the estimates are derived from a sample they are subject to sampling error. For instance, the survey's 'best estimate' of the number of incidents of burglary is 904,000: with 95% certainty the number falls between 808,000 and 1,000,000.

As is clear from Fig. 15.1, the vast majority of crimes do not involve violence against the person but are offences against property. Motor vehicles emerge as a strikingly common target: a third of all incidents uncovered by the BCS involved theft of, theft from, or damage of cars, vans or motorcycles, and 20% of owners were the target at least once of some form of vehicle crime in 1983. In most thefts — whether or not they involved motor vehicles — losses were relatively low, exceeding £50 in only about a quarter of cases.

Together, crimes of violence and common assault (which is not a notifiable offence) comprised 17% of the total. Wounding, robbery and sexual offences by themselves formed 5% of all offences. Most assaults and crimes of violence did not result in any serious physical injury; in only 12% of cases did the victim need any sort of professional medical attention, and in 1% of cases

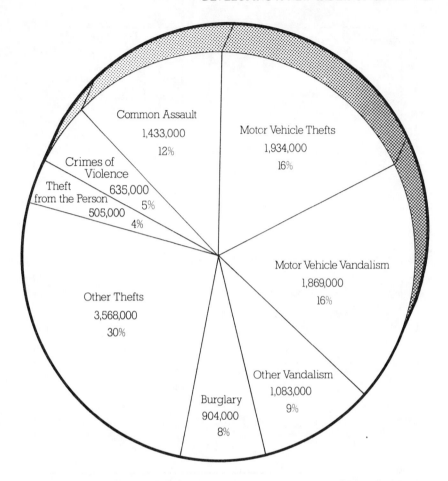

Figure 15.1 Offences in England and Wales, 1983: British Crime Survey estimates. 'Crimes of violence' comprise wounding, robbery and sexual offences. (Unlike common assault, these are all 'notifiable' offences.) 'Motor vehicle thefts' include attempted thefts. 'Other thefts' comprise personal thefts not involving contact with an offender, together with thefts in a dwelling, bicycle thefts and other household thefts not involving vehicles. Percentages do not total 100% because of rounding. Reproduced by permission of the Controller of Her Majesty's Stationery Office.

the victim was admitted to hospital. Victim and offender were unknown to each other in half of cases; one in eight incidents involved family, lovers or ex-lovers—but the BCS probably undercounts domestic violence.

Without any doubt, too, the number of sexual offences is also an underestimate, particularly for offences committed by non-strangers. The screen questions about sexual attack were changed in the 1984 BCS to reduce the evident reticence of victims in the 1982 survey to mention incidents to interviewers. Even so, the number of sexual offences uncovered by the second

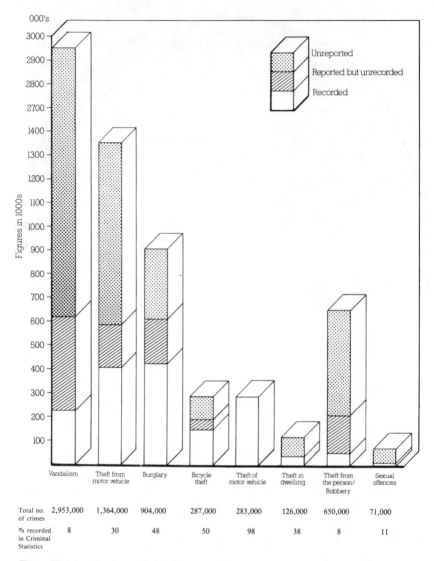

Figure 15.2 Levels of recorded and unrecorded crime, 1983: British Crime Survey estimates. Reproduced by permission of the Controller of Her Majesty's Stationery Office

survey was still very small. The estimate for rape is low, for example. Each sweep of the BCS, interviewing almost 6000 women, uncovered only one attempted rape. On the basis of the number of rapes recorded by the police alone (1800 in 1985), the BCS should uncover on average one rape or attempt every second or third sweep. Making the assumption that only one in ten rapes are recorded, each sweep should uncover four such offences; and if one in 50 rapes gets into police records, each sweep should uncover 20. Women were asked a further question about sexual harassment, though the results were not included in estimates of the extent of crime. Only one in 40 mentioned such incidents. The great majority of these involved strangers, suggesting that respondents did not define incidents involving workmates, friends and relatives according to the terms of the question—or else were not prepared to mention them in a survey interview.

By combining information from the BCS with police statistics, estimates can be derived of the proportion of crimes reported to, and recorded by the police. For crime types which can be compared, Fig. 15.2 shows unreported incidents, those which were reported but not recorded and those which found their way into police records.

Reporting to the Police

A large proportion of incidents went unreported for all categories of crime except vehicle theft. The overall reporting rate for crimes shown in Fig.15.2 was 38%. Rates for selected categories are shown in Table 15.1.

Victims who notified the police were asked why they reported incidents to the police; responses were balanced between self-interest (recovering goods, making insurance claims etc) and a sense of obligation ('You ought to', 'It was a serious crime' etc). Most 'non-reporters' gave as their reasons the triviality of the incident, or the fact that the police would be able to do little. There was, however, a significant number of serious incidents which went unreported. In general, then, reporting to the police turned—almost by definition—on perceptions of offence seriousness. But overlying victims' sense of what properly was or was not grist for the mill of formal justice was a calculation of the costs and benefits to themselves in reporting, and of the chances that the police could actually achieve anything if informed.

Thus Table 15.1 shows that overall, 'seriousness ratings' were high for crimes which were well reported and low for those which were poorly reported. But there were anomalies. Bicycle thefts and thefts from cars were better reported than their average seriousness scores would suggest— presumably because victims wanted to recover property or file insurance claims. And sexual offences showed a very low reporting rate but the highest ratings for seriousness. (This is consistent with the idea that women are reluctant to bring in the police over sexual offences, though it could reflect a quirk of sampling, as so few sexual offences were uncovered by the survey.)

Recording by the Police

Figure 15.2 shows that many of the offences reported to the police do not get recorded as crimes—or do not get recorded in the crime categories shown.

Table 15.1 Percentage of Crimes Reported to Police and Seriousness Ratings, for Selected Crime Categories.

	% reported	Average rating for seriousness
Well-reported crimes		
Theft of cars	99	7.6
Burglary with loss	87	7.9
Bicycle theft	68	4.7
Vandalism over £20 to the home	62	7.2
Wounding	60	7.7
Robbery	57	7.6
Less well-reported crimes		
Attempted and no-loss burglaries	51	6.1
Theft from cars	44	4.2
Common assault	31	5.0
Theft from the person	31	5.0
Poorly-reported crimes		
Theft in a dwelling	23	4.8
Vandalism over £20 to cars	30	4.5
Vandalism under £21 to the home	19	3.8
Sexual offences	10	9.1
Vandalism under £21 to cars	9	2.6

Question on seriousness: 'On this card is a scale to show the seriousness of different crimes, with the scale going from 0 for a very minor crime like theft of milk bottles from a doorstep to 20 for the most serious crime, murder. How would you rate this crime on the scale from 0 to 20? Weighted data: unweighted n = 3425; source BCS, 1984. Reproduced by permission of Her Majesty's Stationery Office.

Overall, for instance, the police would appear to record two-thirds of the property crimes known to them. The BCS offers only imprecise estimates of this 'recording shortfall', both because of errors in the survey estimates and because of the difficulties in comparing like with like when matching BCS offence categories to those used by police statistics. However, the first and second surveys yielded similar estimates, and there can be little doubt that many reported incidents are not recorded in those crime categories suggested by victims' descriptions.

One likely reason for the shortfall is that the police do not accept victims' accounts of incidents; they may—quite rightly—think that a report of an incident is mistaken or disingenuous, or may feel that there is simply insufficient evidence to say that a crime has been committed. Some incidents *will* have been recorded, of course, but in different crime categories—where, for example, it is indisputable that criminal damage has been committed, but less clear that a burglary has been attempted. Some incidents may have been regarded as too trivial to warrant formal police action—particularly if complainants indicated they wanted the matter dropped or were unlikely to give evidence, or if the incident had already been satisfactorily resolved.

Three offence categories show no shortfall at all — sexual offences, thefts of motor vehicles and theft in a dwelling; in the fact the BCS estimates of *reported* crime are lower than the number of recorded crimes. As the BCS estimate for sexual offences is unreliable, little can be said about the discrepancy here. For thefts of motor vehicles the discrepancy was small, and may have arisen simply through BCS measurement error. For thefts in a dwelling, the discrepancy was large, and may be accounted for by differences in classification: some of the incidents which the BCS would classify as burglary may have been judged by the police to be the lesser offence of theft in a dwelling, perhaps because there was insufficient evidence of trespass.

Changes in Crime over Time

Now that two sweeps of the BCS have been carried out, it is possible to say a little about the movement in crime. What can be said, of course, is rather limited, as two surveys do not provide a strong base on which to make inferences. The sampling errors attached to victimisation rates for the respective years mean that only large changes register as statistically significant. And even significant changes may not necessarily reflect a change in underlying reality: they could arise, for example, from unintended changes in survey procedure.

As shown in Table 15.2, there was over the period 1981–1983 a statistically significant 10% rise in the number of household offences taken together ($p < 0.05$). However, within the household offences category, only the increase in burglary was statistically significant at the 5% level, although the increase in bicycle thefts approached it. The 21% increase in burglary reflects a rapid rise in the number of *attempts*; when these are excluded, there is a much shallower increase of 11% (ns; $p > 0.10$). Part of the increase in bicycle theft is probably attributable to increased ownership amongst adults and especially amongst children. (The vogue for 'BMX' bikes only emerged after 1981.) The 6% increase in all personal offences was not statistically significant. The increase in sexual offences is unreliable, as explained, because of deliberate questionnaire changes.

Do recorded crime figures show a similar increase to that identified by the BCS? Limiting comparison to those crime types which can most reliably be compared, the BCS shows a 10% increase in crime — broadly in line with the 12% increase in recorded crime figures. Nevertheless, there is a divergence of 2%. This is not statistically significant; in other words, the divergence could simply reflect sampling error. But it might also have arisen from increased reporting or recording. The former seems likely, as the survey found that reporting levels increased between 1981 and 1983. Overall, there was a (statistically significant, $p < 0.05$) rise from 31% to 34% in the proportion of offences reported to the police.

Table 15.2   Offences in England and Wales, 1981 and 1983: British Crime Survey Estimate

		1981	1983	% change
1.	Vandalism	2,714,000	2,953,000	+ 9
2.	Theft from motor vehicle	1,272,000	1,364,000	+ 7
3.	Burglary in a dwelling	745,000	904,000	+21**
4.	Theft of motor vehicle	283,000	283,000	—
5.	Bicycle theft	214,000	287,000	+34*
6.	Theft in a dwelling	124,000	126,000	+ 2
7.	Other households thefts	1,535,000	1,671,000	+ 9
8.	Assaults	1,909,000	1,852,000	− 3
9.	Theft from person/robbery	596,000	650,000	+ 9
10.	Sexual offences	33,000	71,000	[+ 115]
11.	Other personal thefts	1,559,000	1,770,000	+14
	All household offences (1–7)	6,887,000	7,588,000	+ 10**
	All personal offences (8–11)	4,097,000	4,343,000	+ 6

Double-starred figures are statistically significant at the 5% level (one-tailed test, taking complex standard error into account). This means that the chances are less than one in 20 that the increase has arisen simply through sampling error. Single-starred figures are statistically at the 10% level. The increase in sexual offences will be due to questionnaire changes.
Categories 3, 7, 9, 10 and 11 include attempts. Reproduced by permission of the Controller of Her Majesty's Stationery Office

Comparison of survey estimates with police statistics is possible over a longer period for household burglary. Combining the GHS and the BCS, survey estimates can be calculated for the years 1972, 1973, 1979, 1980, 1981 and 1983. Figure 15.3 compares survey estimates of burglaries involving loss to police statistics over the 11-year period. The latter have doubled while together the surveys indicate an increase of the order of 20%. This divergence is sufficiently marked as to leave little doubt that police statistics exaggerate the increase since 1972 in burglary rates; the divergence between the two sets of figures can be explained by increased reporting to the police and increased recording by the police.

Other Findings

The British Crime Survey was one of the first studies in Britain to attempt any comprehensive assessment of fear of crime. Table 15.3, which originates from the first sweep of the survey, compares, by age and sex, fear of crime and the extent to which people fall victim to 'street crime'. (This term is used to refer to any robbery, theft from the person, assault or other attack in public open space.) Those who felt most unsafe were women and the elderly; the table demonstrates the apparent paradox that those who are most fearful are least often victims. These findings do not necessarily mean that fear of crime is irrational or excessive, however. In the first place, some people —

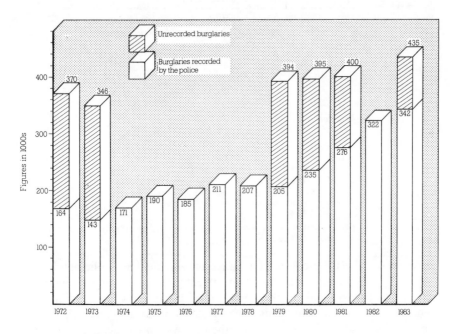

Figure 15.3 Recorded and unrecorded burglaries involving loss, 1972–1983. Figures for unrecorded burglaries (hatched) are derived from the GHS for 1972, '73, '79 and '80, and from the BCS for '81 and '83. The BCS figures have been calculated to be comparable to the GHS figures. The unhatched part of the columns are burglaries involving loss recorded by the police (ie, residential burglaries minus nil-value cases). GHS respondents were asked about their experiences 'during the last 12 months', a period which usually began before the relevant calendar year shown in the figure. Reproduced by permission of the Controller of Her Majesty's Stationery Office

the elderly in particular—are far more vulnerable to the consequences of victimisation. And secondly, those who are most fearful may expose themselves to least risk, thus avoiding victimisation. For example, the elderly go out less than others, and consequently they are less at risk of street crime and their homes less at risk of burglary. Again, young men are not afraid of a fight, and get into fights; older people do not. The BCS cannot claim to have solved the question of the 'rationality' of fear, but its findings have helped place the issue firmly on the agenda of criminological debate.

Another area where the BCS has been made a substantial empirical contribution is public attitudes to the punishment of offenders. It has generally been assumed—especially in the media—that the general public is intolerant of the supposed leniency of the courts in dealing with

Table 15.3   Fears for Personal Safety after Dark and
Risks of 'Street Crime'.

	feeling 'very unsafe' (%)	*victims of 'street crime' (%)*
Men		
16–30	1	7.7
31–60	2	1.6
61 +	9	0.6
Women		
16–30	15	2.8
31–60	17	1.4
61 +	34	1.2

Question: 'How safe do you feel walking alone in this area
after dark?'
Weighted data: unweighted n = 10,905
Source: 1982 British Crime Survey
Reproduced by permission of the Controller of Her Majesty's
Stationery Office

offenders. The BCS, however, has suggested that neither public opinion nor victims' views are more punitive than current practice. Though people think the courts are too lenient, this seems to be because they overestimate the lenience of current sentencing. When asked what sentences they think specified offenders ought to receive, their answers are generally in line with current court practice (Hough and Moxon[9]).

The Acorn classification of neighbourhoods developed by CACI has proved an especially useful analytic tool. Acorn stands for 'A Classification of Residential Neighbourhoods'; it is a system for classifying households according to the demographic, employment and housing characteristics of their immediate area, based on data from the 1981 Census. In the second BCS, postcodes of all BCS respondents were recorded, enabling an Acorn code to be assigned to each. In assessing the geographical distribution of crime, the 11-fold classification of neighbourhood groups describes high- and low-risk areas very well: attitudes to crime and criminal justice also vary considerably across the 11 groups.

Though there is not enough space to discuss other results of interest here, some idea of the range of published findings can be derived from the following list of titles:

(a) Elderly Victims of Crime and Exposure to Risk.
(b) Victims of Crime: the Dimensions of Risk.
(c) Building Design and Burglary.
(d) Residential burglary: Findings from the BCS.
(e) Fear of Crime in England and Wales.
(f) Target-hardening: How much of an Answer?

(g) Crime in England and Wales and Scotland: a BCS Comparison.

(h) Self-reported Cannabis Use in Great Britain in 1981.

(i) Public Reactions to Police Behaviour: Some Findings from the BCS.

(j) Drivers' Beliefs about Alcohol and the Law.

(k) Contacts between Police and Public: Findings from the BCS.

(l) Victims of Violent Crime.

(m) The Impact of Victimisation: Findings from the BCS.

(n) Dealing with Offenders: Popular Justice and the Views of Victims'.

(o) Drinking Drivers: the Limits to Deterrence?

(p) Attitudes to Neighbourhood Watch.

(q) Crime Seriousness: Findings from the 1984 BCS.

(r) Obscene Telephone Calls in England and Wales.

(s) Incidents of Violence: Findings from the British Crime Survey.

(t) Penal Hawks and Penal Doves: Attitudes to Punishment in the BCS.

(u) If at First you don't Succeed: BCS Findings on Attempted Burglary.

TAKING STOCK

The two sweeps of the BCS carried out so far have yielded a very large amount of information about crime. They have demonstrated the extent of a range of crimes against people and property, including unreported and unrecorded incidents. They have yielded a great deal of additional information on people's attitudes to crime and the criminal justice system. The BCS has undoubtedly had an impact on the discussion of crime and criminal justice: before a national survey of victimisation, few acknowledged the problems in using police statistics as an index of crime, and those who did so generally ignored them. There is now a far greater awareness of the capacity of such statistics to mislead.

If the core contribution of the BCS is to offer an alternative index of crime, it has increasingly paid its way via the information it can generate about the risks of crime and about attitudes to crime. Its contribution necessarily has been in the definition and clarification of policy issues, rather than in their solutions. It is probably true to say that within the boundaries of criminology, the survey is the most heavily referenced piece of empirical research in the eighties.

A further — and still emergent — contribution of the BCS is as a resource for independent academic research. With large data sets, the commissioning agencies are rarely able to exhaust the potential for analysis: nor is it especially desirable that such analysis should be informed by the perspective of a single group of researchers. Both data sets have been lodged with the ESRC Data Archive, (location: University of Essex, Wivenhoe Park, Colchester, Essex CO4 3QS) and at the last count one or both were mounted in a dozen universities and polytechnics. Secondary analysis should help exploit the data sets more fully, and in the longer term, the availability of the data should help foster analytic expertise amongst criminologists, with consequent benefits to future sweeps of the BCS and to other survey research.

As for the future of the survey, the third and further sweeps should yield more firmly based crime trends and provide additional information on people's attitudes to crime and criminal behaviour. There are inherent limitations to surveys of victimisation, and their costs are high. But crime surveys provide the only available yardstick on the extent of crime which includes incidents unrecorded by the police: without them, it is hard to know whether police statistics accurately reflect underlying trends. Now that such measures are available, it is difficult to argue convincingly that they should not be used.

REFERENCES

1. Hough, M. and Mayhew, P., *The British Crime Survey: First Report*, Home Office Research Study No. 76, HMSO (1983).
2. Chambers G. and Tombs, J. (Eds). *The British Crime Survey: Scotland*, A Scottish Office Social Research Study, HMSO (1984).
3. Hough, M. and Mayhew, P., *Taking Account of Crime: Key Findings from the 1984 British Crime Survey*, Home Office Research Study No. 85, HMSO (1985).
4. Farrington, D. P. and Dowds, E. A. (1985). 'Disentangling criminal behaviour and police reaction', In *Reaction to Crime: the Public the Police Courts and Prisons* Farrington, D. P. and Gunn, J. John Wiley & Sons (1985).
5. Kinsey, R., *Merseyside Crime Survey: First Report November 1984*, available from the Police Committee Support Unit, Metropolitan House, Old Hall Street, Liverpool L69 3EL (1984).
6. Young, J. *et al.*, *The Islington Crime Survey*, Middlesex Polytechnic (1986).
7. Skogan, W. G. *Issues in the Measurement of Victimization*, Bureau of Justice Statistics, US Department of Justice, US Government Printing Office (1981).
8. Sparks, R. F., *Research on Victims of Crime: Accomplishments Issues and New Directions*, National Institute of Mental Health, Centre for Studies of Crime and Delinquency, Rockville, MD, USA (1982).
9. Hough, M. and Moxon, D.,[1] Dealing with offenders: Public Opinion and the Views of Victims. *Howard Journal*, **24** (1985) 160–175.

ACKNOWLEDGMENT

The figures and tables in this chapter are reproduced by permission of the Controller of Her Majesty's Stationery Office and the questionnaires by courtesy of NOP.

APPENDIX 15.1   *1984 BRITISH CRIME SURVEY*

The Questionnaire comprises four parts, which are completed as indicated.

(i) Main Questionnaire	:	all respondents.
(ii) Victim Form	:	one for each victimisation, up to a limit of four
(iii) Follow-up Questionnaire	:	all victims, two-fifths of others.
(iv) Demographic Questionnaire:		all respondents.

There are two versions of the Main Questionnaire. On Version 1 (black on coloured copies) at Q. 49 positive answers to the 'screener' questions at Qs 18, 30, 38 and 42 lead to a Victim Form. On Version 2 (blue on coloured copies) they do not, this to halve the number of Victims Form completed for vandalism incidents. Version 2 is shown here.

There are also two versions of the Follow-up Questionnaire. There is only one small difference between them. At Q. 18(b) on Version 1 (orange on coloured copies), the 'typical' offender is a male aged 17, who has previously been in trouble. On Version 2 (green on coloured copies), the offender is aged 25. Version 1 is shown here.

Respondents use a series of showcards. Showcards are not attached. However, items on most showcards are clear from the Questionnaire.

NOP/9888   AREA CODE

(5)   (6)   (7)

SERIAL NO.

(8)   (9)

1984 BRITISH CRIME SURVEY
MAIN QUESTIONNAIRE

Complete this questionnaire for all respondents
with serial numbers ending in an even number   (02)   (10/11)

TIME MAIN QUESTIONNAIRE STARTED ....   (2)   (12)

Q.1   I would like you first of all to think of the area round here, and what you think are the best and worst things about living here. Firstly, can you tell me what you personally think are the best things about living in this area? Anything else? *Code all that apply*

	(13)	
Transport/access to places	1	
Shops	2	
Parks/sports/leisure facilities	3	
Schools/colleges	4	
Housing	5	
Quiet/peaceful.	6	
Friendly/near friends/good		
neighbours	7	
Safe/lack of crime	8	
General convenience of the area	9	
Good area/just like it	0	
In countryside/near		
countryside.	X	
Know the area/it's familiar	Y	(13/14)
Other (*Write in fully and code*)		

	(14)
_____	1
Nothing	2
Don't know	3

Q.2 And what would you say are the worst things about living in this area? Anything else?

```
                                                        (15)
_____            1  2  3
_____            4  5  6
_____            7  8  9
_____            0  X  Y
```

If more than one thing mentioned ask: Of the problems you have mentioned, which *one* do you think is the worst problem?

```
                                                        (16)
_____            1  2  3
_____            4  5  6
_____            7  8  9
_____            0  X  Y
```

Q.3 Overall, how satisfied or dissatisfied are you with living in the area?

Very satisfied.	1	(17)
Satisfied	2	
Dissatisfied.	3	
Very dissatisfied	4	
Don't know	5	

Q.4 In some neighbourhoods people do things together and try to help each other while in other areas people mostly go their own way. In general, what kind of neighbourhood would you say you live in; is it one where people mostly help each other, or where people mostly go their own way?

Help each other	1	
Go own way	2	(18)

Mixture........................... 3
Don't know........................ 4

Q.5 How difficult is it for you to tell a stranger in your neighbourhood from someone who lives here? Is it . . .
Read out
Very easy 1
Fairly easy 2
Fairly difficult.................... 3   (19)
Very difficult..................... 4
Don't know........................ 5

Q.6 How long have you lived in this area?
Under 1 year...................... 1
1 but under 5 years 2
5 but under 10 years 3   (20)
10 but under 20 years 4
20 years or more.................. 5

Q.7 (a) How safe do you feel walking alone in this area after dark. Would you say you feel . . . (*read out*) (*Note: If respondent never goes out alone at night, Probe . . . 'How safe would you feel . . . ?*)

Very safe .... 1 GO TO Q.8
Fairly safe 2

A bit unsafe .... 3 ASK Q.7(b)   (21)
or Very unsafe 4

Q.7 (b) Why do you feel unsafe?
Fear of being mugged 1
Too dark 2
No-one about 3
Hearsay (what other people say) 4
People hanging about/gangs/
    strange people 5
General fear something may happen ... 6   (22)
Other (*write in and ring*)
_____ 7
Don't know........................ 8

Ask all
Q.8 Most of us worry at some time or other about being the victim of a crime, and I would like you to tell me how worried you are about being the victim of different types of crime.
Showcard A Using one of the phrases on this card, could you tell me how worried you are about . . . having your home broken into . . .
Read out each crime in turn

		Very worried	Fairly worried	Not very worried	Not at all worried	Don't know	
(a)	Having your home broken into and something stolen	1	2	3	4	5	(23)
(b)	Being mugged and robbed	1	2	3	4	5	(24)

(c)–(d) Ask women only. Men go to (e)

(c)	Being raped	1	2	3	4	5	(25)
(d)	Being sexually molested or pestered	1	2	3	4	5	(26)

Ask all

(e)	Having your home or property damaged by vandals	1	2	3	4	5	(27)
(f)	Being attacked by strangers	1	2	3	4	5	(28)
(g)	Being insulted or bothered by strangers	1	2	3	4	5	(29)

Q.9 (a) I would now like to talk about the chance of certain crimes happening. Some crimes are of course, more likely to happen to some people than to others. I am going to read out a list of crimes and for each one, I would like you to tell me from this card *Showcard B* how likely you think this crime is to happen to you in the next year. *Read out each in turn and code below.*

	Certain to	Very likely	Fairly likely	Fairly unlikely	Not at all likely	Certain not to	Don't know	
Having your home or property damaged by vandals	1	2	3	4	5	6	7	(30)
Being mugged and robbed	1	2	3	4	5	6	7	(31)
Being attacked by strangers	1	2	3	4	5	6	7	(32)
Having your home broken into and something taken	1	2	3	4	5	6	7	(33)

Ask women only

Being raped ....1 .....2 ..... 3 ......4 .... 5 ......6 7   (34)

Being sexually molested
or pestered .... 1 .....2 ..... 3 ......4 .... 5 ......6 7   (35)

Q.9   (b) Thinking about a hundred houses around here, about how many
      of these hundred houses do you think will be burgled in the next year?
      If don't know ask: Well how many would you guess?

      WRITE IN   [| |]   (36/38)

      (No idea = XXX)   (36)   (37)   (38)

Q.9   (c) Do you think your own chances of being burgled are about the
      same as everyone else's around here, or more, or less than everyone
      else's around here?

      About the same   1
      More than everyone else's............   2
      Less than everyone else's   3   (39)
      No idea...........................   4

Q.9   (d) And thinking about a hundred average people around here of all
      different types, about how many of these hundred people do you think
      will be mugged in the next year? *If don't know ask:* Well how many
      would you guess?

      WRITE IN   [| |]   (40/42)

      (No idea = XXX)   (40)   (41)   (42)

Q.9   (e) Do you think your own chances of being mugged are about the
      same as everyone else's around here or more, or less than everyone
      else's around here?

      About the same   1
      More than everyone else's............   2
      Less than everyone else's   3   (43)
      No idea...........................   4

Q.10 For the following things I read out, can you tell me if they are very
      common, fairly common, not very common, or not at all common
      in your area. Firstly, how common or uncommon are . . . *Read out
      each in turn and code below*

		Very Common	Fairly Common	Not very Common	Not at all Common	Don't know	
(a)	Noisy neighbours or loud parties	1	2	3	4	5	(44)
(b)	Graffiti on walls or buildings	1	2	3	4	5	(45)
(c)	Teenagers hanging around on the streets	1	2	3	4	5	(46)
(d)	Drunks or tramps on the streets	1	2	3	4	5	(47)
(e)	Rubbish and litter lying about	1	2	3	4	5	(48)

EXPERIENCE AS A VICTIM

The next few questions concern things that may have happened to you over the *thirteen/fourteen* months since the first of January 1983, in which you may have been the victim of a crime or offence. I am only concerned with incidents which have happened to you personally or to other members of your household — that is people living with you and catered for by the same person as you.

I don't just want to know about serious incidents — I want to know about small things too. It is often difficult to remember exactly when things happen, so I will take the questions slowly and I would like you to think carefully about them.

First, I need to ask a few questions to find out which parts of the questionnaire apply to you and which don't.

Q.11 First of all does anyone in this household own or have the regular use of a motorcycle, scooter or moped?

Yes	1 GO TO Q.13
No	2 ASK Q.12

(49)

Q.12 Can I check, has anyone in this household owned or had the regular use of a motorcycle, scooter or moped at any time since the first of January 1983?

Yes 1

No 2   (50)

Ask all

Q.13 Does anyone in this household own or have the regular use of a car, van or other motor vehicle?

Yes .... | 1 GO TO Q.15
No.............................. | 2 ASK Q.14   (51)

Q.14 Can I just check: has anyone in this household owned or had the regular use of a car, van or other motor vehicle at any time since the first of January 1983?

Yes 1
No.............................. 2   (52)

Q.15 *Interviewer check — Is there a 'Yes' answer at Q.11 or Q.12 or Q.13 or Q.14*

Yes .... | A ASK Q.16
No.............................. | B GO TO Q.19

Q.16 During the *thirteen/fourteen* months since the first of January 1983 have you or anyone else now in your household had their car, van, motorcycle or other motor vehicle *stolen* or driven away without permission? How many times?

Write in number of times, if none code 00   (53/54)

(53) (54)

Q.17 And in the time since the first of January 1983 has anyone had anything *stolen off their vehicle or out of it* (parts of the vehicle, personal possession or other things)? How many times?

Write in number of times, if none code 00   (55/56)

(55) (56)

Q.18 And apart from this, in that time has anyone had their vehicle *tampered with or damaged* by vandals or people out to steal? How many times?

Write in number of times, if none code 00   (57/58)

(57) (58)

Ask all

Q.19 Does anyone in this household own a bicycle?

Yes	1 GO TO Q.21	(59)
No...............................	2 ASK Q.20	

Q.20 Can I just check, has anyone in this household owned a bicycle at any time since the first of January 1983?

Yes	1 ASK Q.21	(60)
No...............................	2 GO TO Q.22	

Q.21 During the *thirteen/fourteen* months since the first of January 1983, have you or anyone else now in your household had a bicycle stolen? How many times?

Write in number of times, if none code 00   (61/62)

(61)   (62)

NB: If two bicycles taken at one time, count as one incident

Q.22 Can I just check: how many years have you lived at this address?

Less than 1 year	1 GO TO Q.24	
1 but less than 2 years...............	2 ASK Q.23	
2 but less than 5 years...............	3	(63)
5 but less than 10 years..............	4 GO TO	
10 years or more.....................	5 Q.32	

Q.23 Were you living at this address on the first of January 1983?

Yes	1 GO TO Q.32	(64)
No.............................	2 ASK Q.24	

Q.24 I would like you to think back to the place or places you were living between the first of January 1983 and the time you moved here. Between the first of January 1983 and the time you moved here, did anyone get into the place you were living without permission and steal or try to steal anything? How many times?

Write in number of times, if none code 00   (65/66)

(65)   (66)

Q.25 Apart from this, in that time did anyone get into your *house/flat* without permission and cause damage? How many times?

Write in number of times, if none code 00 (67/68)

(67) (68)

Q.26 Apart from this, in that time have you had any evidence that someone had *tried* to get in without permission to steal or to cause damage? How many times?

Write in number of times, if none code 00 (69/70)

(69) (70)

Q.27 Apart from this, in that time was anything stolen out of your *house/flat*? How many times?

Write in number of times, if none code 00 (71/72)

(71) (72)

Q.28 Apart from this, in the time between the first of January 1983 and the time you moved here did you ever have the milk stolen from outside your *house/flat*? How many times?

Write in number of times, if none code 00 (73/74)

(73) (74)

Q.29 And apart from anything you have told me about already, in that time was anything else that belonged to someone in your household stolen from *outside* the *house/flat* — from the doorstep, the garden or the garage for example? How many times?

Write in number of times, if none code 00 (75/76)

(75) (76)

Q.30 And again, apart from anything you have told me about already, in that time did anyone deliberately deface or do damage to your *house/flat* or to anything outside it that belonged to someone in your household? How many times?

Write in number of times, if none code 00 (77/78)

(77) (78)

Q.31 I would now like you to think about the time since you moved here. Since you moved here has anyone got into this *house/flat* without permission and stolen or tried to steal anything? How many times?

Write in number of times, if none code 00 | | | *Now go to Q.33*   (79/80)

(79) (80)

NEW CARD
DUP COLS
1–9

Ask only those who have lived at their present address since January 1st 1983 others go to Q.33   (03)   (10/11)

Q.32 In the *thirteen/fourteen* months since the first of January 1983 has anyone got into this *house/flat* without permission and stolen or tried to steal anything?

Write in number of times, if none code 00 | | | (12/13)

(12) (13)

Ask all

Q.33 Apart from this, in that time did anyone get into your *house/flat* without permission and cause damage? How many times?

Write in number of times, if none code 00 | | | (14/15)

(14) (15)

Q.34 Apart from this, in that time have you had any evidence that someone had *tried* to get in without permission to steal or to cause damage? How many times?

Write in number of times, if none code 00 | | | (16/17)

(16) (17)

Q.35 Apart from this, in that time was anything stolen out of your *house/flat* How many times?

Write in number of times, if none code 00 | | | (18/19)

(18) (19)

Q.36 Apart from this, in that time did you ever have the milk stolen from outside your *house/flat*? How many times?

Write in number of times, if none code 00

(20)   (21)

(20/21)

Q.37 And apart from anything you have told me about already, in that time was anything else that belonged to someone in your household stolen from *outside* the *house/flat*—from the doorstep, the garden or the garage for example? How many times?

Write in number of times, if none code 00

(22)   (23)

(22/23)

Q.38 And again, apart from anything you have told me about already, in that time did anyone deliberately deface or do damage to your *house/flat* or to anything outside it that belonged to someone in your household? How many times?

Write in number of times, if none code 00

(24)   (25)

(24/25)

Ask all

Q.39 The next few questions are about things that may have happened to *you personally—not* the other people in your household—in the *thirteen/fourteen* months since the first of January 1983. Please include *anything* that happened to you during that time—at home, in the street, at work, in a shop, in a park, on a train or anywhere else. Apart from anything you have mentioned already, since the first of January 1983, have you had anything you were carrying stolen—out of your hands or from your pockets or from a bag or case? How many times?

Write in number of times, if none code 00

(26)   (27)

(26/27)

Q.40 Apart from this, in that time has anyone *tried* to *steal* something you were carrying—out of your hands or from your pockets or from a bag or case? How many times?

Write in number of times, if none code 00

(28)   (29)

(28/29)

Q.41 And apart from this, in that time has anything else of yours been stolen, from a cloakroom, an office, a car or anywhere else you left it? How many times?

Write in number of times, if none code 00   (30/31)

(30)   (31)

Q.42 And apart from this, in that time has anything else of yours been deliberately damaged or tampered with by vandals or people out to steal? How many times?

Write in number of times, if none code 00   (32/33)

(32)   (33)

Q.43 And again apart from anything you have already mentioned, since the first of January 1983 has anyone (including people you know well) deliberately hit you with their fists or with a weapon of any sort or kicked you or used force or violence on you in any other way? How many times?

Write in number of times, if none code 00   (34/35)

(34)   (35)

Q.44 And in that time, has anyone threatened to damage things of yours or threatened to use force or violence on you in a way that actually frightened you? How many times?

Write in number of times, if none code 00   (36/37)

(36)   (37)

Female respondents only, male go to Q.49

Q.45 Since the first of January 1983, have you been sexually interfered with, assaulted or attacked, either by someone you knew or by a stranger? How many times?

Write in number of times, if none code 00   (38/39)

(38)   (39)

Q.46 Apart from anything you have mentioned already, since the first of January 1983 have you been sexually pestered or insulted by anyone?

Yes	1 GO TO Q.47	(40)
No	2 ASK Q.49	

Q.47 How many times since January 1st 1983?

<table>
<tr><td></td><td></td></tr>
</table>

(41) (42)

(41/42)

Q.48 Can you tell me what happened (on the last occasion)? *Probe for:* Who was involved, where it occurred, and what happened. *Write in fully and then code below*

_____

_____

_____

(43)
1 2 3
4 5 6
7 8 9
0 X Y

Location	(44)	*Person responsible*	(45)	
At work	1	Someone at work	1	
On street	2	Someone else known to respondent	2	(44/45)
Other	3	Someone not known to respondent	3	

Ask all

Q.49 I have now just got to copy the answers about incidents you have experienced onto this page. *Check back to questions listed below. For each, code the number of incidents—If none code 0, if 10 or more code 9. Note that Q's 18, 28, 30, 36, 38, 42 and 47 are not* recorded here.

Q.16	Vehicle theft	☐		Q.31	*Present Home* or Q.32 Burglary	☐
Q.17	Theft from vehicle	☐		Q.33	Break-in with damage	☐
Q.21	Bicycle theft	☐		Q.34	Attempted burglary	☐
				Q.35	Theft from dwelling	☐
	Former Home (If applicable)			Q.37	Theft outside dwelling (not milk bottles)	☐
Q.24	Burglary	☐		Q.39	Theft from person	☐
Q.25	Break-in with damage	☐		Q.40	Attempted theft from person	☐
Q.26	Attempted burglary	☐		Q.41	Other theft	☐
Q.27	Theft from dwelling	☐		Q.43	Assault	☐

Q.29 Theft outside building
(not milk bottles) □   Q.44 Threats □
                          Q.45 Sexual assault
                                (female only) □

Check Q.49. If all crimes are 0 or not applicable go to Q.53. If no crime has more than one incident, go to Q.51. If any crime has two or more incidents ask Q.50 for each crime with two or more incidents.

Q.50 You mentioned . . . (NUMBER) incidents of . . . (TYPE OF OFFENCE). Were any of these very similar incidents, where the same thing was done under the same circumstances and probably by the same people?

Yes	1 RECORD DETAILS BELOW
No	2 GO TO Q.51

(46)

Question number   Number of similar incidents in series

_____   _____
_____   _____
_____   _____
_____   _____

If any incidents recorded at Q.49
Q.51 So can I just check . . .

a) Re-record total number of *series*
   of incidents from Q.50 (47/48) [|] Series (47/48)

b) Re-record total number of other
   single incidents from Q.49 (49/50) [|] Incidents (49/50)

c) Code overall total—a)+b) (51/52) [|] Series or Incidents (51/52)

If total at c) is 1, 2, 3, or 4—Complete victim form for each incident or series of incidents—complete Qs.53 and 54 before completing victim forms.

If total at c) is 5 or more   —Complete only *four* victim forms. Work back from the end of the list at Q.49, and complete victim forms for the four incidents or series you come to first.

— If this means choosing out of incidents at the same question, take the most recent.

— Record at Q.52 overleaf the incidents or series recorded at Q.49 for which a victim form was *not* completed.

If 5 or more incidents or series recorded at Q.51(c)

Q.52 Record below any incidents or series for which victim forms were *not* completed. Write in number of incidents at each question for which a victim form was not completed — if 10 or more at any question, write in 9.

				Present Home		
Q.16 Vehicle theft	☐	(53)		Q.31 or Q.32		
Q.17 Theft from vehicle	☐	(54)		Burglary	☐	(63)
SKIP COL. 55				Q.33 Break in with damage	☐	(64)
Q.21 Bicycle theft	☐	(56)		Q.34 Attempted burglary	☐	(65)
Former Home				Q.35 Theft from dwelling	☐	(66)
(If applicable)				Q.37 Theft outside dwelling		
Q.24 Burglary	☐	(57)		(not milk bottles)	☐	(67)
Q.25 Break in with damage	☐	(58)		SKIP COL. 68		(53/75)
Q.26 Attempted burglary	☐	(59)		Q.39 Theft from person	☐	(69)
Q.27 Theft from dwelling	☐	(60)		Q.40 Attempted theft from		
Q.29 Theft outside building				person	☐	(70)
(not milk bottles)	☐	(61)		Q.41 Other theft	☐	(71)
SKIP COL. 62				SKIP COL. 72		
				Q.43 Assault	☐	(73)
				Q.44 Threats	☐	(74)
				Q.45 Sexual assault		
				(female only)	☐	(75)

Ask all

Q.53 *Interviewer* record if anyone else was in the room during main questionnaire — code all that apply

No — no-one	1	
Yes — child/children under 16	2	(76)
Yes — adult/adults	3	

Q.54 Interviewer record — are there any victim forms to be completed for this respondent

Yes	1 FILL IN TIME BELOW THEN GO TO VICTIM FORM	(77)
No	2 GO TO Q.55	

Q.55 Interviewer check—what is the last digit of the serial number?

0, 1, 2, 3	1 FILL IN TIME BELOW THEN GO TO FOLLOW-UP QUESTIONNAIRE
4–9	2 FILL IN TIME BELOW AND CLOSE INTERVIEW

Time main questionnaire ended   _____

Length of main questionnaire | | | Minutes   (78/79)
                                  (78) (79)

Note: in the reproduction of these questionnaires and victim forms the original question layout has been retained as far as possible, but not the page layout.

NOP/9888

AREA CODE

(5)   (6)   (7)

SERIAL NO.

(8)   (9)

1984 BRITISH CRIME SURVEY
VICTIM FORM

COMPLETE ONE VICTIM FORM FOR EACH
INCIDENT OR SERIES OF INCIDENTS
INDICATED BY MAIN QUESTIONNAIRE Q.51   (04)(10/11)

VICTIM FORM NO.

(1–4)   (12)

TIME THIS VICTIM FORM STARTED ....

Re-record from main questionnaire Q.49
Q.1 (a) Screening question at which this incident/series of incidents was mentioned

(13)   (14)

Q.   (13/14)

Q.1 (b) This form refers to:

One incident only...................	1 GO TO Q.4	(15)
A series of incidents.................	2 ASK Q.2(a)	

If series of incidents at Q.1(b)

Q.2 (a) Number of incidents in series (from Q.50)?

(16)   (17)

WRITE IN   (16/17)

Q.2 (b) You mentioned a series of . . . (NUMBER) similar incidents of (TYPE OF OFFENCE) since January 1983. When did these incidents happen?

Record a number for each time period. If there were no incidents in a particular period code '00'.

January–March 1983	□□ incidents	(18/19)
April–June 1983	□□ incidents	(20/21)
July–September 1983	□□ incidents	(22/23)
October–December 1983	□□ incidents	(24/25)
January ⟶ 1984	□□ incidents	(26/27)
Can't say when	□□ incidents	(28/29)

Q.3   In which *month* did the most recent of these incidents happen?

Record below Q.4. From now on all questions refer to the most recent incident in series. If single incident only at Q.1(b)

Q.4   You said that, since January 1983, you or your household had ....
(TYPE OF OFFENCE). In which *month* did that happen? *Record below*

RECORD ANSWER TO Q.3 *OR* Q.4 BELOW

	MONTH	YEAR	
	(30) (31)	(32)	(30/32)
Write in exact month (if at all possible)			
(e.g. JANUARY = 01	□□	1983 1	
DECEMBER = 12		1984 2	
DON'T KNOW = 99)			

If exact month not known probe for quarter

	(33)
January–March 1983	1
April–June 1983	2
July–September 1983	3
October–December 1983	4
January → 1984..................	5
Can't say	6

NOTE: If you find that incident occurred before January 1983 note this and close victim form here.

If happened this month or last month ask Q.5. If longer ago go to Q.6.

Q.5   Did it happen . . . READ OUT

                                                    (34)
    Less than a week ago 1
    In the last 2 weeks 2
    In the last 3 weeks 3
    In the last 4 weeks 4   (34)
    or Over 4 weeks ago 5
    (Don't know)................ 6

Ask all

Q.6   Can you tell me, very briefly, what happened? *Probe for outline details of nature and circumstances of incident. Record key details only.*

_____

_____

_____

_____

_____

_____

_____

OFFICE USE ONLY

(35)   (36)

Q.7   At what time of day did it happen? (*Prompt with categories if necessary*)

    During morning 1
    During afternoon 2
    Morning/afternoon (can't say which)... 3
    During evening (6 p.m.–midnight)...... 4   (37)
    During night (midnight–6 a.m.) 5
    Evening/night (can't say which) 6
    Don't know 7

Q.8   Did it happen during the week or at a weekend?
    NOTE: Take weekend as Friday 6 p.m. to Monday 6 a.m.

    During week 1
    At weekend 2   (38)
    Don't know 3

Code if obvious otherwise ask:

Q.9   Can I just check; did it happen in England or Wales or did it happen somewhere else?

England or Wales.................	1 ASK Q.10(a)	(39)
No...............................	2 CLOSE VICTIM FORM HERE	

Ask all

Q.10 (a) Where did it happen? *Prompt as necessary with categories. Code all doubtful cases as 'other'.*

Own home

Inside own home (include attempted break-in)........................	1 GO TO Q.11(a)	
In garage specifically for this house/flat.......................	2 ASK Q.10(b)	
Immediately outside home In row of garages for block of flats/estate......................	3	(40)
Outside own home but on same premises (doorstep, corridor of flat block, garden, carport, yard or car park attached to flat/block)	4	
In street immediately outside home	5	
In or near victim's regular place of work At place of work	6	
In car park at place of work	7	
In street near place of work..........	8 GO TO Q.14	
Other: Specify details of type of location	9	

Q.10 (b) Does the garage have a connecting door to the house itself?

Yes	1 NOW ASK	(41)
No...............................	2 Q.11(a)	

Q.11 (a) Can I just check was the *person/were the people* who did it actually *inside* your home (or your garage) at all during the incident?

Yes	1 GO TO Q.12	(42)
No...............................	2	
Don't know	3 ASK Q.11(b)	

Q.11 (b) Did they try to get inside?

Yes	1	(43)
No...............................	2 NOW GO	
Don't know	3 TO Q.13	

If offender inside

Q.12 Did the *person/the people* who did it have a right to be inside? For example waas it done by people who were invited in, workmen doing a job or guests or people who lived with you?

Yes	1 NOW GO	(44)
No	2 TO Q.13	

Ask Q.13 if in or just outside own home (codes 1–5 at Q.10). Others go to Q.14.

Q.13 Were you or anyone else in your household at home at the time?

Household member at home	1	
No household member at home........	2	(45)
Don't know	3	

Ask all

Q.14 *Interviewer: Code from what has already been said if answer is wholly obvious. Otherwise ask:*

Can you say anything at all about the people who did it — how many there were or what sort of people they were?

Yes	1 ASK Q.15	(46)
No	2 GO TO Q.23	

Q.15 How many were there?

One	1	
Two...............................	2	
Three.............................	3	
Four or more	4	(47)
Don't know	5	

Q.16 Was the *person/were the people* who did it male or female?

Male	1	
Female	2	
People of both sexes	3	(48)
Don't know	4	

Q.17 How old was *the person/were the people* who did it? Would you say *it was/they were* . . .

CODE ALL THAT APPLY

A child/children under school age	1	
A child/children of school age	2	
A young person/people between		
16 and 25	3	(49)
or an older person/older people	4	
(Don't know)......................	5	

Q.18 As far as you know was *the person/were the people* who did it . . .

READ OUT   CODE ALL THAT APPLY
....White.......................... 1
....Black (West Indian or African) 2
....Indian, Pakistani or Bangladeshi 3   (50)
or something else (write in and ring)
_____ 4
....(Don't know) 5

Q.19 *Code from what has already been said if answer is wholly obvious otherwise ask:*

Why do you think this *was the person/these were the people* who did it?

CODE ALL THAT APPLY

I saw them myself/was personally
  involved 1
Someone else saw them 2
The police arrested them............. 3
The police told me 4
They were convicted of the crime 5
They admitted to it 6
They have done it before/they are
  responsible for similar crimes........ 7   (51)
They were behaving suspiciously/
  strangly, just before or after the
  incident......................... 8
Have seen them about and thought
  they looked suspicious............. 9
Hearsay (what other people say) 0
Other (write in and ring)
_____ X

Don't know — just think it was .... Y

Q.20 *Was it someone/were any of them people* you knew before it happened or *was it a stranger/were they all strangers?*

All known	1 ASK Q.21
Some known, some not known	2
None known	3 GO TO Q.23

(52)

If any know
Q.21 How did you know them? Just by sight *or* just to speak to casually, *or* did you know (any of) them well?

CODE ALL THAT APPLY
(All/some) just by sight 1
(All/some) just to speak to casually 2   (53)
(All/some) known well 3

If any known well ask Q.22. Others go to Q.23

Q.22 What was their relationship to you?

CODE ALL THAT APPLY

Spouse/cohabitee	1
Other household member	2
Current boyfriend/girlfriend	3
Former spouse/cohabitee	4
Former boyfriend/girlfriend	5
Other relative	6
Friend/colleague	7
Neighbour	8
Other (write in and ring)	
_____	9

(54)

Ask all

Q.23 *Code if wholly obvious. Otherwise ask:* Was anything at all stolen that belonged to you or anyone else in your household?

Yes	1 ASK Q.24
No	2 GO TO Q.28

(55)

Q.24 What was taken? What else? Anything else? *Probe to 'No'*

(56)

Handbag...........................	1 COLLECT
Wallet	2 DETAILS OF
Purse..............................	3 CONTENTS
Cash (not from meter)...............	4
Money from meter	5
Cheque book/credit card	6
Car/van	7
Motorcycle/scooter/moped...........	8
Vehicle parts/accessories	9

(57)

Bicycle	1
Video equipment....................	2
Television	3
Stereo/hi fi equipment	4
Camera............................	5
Jewellery...........................	6
Silverware..........................	7
Other (write in and ring)	
_____	8

(56/57)

Code if wholly obvious. Otherwise ask:

Q.25 Were the things stolen from a motor vehicle—off or out of a car or off a motorcycle?

Yes	1
No	2

(58)

Q.26 (a) (Including cash), what would you estimate was the total value of what was stolen? *Prompt with precoded categories if necessary.*

Interviewer: If asked say we mean *replacement value.* Cheques/credit cards count as no value.

Nothing	1
Under £5	2
£5 but under £25	3
£25 but under £50	4
£50 but under £100	5
£100 but under £250	6
£250 but under £500	7
£500 but under £1,000..............	8
£1,000 + ...	9
No idea...........................	0

(59)

Q.26 (b) Was anything stolen which was of sentimental value to you? IF YES: Did it have a lot of sentimental value for you or just a little?

No, nothing	1
Yes — a lot	2
Yes — a little	3

(60)

Q.27 Was any of the stolen money or property recovered? *Probe as necessary.*

Yes — all	1
Yes — some.........................	2
No — none	3

(61)

Ask all

Q.28 (Apart from things that were actually stolen) did the person/people who did it damage, deface or mess up anything that belonged to you or to anyone else in your household (including any damage which may have been done getting in or out)?

Yes	1 ASK Q.29
No	2 GO TO Q.31

(62)

Q.29 What did they do? *Probe fully* What else? Anything else?
Write in

(63)

1 2 3
4 5 6
7 8 9
0 X Y

Q.30 What was the total value of the damage they did? *If 'Don't know'* *probe for an estimate. Prompt with categories if necessary.*

Nothing	1
£20 or under	2
£21 but under £50	3
£50 but under £100	4
£100 but under £250	5
£250 but under £500	6
£500 but under £1,000...............	7
£1,000+	8
No idea............................	9

(64)

Q.31 *Interviewer check Q.23 and Q.28. Was any property stolen or anything damaged/defaced?*

Yes	1 ASK Q.32
No	2 GO TO Q.37

(65)

Q.32 Was any of the property which was stolen or damaged covered by an insurance policy?

Yes	1 ASK Q.33
No..............................	2 GO TO Q.37
Don't know	3

(66)

Q.33 Did you or anyone else in your household make a claim for the property which was stolen or damaged?

Yes	1 ASK Q.34
No..............................	2 GO TO Q.37
Don't know	3

(67)

Q.34 Did the insurance company give you all the money you claimed, some of it or none of it?

All..............................	1 ASK Q.35
Some............................	2
None............................	3 GO TO Q.37
Still waiting for a settlement	4
Don't know	5

(68)

Q.35 Bearing in mind any money you got from insurance and any property you got back, would you say you were financially better off or worse off in the end?

Better off	1 GO TO Q.37	
Worse off..........................	2 ASK Q.36	(69)
About the same	3 GO TO Q.37	
Don't know	4	

If worse off

Q.36 By how much would you say you were worse off? If 'Don't know' probe for an estimate. Prompt with categories if necessary.

Under £5	1	
£5 but under £25	2	
£25 but under £50	3	
£50 but under £100	4	
£100 but under £250	5	
£250 but under £500	6	(70)
£500 but under £1,000	7	
£1,000 + ...	8	
No idea...........................	9	

Ask all

Q.37 (Apart from what was actually stolen), to the best of your knowledge, did the *person/people* who did it *try* to steal anything (else) that belonged to you or any other member of your household?

Yes	1 ASK Q.38	(71)
No..............................	2 GO TO Q.39	
Don't know	3	

Q.38 What did they try to steal? What else? Anything else? *Probe to 'No'.*

(72)

Handbag..........................	1 COLLECT	
Wallet	2 DETAILS OF	
Purse............................	3 CONTENTS	
Cash (not from meter)..............	4	
Money from meter	5	
Cheque book/credit card	6	
Car/van	7	
Motorcycle/scooter/moped...........	8	
Vehicle parts/accessories	9	(72/73)

(73)

Bicycle	1
Video equipment....................	2
Television	3
Stereo/hi fi equipment	4
Camera...........................	5
Jewellery..........................	6

Silverware. 7

Other (write in and ring)

_____ 8
_____

Ask all

Q.39 Would you say that you or anyone else *apart* from the offenders were responsible in *any* way for what happened, because of something you or they did or forgot to do? *Probe:* Who?

No — No-one	1 GO TO Q.41
Yes — Respondent	2
— Other household member	3
— Other (write in and code)	
_____	4 ASK Q.40

Q.40 In what way were *you/they* responsible?

CODE ALL THAT APPLY

Provoked offender 1

Failed to *lock* (door, window, etc.) 2

Failed to *close* — left door etc. open . . . 3

Failed to *lock away* (e.g. didn't
put in safe) 4

Failed to *put away* (e.g. left in
open/visible) 5   (75)

Other (write in and code)

_____ 6

Ask all

Q.41 *Code if wholly obvious. Otherwise ask:* At the time it happened, were you or anyone else aware of what was happening?

Yes	1 ASK Q.42	(76)
No	2	
Don't know	3 GO TO Q.52	

Q.42 Who was aware of it?

CODE ALL THAT APPLY

Respondent 1

Other household member 2

Other (write in and ring)

_____ 3

If anyone aware

Q.43 Did *the person/any of the people* who did it have a weapon or something they used or threatened to use as a weapon?

Yes	1 ASK Q.44
No...............................	2 GO TO Q.45
Don't know	3

(78)

Q.44 What was the weapon?
WRITE IN

(79)

1 2 3
4 5 6
7 8 9
0 X Y

_____
_____
_____
_____

NEW CARD
DUP COLS
1–9
(05)   (10/11)
DUP COL. 12

Code if obviously 'Yes' otherwise ask:
Q.45 Did *the person/any of the people* who did it actually hit anyone or use force or violence on anyone in any way?

Yes	1 ASK Q.46
No...............................	2 GO TO Q.49
Don't know	3

(13)

Code if obvious otherwise ask:
Q.46 On whom did they use force or violence?

CODE ALL THAT APPLY
Respondent 1
Other household member 2
Other person outside household 3

(14)

Ask Q.47 and Q.48 for each person mentioned at Q.46
Q.47 In what way did they use force or violence on .... (PERSON)?
RECORD BELOW

Q.48 Were you/was .... (PERSON) bruised, scratched, cut or injured in any way? *If yes ask:* In what way? RECORD BELOW

	Respondent	Other Household Member	Other Person
Q.47 *Code all that apply*	(15)	(17)	(19)
Grabbed/pushed	1	1	1
Punched/slapped	2	2	2

Kicked ....3 .... 3 3
Hit with weapon/
  something used as
  weapon .... 4 .... 4 4

RING ONLY ⌈ Raped .... 5 .... 5 5
FIRST CODE | Attempted rape .... 6 .... 6 6
TO APPLY ⌊ Sexually assaulted .... 7 ....7 7   (15/20)
Other (write in
  and ring)

_____ 8 .... 8 8

   Q.48   (16)   (18)   (20)
No — not injured .... 1 .... 1 1
Yes — Bruises/black eyes ....2 .... 3 2
Yes — Scratches .... 3 ....3 3
Yes — Cuts .... 4 .... 4 4
Yes — Broken bones .... 5 ....5 5
Yes — Other (write in
      and ring)

_____ 6 ....6 6

If anyone aware of what was happening
Q.49 Did the person/people who did it *threaten* to use force or violence
on anyone there or harm them in any (other) way?

Yes	1 ASK Q.50	(21)
No	2	
Don't know	3 GO TO Q.52	

Q.50 Whom did they threaten?

                                    CODE ALL THAT APPLY
Respondent 1
Other household member 2   (22)
Other person outside household 3

Ask Q.51 for each person mentioned at Q.50
Q.51 What did they threaten to do to .:............... (PERSON)?

	Respondent	Other Household Member	Other Person
CODE ALL THAT APPLY	(23)	(24)	(25)
Punch/slap/kick/beat up	1	1	1
Hit with weapon/something used as weapon	2	2	2
Sexual assault/rape	3	3	3
Kill	4	4	4

Other (write in and ring)   (23/25)

_____ 5

_____ 5

_____ 5

462 APPLIED MARKETING AND SOCIAL RESEARCH

Ask all
Q.52 Can I just check, as a result of what happened did you or anyone else in your household have attention from a Doctor?

Yes	1 ASK Q.53	(26)
No	2 GO TO Q.56	

Q.53 Who had attention from a doctor?

Respondent	1	(27)
Other household member	2	

Ask Q.54 for each person who had attention from doctor
Q.54 What was the reason why you/why .... (other household member) needed attention from a doctor?

	Respondent (28)	Other Household Member (29)	
CODE ALL THAT APPLY			
Had physical injury/pain	1	1	
Had difficulty sleeping	2	2	
Felt worried/anxious/nerves	3	3	
Felt depressed	4	4	
Shock	5	5	
Headaches	6	6	
Nausea	7	7	
Other physical symptoms (write in and ring)			(28/29)
_____ 8			
_____		8	
Other psychological symptoms (write in and ring)			
_____ 9			
_____		9	
Don't know	0	0	

Q.55 Did you/did .... (other household member) need to stay one night or more in hospital at all?

	Respondent (30)	Other Household Member (31)	
Yes	1	1	(30/31)
No	2	2	

Ask all
Q.56 As a result of the incident, did you or any other member of your household lose time from work at any stage?

Yes	1 ASK Q.57	(32)
No	2 GO TO Q.59	

Q.57 Who lost time from work?

Respondent 1
Other household member 2   (33)

Ask Q.58 for each person who lost time at work
Q.58 How many days did you/ .... (other household members) lose?

	Respondent (34)	Other Household Member (35)	
1 day or less	1	1	(34/35)
2 days	2	2	
3–5 days	3	3	
Over one week	4	4	
Over one month	5	5	

Ask all
Q.59 (a) Looking back over the time since it happened could you describe to me any kinds of practical problems or particular inconvenience which this incident has caused you or your household? What else? Anything else? *Probe fully*

(36)
1 2 3
4 5 6
7 8 9
0 X Y

Q.59 (b) And could you also describe to me any kinds of emotional or personal problems which this incident has caused you or your household? What else? Anything else? *Probe fully*

(37)
1 2 3
4 5 6
7 8 9
0 X Y

Q.60 Thinking back to the *first few days* after it happened, how much would you say the incident affected you or your household at that time?

Q.61 And how much would you say the incident is affecting you or your household *now*?

	Q.60 (38)	Q.61 (39)	
Very much	1	1	(38/39)
Quite a lot	2	2	
A little	3	3	
Not at all	4	4	

Ask Q.62 if any problems at Q.59(a) or Q.59(b) if no problems at all go to filter before Q.64

Q.62 What has been *the worst problem* that you or your household have had because of this incident? *Probe fully*

(40)

1	2	3
4	5	6
7	8	9
0	X	Y

_____

_____

_____

Q.63 (a) Were there any kinds of information, help or advice, such as the things listed on this card *show card C* which you needed but did not get? What else? Anything else?

Information or advice about:

crime prevention....................	1
insurance	2
immediate financial help.............	3
problems with gas/electricity board	4
compensation......................	5
repairs............................	6
legal advice	7
Someone to talk to about the crime and your feelings	8
Advice about effects on children.......	9
Information on the progress of the case	0
None of these	X

(41)

Q.63 (b) Would you have liked help, information or advice about anything else?

No, nothing........................	1
Yes (RECORD FULL DETAILS BELOW)	2

(42)

		3
4	5	6
7	8	9
0	X	Y

_____

_____

_____

Only ask Q.64 to Q.68(d) if this is the first victim form for this respondent on second, third or fourth victim forms go to Q.69

Q.64 Victim Support Schemes are groups of volunteers trained to offer information, help and advice to the victims of crime. Had you heard of Victim Support Schemes before now?

Yes	1
No...............................	2
Don't know	3

(43)

Q.65 Well to explain briefly what they do . . .
In some areas the police ask Victim Support Schemes to call round to see if victims of crime need any further information, advice or assistance, for example about insurance claims, repairs or court appearances; or if people are upset they can talk about their feelings.

Do you think *all* victims of crime should be contacted by such schemes or not? *Do not prompt*

Yes — all	1 ASK Q.66	
Only serious crimes	2	
No — not all	3	(44)
No — none	4 GO TO Q.68(a)	
Don't know	5 ASK Q.66	

Q.66 Would you have liked to have been contacted by a Victim Support Scheme or not?

Yes	1	
No	2	
Was actually contacted	3	
Don't know	4	(45)

Q.67 Would you have accepted (did you accept) an offer of assistance from such a scheme?

Would have accepted	1 ASK Q.68(a)	
Would not have accepted	2	
Had offer and accepted	3	(46)
Had offer and did not accept	4 GO TO Q.68(b)	
Don't know	5	

Q.68 (a) When would their call have been *most* welcome?

The day of the incident	1	
The next day	2	
Two days to a week later	3	(47)
Between a week and a month later	4	
or More than a month later	5	
(Don't know)	6	

Ask all (If first victim form)

Q.68 (b) The Government is considering schemes in which victims and offenders would meet out of court in the presence of an officially appointed person to agree a way in which the offender could make a repayment to the victim for what he had done. Would you have accepted a chance of such a meeting after this crime?

Yes	1 GO TO Q.68(d)	
No	2	(48)
Don't know	3 ASK Q.68(c)	

Q.68 (c) If an out of court agreement like this could be arranged *without* you having to meet the offender(s) would you like this to happen or not?

Yes	1 GO TO Q.68(d)	
No................................	2 GO TO Q.69	(49)
Don't know	3	

Ask Q.68(d) if 'Yes' at either Q.68(b) or Q.68(c). Others go to Q.69

Q.68 (d) If an agreement could be reached would you want the offender(s) to be prosecuted and punished as well?

Yes	1	
No................................	2	(50)
Don't know	3	

Ask all

Q.69 Going back to the crime itself, did the police come to know about the matter?

Yes	1 GO TO Q.71	(51)
No................................	2 ASK Q.70	

If no at Q.69

Q.70 Why not? *Probe fully*
Write in

_____
_____
_____
_____

(52)		
1	2	3
4	5	6
7	8	9
0	X	Y

NOW GO TO Q.75

If yes at Q.69

Q.71 How did they come to know about it?

Police told by respondent	1 ASK Q.72	
Police told by other person on respondent's behalf	2	
Police told by other person	3	
Police were there	4	(53)
Police found out another way (write in and ring) _____	GO TO Q.73 5	
(Don't know)......................	6	

If police told by respondent or on respondent's behalf ask Q.72. Others go to Q.73

Q.72 People do not always tell the Police about crimes which are committed. Can you tell me why you decided to report this crime to the police? Any other reasons?

(54)
1 2 3
4 5 6
7 8 9
0 X Y

_____

_____

ASK Q.73

If police came to know about matter (Yes at Q.69)

Q.73 Overall were you satisfied or dissatisfied with the way the police dealt with the matter?
If satisfied ask: Very satisfied or just fairly satisfied?
If dissatisfied ask: A bit dissatisfied or very dissatisfied?

Very satisfied.......................	1
Fairly satisfied.......................	2 GO TO Q.75
A bit dissatisfied....................	3 ASK Q.74
Very dissatisfied	4
Don't know/Can't say	5 GO TO Q.75

(55)

Q.74 Why were you dissatisfied? What other reason? Any other reason?

They were slow to arrive when sent for.........................	1
They did not come when sent for	2
They didn't investigate matter/did did not do enough to investigate matter...........................	3
They seemed uninterested	4
They made mistakes/handled matter badly	5
They didn't recover property	6
They didn't apprehend the offenders ...	7
They failed to keep the respondent informed of progress of investigation......................	8
They were impolite/unpleasant	9
They didn't believe me/they accused me.......................	0
Other (write in and ring)	
_____	X
_____	Y
(Don't know).......................	Y

(56)

Ask all

Q.75 *Code if obvious otherwise ask:*
Do you know if the police ever found out who did it?

Yes they did	1
No they did not	2
Don't know if they did or not.........	3

(57)

Q.76 I would now like to ask you how serious a crime you personally think this was. On this card (*show card D*) is a scale to show the seriousness of different crimes, with the scale going from 0 for a very minor crime like theft of milk bottles from a doorstep, to 20 for the most serious crime, murder. How would you rate this crime on the scale from 0 to 20?

DONT KNOW = 99 ☐☐   (58/59)

(58)   (59)

Q.77 *Show card E* When the police are told about a crime like the one you suffered, how much priority do you think they *should* give to solving it?

Very high priority....................	1
High priority.......................	2
Average priority....................	3
Low priority.......................	4
Very low priority....................	5
or Should they take no action at all....	6
(Don't know).......................	7

(60)

Q.78 On this card (*show card F*) are the actions the police can take and the various sentences which a Court can give to people. Which of these do you think should have happened to the *person/people* who did it? *If 'Compensation' mentioned ask:* 'Should the *person/people* be given any other sentence as well as having to pay compensation'? CODE *ONE* ITEM ONLY *OR* COMPENSATION PLUS *ONE* ITEM ONLY

(61)

No action taken/not a matter for the police.......................	1
Get an informal warning from the police...........................	2
Get a formal caution from the police...	3
Go to Court but only get a warning....	4
Have to pay compensation...........	5
Get a suspended prison sentence.......	6
Have to do community service........	7
Be put on probation................	8
Be fined under £50..................	9
Be fined £50 or more................	0
Go to prison or similar for under a year...........................	X
Go to prison or similar for 1 to 5 years..........................	Y

(61/62)

(62)

Go to prison of similar for over 5 years..........................	1
(Other)............................	2
(Don't know).......................	3
It depends.........................	4

Q.79 *Interviewer: Record if anyone else was in the room during victim form.*
Code all that apply.

No-one else present 1
Yes — child/children under 16 2   (63)
Yes — adult/adults 3

Fill in time below, then go to follow-up questionnaire

Time victim form ended _____

Length of victim form   [|]   Minutes

           (64)   (65)

NOP/9888

AREA CODE

(5)   (6)   (7)

SERIAL No.

(8)   (9)

1984 BRITISH CRIME SURVEY
FOLLOW-UP QUESTIONNAIRE

COMPLETE THIS QUESTIONNAIRE FOR
1. ALL RESPONDENTS FOR WHOM VICTIM
   FORMS WERE COMPLETED
2. ALL OTHER RESPONDENTS WITH ADDRESS
   NUMBERS ENDING IN 0, 1, 2, OR 3   ⑥   (10/11)
TIME THIS QUESTIONNAIRE STARTED: ....   ①   (12)

Q.1   (a) Do you personally know anyone who has been mugged and robbed
       since the beginning of last year, that is since January 1983?

Yes	1 ASK Q.1(b)	(13)
No	2 GO TO Q.2(a)	

Q.1   (b) Did this/any of these incidents happen in this area?

Yes	1	
No	2	(14)
Don't know	3	

Q.2   (a) Do you personally know anyone who has been sexually attacked
       or molested since January 1983?

Yes	1 ASK Q.2(b)	(15)
No	2 GO TO Q.3(a)	

Q.2   (b) Did this/any of these incidents happen in this area?

Yes	1	
No	2	(16)
Don't know	3	

Q.3 (a) Apart from your own household, do you personally know anyone who has had their home burgled or broken into since January 1983?

Yes	1 ASK Q.3(b)	(17)
No	2 GO TO Q.4	

Q.3 (b) Did this/any of these incidents happen in this area?

Yes	1	
No	2	(18)
Don't know	3	

Q.4 What sort of crimes do you think happen most often in this area?

Burglary/break-ins	1	
Vandalism	2	
Mugging	3	
Pickpocketing	4	
Petty theft	5	(19)
Assault	6	
Sexual crimes.......................	7	
Car theft/theft from cars	8	
Other (write in and ring)		
_____	9	
No crime round here	0	
Don't know	X	

Q.5 Do you think that in the last two years, the level of burglary in this area has . . . READ OUT

Decreased..........................	1	
Increased	2 ASK Q.6(a)	
or Stayed the same..................	3	
(Don't know).......................	4	(20)
No burglaries around here	5 GO TO Q.7	

Q.6 (a) Do you think most burglaries in this area are committed by people who live in the area or by people from outside the area?

People from the area.................	1	
People from outside..................	2	
Both equally	3	(21)
Don't know	4	

Q.6 (b) And are most burglaries in this area committed by . . . READ OUT

Children under 16	1	
People aged 16–20	2	
or People over 20...................	3	(22)

(All ages) 4
Don't know 5

Q.6   (c) And do you think these people are mainly . . . READ OUT

Professional criminals 1
or Casual thieves or opportunists 2
(Mixture of both) 3   (23)
(Don't know)....................... 4

Q.7   What kinds of people do you hear about being mugged and robbed
in this area? Are they mainly men or women, or both equally?

Mainly men	1	
Mainly women	2 ASK Q.8	(24)
Both equally	3	
Don't know	4	
No mugging in area	5 GO TO Q.9(a)	

Q.8   And in terms of age, what kinds of people do you hear about
being mugged and robbed in this area—are they mainly younger
people, older people or somewhere in-between or are they of all ages
equally?

Mainly young 1
Mainly old 2
Mainly in-between 3   (25)
All equally 4
Don't know 5

Ask all
Q.9   (a) Can I check, do you currently have a paid job?

Yes	1 ASK Q.9(b)	(26)
No	2 GO TO Q.10	

Q.9   (b) Do you ever travel to work or come back from work between
nine o'clock at night and six o'clock in the morning? *Probe as
necessary*

Yes—regularly 1
Yes—sometimes 2
Yes—very occasionally 3   (27)
No—never 4

Ask all

Q.10 In the last seven days, have you spent any evenings outside your home on leisure, social or other spare time activities? Which evenings? Any others?

No — none	1 ASK Q.11(a)	
Yes — Sunday......................	2	
— Monday......................	3	
— Tuesday......................	4	(28)
— Wednesday	5 GO TO Q.12	
— Thursday....................	6	
— Friday	7	
— Saturday	8	

Q.11 (a) You say you haven't been out in the evening at all for leisure, social or other spare time activities during the last seven days. How often *on average* do you go out after dark for leisure? *Show card G*

At least once a week	1	
At least once a fortnight.............	2 GO TO Q.12	
At least once a month...............	3	(29)
Less often than once a month	4	
Never	5 ASK Q.11(b)	

Q.11 (b) Why not? *Probe fully:* Any other reasons?

(30)

1 2 3
4 5 6
7 8 9
0 X Y

_____

_____

_____

_____

NOW GO TO Q.14

Q.12 What was the main thing you did on the last time you went out in the evening for leisure?

Visited friends/relatives..............	1	
Went to pub/club/other licensed premises	2	
Went to cafe/restaurant	3	
Went to dance/disco/party...........	4	
Went to church.....................	5	
Went to evening class	6	
Took part in sport	7	
Watched sport......................	8	(31)
Went to meeting of club/committee	9	
Went to cinema/theatre	0	
Other (write in and ring)		
_____	X	

Q.13 The next questions are about some things people might do simply as a precaution against crime when they go out after dark. When you are out after dark, how often do you . . . avoid walking near certain types of people? *Record below. Repeat for each item. Show card H*

How often *simply* as
a *precaution* do you...

		Always	Usually	Some-times	Rarely	Never	Don't know	Not Applicable	
(a)	Avoid walking near certain types of people	1	2	3	4	5	6	7	(32)
(b)	Stay away from certain streets or areas	1	2	3	4	5	6	7	(33)
(c)	Go out with someone else rather than by yourself	1	2	3	4	5	6	7	(34)

And how often,
simply as a precaution
do you...

		Always	Usually	Some-times	Rarely	Never	Don't know	Not Applicable	
(d)	Avoid using buses or trains	1	2	3	4	5	6	7	(35)
(e)	Use a car rather than walk	1	2	3	4	5	6	7	(36)

Ask all
Q.14 Are there any events and activities which you would like to go to but do not because of crime or violence?

Yes	1 ASK Q.15	(37)
No	2 GO TO Q.16	

Q.15 Why do you say that? *Probe:* What events?

(38)
1 2 3
4 5 6
7 8 9
0 X Y

Q.16 Yesterday (last weekday) how many hours did you spend outside your home during the day?

None	1	
Under 1	2	
1 but under 3	3	(39)
3 but under 5	4	
5 but under 7	5	
7 or more	6	

Q.17 I would now like to talk to you about how serious you personally think different crimes are.
Place down the loose cards headed 'Q.17' and give respondent all 14 crime cards

Written on these cards are descriptions of different crimes. Please will you sort them into different piles according to how serious you think they are. For example if you think a crime is very serious put it on this pile—*point to 'very serious' card.*

Please have a look through all the crimes before you sort them into piles. *Allow respondent to look through cards.*

There are no right or wrong answers to this question and you can put all the crimes into one pile if you want to, or sort them out in any other way, it is just your personal opinion we are interested in.
When respondents have done this ask them to read out the crimes in each category and record the answers below.

		Very serious	Fairly serious	Not very serious	Trivial	Don't know	
1.	Someone being mugged and robbed	1	2	3	4	5	(40)
2.	Someone fiddling their income tax	1	2	3	4	5	(41)
3.	A car being stolen for a joy ride	1	2	3	4	5	(42)
4.	A home being broken into and something stolen	1	2	3	4	5	(43)
5.	Someone regularly driving a car while over the legal alcohol limit	1	2	3	4	5	(44)
6.	A woman being sexually molested or pestered	1	2	3	4	5	(45)
7.	Someone smoking cannabis or marijuana	1	2	3	4	5	(46)
8.	A woman being raped	1	2	3	4	5	(47)
9.	Someone stealing £5 worth of goods from a shop	1	2	3	4	5	(48)
10.	A prostitute soliciting for trade	1	2	3	4	5	(49)
11.	A private home or property being damaged by vandals	1	2	3	4	5	(50)
12.	Someone being insulted or bothered by strangers but not in a sexual way	1	2	3	4	5	(51)

13. Someone fiddling Social
    Security .... 1 .... 2 ..... 3 .... 4 5   (52)

14. Someone being attacked by
    strangers .... 1 .... 2 ..... 3 .... 4 5   (53)

Q.18 *Show card J* On this card are just some of the sentences which a court can give to people. Not everyone agrees about how severe these various sentences are, and I would like to know what you think.
First of all, which of these sentences do you think is the most severe?
And which next?
And which next?
And which next?
And which do you think is the least severe?

	Most (54)	2nd (55)	3rd (56)	4th (57)	5th (58)	
Suspended prison sentence.............	1	1	1	1	1	
Community service	2	2	2	2	2	
Probation	3	3	3	3	3	(54/58)
Fine of under £50	4	4	4	4	4	
Fine of £50 or more ...	5	5	5	5	5	
Don't know	6	6	6	6	6	

Q.18 (b) *Show card K* On this card are the actions the police can take or the various sentences which a court can give to people. I am going to read out a number of different crimes and for each one I would like you to tell me what you think should have happened to the person committing the crime.
You should assume in each case that this person is male, aged 25 and has previously been in trouble for similar crimes and that . . . *Read out each crime in turn and code below*

a) he has mugged and robbed someone
b) he has broken into a home and stolen something
c) he has committed a rape
d) he has stolen £5 worth of goods from a shop
e) he has stolen a car for a joy ride
f) he has smoked cannabis or marijuana

> *If compensation mentioned, ask:* Should the person be given any other sentence as well as having to pay compensation? What other sentence?

And finally, can you assume that this last is done by a woman aged 25, who has previously been in trouble for similar offences . . .

g) and she is a prostitute soliciting for trade

Code one item only or compensation plus one item only

	a) (59)		b) (61)		c) (63)		d) (65)		e) (67)		f) (69)		g) (71)
No action/Not matter for Police	1	..	1	..	1	..	1	..	1	..	1	..	1
Informal warning from Police ..	2	..	2	..	2	..	2	..	2	..	2	..	2
Formal caution from Police ..	3	..	3	..	3	..	3	..	3	..	3	..	3
Court warning .	4	..	4	..	4	..	4	..	4	..	4	..	4
Pay compensation	5	..	5	..	5	..	5	..	5	..	5	..	5
Suspended prison sentence	6	..	6	..	6	..	6	..	6	..	6	..	6
Community service	7	..	7	..	7	..	7	..	7	..	7	..	7
Probation	8	..	8	..	8	..	8	..	8	..	8	..	8
Be fined under £50	9	..	9	..	9	..	9	..	9	..	9	..	9
Be fined £50 or more........	0	..	0	..	0	..	0	..	0	..	0	..	0
Prison for under a year	X	..	X	..	X	..	X	..	X	..	X	..	X
Prison for one to five years	Y	..	Y	..	Y	..	Y	..	Y	..	Y	..	Y

(59/72)

	(60)		(62)		(64)		(66)		(68)		(70)		(72)
Prison for over 5 years	1	..	1	..	1	..	1	..	1	..	1	..	1
Other	2	..	2	..	2	..	2	..	2	..	2	..	2
Don't know....	3	..	3	..	3	..	3	..	3	..	3	..	3

Q.19 What proportion of people aged 21 or over who are convicted of burglary do you think get sent to prison? Is it . . . *Read out*

Around a third 1
Around a half...................... 2
or Around two-thirds 3   (73)
(Don't know)...................... 4

Q.20 (a) There has been much discussion recently about the size of Britain's prison population and ways in which it might be reduced, and I would like to ask for your views on this. All prisoners except those on life sentences are released on remission after serving two-thirds of their sentence, providing they have behaved well. Would it be a good or bad idea if they were released after serving *half* their sentence, providing they had behaved well? *Code below*

Q.20 (b) Some prisoners are released on parole before serving two-thirds of their sentence, under the supervision of a Probation Officer. Would it be a good or bad idea if the system were changed so that more prisoners were selected for parole? *Code below*

	Q.20(a) (74)	Q.20(b) (75)	
Good idea	1	 1	(74/75)
Bad idea	2	 2	
Don't know	3	 3	

Q.21 I am going to read out some other ways people have suggested for reducing the prison population, and for each one I would like you to say if you think it would be a good or bad idea?

		Good Idea	Bad Idea	Don't know	
a)	Judges and magistrates giving shorter sentences to people guilty of non-violent crimes	1	 2	 3	(76)
b)	Making some non-violent offenders do community service instead of going to prison	1	 2	 3	(77)
c)	Making some non-violent offenders pay compensation to their victims instead of going to prison	1	 2	 3	(78)
d)	Fining people guilty of non-violent crimes instead of sending them to prison	1	 2	 3	(79)

NEW CARD
DUP COLS.
1–9
⑰ (10/11)

Q.22 Some countries have schemes where people with dependents or jobs, who are sentenced to prison do not serve their sentence all at once. Instead they serve their sentence over a number of weekends. Do you think that in principle this is a good or bad idea for people guilty of non-violent crimes?

Good idea	1	
Bad idea	2	(12)
Don't know	3	

Q.23 Taking everything into account, would you say the police in this area do a good job or a poor job?
If good: Very good or fairly good?
If poor: Very poor or fairly poor?

Very good	1	
Fairly good	2	
Fairly poor.......................	3	(13)
Very poor........................	4	
Don't know	5	

Q.24 When did you *personally* last see a police officer on foot in this area?

Today/yesterday	1	
2–3 days ago	2	
4–7 days ago	3	
8–14 days ago	4	(14)
Longer ago	5	
Never	6	
Can't remember	7	

Ask heads of household or spouses only, others go to Q.42

Q.25 I would now like to talk about ways of preventing burglary. Firstly, are the contents of your home insured against theft?

Yes	1 GO TO Q.27	(15)
No...............................	2 ASK Q.26	
Don't know	3 GO TO Q.27	

Q.26 Why is that?

Not worth it	1	
Too expensive	2	
No risk of burglary	3	
Nothing worth insuring	4	
Can't get insurance	5	
Haven't got round to it..............	6	
Can't be bothered	7	(16)
Other (write in)		
_____	9	
_____		
Don't know	9	

Q.27 What, in your opinion, is the best thing the police could do to prevent burglary? *Code first mentioned only*

More police (unspecific)	1	
More patrols	2	
More police on foot.................	3	
Devote more time to it	4	
Other (write in)		
_____	5	(17)
Don't know	6	

Q.28 And what is the best thing people themselves can do to prevent burglary? *Code first mentioned only*

More/better locks (doors and windows)	1	
Stronger doors	2	
Cancel milk/papers	3	
Leave lights/radio on	4	
Burglar alarm	5	
Dog................................	6	(18)
Tell neighbours	7	
Tell police	8	
Other (write in)		
_____	9	
Don't know	0	

Q.29 Thinking of the various things which people can do to protect their homes from burglary — things like better door locks, window locks, stronger doors and so on — how much safer do you think this makes them? *Read out*

A lot safer	1	
A little safer	2	
or Not safer........................	3	(19)
(Don't know).......................	4	

Q.30 Thinking of the people who live in this area, how many would you regard as friends or acquaintances? *Read out*

Most of them	1	
Some of them	2 ASK Q.31	
Just a few of them..................	3	(20)
or None of them....................	4 GO TO Q.32(a)	

Ask only where layout of houses makes it appropriate. Others go to Q.32(a)

Q.31 Does this include the people next door, or across the road, or whose garden backs onto yours?

Yes	1	
No................................	2	(21)
Not applicable.....................	3	

Q.32 (a) The last time you were away from home for more than a few days did you . . . *Read out and code all that apply*

Ask someone to come and stay in it ...	1	
Ask someone to come in to make sure things were alright	2 ASK Q.32(b)	
or Ask someone to keep an eye on your home	3	(22)

or Did you do none of these things 4
(Never go away/house not left empty).. 5 GO TO Q.33

Q.32 (b) Who did this for you? *Probe if necessary:* Where do they live?

People from next door/opposite/
back 1
Other people who live nearby 2
Police 3
Other (write in)

_____ 4
Can't remember 5

(23)

Q.33 *Show card L* Would you please read this card, which gives a brief description of Neighbourhood Watch Schemes. *Wait for the respondent to read card.* Have you heard of these schemes before?

Yes 1
No 2

(24)

Q.34 (a) Do you think schemes like this would be effective in preventing burglary?

Yes .... 1 GO TO Q.35(a)

No 2
Don't know .... 3 ASK Q.34(b)

(25)

Q.34 (b) Why do you say that?

_____
_____
_____
_____

(26)
1 2 3
4 5 6
7 8 9
0 X Y

Q.35 (a) Do you think a scheme like this would work in this area?

Yes .... 1 GO TO Q.36(a)

No 2
Don't know .... 3 ASK Q.35(b)

(27)

Q.35 (b) Why do you think it would not work?

_____
_____
_____
_____

(28)
1 2 3
4 5 6
7 8 9
0 X Y

Ask all who think a scheme would work in this area

Q.36 (a) Would you personally be prepared to join one of these schemes?

Yes — would be prepared	1	GO TO Q.37
Already a member	2	
No — would not be prepared	3	ASK Q.36(b)
Don't know	4	

(29)

Q.36 (b) Why do you say that?

(30)

1 2 3
4 5 6
7 8 9
0 X Y

_____

_____

_____

Q.37 Would you be prepared to put Neighbourhood Watch stickers or posters in your window, to show you were a member?

Yes	1
No	2
Don't know	3

(31)

Ask all

Q.38 How easy would it be for your neighbours to keep a watch on your property while you were out?

Very easy	1
Fairly easy	2
Fairly difficult......................	3
Very difficult.......................	4
Don't know	5

(32)

Q.39 Such schemes rely on people telling their neighbours when their house is empty. Would you be willing to tell people living around here when your home is usually empty?

Yes	1
No	2
Don't know	3

(33)

Q.40 Do you think that the idea of neighbours looking after each other's homes needs to be organised, or should people be left to make their own arrangements?

Needs to be organised	1
Make own arrangements	2
Don't know	3

(34)

Q.41 When the police receive a call from a Neighbourhood Watch Scheme, what priority do you think the police would give to it? *Show card M*

Very high priority....................	1
High priority	2

```
Low priority .......................   3
Very low priority ...................   4        (35)
Don't know ........................   5
```

Ask all

Q.42 There are lots of things which are actually crimes, but which are done by lots of people, and which many people do not think of as crimes. On this card (*show card N*) are a list of eight of them. For each one can you tell me how many people you think do it — most people, a lot of people, some people, or no-one.

    (i) Firstly Item A — how many people do you think do this? *Code below*

    (ii) And have you personally done this in the last year?

Repeat (i) and (ii) for each item from at to H.

	Most people	A lot of people	Some people	No-one	Don't know	Done	Not done	Refused	
A	1	2	3	4	5	6	7	8	(36)
B	1	2	3	4	5	6	7	8	(37)
C	1	2	3	4	5	6	7	8	(38)
D	1	2	3	4	5	6	7	8	(39)
E	1	2	3	4	5	6	7	8	(40)
F	1	2	3	4	5	6	7	8	(41)
G	1	2	3	4	5	6	7	8	(42)
H	1	2	3	4	5	6	7	8	(43)

The columns (i) cover: Most people, A lot of people, Some people, No-one, Don't know. The columns (ii) cover: Done, Not done, Refused.

Q.43 *Interviewer: Record if anyone else was present in the room during follow-up questionnaire. Code all that apply*

```
No-one else present ..................   1
Child/children under 16 ..............   2        (44)
Adult/Adults ........................   3
```

Fill in time below then go to demographic questionnaire

Time follow-up questionnaire ended ....

Length of follow-up questionnaire | | | Minutes   (45/46)

          (45)   (46)

NOP/9888

AREA CODE

(5)   (6)   (7)

SERIAL No.

(8)   (9)

1984 BRITISH CRIME SURVEY
DEMOGRAPHIC QUESTIONNAIRE

COMPLETE THIS QUESTIONNAIRE FOR *ALL* RESPONDENTS

TIME THIS QUESTIONNAIRE STARTED: ....   (08)   (10/11)

Q.1   I would like to finish by collecting some details about you and your
      household to help us analyse the results. Firstly, are you . . . *Read out*

Single — (never married)	1	
Married............................	2	
Separated	3	(12)
Divorced...........................	4	
or Widowed........................	5	

Q.2   Last week were you in paid employment, or looking for work, or doing
      something else?

Working full-time (over 30 hours per week)	1 ASK Q.3
Working part-time (10–30 hours per week........................	2
Working part-time (under 10 hours per week........................	3
Unemployed and seeking work	4 GO TO Q.4
Sick or disabled and unable to work	5
Retired	6 ASK Q.3
Housewife	7
In full-time education	8

Q.3   Have you spent any time out of work and looking for work since the
      first of January 1983?

Yes	1	
No................................	2	(14)

Ask all

Q.4 How old were you when you completed your full-time education at school or college?

Under 15	1
15	2
16	3
17	4
18	5
19	6
20 or over	7
Still in full-time education	8

(15)

Q.5 Can I check some details of the members of your household? First, how many people aged 16 and over are there in your household, *including yourself?*

Write in number, then record details of each household member

(16)

	Sex	Age	Relationship to respondent	Head of household	
	Male .... 1 Female .. 2	Don't know = 98 Refused = 97	Spouse/cohabitee 1 Parent/Parent-in law .... 2 Brother/sister (or in-law) ...... 3 Son/daughter (or in-law) ...... 4 Other relative .. 5 Non-relative .. 6..	Code one only	
Respondent	(17)	(18) (19)	(20)	(21) 1	(17–21)
Person 2	(22)	(23) (24)	(25)	(26) 1	(22–26)
Person 3	(27)	(28) (29)	(30)	(31) 1	(27–31)
Person 4	(32)	(33) (34)	(35)	(36) 1	(32–36)
Person 5	(37)	(38) (39)	(40)	(41) 1	(37–41)
Person 6	(42)	(43) (44)	(45)	(46) 1	(42–46)

	(47)	(48)	(49)		(50)	(51)	
Person 7						1	(47–51)

	(52)	(53)	(54)		(55)	(56)	
Person 8						1	(52–56)

Q.6   Establish details of present or last main job of head of household.
If head of household has never worked, record below and go to Q.7

Head of household never worked	1	(57)

a) Title of job _____

b) Description of work done — probe for machinery used

_____

_____

c) Skill or training needed _____

d) Head of household is/was

	(58)	
Employee	1	(58)
Self-employed	2	

e) *Does/did* (HOH) supervise the work of other people? How many?

	(59)	
No	1	(59)
Yes	2	

Number _____

h) What industry *does/did* (HOH) work in? What *does/did* (HOH)'s
employer make or do?

_____

_____

i) How many people *are/were* employed at (HOH)'s place of work?

	(60)	
1	1	
2–24	2	(60)
25 or more	3	

Ask all
Q.7   Are there any children aged under 16 in this household?

Yes	1 ASK Q.8	(61)
No	2 GO TO Q.10	

Q.8   How many?

(62)

(62)

Q.9 How many, if any are aged under 5? *Write in number. If none code 0*

(63)

(63)

OFFICE USE ONLY

(64) (65)

·*Ask all*
Q.10 Does your household own this accommodation or rent it? *Probe as necessary*

Owned/being bought	1
Rented from Council	2
Rented from Housing Association	3
Rented from private landlord..........	4
Tied to job	5
Other (write in and code)	
_____	6

(66)

Ask head of household or spouse only. Others close interview
Q.11 To analyse the results we need to look at different types of households, and to help us do this can you tell me the letter in this card for the group in which you would place your *total household income* from all sources *before* tax and other deducations? *Show card P*

A. Under 2000	1
B. 2000–4999.......................	2
C. 5000–9999.......................	3
D. 10,000–14,999	4
E. 15,000–19,999	5
F. 20,000 or more	6
Dont know.........................	7
Refused...........................	8

(67)

Time this questionnaire finished   _____

(68)   (69)

Total length of this questionnaire   [|]   Minutes   (68–69)

INTERVIEWER ASSESSMENT—all respondents

A. Are the houses in this area in a good or bad physical state?

Mainly good 1
Mainly fair........................ 2
Mainly bad 3   (70)
Mainly very bad 4

B. Is there much rubbish and litter around on the streets?

A lot............................. 1
A little 2   (71)
None............................. 3

C. Code respondent type

1
2
3   (72)
4